Relaxing reefs, exhilarating drift dives and some seriously diverse marine life. From the tiniest critters to massive wrecks... Dive Bequia has got it all.

Opening Hours:

Mon - Sat 8am to 4.30pm.

Sun - By Appointment.

We offer scheduled guided dives departing the dock at 9am, 11.30am and 2.30pm

Private charters available on request

Snorkel Tours to Devil's Table or Moonhole

at 2.30pm

Not a Diver? Want to try?

Come and try a Discover Scuba

Beginners sessions offered daily at 1.00pm

Tuesday at 1.00pm come and give scuba a try FREE!

Spaces are limited, please reserve

Using the PADI system beginners sessions can be counted towards Open Water certification

SPECIAL 10% OFF GUIDED DIVING FOR VISITING YACHTS - JUST MENTION IT!

DIVE BEQUIA

TEAM

DIVERSE MARINE LIFE

FRIENDLY DIVE CENTER

BEST DIVE BOATS

© www.teup.co.uk

SAILORS GUIDE TO THE

Chris Doyle	Text, charts, layout
Sally Erdle	Illustrations
Chris Doyle	Photos
Polly Philipson	
Jeff Fisher	
John Douglas	
Virginia Barlow	Editor

DISTRIBUTION

USA AND WORLDWIDE
Cruising Guide Publications
P.O. Box 1017
Dunedin, Florida 34697-1017
Tel: 727-733-5322
Fax: 727-734-8179
info@cruisingguides.com

ST. VINCENT AND THE GRENADINES
Sophie Punnett, Box 17
St. Vincent, W. I.
Tel: 784-458-4246
Fax: 784-457-4851

ST. LUCIA
Ted Bull, P.O. Box 125
Castries, St. Lucia
Tel/Fax: 758-452-8177
windshift@candw.lc

GRENADA
Alan Hooper, Box 308
St. George's, Grenada
Tel: 473-409-9451
sark@spiceisle.com

Cover photos:
Background: Green Flash taken at St. Anne. Did you notice it?
Main: Yoles racing from St. Lucia to Martinique
Small: Linn Svendsen from JT Pro Kitesurf center, Union catches the sunset at Happy Island

AUTHOR'S NOTES

In the text we give a very rough price guide to the restaurants. This is an estimate of what you might spend to eat out and have a drink:

$A is $60 U.S. or more
$B is $30 to $60 U.S.
$C is $15 to $30 U.S.
$D is under $15 U.S.

We are happy to include advertising. It gives extra information and keeps the price of the book reasonable. If you wish to help us keep it that way, tell all the restaurateurs and shopkeepers, "I read about it in the Sailors Guide." It helps us no end.

If you like, tell us about your experiences, good or bad. We will consider your comments when writing the next edition.

Chris Doyle
email: sailorsguide@hotmail.com
or: c/o Cruising Guide Publications
P. O. Box 1017, Dunedin
FL 34697-1017
Fax: 727-734-8179

ACKNOWLEDGEMENTS

To everyone who helped; those who sat me down in their bars and shops to explain what they are trying to achieve; those who tapped me on the shoulder and said "know what you should say..."; but especially to all those who have emailed me in suggestions and information – a big thank you to all of you! This book would not be the same without your input. Thanks also to Bob Sachs for use of his plane and his skills as a pilot.

Chris Doyle

WINDWARD ISLANDS

**PUBLISHED BY
CHRIS DOYLE PUBLISHING**

in association with

**CRUISING GUIDE
PUBLICATIONS**

ISBN_9780-944428-94-8

First edition published............. 1980
Second edition published 1982
Third edition published 1984
Third edition revised   1985
Third edition revised   1986
Fourth edition published 1988
Fifth edition published 1990
Sixth edition published 1992
Seventh edition published 1994
Eighth edition published 1996
Ninth edition published.......... 1998
Tenth edition published.......... 2000
Eleventh edition published..... 2002
Twelfth edition published........2004
Thirteenth edition published ...2006
Fourteenth edition published...2008
Fifteenth edition published 2010
Sixteenth edition published.....2012

Please check for updates at
www.doyleguides.com

SKETCH CHART INFORMATION

Our sketch charts are interpretive and designed for yachts drawing 6.5 feet or less. Deeper yachts should refer to the depths on their charts.

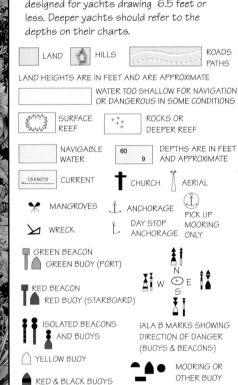

LAND

HILLS

ROADS PATHS

LAND HEIGHTS ARE IN FEET AND ARE APPROXIMATE

WATER TOO SHALLOW FOR NAVIGATION OR DANGEROUS IN SOME CONDITIONS

SURFACE REEF

ROCKS OR DEEPER REEF

NAVIGABLE WATER

60   9   DEPTHS ARE IN FEET AND APPROXIMATE

1.5 KNOTS CURRENT

CHURCH

AERIAL

MANGROVES

ANCHORAGE

PICK UP MOORING ONLY

WRECK

DAY STOP ANCHORAGE

GREEN BEACON
GREEN BUOY (PORT)

RED BEACON
RED BUOY (STARBOARD)

N
W E
S

ISOLATED BEACONS AND BUOYS

IALA B MARKS SHOWING DIRECTION OF DANGER (BUOYS & BEACONS)

YELLOW BUOY

MOORING OR OTHER BUOY

RED & BLACK BUOYS

SECTOR

WHITE (W)

GREEN (G)

YELLOW (Y)

RED (R)

LIGHTS

FL = FLASHING, F = FIXED, L = LONG, Q = QUICK, M = MILES
LIGHT EXPLANATION:
FL (2) 4S, 6M
LIGHT GROUP FLASHING 2 EVERY FOUR SECONDS, VISIBLE 6 MILES

SNORKELING SITE

SCUBA DIVING SITE

ONLY THOSE SITES THAT ARE EASILY ACCESSIBLE ARE SHOWN

SAILORS GUIDE

TO THE

by Chris Doyle
16th edition

Bequia Regatta

WINDWARD ISLANDS

Hiking with Henry Safari, Seven Falls

TABLE OF CONTENTS

ANCHORAGES IN THE WINDWARD ISLANDS

CONTINUED ON NEXT PAGE

SKETCH CHARTS

CONTINUED ON NEXT PAGE

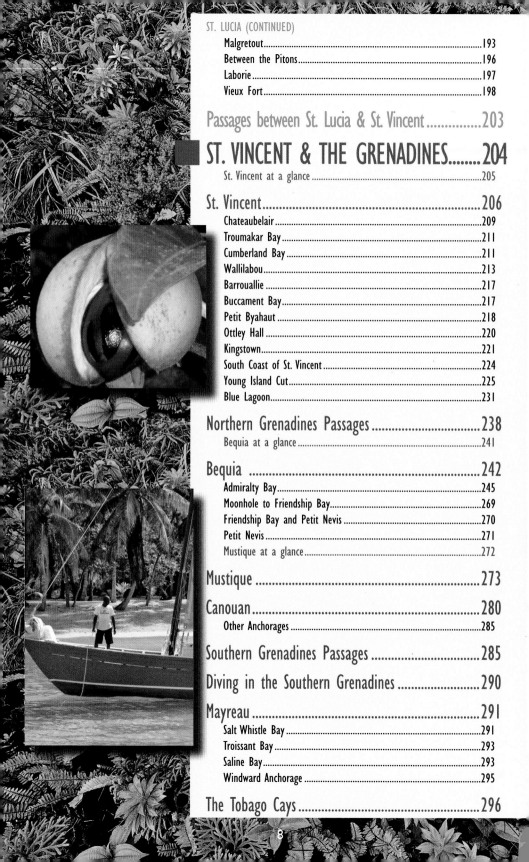

PSV

PLANNING & CRUISING

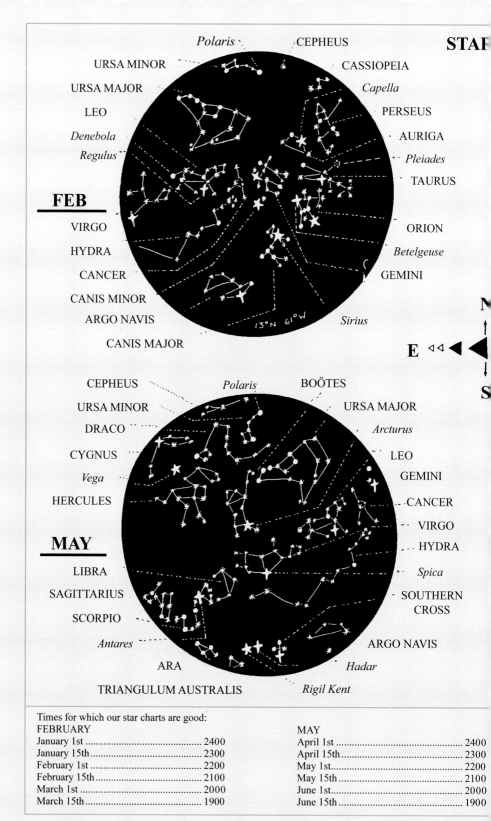

STAR

FEB

Polaris · CEPHEUS
URSA MINOR · CASSIOPEIA
URSA MAJOR · Capella
LEO · PERSEUS
Denebola · AURIGA
Regulus · Pleiades
· TAURUS
VIRGO
HYDRA · ORION
CANCER · Betelgeuse
CANIS MINOR · GEMINI
ARGO NAVIS
CANIS MAJOR · Sirius

13°N 61°W

N
E ◁◁ ◀
S

MAY

CEPHEUS · Polaris · BOÖTES
URSA MINOR · URSA MAJOR
DRACO · Arcturus
CYGNUS · LEO
Vega · GEMINI
HERCULES · CANCER
· VIRGO
· HYDRA
LIBRA · Spica
SAGITTARIUS · SOUTHERN CROSS
SCORPIO
Antares · ARGO NAVIS
ARA · Hadar
TRIANGULUM AUSTRALIS · Rigil Kent

Times for which our star charts are good:

FEBRUARY		MAY	
January 1st	2400	April 1st	2400
January 15th	2300	April 15th	2300
February 1st	2200	May 1st	2200
February 15th	2100	May 15th	2100
March 1st	2000	June 1st	2000
March 15th	1900	June 15th	1900

CHARTS

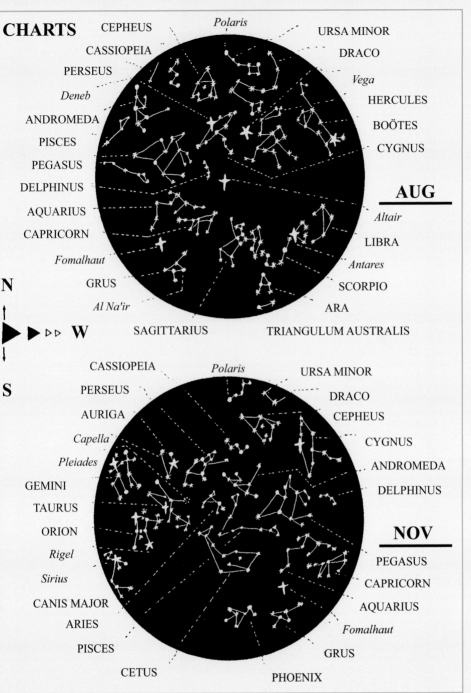

CEPHEUS   *Polaris*   **URSA MINOR**

CASSIOPEIA   **DRACO**

PERSEUS   *Vega*

Deneb   **HERCULES**

ANDROMEDA   **BOÖTES**

PISCES   **CYGNUS**

PEGASUS

DELPHINUS   **AUG**

AQUARIUS   *Altair*

CAPRICORN   **LIBRA**

Fomalhaut   *Antares*

N   **GRUS**   **SCORPIO**

Al Na'ir   **ARA**

▶ ▶ ▷▷ **W**   **SAGITTARIUS**   **TRIANGULUM AUSTRALIS**

S

CASSIOPEIA   *Polaris*   **URSA MINOR**

PERSEUS   **DRACO**

AURIGA   **CEPHEUS**

Capella   **CYGNUS**

Pleiades   **ANDROMEDA**

GEMINI   **DELPHINUS**

TAURUS

ORION   **NOV**

Rigel   **PEGASUS**

Sirius   **CAPRICORN**

CANIS MAJOR   **AQUARIUS**

ARIES   *Fomalhaut*

PISCES   **GRUS**

CETUS

PHOENIX

Note: Hold this book over your head with the east arrow pointing to the east (normally your bow).

AUGUST		NOVEMBER	
July 1st	2400	October 1st	2400
July 15th	2300	October 15th	2300
August 1st	2200	November 1st	2200
August 15th	2100	November 15th	2100
September 1st	2000	December 1st	2000
September 15th	1900	December 15th	1900

Approaching Bequia *BequiaPhotoAction*

Introduction

he islands of the Caribbean sweep southward in a huge arc, like a string of giant-sized stepping stones from Florida to Venezuela. On the eastern or windward side, the Atlantic Ocean pounds the shore. On the leeward side, the calmer Caribbean Sea lies tranquil, sparkling in the sun.

The Windward Islands are at the southern end of this chain, the last links before Trinidad and South America. The British called them the Windwards, because you had to beat to windward to get there from many of their other possessions.

They lie almost across the easterly trade winds, which makes for easy passages north or south, and they are just far enough apart to allow for some wild romps in the open ocean before tucking into the calm of the next lee shore.

The four main Windward Islands ~ Martinique, St. Lucia, St. Vincent, and Grenada ~ are lush and richly tropical, with high mountains that trap the clouds and pro-

duce dense green vegetation. Here you can find excellent examples of tropical rainforest, easily accessible to those who hike.

Between St. Vincent and Grenada lie the Grenadines ~ a host of smaller islands, some with hills of a thousand feet, others no more than a reef-enclosed sand cay sprouting a few palms. Drier than the large islands, they all have perfect white beaches, crystal clear waters, and colorful reefs.

Over 2000 years ago the islands were colonized by the Arawaks, an oriental-looking people who were great navigators, artists, and sportsmen. They were somewhat peaceful. Those in residence when Columbus arrived were a more warlike tribe called the Kalinargo who Columbus renamed Caribs. The Kalinargo resisted the Europeans and refused to be slaves. In Grenada, the northern town of Sauteurs marks the spot where the last of the Grenada Kalinargo leapt to their deaths rather than be taken captive. They held out the longest in St. Vincent, where the steep terrain made colonization harder. Even here the European colonists

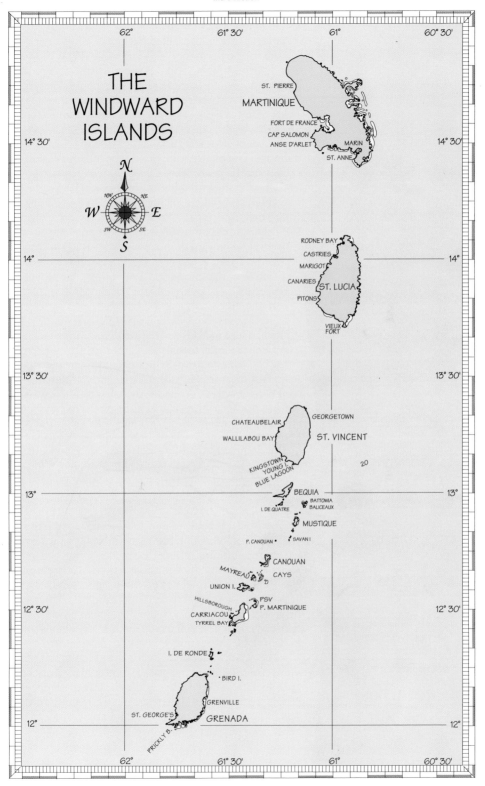

THE
WINDWARD
ISLANDS

N
NW · NE
W · E
SW · SE
S

MARTINIQUE
ST. PIERRE
FORT DE FRANCE
CAP SALOMON
ANSE D'ARLET
MARIN
ST. ANNE

ST. LUCIA
RODNEY BAY
CASTRIES
MARIGOT
CANARIES
PITONS
VIEUX FORT

ST. VINCENT
CHATEAUBELAIR
GEORGETOWN
WALLILABOU BAY
KINGSTOWN
YOUNG I.
BLUE LAGOON

20

BEQUIA
I. DE QUATRE
BATTOWIA
BALICEAUX
MUSTIQUE
P. CANOUAN
SAVAN I

CANOUAN
MAYREAU
CAYS
UNION I.
HILLSBOROUGH
PSV
P. MARTINIQUE
CARRIACOU
TYRREL BAY

I. DE RONDE
BIRD I.

GRENVILLE
ST. GEORGE'S
GRENADA
PRICKLY B.

62° 61° 30' 61° 60° 30'
14° 30'
14°
13° 30'
13°
12° 30'
12°

Planning & Cruising

Seven Falls, Grenada

Honeymoon falls, Grenada

Ziplining, St. Lucia

eventually drove them out. Today, just a handful of Kalinargo remain in the Windwards, on the north end of St. Vincent in a village called Fancy.

Years of colonization followed and the Windward Islands were fought over by the British and French. Plantation owners became rich from the production of sugar, and slaves were brought from Africa to work in the fields. After slavery was abolished, many former slaves showed a healthy disinclination to work for their previous masters, preferring to eke out a living fishing and farming. The planters imported East Indian laborers to take over the fieldwork.

Today, the intermingling of the races has produced an interesting blend of people who live in harmony together.

During its colonial history, Martinique, the northernmost Windward Island, was nearly always in French hands. Today, it is still part of France and therefore a member of the European Community. The language and ambiance are French and, while not essential, it certainly helps to speak the language.

St. Lucia, St. Vincent, and Grenada are now all independent nations with a British tradition. Each has its own laws and customs.

The main industries throughout this area are tourism, farming, fishing, and, more recently, international company services. While all the islands produce some rum, Martinique has a large industry producing their own specially flavored product, "Rhum Agricole." Farmers in Martinique also grow excellent pineapples. Grenada has traditionally grown nutmeg and cocoa. St. Lucia and St. Vincent have been heavily involved in bananas, but with protective arrangements with Europe ending, farmers are looking for alternative products, and tropical flowers seem to be an increasing market.

Tourism is probably responsible for much of the rise in the standard of living that has been visible over the last 30 years. In recent times, selling land to visitors has become a major money earner, though this is not ultimately sustainable. Yachting tourism has become a significant factor in the economy of many of these islands, and has encouraged the growth of restaurants, shops, handicraft artisans, and support services. The dollars you spend in the islands really do help the local economy.

The Windwards are a joy for the sailor. Good trade winds ensure exhilarating passages and delightful anchorages abound. The weather is pleasant year round, the people are friendly, and there are not too many annoying regulations. You are free to sail and enjoy some of the most beautiful islands on earth.

Welcome to the Windwards!

palm shadow, Bequia

Local Lore

Currency

In Martinique the currency is the Euro, currently worth more than the US dollar. Change bureaus give better rates than banks, some tourist shops offer up to a 20% discount on purchases made with traveler's checks.

In the other islands the currency is the Eastern Caribbean (EC) dollar at a fixed bank rate of 2.67 to one US dollar. This is usually a slightly better rate than that offered by shops or taxi drivers, though most people are willing to take US dollars. You get a lot of EC dollars for the US ones, but they are much more quickly spent. Oh well, "EC come, EC go," or as Jimmy Buffet said: "It's much more fun to spend money with pictures of flowers and palm trees on it than money with pictures of green old men." Spend it all or change it back locally. Bankers just laugh if you try to change it back home.

Credit cards, especially the Visa/MasterCard/Discover group, are now very widely accepted and they are much safer and more convenient than sporting big wads of cash. Let your credit card company know you are traveling so they do not block your card.

Language

In Martinique the language is French, and though an increasing number of people speak English, it is by no means a bilingual society. Some knowledge of French is very helpful. *French for Cruisers* by Kathy Parsons, is a good aid and, unlike most phrase books, it is thoroughly researched, beautifully laid out, and includes boat and engine parts.

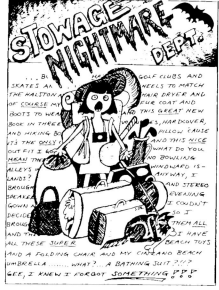

In the other Windwards, the official language is English, though the dialect can be hard to understand when locals talk fast among themselves. In St. Lucia, nearly everyone is bilingual. When you sit on a bus or hear people talking in the streets they are usually speaking in Patois, a dialect of French, influenced by English and African, which is the most commonly spoken language. However, English is used when writing or talking to visitors.

Tourist season

Charter and hotel rates vary with the time of year. Most people want to visit when it is cold up north, so the winter

Carriacou fish market

OVERSEAS CALLS
From local private, public, and GSM phones.
This is what you dial from the following islands:

Martinique: 00 + country & area code + number for Zone A & B*

St. Lucia/Grenada/St, Vincent: country & area code + number for Zone A

St. Lucia/Grenada: 011 + country & area code + number for Zone B

St. Vincent: 0 + country & area code + number for Zone B

Except within French territories, where you just dial the area code and number.

When dialing overseas, if the first digit of an area code is 0, leave it off.

When dialing Martinique from overseas, the number is + 596 596 + 6 digits (regular phones) or +596 696 + 6 digits (mobile phones)

SATELLITE PHONES
For each phone we give the same example for calling Grenada, 444-4266

GLOBALSTAR
If you use a Globalstar phone set up for the Americas, it works just like a USA phone: For USA and NANP countries dial 1 + the country & area code, + 7 digits. To call overseas dial 011 + country & area code, + number, Example, dial: 1-473-444-4266

IRIDIUM
Dial 00 + the country & area code - e.g. for the USA dial 001 then the area code + 7 digits, Example, dial: 00-1-473-444-4266

INMARSAT
Dial 00 + the country & area code - e.g. for the USA dial 001 then area code + 7 digits + #. The # key is used after all numbers are entered to initiate the call. Example, dial: 00-1-473-444-4266-#

Country Codes
Zone A NANP
(North American Numbering Plan)

USA	1-(area code)
Anguilla	1-(264)
Antigua	1-(268)
Barbados	1-(246)
Dominica	1-(767)
Grenada	1-(473)
Montserrat	1-(664)
St. Lucia	1-(758)
St. Vincent	1-(784)
St. Kitts	1-(869)
Trinidad	1-(868)

Zone B

UK	44
Australia	61
New Zealand	64
Austria	43
Germany	49
Guadeloupe	590
Martinique	596
Denmark	45
France	33
Italy	39
Sweden	46
Switzerland	41

months (November to April) are the high (expensive) season; the rest of the year is low season. Restaurant and bar prices are generally the same year round. During the quietest months (September and October), some small hotels close down and the staff go on holiday.

What to bring

Nearly all visitors bring too much luggage and do not realize that it is almost impossible to stow hard cases on a yacht. Only soft bags should be used. One of my charterers once arrived without luggage, the airline having spirited it away. Rather than wait, he bought a bathing suit, two pairs of shorts, and a shirt and wondered why he had ever bothered packing anything else.

If you need prescription drugs, bring an ample supply and make sure they stay in your carry-on bag.

Life is very informal here and even in the best of eating-places men can get by with a pair of slacks and a sports shirt, women with a simple dress.

Communications

The Windwards have excellent communications with the rest of the world and even in quite small islands you will find internet cafes. Public card phones are the obvious place to target the tourist, so calls from such phones often cost far more than the same call made on a private phone. Many internet cafes offer significantly better rates.

However, these days there is no reason not to have the convenience of a phone on the boat at reasonable rates. The introduction of GSM technology and the opening of the market to new companies have revolutionized the industry. From a yachting point of view, the most convenient are the phones that use prepaid cards, so there is no billing. You can buy a GSM phone locally, or bring your own and get a local SIM card ($25-50 EC).

Both Digicel and Lime (Cable and Wireless) are fairly seamless through all the islands from Grenada to St. Lucia (Barbados included). Take your phone with you when you want a recharge. They work well for local and regional calls. Calls outside the region from an island other than the one where you bought your SIM are prohibitive so it is best to buy another SIM. If you use your phone a lot, then Lime's "anywhere minutes" can be a good deal; ask for details. Martinique is on a different system: Digicel will work in Martinique, but for more than few calls it may be worth getting a Martinique SIM. To make a call in Martinique on a SIM from the other islands, you have to enter a + in front of the phone number. Orange Martinique have an excellent deal: for a few Euros you can buy a three-week Caribbean pass, which makes calls to the USA and the Caribbean the same price as the local calls.

The most popular internet solution is wifi, widely available, and a few stations are free. Unless you want to take your computer ashore, you will need to buy a booster wifi aerial to plug into your USB port. At anchor, turn on your computer and try connecting to likely stations. Once you are connected, just try to open any internet page and, if it is an appropriate station, that should initiate the registration.

Internet via a SIM card using a USB adapter is just becoming popular. Satellite phones work everywhere and some can also handle email. Some cruisers also use an SSB-based service.

Local etiquette

Clothing. Unlike many other western seaside towns, people in the Caribbean will look somewhat askance if you wander away from the beach in a bathing suit or, perish the thought, a bikini. Away from the beach, even in that tiny waterfront village, people generally wear at least a shirt and pair of shorts or skirt. In the major towns people dress much as you would if you were going to your local town.

For women, toplessness, for a while fashionable in Martinique, seems to have died owing to increasing awareness of skin cancer. It is illegal in most other islands. Complete nudity is best confined to anchorages where you can be sure of not being seen.

Greetings. Manners here are different and great store is set on greetings: "good morning" or "good afternoon" (or in Mar-tinique "bonjour" or "bonne nuit"). It is considered rude to approach people with a question or to transact business without beginning with the appropriate greeting.

Tipping. Everyone likes to be tipped, but it is not always expected. In restaurants where no service charge is added, a 10% tip is normal. If service has already been included (as it is by law in Martinique), a little extra is appreciated, but not essential. Taxi drivers do not normally expect to be tipped, but if they go out of their way to help you, you can add a few dollars to the fare to show your appreciation. If you get help from kids carrying your suitcases, they will expect an EC dollar or two.

Water skiing, jet-skis

Local laws require that a water ski vessel has at least two people on board. Water skiing or jet-skiing within 100 yards of a beach or in harbors where yachts are anchored is strictly forbidden. St. Vincent and the Grenadines have some enlightened environmental laws and jet-skiing is completely forbidden throughout the country. Jet-skis are also forbidden in the Soufriere Marine Management Area in St. Lucia. Legislation is being considered in other islands.

Drugs

Marijuana grows in the Windwards and is part of the local Rasta religion. It is, however, illegal, as are most other mind-bending substances except alcohol and tobacco. Laws are very strict and those caught can expect yacht confiscation and up to life imprisonment (a longer vacation than you may have intended).

Suntanning

Whatever the season, the sun is intense and adequate protection is essential. It is advisable to bring down plenty of sunscreen (30+) and use it from the start, building up exposure slowly. The tops of your feet are vulnerable and light cotton socks can help. Loose, long-sleeved, cotton clothing, hats, and sunglasses are essential. Heavy burning can still take place on cloudy days and in shade.

IATA (FAA) Airport Codes

For online booking or finding out if your travel agent has booked you to the right airport

Martinique
FDF - Fort de France

Grenada
GND - Point Saline
CRU - Carriacou

Barbados
BGI - Bridgetown

St. Lucia
SLU – Vigie, Castries
UVF - Vieux Fort, Hewanorra

Trinidad
POS - Port of Spain (Piarco)

St. Vincent and the Grenadines
UNI - Union Island
MQS - Mustique,
CIW - Canouan,
BQU - Bequia
SVD - Arnos Vale (Kingstown)

Local food products

Many local products, some unavailable anywhere else, are sold in the islands. Some make great presents. Locally bottled peanuts and cashews taste much fresher and better than imported ones. Grenada has an inspired chocolate factory where organic cocoa beans are made into gourmet chocolate by means of vintage machinery. Most islands have local rums, and on every island you will find a big variety of hot sauces, a local specialty.

Coconut water is sold in bottles in some islands and is delicious. Unfortunately, it has a short shelf life, so is not good to take back home.

All the main islands have great fruit and vegetable markets. These are always colorful, but Saturday morning is the best and busiest time, with the greatest selection (Friday in St. Lucia). Never be afraid to ask about things you do not recognize. The market ladies are helpful and will tell you how to cook different vegetables. Some things are not what they appear to be. For example, many fruits that look like bananas have to be cooked. (For more local food information, see our *Island foods* section.)

Transport

If you don't like to hoof it, you have a choice between taxis, buses, communal taxis, and rental cars.

Taxis are plentiful and come in all shapes and sizes. For long trips, some bargaining is usually possible. In any case, always ask for the fare in EC dollars (or Euros) before you start. If you think you are being quoted too high a figure, try another driver. Fares are likely to increase as gas gets more expensive.

Colorful, noisy, and cheerful, the buses in the English speaking islands are the mainstay of the transport system. They often bear such names as "Trust No Man," "De Bad Ride," "In God We Trust," and similar reflections. Not only is this an inexpensive way to travel, but you get to experience some local life. Most nowadays are minibuses. They are not for the claustrophobic, for there is always room for one more on a local bus. Just when you think the whole thing is packed to bursting, the driver's assistant manages to create a tiny square of spare air and, like a conjuror, he whips out yet another seat ~ a pullout piece of wood that is jammed in to take the extra person. Most buses have stereo systems and the drivers like to run them, like their buses, at full-bore. The buses are a wonderful example of the kind of service you can get with free enterprise. If you are carrying heavy shopping and wish to go off the normal route, this can be negotiated. In some islands buses will stop to pick you up anywhere, in others (including St. Lucia) they are only allowed to pick up at designated stops. Buses do get rather few and far between after dark, and may be very limited when going to a distant spot. Before taking off to the other end of an island, make sure there will be a bus coming back.

If you arrive by air at a reasonable hour, without too much luggage, and can make it to the nearest main road, St. Lucia's Hewanorra Airport and the airport in St. Vincent are on bus routes, and Martinique's airport is on a communal taxi route.

Manchineel
leaf and flower,
Below: Sea grape

Bugs, Beasts, Plants, and People

Don't let the cockroaches bug you

The unmentionable, indomitable cockroach thrives. If you are on a yacht, the odds are that eventually you will find yourself face to face with one of these miniature, armor-plated monstrosities. No need to panic. Despite their off-putting appearance, they are quite harmless, make good pets, and in reasonable quantities are not a reflection of the cleanliness of the boat. A good dose of spray will keep them out of sight for a couple of days. (This will be done automatically on a skippered yacht.) If you are on a boat with a bad infestation, the permanent cure is as follows: First, give a good spray to reduce the numbers (not necessary if you only have one or two). Then, using a mortar and pestle, grind equal quantities of boric acid and white sugar together and distribute freely under drawers, in bottoms of lockers, etc. This will normally give at least six months of cockroach-free living. Some people prefer to mix the boric acid into a gooey mess with condensed milk because they can then stick it on walls and ceilings. I also find some large versions of the "Sticky Box" (usually found in Martinique) to be very

22

effective. Cockroaches generally arrive on board as stowaways in cardboard cartons or amid fruits and vegetables. It helps to keep "cockroach free" crates and boxes on board and transfer all incoming supplies into them. Examine fruits and vegetables before you stow them. So much for the bad news. The good news is that the boat variety, known as the German cockroach, is relatively small, quite unlike the huge shoreside monsters that grow up to two inches long and are aptly called "mahogany birds."

Mosquitoes are not usually a problem on board because of the breeze, but jungly anchorages or enclosed lagoons on the lee of the large islands are occasionally buggy. If you find yourself in such a bay, you can always resort to the mosquito coil. This is not a contraceptive device for mosquitoes, but a spiral of incense-like material that burns slowly and puts the mosquitoes to sleep. It is effective, but you should be warned that it does not usually kill the bugs and, should the coil go out before you awake, they will be up first and you will be breakfast.

In the evening, beaches can be buggy, especially on a still night in the rainy season, July to November. Worse than mosquitoes are the minute sand flies known as no-see-ums. Any brand of bug repellent will help prevent your sunset barbecue from becoming a free-for-all slapping match.

Dangers

Perhaps we should start with the rum punch. This delicious concoction, a mixture of rum and fruit juice, is available in any waterside bar. It can be positively euphoric in small doses and lethal in large. Strongly recommended at sunset, but be warned that the potency is often stronger than the flavor would suggest.

There are poisonous scorpions and centipedes on the islands, but luckily they are rare and not generally deadly. Still, take a good look at that old pile of twigs and leaves before you sit and take care when picking up coconut husks to burn for your barbecue.

A real danger is the manchineel tree (*Hippomane mancinella*), which grows abundantly along some beaches. This pretty tree with yellow-green apples is toxic. The leaves can produce a rash like poison ivy. It is all right to take shade under the tree, but never stand under a manchineel in the rain, and avoid using the branches for firewood, or that song "Smoke Gets in Your Eyes" may take on new meaning. If you eat the apples, they will cause blisters from stem to stern and are very dangerous.

Martinique and St. Lucia are also home to a deadly snake, the fer de lance, which is thankfully quite rare. Various parasites can live in fresh water. Usually they need entry via a break in the skin. It is safest to stick to clear, fast flowing streams. Swimming in murky, swollen rivers in the rainy season increases the risk.

The main dangers in swimming and snorkeling are negligent and speeding fishermen, yacht tender drivers, and water taxis. There have been some serious accidents over the years, so swimmers and snorkelers should be aware of small craft movement at all times. Lesser dangers include sea urchins. These are spiny creatures whose prickles penetrate the skin and break off on contact. This is quite painful, especially for the first few hours. They are virtually impossible to pull out once embedded, as they break into little pieces. It is best to leave them in and treat them with hot lime juice, as the acid helps dissolve them.

There are sharks and barracudas but, unlike their cousins in the movies, they have yet to attack anyone in these waters unless harassed and so are not considered dangerous here. There is no question that spearfishing can excite these fish. I have dived and snorkeled at night with no problem, but since so few people swim at night, it is impossible to assess how safe it is. Despite their reputation, moray eels are short sighted and timid, but it would be pushing your luck to stick your hand into holes in rock or coral. Corals eat by stinging their prey, and many can sting you, so look and do not touch. This is also better for the coral. Coral scratches can become infected. If you get one, scrub it well with soap and fresh water. Stinging jellyfish are not frequent, but do exist, and occasionally the swimmer may feel a mild tingling from minute animals known as sea ants. If you do get a jellyfish sting, soaking with vinegar can help

A good book on dangerous marine animals would certainly list some more horrors, but the truth is that harm from any of these is extremely rare and, provided you watch where you put your hands and feet and keep an eye on the sea conditions and current, snorkeling is safer than doing the weekly ironing and a lot more fun.

Taxi drivers

Taxi drivers are often colorful characters, owners of highly individualized cars, and they have a fund of local knowledge. The ambitious ones who used to act as commission agent as well, running around shopping, tracing lost luggage, and obtaining hard to find parts, have morphed into yacht agents. In Martinique, only a few of the drivers speak English, though they will bear with your French.

Unfortunately, among the good ones there are an overenthusiastic few who will bully or confuse the unwary passenger into going on a tour he or she really does not want. There are two basic rules: always discuss and agree on a price before you embark on a taxi ride and make sure you are both talking the same kind of dollars (EC or US) or, in Martinique, Euros.

Boat vendors

At some point, there will be a thump on your topsides and a voice shouting "Hey skip, want some limes? How about a nice T-shirt? Or a coconut boat? It sails very good." You are in islands with a great spirit of free enterprise ~ better get used to it. From the skipper's point of view, the most harrowing thing is trying to persuade these vendors that you really do not want several hundred pounds of rough wood and exposed nail heads (a local dinghy) banging your topsides. The vendor's cheerful cry of "no problem, skip" does nothing to remove the scratch.

The problem is exacerbated in some areas where the competition is so keen that you may be approached two miles from port. This most often occurs in the Soufriere/Pitons area in St. Lucia and the Cumberland/Wallilabou area in St. Vincent. In these places it is quite a useful service because it is

necessary to tie to a palm tree, owing to the depth of water. However, some vendors you meet way out will want you to tow them in. It is unwise to tow these heavy boats a long way and there are always line handlers close to the shore, so refuse these long distance offers. You can tell them your insurance does not allow for towing. When you get closer to shore, come to a standstill and negotiate the price before handing over any lines. (I offer a set fee of $10-20 EC on a "take it or leave it" basis.) When finally at anchor, put out at least two big fenders and make sure any local boats coming alongside stay on them.

You will probably be offered, at various times, t-shirts, jewelry, fruit, scrimshaw, model boats, ice, and bread. It is worthwhile to consider what is offered.

Vendors are part of the local scene and endemic to undeveloped countries with struggling economies. Some people enjoy the interactions and opportunity to do business in this way; most vendors are friendly and helpful. However, since most visitors have no prior experience with vendors, some find them irritating and I have had letters from people saying they would not revisit some anchorages because of their experiences with vendors.

Dealing with vendors is easier once you know to expect them. Be straightforward, look them in the eye, always demand professional behavior, and keep your sense of humor and you will be okay. If you imagine yourself in their position, it is not hard to figure out how they operate and why.

You will find vendors in the Grenadines, St. Vincent, and St. Lucia. In the Grenadines, most are very professional. If you say no, they will leave you in peace. On the other hand, the situation on the west coast of St. Vincent reminds me of the airport in Grenada back in the early 70s when it was very amusing to watch the hapless and unsuspecting passenger stagger forth into the daylight with his three or four suitcases. Within seconds three or four taxi drivers would rush up and each grab a bag and head in a different direction, entreating the passenger to follow as loudly as they could. He would stand confused and sweating in his traveling suit, wondering if this was the

start of a trip to hell. Clearly, things could not go on that way, and a taxi drivers union was formed to get everyone organized. I feel we need such organization for boat vendors in St. Vincent, where people sometimes find themselves surrounded by vendors all shouting at once, but this is not going to happen soon. In St. Lucia, where it used to be like that, some strides have been made in the Soufriere Marine Management Area, and now many vendors and taxis are licensed and are very helpful.

People sometimes complain that while vendors are fine, there are just too many of them. If I were a charterer (prime customers for vendors; cruising folk don't have as many problems), I think I would make a couple of clearly visible signs I could hang from the lifelines near the cockpit saying "I am not buying now, leave me in peace ~ visit again when this sign is down."

You may also get vendors you should clearly not do business with. Sometimes someone will come out to your boat touting a local restaurant. This is fair enough, but when he or she tells you not to visit the other restaurant because the food is bad and the cockroaches in the kitchen are the size of small rats, common sense should tell you this is not an unbiased judgment. Yet some visitors are naive enough to heed such advice and usually end up with the worst meal in the harbor as a result. (There is logic to this: restaurateurs who encourage such unscrupulous behavior are likely to be equally dastardly in the kitchen and in dealing with customers.) People have paid youths to watch their dinghy, which has resulted in the creation of an unnecessary service, with the dinghy watchers often being rude. Lock your dinghy on with a cable and refuse all such services. Make sure your locking line is at least 16 feet long so that you do not block others approaching the dock.

Some kids beg. "It's my birthday, what are you going to give me?" is a favorite line. It is important to bear in mind that wages for an unskilled adult may only be $50 to $100 EC a day. If young kids end up getting twice that much liming around the docks, begging from tourists, or getting grossly overpaid for watching dinghies, they skip school and it is

Planning & Cruising

PROTECT YOURSELF AGAINST PETTY THEFT

If you take the following precautions, you are unlikely to have a problem.

✔ Lock up when you leave the boat, and leave someone on board at night in main towns like St. George's, Castries, and Kingstown.

✔ Lock your outboard onto your boat at night.

✔ Lock your dinghy to the dock by day and onto your yacht by night.

✔ Be cautious about inviting strangers on board.

✔ Do not bring big wads of cash; use credit cards instead. Do not leave cash on the boat. Insure valuables such as cameras.

✔ Don't leave things unattended on the beach or in the dinghy in public places.

✔ Bring copies of CDs rather than your orginals.

hard for them to adjust later when they need to go out to work. By all means, employ kids and find something useful for them to do. That helps the economy, but just throwing money around can be harmful. For those who like to give away money, there are a few beggars who have handicaps. Local associations for the handicapped are also happy to accept donations.

"Tiefs"

Most islanders and yachtspeople are very honest, but obviously there are shady characters, too: thieves, con men, and extortionists. Dinghies and outboards are sometimes stolen at night. It is hard to say how many, because no one wants to admit that his dinghy disappeared after that final rum punch because the "rabbit" lost its way while going through the "hole" to make the bowline. There have been cases when a dinghy is returned the next day and the

finders demand huge sums for the "rescue." Boats occasionally get robbed when people are ashore. The thieves are mainly looking for cash and easily saleable items. Instead of cash, use credit cards (Visa, MasterCard and Discover are most widely accepted). Insure valuables such as cameras and binoculars. This way, if you do get affected, the results will not be as bad.

There are a few who will provide a service and then demand outrageous sums, so always ask the price before accepting any service, including taxis. Make sure you are both referring to EC dollars.

Violent crimes, including armed robbery and rape, are rare but not unknown on yachts.

If you are planning to walk at night or hike into remote places, it doesn't hurt to ask around first, especially if you are alone or with just one other person. Keep in mind that while the islands are generally safe, there are isolated incidents, as there are anywhere in the world. Occasionally, someone turns bad and goes on a robbing spree, doing a "your money or your life" bit with the aid of a cutlass. Usually they run amok for a month or two before they get well and truly nailed. Once they are put away everything returns to normal. For current information on where there are problems, ask in any charter company office and check my website (www.doyleguides.com), read the updates, and go to the security links on the advisories page. Also, read the free waterfront newspaper, *Caribbean Compass*, which often highlights areas where there are problems.

Bequia Regatta

Photography, Medical & Fishing

Photography

These days we are all using digital cameras, which makes photography much easier; instant results and no more running around looking for film.

The light in the Windwards is so bright that colors often photograph better in the early morning or late afternoon. This changes radically when you venture into the rainforest, where light levels are so low that a tripod is useful for long exposures.

Learn enough about the setup of your camera so that when you venture into the forest you can take pictures with the camera set at an equivalent of 400 ASA.

A polarizing filter can really enhance sea shots, giving dramatic results. You can watch the colors change as you twist the filter. Keep an eye on the sky as well as the sea, as it will turn gray at some angles.

It is only polite to ask when you want to photograph someone. Local attitudes can be a little strange. People with cameras sometimes become a focal point for frustrations and feelings of being exploited. If you try to take a crowd scene, someone will often object and, funnily enough, that person might not even be in the picture. Vendors who deal with tourists are usually happy to say "yes," especially if you are buying something. Digital cameras help, as you can show the subject their image on the screen after you have taken it.

Medical care

There is adequate medical care for most ailments in all the larger islands and any hotel or charter company will help you get in touch with a doctor. In emergencies, remember that all cruise ships stand by on VHF: 16 and carry doctors on board. If you have a life-threatening situation or a serious head injury, plan on immediate transport to Martinique or Barbados. SVG Air (784-457-5124) do medical flights; the big hospitals may be able to organize a helicopter ambulance.

For diving accidents needing decompression, call Martinique's main hospital or Tapion, St. Lucia, or Barbados (246) 436-6185, for immediate evacuation.

Martinique: The main hospital is Hopital Pierre Zobda-Quimann (0596) 55 20 00. For advice on facilities try Douglas Yacht Services: 0696 45 89 75. For lesser ailments: Dr. Jean Louis Deloge and Dr. Veronique Claisse, (office 0596 74 98 24) in Marin.

St. Lucia: For most problems, the Rodney Bay Medical clinic is good and convenient (Dr. Beaubrun, 452-8621/0785). If you need more, check Tapion Hospital, (758) 459-2000, a kind of medical mall with all kinds of doctors. Dr. Andrew Richardson, the general surgeon, a sailing man, is good, and may also be consulted as a regular doctor. Tapion has a hyperbaric chamber for divers

For dental care, Dr. Glace, in Rodney Bay can handle everything from fillings to implants (758) 458-0167.

St. Vincent: Maryfield Hospital (highly recommended by some of our readers), Gunn Hill, Kingstown: (784) 457-2598/2929, or the Botanic Hospital: (784) 457-1747.

In the **Grenadines**, Mustique is a good place to get sick. There is an excellent small clinic, (784) 458-4621 (ask for the clinic), situated next to the airport, in case you need fly out for further treatment. Bequia (784) 458-3294, VHF: 74 (24 hours) has a doctor and a fair little clinic in Port Elizabeth that responds to emergency calls. For dental care Profamdental: (784) 459-0745, run by Johanna Osborne, dental and maxillofacial surgeon, opens Saturday mornings only.

Grenada: If you need hospitalization, try the St. Augustine's Medical Clinic: (473) 440-6173/5. It is quite complete, with a lot of modern equipment.

For a doctor visit Dr. Michael Radix, (473) 444-4850, 440-4379 surgery, or (473) 443-5330 home. Mike is a good old-school doctor, very pleasant to visit, and he makes house calls.

If you need surgery, Dr. Yearwood is a general surgeon, a urologist, and a competitive yachtsman: Ocean House, Grand Anse (473) 444-1178.

Remember also the St. George's School of Medicine: (473) 444-4271.

Dr. Roxanne Nedd is excellent for general dental care. Her office (473) 444-2273 is next to the Excel Mall in Grand Anse.

Island Dental Care, run by Dr. Tara Baksh and Dr. Victor Samaan in Grand Anse, also come highly recommended (473) 437-4000, islanddentalcare@yahoo.com

Fishing

Forget spearfishing, Hawaiian slings, pots, nets, and diving down to pick up conch or sea urchins; it is illegal for visitors to engage in these activities. Fishing regulations are very strict. Even though trolling and handlining may not be strictly legal unless you have a license, most islands have agreed to turn a blind eye to these activities, unless you are in a marine park or protected area. This courtesy does not extend to sports fishing boats, which often need a license. So, leave the rest, but get out your rod and enjoy.

Trolling for fish is fun, and those you catch yourself always taste better. If you are on a short holiday you can just walk into any fishing tackle shop and buy a couple of ready-to-go lines, complete with lures. Shell out extra for (or create) a good device that will let you know you have caught a fish. If you do not know a fish is there, it will likely break the line and you will lose both lure and fish. Setting two lines, one from each side of the boat doubles your chance of catching a fish (but take one in when you tack). Set the lee one long (about 150 yards) and keep the other short (half that or less ~ a little skipping does not hurt). Haul in for a weed check every 40 minutes or so. Remove any weed.

When you catch a fish, you may need to slow the boat. If you have two lines out, have someone reel in the empty one so it doesn't get tangled. One easy way to slow down is to furl the jib. Luff also, if necessary, but not until the spare line is in. Gloves are a big plus for the last part, when you have to heave your catch out of the water and into the cockpit, or at least on deck where someone can hold it.

skipjack tuna
not shown:
blue fin tuna
yellow fin tuna
big eye tuna

yellow tail snapper

rainbow runner

tuna is thon
in French

great baraccuda

Spanish mackeral

black fin tuna

albacore

wahoo, thazar in French

unmistakable
shape of the
dolphin
(dorado)
dorade in
French

kingfish

caripe or tuny fish
ti thon in French

Planning & Cruising

31

It is better to use a proper reel. Not only will you instantly know when you have a fish, but the give of the reel will stop you losing the occasional fish when it strikes.

If you are making your own rig, you do need a swivel on the end of your line, and a wire leader is best. Have the wire leader about 10 lbs. lower breaking strain than the line so that if you get a monster you do not break the line. Around 80-lb. test line should bring in most of the fish you will catch. The lighter the line and gear, the more strikes you will get, but you have a greater chance of losing the fish.

You could also try adding a fish attractor on one line. This looks like a lure but is flat headed. The lure and hook go on a leader, a couple of feet beyond the attractor.

Any fish you catch out in open water will almost certainly be good to eat. Ciguatera fish poisoning, common farther north, is a rarity here. One might be suspicious of a really large barracuda that could be down from up north visiting relatives, but smaller barracuda (around five lbs.) are delicious. Dolphins, tuna family, (including caripe), albacore, and wahoo are not considered risky even in bad areas up north.

The photos of the most common catches are to help with identification. The photos were taken after the fish had been caught so most have lost a lot of color. The dolphin (or dorado; no relation to flipper) is the most dramatic at this ~ it gives a brilliant display of bright color then fades to nothing. Most fish will change color significantly before your eyes, so shape and markings need to be taken even more seriously than color when making an identification. If you get a fish with a really large eye, it is probably a horse-eye jack. They are not choice, and are very bony, but some people eat them.

Fish can have worm-like parasites. They don't live on humans for long, but hurt like hell while trying. Both cooking and deep-freezing will kill them. However, if you do the sushi thing, observe the flesh closely, the parasites are said to be of visible size.

Lobster season is usually from the first of October to the end of April. During this time, lobsters may be bought from local fishermen, and the most likely places to find them are Mustique, Union, the Tobago Cays, and P.S.V.

It is against the law to buy lobster out of season, those less than 9 inches long, or lobsters bearing eggs at any time, and the fines are steep. You may be offered one, but please refuse.

.

Entertainment & Special Events

Green flash

In the evenings, sunset brings an opportunity to look for the elusive "green flash." This happens as the sun disappears below the horizon. For about a second (blink and you've missed it), the very last bit of the sun to disappear turns bright green. To see this you need a clear horizon and the right atmospheric conditions. Some say rum punch helps. Binoculars make it a lot clearer. Photographers will need a big telephoto lens and an auto drive.

Entertainment

The most popular form of evening entertainment is the "jump up." This usually happens in one of the bars or hotels and takes the form of a dance, most often to a live band. If enough rum flows, everyone does indeed "jump up." Both Martinique and St. Vincent have casinos, but these are very low-key. Most of the larger hotels offer evening dancing with a floorshow. Some hotels serve Sunday lunch to the accompaniment of a steel band. You can dance, swim, or just enjoy the music.

Special events

There are a variety of local festivals and events for entertainment and partying. If you happen to be here at the right time,

Planning & Cruising

they are worth investigating; some are worth a special trip.

Carnival started as a riotous bacchanal before Lent. Carnivals feature costumed parades, calypso contests, steel bands, and days of dancing in the street. Martinique still has their carnival before Lent, but St. Vincent, St. Lucia and Grenada have switched. Check our information on holidays at the beginning of each island section.

St. Lucia has a jazz festival that lasts about a week in early May. Some of the events are on Pigeon Island and you can anchor your yacht below. Basil, in Mustique, runs a small but good blues festival in both Mustique and Bequia sometime during late January or early February. Carriacou has a great Maroon and String Band Festival around the end of April/beginning of May. Carriacou has a Parang Festival before Christmas.

You can join in sailing events. Martinique has a fun week in early June with races from port to port around the island with plenty of good food and entertainment. If you are here on July 14th, the French national holiday, you may see yole (pirogue) races around Fort de France. Yoles also feature in each coastal village during celebrations for its patron saint. Anyone interested can get a list from the local tourist office. Martinique has a series of races that tour the island over several days in January and a sailing week at Schoelcher in February.

St. Lucia has a big event around Christmas, well timed for those arriving on the ARC.

Bequia's Easter Regatta is well worth attending. It includes yacht races, local "two-bow" fishing boat races, model boat races, and cultural shows.

The Grenada Sailing Festival is held in January. It is a program of race events backed by a well-organized social program. All entrants are welcome, from serious racing boats to live-aboards. The Grenada South Coast Regatta, hosted by Phare Bleu Marina, is great fun and takes place towards the end of February. Another occasional Grenada event is the *Round Grenada Race*.

The Carriacou Regatta, in late July or early August, is a local event featuring races for small fishing boats and the larger cargo carrying sloops. These are some of the finest sailing vessels made in the islands. Ashore there is plenty of fun.

For cruisers there are several rallies to join. The Oragnization of Eastern Caribbean States (OECS) occasionally has a cruising rally after the ARC. It is a great way to see the islands, while being feted and entertained

Club Transcaraibes runs a whole bunch of cruises, including Trinidad for Carnival, Cuba and Venezuela. Check them at www. transcaraibes.com.

People lose more dinghies in regattas and big parties than at any other time; either borrowed by a drunk who does not secure it, or loosed by a drunk as he fumbles to get his untied. Lock it up for security, especially during regatta time!

Protecting the Environment

Most visitors are courteous and well behaved. With the increasing volume of yachts in the area, it definitely helps if people are considerate. Anchorages here have been reasonably free of loud noises, including drunken raucous laughter, stereo equipment, endlessly running generators, and loudly clanking halyards. Luckily, there is plenty of room in most anchorages, so those who want to make noise or need to run generators for much of the time can just stay well away from everyone else. Most of us have to run our engines at some time during the day, but let us at least leave the hour around sunset free so everyone can enjoy it in peace.

A few inconsiderate people still blast the anchorage with the sound of a noisy windmill. Most makes are quiet and unobtrusive, yet one of the most popular brands can be heard well over a hundred yards away. They destroy the natural peace of many a quiet anchorage. Plus, some people who own them seem to think that because they are not using fossil fuels, they are on the side of the angels and can do no wrong. They run them 24 hours a day without giving any consideration to others who find the noise irritating. These windmills do not have to be obnoxious; quiet blades are available from Spreco (silentwindgenerator.com). If you have not yet bought a windmill, make sure the one you buy is quiet or, if you want to

be sure, use solar panels. If you already own a noisy one, and cannot be bothered to get the quiet blades, try to anchor to the back of the fleet, and when your batteries are charged up, stop the blades.

Right now you can don a mask and snorkel and dive in the water anywhere in the Windwards and find the seabed pretty clean. Let's keep it that way.

Fishing and hunting

The days have gone when we could jump over the side, bristling with knives and festooned with spearguns long enough to be sold by the yard, to decimate the local fish population. Spearfishing has proved too damaging and new laws have been passed to control it. It is now illegal for visitors to spearfish (& Hawaiian sling) anywhere from St. Lucia to Grenada. It should be mentioned that spearfishing, apart from being completely illegal, is very harmful to the environment; spears that miss their target can damage coral and allow infection to take hold. Gloved hands grabbing coral, can also stress the reef. Most speared fish are reef cleaners, so fishing them can affect the whole ecosystem. Lobsters, when caught this way, cannot be sized and checked for eggs. For this reason, even locals are not allowed to spearfish lobsters; they must be caught by snare. Try not to give moral support to other

cruisers who boast about their spearfishing exploits. It is a bad thing to do, especially now when reefs are already degraded, at least in part because of us.

Hunters should note that all cows, goats and sheep, even on remote uninhabited islands, are privately owned. They are often put out to graze and left for months on end. They should not be harmed.

Garbage

Yacht garbage can be a problem in the Grenadine Islands, where it can totally overwhelm the available facilities. We need to cut down on what we bring ashore, and we have to be careful what we bring ashore. Food waste of all kinds should be stored in a separate container and dumped when you are out at sea in deep water, far from reefs. Carrying organic matter from one island to another as garbage is a dangerous practice. Island agriculture is very sensitive as we saw some years ago when an introduced pink mealy bug spread rapidly through some of the Windward Islands and cost millions of dollars in lost produce and, more recently, when a mango worm was introduced to Grenada. Organic matter may contain fruit flies, cockroaches, fungi, and other potentially dangerous pests. So take care when transporting and disposing of fresh fruit and vegetable matter. In addition, it is unwise to transport things like woven palm hats and baskets between islands.

Most harbors are open to the west and if you are stuck in such a harbor too long, dinghy the food waste as far out of the harbor as you can and dump it there, preferably at dusk. Never do this in places like the Tobago Cays where there are islands and reef downwind. Rinse all your empty cans and containers in seawater before putting them in the trash.

It is best to buy things with as little packing as possible and use returnable bottles. Take along your own shopping bags and avoid those plastic ones.

In addition, yachtspeople have caused considerable degradation by letting locals dispose of their garbage for a fee. Never give garbage to vendors. Some will offer to take your garbage for a couple of dollars. How-ever, these people have no proper means of disposing of it. The good ones try to burn it, but combustion is never complete and the remains are left strewn around. Others dump your garbage in holes in the bushes and the worst take it to the nearest beach, rummage through for items of interest, and abandon it. You are responsible for your own garbage. If you give it to someone else for a fee, they are considered your employee, and if they litter with your garbage, you are responsible.

Never throw plastics, including bags and bottled water containers, at sea. Leatherback turtles eat jellyfish and many have been found dead, their stomachs filled with plastic bags. Smelly bags can be rinsed in the ocean before storing. Other items that should never be thrown out at sea include string and fishing line which might form a tangle trap somewhere or be eaten, or plastic lined cardboard cartons (juice cartons, etc.) and tin foil. These can be rinsed in seawater before stowing. Similarly, anything that could be the least bit toxic, including aerosol sprays and chemicals, should not be dumped at sea.

Most garbage consists of paper, cardboard, cans and bottles. Should we throw these at sea? Ideally, no. The ocean is not a dumping ground, and if we are not very careful where we dump such garbage we can damage reef structures. On the other hand, we should not take these items ashore and dump them in the Grenadines where the facilities are totally inadequate. So what to do? As far as possible, keep such garbage for an adequate refuse facility in one of the larger islands. Martinique has plenty of places to put garbage, and you will find adequate facilities in Rodney Bay and Marigot Bay in St. Lucia, and in The Yacht Club and Spice Island Marine in Grenada.

If you are unable to do this, then it is probably marginally better to dump non-returnable bottles, cans, shredded paper, and cardboard far from land, with no islands or reefs in the lee, in water over 600 feet deep, than it is to pile them in a heap on land where they are not being collected. Paper and cardboard will eventually dissolve (though we do not know about the toxicity of the inks printed on them). Cans

and bottles will sink and sit on the seabed which, in deep water, is mainly sand or mud; they provide homes for baby fish. Nothing should ever be dumped near a reef or in an anchorage.

Holding tanks

I have not yet seen a convincing study that shows the direct pumping of toilets into our anchorages has a measurable ecological impact. However, it can have an aesthetic one, and it is reassuring to know you are swimming in water that someone has not just dumped in. Some marine parks are now asking people to use holding tanks. If you do not have one, you can make a temporary one using a bucket (and a lid for when not in use), and carrying a bag of sawdust. Sprinkle the sawdust before and after each use. Empty and rinse the bucket after you have left the anchorage. Use the regular head for pee.

Save our reefs

In minutes, anchors can destroy what nature has taken generations to build. A coral structure is a colony of millions of minute animals called polyps. They are fragile and reefs grow very slowly. Always anchor on sand, never on coral. If there is any doubt, have someone snorkeling when you drop your anchor. Dinghy anchors also do harm, so use a sand anchor for your dinghy and anchor on the sand beside the coral, rather than on the coral itself.

When snorkeling or diving, be careful of coral structures. Avoid standing, bumping into, getting swept onto, or grabbing coral. Even a small amount of damage can open a coral to being taken over by sponges and algae. Don't wear gloves when diving and snorkeling, and never take anything from the reef.

Eco-purchasing

Few people realize how powerfully their dollars speak, and one of the very best things you can do for the environment is to spend wisely.

Dollars spent on wood carvings, jewelry made from decorative local seeds, banana craft, straw goods, woven grasses, art, and anything made from coconut shells will really help the economy and the environment. Jewelry made from conch shells is also okay as these are caught for their meat, and the shell is normally thrown away. (However, check importation regulations in your home country.) T-shirts and other locally manufactured items are fine, too.

Avoid buying coral and turtleshell prod-

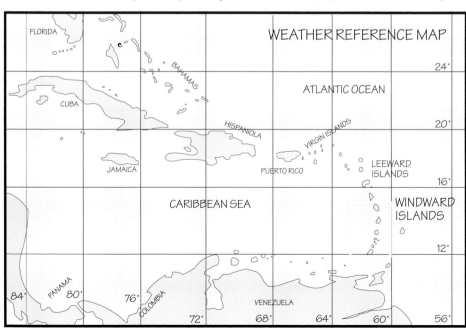

WEATHER REFERENCE MAP

FLORIDA

BAHAMAS

24°

ATLANTIC OCEAN

CUBA

HISPANIOLA

20°

VIRGIN ISLANDS

JAMAICA

PUERTO RICO

LEEWARD ISLANDS

16°

CARIBBEAN SEA

WINDWARD ISLANDS

12°

PANAMA

84°   80°   76°

COLOMBIA

VENEZUELA

72°   68°   64°   60°   56°

ucts. Considerable damage to reef structures is done by youths who take corals to sell to jewelry makers. The hawksbill turtle, most often killed for its shell, is an endangered species, as are all Caribbean sea turtles, and importation of turtle shell is forbidden in most countries. These items are sold mainly to yachts, so let us say "no" to these vendors and support the turtles and reefs. If you visit during the lobster season and are buying lobsters, always turn them over to see if they have eggs underneath (easily seen as red caviar). If they do, refuse to buy them.

I am happy to say that in the years since I included this paragraph, the amount of coral and turtle shell products offered to yachtspeople has diminished significantly. Thank you!

One purchase that might significantly effect the environment is your choice of antifouling. TBT paints have been banned nearly everywhere in the world for their damage to the environment. In the Caribbean they are still legal. Make sure you know what your paint has in it, and choose wisely.

Cruising Information

Weather

Continuous sunshine and balmy trade breezes, right? Well, not too far wrong.

There are two seasons, the dry and the wet, but they are not always well differentiated. During the dry season (February to June), there will often be weeks of clear sunny weather broken only by an occasional small rain shower. In the wet season (July until January) there will still be plenty of sunshine, but with more frequent showers and occasional rainy days with no sun. There is very little temperature difference between the seasons; you can expect 78° to 87°F (25° to 31°C) year round.

The winds nearly always blow from between northeast to southeast at 10 to 25 knots; calms are rare. The wind tends to strengthen around the northern ends of islands. Rain usually arrives in intense squalls that can be seen coming from afar. Sometimes these squalls have a lot of wind in them (40 knots or more); often they do not. There is no way to tell before they arrive. Infrequently, a squall or cold front can produce winds from the west, making the usual anchorages uncomfortable.

During the winter months storms and cold fronts farther north sometimes produce swells that reach the Windwards. These northerly swells can make anchorages that are open to the north or west rolly and occasionally untenable. Few swells are really bad, but when they are, you have to be prepared to move to a calmer spot, even in the middle of the night. Swells have caused the demise of quite a few unattended yachts. Hurricanes also cause swells during the hurricane season. These swells may come from any direction, depending on the position of the storm.

In the winter a big high-pressure area to our northeast is a dominant feature. When the isobars get tight, the wind increases and is sometimes very fresh (25-30 knots). We call these Christmas winds. This high pressure is offset by cold fronts that come down from the northwest. They almost never make it as far as the Windwards, but as they approach, we often get very calm and sunny weather followed by wind and rain, as their tail ends affect this area.

Visibility varies from an exceptional low of five miles to a high of over 50 miles. Extremely hazy days are caused by dust from Africa. Sometimes reddish traces may be found on the cabin and decks. On hazy days avoid dust stains when doing the laundry by wiping off the lifelines before hanging out the washing.

The hurricane season is from June to October. People now talk of "named storms" only about half of which will reach hurricane strength. The months of June, July, and October only produce about one hurricane every three years for the whole western Atlantic, including the Caribbean

LOCAL RADIO
For news, views, and weather

A M

Radio Grenada ----------------------535/540
  (weather after 0700 news) insomniacs
  note that BBC runs late night till 0500
Barbados Broadcasting Corp ---900
  (weather after 0715 news)
St. Vincent Radio ----------------------705

F M

Sun Radio (Grenada)...98.5/87.9/105.5
  weather 0700, noon and 1800.
Waves (St. Lucia) -----------------93.5, 93.7
  weather daily at 0730 & 1630
Sound of the Nation (St. Vincent)----------
---- --------------------------89.7,90.7, 107.5
  weather at 0700 after news and ads
St. Vincent --------------------------100.5,
  weather 0745
Radio Caraibes (French)---------89.9

HAM & SSB (local times)

Caribbean weather net on 8137 USB
  @0700 (Safety and Security net 8104
  USB @0815)
Caribbean weather net on 8104 kHz
  USB @ 0830
Caribbean emergency /weather net on
  3815 kHz LSB @ 1835
NMN Offshore forecast 4426, 6501 &
  8764 USB @ 0530, 1130, 1730 &
  2330
Southbound II, 12359 USB at 1600
Cocktail and weather net 7086 LSB at
  1630 (hurricane season only)
For information on weather Fax
  check: http://weather.noaa.gov/fax/
  marine.shtml

VHF

Cruisers nets (not Sunday) on Channel
68, Grenada at 0730, Bequia at 0800 and
St. Lucia at 0830
In Martinique, COSMA gives forecasts in
  French at 0730 and 1830 on VHF: 11.

Sea and the Gulf of Mexico. During August and September the number is around five a year. Hurricanes frequently start well out in the Atlantic Ocean, often on the latitude of the Windwards, but then they usually swing north and pass through the Caribbean farther north. Very few hit the Windwards and sometimes years go by without one in this area, but it is essential to check the forecasts, especially in these days of rather active hurricane seasons. You can get weather on the radio, but it is hard to find consistently good forecasts.

It is probably easiest to go into an internet cafe and get the weather on the web. (We give links to several forecasts on doyleguides.com.) Cruisers nets are good for weather. Cruisers nets in the Windwards are on VHF: 68, Monday to Saturday. Grenada is at 0730, Bequia is at 0800, St. Lucia (Rodney Bay) is at 0830.

Here are some terms you will hear on the radio and what they mean: "Intertropical convergence zone" affecting the area. This is not any kind of low, but you may get some rain squalls or cloudy weather. "Tropical disturbance," "tropical wave," and "upper level trough" are poorly organized weather systems associated with rain squalls of varying intensity. A "tropical depression" is an organized weather system with sustained winds of up to 35 knots and rain. Sometimes these can be very nasty and other times they turn out to be nothing. A "tropical storm," on the other hand, is definitely something to be avoided as it has lots of rain and sustained winds of 35 to 63 knots. Once the sustained winds become more than 64 knots, it is called a hurricane.

Hurricane winds can come from any direction, so be prepared to get out of the way or run for one of the hurricane holes: Cohe du Lamentin, Trois Ilets, or, better still, Cul de Sac Marin in Martinique; Rodney Bay Lagoon or Marigot Bay in St. Lucia; the mangrove swamp in Tyrrel Bay, Carriacou; and in Grenada, Port Egmont. Drive your boat aground bow first into the mangroves. Tie off to the biggest mangrove trees with all available lines (use at least ten). Put out two anchors astern, turn off all seacocks, remove all sails, awnings and biminis, leave the boat

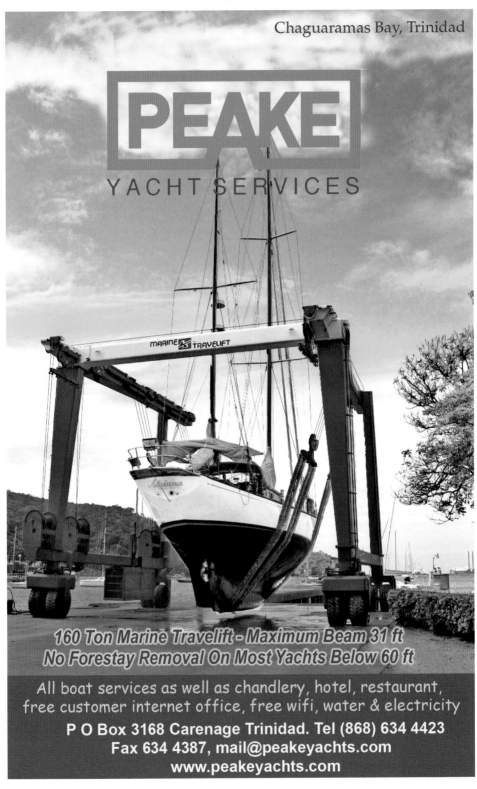

and find somewhere safe ashore.

During one of the few hurricanes that we did get, a charter party was advised by their company to make at once for a safe harbor to ride it out. "Oh no," they said "we have confirmed flights out and don't want to miss them. We will make it in time." They sailed north from St. Vincent to St. Lucia, but by the time they reached Soufriere, it was raining cats and dogs, and the wind was howling, so they anchored and went ashore. The boat soon began to drag and the skipper, aided by a local fisherman, tried to re-anchor. They managed to get their anchor line caught in the prop so they could not use power, and it was blowing too hard to make sail. In the end they drifted all night through the hurricane, and were rescued, after the winds fell, by a French coast guard boat off Martinique. I suppose the moral of the tale is that it is amazing what you can get away with, but better not to try.

Charts

You have a choice between British Admiralty (B.A.), U.S. Defense Mapping Agency (D.M.A) and yachting charts. U.K. charts are much more expensive in the U.S. and vice versa. New charts should be based on WG 84 data so they can be used with GPS.

Nautical Publications supply their charts in kits each kit covering several islands. They are in color and the format is relatively small (23.5 by 16.5 inches) so you never need to fold them. Each kit comes in a handy plastic see-through envelope that you can take into the cockpit with the current chart on top. This also ensures that, rather than losing one chart over the side, the whole kit will blow over, so make a little hole in the plastic and tie the envelope down. Hasko Scheidt of Nautical Publication has done several surveys in the Caribbean, and in those areas he has surveyed (including the east coast of Antigua and the south coast of Barbuda), their charts are particularly good. His charts include very detailed land information as well as nautical information; the kit includes both paper and a digital DVD.

Imray Iolaire also does yachting charts and these are printed on plastic so they almost last forever and you can get them wet. However, vigorous rubbing will take the color right off them, so experiment a little before you cover them with temporary pencil lines. These charts are sold individually so you can tailor your collection to your needs, and while they are large format, like the hydrographic charts, you need fewer of them as most include detailed harbor plans. They also come in digital format but these are sold separately.

I have found the Garmin Blue Map series of electronic charts, which works on my little Garmin mapreader, to be exceptionally good at placing you in the right place with respect to land. These charts are somewhat simple and sometimes lack adequate depth data.

Buoyage

All the islands now use the IALA B buoyage system. Main channels are marked with red and green buoys or beacons with red to starboard when entering: in other words "Red Right Returning." Other shoals and channels are indicated by black and yellow buoys or beacons coded both with respect to color and triangulation (using cones), as shown in the diagram on page 44.

Lights and buoys in the Windwards are unreliable. Lights do not always work, buoys go adrift, and beacons lose color and cones. Treat navigational aids with great caution.

Tides and currents

The tidal range is around two feet, not enough to be critical except in a few places. The lowest tides are in the summer. An equatorial current sets to the west-northwest. This current is affected by the tide when you are within a few miles of land. A counter-current begins about one hour before low water, offsets the equatorial current, and can run up to one knot to the east. This continues for about five hours, until about four hours after low water. Skippers of boats that are very slow to windward can make use of this to help them when sailing between islands. However, it is a mixed blessing because the counter-current usually sets up much rougher seas.

MILEAGE CHART

This table is approximate and offered as a guide to planning. Distances sailed are often in excess of those shown due to wind and current.

Origin	Ft. de France	G. Anse D'Arlet	Anse Mitan	Ste. Anne	Rodney Bay	Castries	Marigot	Pitons	Vieux Fort	Wallilabou	Kingstown	Young Island	Admiralty B.	Friendship B.	Mustique	Canouan	Mayreau	Tobago Cays	Union I.	P.S.V.	Hillsborough	Tyrrel Bay	St. George's	Prickly Bay	Mt. Hartman B.
St. Pierre	12	14	16	30	42	45	47	56	67	90	97	99	105	109	115	122	127	130	133	136	139		166	172	173
Fort de France		3	7	21	33	37	39	47	57	83	92	98	102	108	115	120	123	126	130	132			159	165	166
Anse Mitan			6	20	32	36	38	46	57	82	91	97	101	107	114	119	122	125	129	131			158	164	165
Gd Anse D'Arlet				15	26	30	32	41	52	77	84	89	96	102	108	113	116	119	123	125			152	158	159
St. Anne					21	26	30	39	50	76	83	85	91	95	101	108	113	114	117	123	126		156	161	162
Rodney Bay						5	8	18	29	55	62	64	70	74	80	87	92	95	98	102	105		126	135	140
Castries							4	13	24	50	57	59	65	69	75	82	87	90	93	97	100		126	131	135
Marigot								10	21	46	53	55	61	65	71	78	83	87	90	93	96		121	126	131
Pitons									11	36	43	45	51	55	61	68	73	77	80	83	86		116	121	122
Vieux Fort										34	41	43	49	53	59	66	71	74	77	81	84		114	119	120
Wallilabou											7	9	15	19	25	32	37	40	43	47	50		80	85	85
Kingstown												2	8	11	16	27	32	35	38	42	45		75	80	81
Young Island													9	10	15	25	32	35	38	42	45		75	80	81
Admiralty Bay														8	11	19	27	32	35	38	45		66	71	72
Friendship Bay															7	15	24	29	33	35	38		61	66	67
Mustique																7	18	20	24	26	31		54	66	72
Canouan																	7	12	19	24	26	31	49	54	55
Mayreau Saline Bay																		4	6	10	16	14	42	47	48
Tobago Cays																			4	7	11	12	44	49	50
Union (Clifton)																				4	7	9	39	44	45
Hillsborough																					4	7	34	39	40
P.S.V.																						4	30	35	36
Tyrrel Bay																							9	35	36
St. George's																								7	8
Prickly Bay																									2

GPS

GPS is the biggest leap in navigational science since the invention of the chronometer. Now we can always know our position anywhere in the world. Accurate though this system is, there are limitations. I have noticed occasional inaccuracies, up to a tenth of a mile, even when the GPS suggested better accuracy. Therefore, I would not advise using a GPS to navigate reef-strewn passages at night or in poor visibility. Older charts were created on unspecified formats, and inaccuracies of up to half a mile may occur. Newer charts are based on WG 84 data and work with GPS. The charts in this book are on GPS grids created by using a Garmin on WG 84 data, using much interpolation. No guarantee is offered about their accuracy. We include a table of GPS positions for route planning. You can download them from www.doyleguides.com. Remember, land and shoals may be on your line of approach, depending on your route.

Customs and immigration

The Windwards contain four separate countries: Martinique, St. Lucia, St. Vincent (including the Grenadines to Petit St. Vincent), and Grenada (which includes Carriacou and Petite Martinique). Each has its own customs regulations and it is necessary to clear in and out of each country. On arrival, you should hoist a yellow flag and anchor in a port of entry. After that, you can go ashore in search of customs and immigration officers. Take passports, ship's papers, and the clearance from your last port with you. All the Windwards now have simple one-page forms.

A pre-clearance system called eseaclear (www.eseaclear.com) can greatly ease formalities. You can preclear from any internet connection. You receive a number, which you give to the officer on arrival, and it saves you filling in all the forms. All your data are stored on the site making it easy the next time. It currently works in all ports in St. Lucia and in Bequia in St. Vincent and the Grenadines.

Customs and immigration officers will refuse to deal with anyone not wearing a shirt and looking reasonably presentable. Charges and other details are given under island and harbor headings.

Officers are often late to the office, so if you need to get going, clear the night before.

Dogs

So you've brought your pet all the way over the ocean and now you want to take it for a walk. Well, here is what you can expect from the local authorities: In Martinique and Grenada, if you have a rabies vaccination certificate handy when you clear in, you can walk your dog ashore. St. Vincent and St. Lucia are both rabies free and animals are not allowed ashore without a vast amount of paper work and a vet visit.

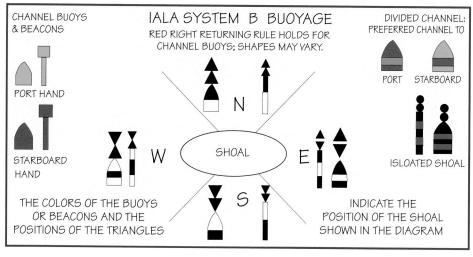

Some people do not realize that dogs in the Caribbean are subject to a deadly heart worm. Check with a vet for appropriate counter-measures before leaving, or as soon as you get here.

Anchoring

It amazes me that you can safely keep a yacht in place with an anchor. Many yachts weigh from six to twenty tons, and provide a stack of windage, yet we hold them in place with a tiny (35-60 lb.) anchor. But it does work, most of the time. Anchoring can be simple or fraught with dangers to your yacht, your relationship with your crew (especially your spouse), and to other yachts.

The first critical decision is where to drop the anchor. Check your chart for no-anchoring channels and for depths, then look at the boats and harbor for possible anchoring spots, and places best avoided (like fish pots and moorings). Clear the foredeck for action, and shorten the dinghy painter so it does not end up in the prop.

In normal conditions the wind in the Windwards will be blowing somewhere from the east, and you can expect to end up as the other anchored yachts are lying. It is safest to anchor behind the other yachts so there is no one for you to drag into. You can drop anchor as close as 50 feet behind another boat in most conditions. If you go in front of another yacht, you need to drop the anchor at least a hundred yards in front of them, or you will end up on top of them.

The wind often shifts 20 or 30 degrees: Will that put your boat over someone's anchor, or you over theirs?

In rare calm conditions with boats facing all directions, you have no idea which way chains are laid out. All you can do is anchor well clear of all other boats. Even if the wind is constant, boats swing from side to side, and each does it differently, so you do not want to end up close beside anyone.

It is best to anchor when the sun is high, so you can choose a light colored, sandy patch, where the holding will be good, rather than a dark colored, weedy patch, where you may drag. Always approach your spot into the wind.

To give the anchor a chance to hold, you need to let out at least five times as much chain or rope as the depth of water you anchor in, plus the height of your bow. (Let out more if bad weather is expected.) If you are anchoring on chain, the chain needs to be marked so you know how much you are letting out. This is imperative. Chandleries sell clever plastic chain markers in different colors, which sit inside the chain and do not interfere with the windlass. Cruisers can use these, or paint the chain. Charterers should ask the company how they have marked the chain (and they should have). If they have not, you will need to flake it out on deck while you are still on the dock and mark it yourself. Good temporary markers are plastic electrical ties in different colors; use two or three for each mark, in case one breaks. Put the bulky bit inside the chain where it will not get crunched by the windlass. If these are not available, you could try whipping twine. You are never going to use less than 50 feet of chain, so this can be your first mark, then mark every 20 feet up to about 150 feet.

If you have a chain/rope combination, it is much easier to estimate how much you are letting out and also to see whether you have let out enough by the angle of the rode after it is set (see diagram on page 46). While rope alone, or rope and 12 feet of chain will work in sand and some other seabeds, you will need at least 50 feet of chain for beds of dead coral. If you use mostly rope, you will wander around more should the wind drop, and need to allow for this.

To look good while anchoring, always bring the boat to a complete stop before dropping the anchor. Let out enough chain for the anchor to reach the bottom, then as the boat swings back with the wind, keep letting out more, bit by bit, till you have let out the right amount. Never dump the chain or rope all at once. When the boat has settled down, facing the same way as all the others, nudge the engine into reverse at low revs till the rode becomes tight. If the boat does not drag, keep increasing the revs (take bearings ashore), and make sure you are holding. If the anchor holds at high revs in reverse you are probably okay, but it is always good to dive on your anchor and make sure it is well dug in. If you do drag, the spot you are in is poor holding, so move to a different place and try again. Do not try the hard reverse if you are anchoring on soft mud; in that case the anchor may need a very long time to settle.

The crew on the bow cannot hear the helmsman with the engine running, and the helmsman certainly cannot hear the crew. Hand signals look more professional and work better than screaming, but only if you figure out a signal system in advance.

If you do end up a little too close to someone else, you can often solve this by putting out a second anchor, at about 30 degrees to your first, which will pull you clear and restrict your swinging room.

Make sure the rope is cleated properly or the chain secure (the windlass does not secure it). Leave the foredeck clear of clutter so, if you have to move in the middle of the night, you are not fighting windsurf boards and hammocks. Check your bearings periodically to make sure you have not dragged.

Mooring

Moorings are rapidly becoming much more widespread in the islands, which is a mixed blessing. Moorings do sometimes help protect the seagrass, which encourages turtles, echinoderms, and many kinds of fish.

Owners of rentable moorings include towns (especially Martinique), marinas, marine parks, charter companies (St. Vincent) and private individuals. The technology to properly design, place and maintain moorings at level where they will not fail has existed for years. Where I grew up in the UK, hundreds of boats were on town moorings, these were hauled and inspected annually, and they had to withstand major storms; I do not remember a single failure

Unfortunately, moorings in the Carib-

bean are not well maintained and, as nearly every bad consequence of failure (and there have been many), has landed on the yacht owner, not the mooring owner, there has been no incentive for improvement. Official moorings are generally correctly put down, but there is often little or no maintenance. In some places mooring use is compulsory. I avoid using moorings where possible, and snorkel on them if there is no alternative. Never run a line from one side of your boat, though the mooring to the other, or as the boat swings it will chafe through. Use a separate line on each side.

In the Grenadines, outside the marine parks, locals view moorings as a kind of personal parking meter to gather income. Most of these are poorly designed and constructed, and the guiding philosophy for most mooring owners is to rent it till it breaks, and then fix it. I would not trust any of them without a very close underwater inspection. They are almost never properly installed and often not a single shackle has been wired, so they can fall apart. Lines can often catch on the concrete block and chafe right through, and the size of the block or the means of attachment is frequently inadequate. They have no legal status; there is even a warning about them in the Bequia customs office. You can anchor right beside one, the owner has absolutely no rights over the seabed and cannot make you move, though he is quite likely to act like a jerk. If you take one, and it is too close to a boat that is already anchored, you must move; such moorings carry no rights. If you decide to take one of these moorings, you are taking substantial risk, so make sure your insurance covers it.

If moorings are okay, we will mention that in the text.

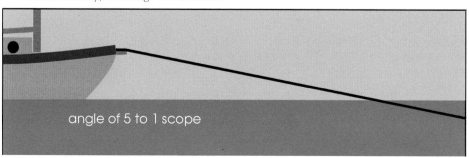

angle of 5 to 1 scope

SAILING, CREWED & POWER YACHTING VACATIONS

The Moorings will bring your dream to reality by providing the newest yachts along with unparalleled customer service to ensure you have the most exceptional boating vacation possible. Our 40-year reputation for integrity, quality and reliability has satisfied the most discriminating boaters. Experience your most unforgettable vacation ever with The Moorings.

www.moorings.com   888.952.6014

NORTH AMERICA I CARIBBEAN I MEDITERRANEAN I SOUTH PACIFIC I INDIAN OCEAN I FAR EAST

GPS WAYPOINTS

For planning purposes only. These waypoints may be downloaded from
www.doyleguides.com along with links to help you put them on your GPS.

All miles are nautical miles.

ID	Latitude	Longitude	Comment
	MARTINIQUE		
WMTQ01	N14°26.00'	W061°05.00'	Approach to Martinique's SW coast
WMTQ02	N14°44.50'	W061°10.70'	Off main dock St. Pierre
WMTQ03	N14°38.40'	W061°08.50'	0.1 miles W of harbor wall, Case Pilote
WMTQ04	N14°37.80'	W061°09.20'	Approach to Case Pilote
WMTQ05	N14°36.80'	W061°06.40'	Schoelcher
WMTQ06	N14°35.00'	W061°05.00'	Approach to Fort de France
WMTQ07	N14°35.70'	W061°04.50'	Approach Fort de France anchorage
WMTQ08	N14°32.90'	W061°02.10'	Approach to Trois Ilets
WMTQ09	N14°33.60'	W061°02.80'	Approach to Trou Etienne
WMTQ10	N14°33.70'	W061°03.40'	Pointe du Bout
WMTQ11	N14°33.00'	W061°04.00'	Approach for Anse A L'Ane
WMTQ12	N14°31.80'	W061°05.40'	Anse Noir
WMTQ13	N14°30.00'	W061°06.00'	Grand Anse D'Arlet
WMTQ14	N14°29.20'	W061°05.20'	Petit Anse D'Arlet (middle of bay)
WMTQ15	N14°27.70'	W061°00.50'	Approach for Baie du Marigot
WMTQ16	N14°25.00'	W060°55.00'	Approach to St. Anne & Marin
WMTQ17	N14°26.70'	W060°54.00'	Cul de Sac Marin (entrance)
WMTQ18	N14°26.20'	W060°53.20'	Ste. Anne (western part of anchorage)
WMTQ19	N14°24.90'	W060°49.80'	Baie Des Anglais (entrance)
WMTQ20	N14°24.00'	W060°53.80'	Approach to Grande Anse des Saline
	ST LUCIA		
WSLU01	N14°05.50'	W060°58.20'	0.1 miles west of Pigeon Island
WSLU02	N14°04.73'	W060°57.40'	Rodney Bay Lagoon (entrance)
WSLU03	N14°04.10'	W060°58.70'	Southern approach, inside Barrel of Beef
WSLU04	N14°01.20'	W061°00.50'	Castries (entrance)
WSLU05	N13°58.05'	W061°01.90'	Marigot (entrance)
WSLU06	N13°56.40'	W061°03.20'	Anse La Raye (entrance)
WSLU07	N13°55.60'	W061°03.70'	Anse Cochon
WSLU08	N13°54.70'	W061°04.30'	Anse de Canaries
WSLU09	N13°51.50'	W061°05.20'	0.4 miles SW of Anse Chastanet reef
WSLU10	N13°51.20'	W061°03.80'	Soufriere
WSLU11	N13°48.50'	W061°05.00'	0.2 miles west of Gros Piton
WSLU12	N13°43.00'	W060°58.00'	0.75 miles WSW of dock Vieux Fort
WSLU13	N13°46.00'	W061°05.00'	2.3 miles south of Gros Piton
WSLU14	N13°44.50'	W061°00.00'	Entrance to Laborie
	ST VINCENT		
WSTV01	N13°20.00'	W061°15.00'	2 miles northwest of Chateaubelair
WSTV02	N13°16.00'	W061°15.80'	Cumberland Bay (center of entrance)
WSTV03	N13°14.90'	W061°16.50'	Wallilabou (center of entrance)
WSTV04	N13°14.40'	W061°16.90'	0.1 miles W of Bottle & Glass
WSTV05	N13°11.40'	W061°16.20'	Buccament Bay (center)
WSTV06	N13°10.90'	W061°16.20'	Petit Byahaut

ST VINCENT (cont.)

WSTV07	N13°09.50'	W061°14.90'	Ottley Hall (entrance)
WSTV08	N13°09.00'	W061°14.00'	Kingstown (center of bay)
WSTV09	N13°07.60'	W061°12.40'	0.1 miles SW of Fort Duvernette
WSTV10	N13°07.50'	W061°11.90'	Approach to Blue Lagoon

GRENADINES

WGNS01	N13°00.70'	W061°15.10'	0.1 miles west of Devil's Table, Bequia,
WGNS02	N12°59.50'	W061°17.60'	Bequia, West Cay (just off W end)
WGNS03	N12°59.10'	W061°14.00'	Bequia, Friendship Bay
WGNS04	N12°53.50'	W061°12.00'	Mustique approach, north of Montezuma
WGNS05	N12°52.50'	W061°12.00'	Mustique approach, south of Montezuma
WGNS06	N12°52.80'	W061°11.50'	Mustique Britannia Bay
WGNS07	N12°44.40'	W061°20.00'	Canouan, northwest point
WGNS08	N12°42.70'	W061°20.20'	Canouan, Charlestown Bay (center of)
WGNS09	N12°42.40'	W061°21.40'	Just northwest of Glossy Hill, Canouan
WGNS10	N12°39.50'	W061°23.00'	0.5 miles west of Baline Rocks
WGNS11	N12°38.20'	W061°21.80'	0.1 miles W of Petit Rameau, Tobago Cays
WGNS12	N12°39.00'	W061°23.70'	Mayreau, Salt Whistle Bay
WGNS13	N12°38.00'	W061°24.50'	Mayreau, Saline Bay
WGNS14	N12°36.00'	W061°28.00'	0.25 miles W of Chatham Bay, Union
WGNS15	N12°36.00'	W061°24.20'	Union, northen approach to Union/Palm
WGNS16	N12°35.00'	W061°25.00'	0.25 miles W of Grand de Coi, Union
WGNS17	N12°32.90'	W061°24.10'	0.2 miles N of Mopion Channel, PSV
WGNS18	N12°32.00'	W061°23.50'	0.5 miles west of PSV dock
WGNS19	N12°32.00'	W061°27.00'	0.7 miles WNW of north end of Carriacou
WGNS20	N12°30.00'	W061°30.80'	2.8 miles west of Jack a Dan, Carriacou
WGNS21	N12°29.70'	W061°28.20'	Just west of Jack a Dan, Carriacou
WGNS22	N12°27.00'	W061°30.00'	Tyrrel Bay (entrance)
WGNS23	N12°19.00'	W061°36.00'	Isle de Ronde

GRENADA

WGDA01	N12°15.00'	W061°40.00'	1 mile N of David Point
WGDA02	N12°06.70'	W061°45.00'	Halifax Harbour (entrance)
WGDA03	N12°05.20'	W061°45.90'	Dragon Bay (entrance)
WGDA3A	N12°05.50'	W061°45.90'	Happy Hill (approach)
WGDA3B	N12°04.40'	W061°45.70'	Grand Mal Bay (approach)
WGDA04	N12°02.70'	W061°45.50'	0.25 miles W of entrance to St. George's
WGDA05	N12°00.20'	W061°48.40'	Point Saline (just off tip of land)
WGDA06	N11°59.60'	W061°46.20'	True Blue (entrance)
WGDA07	N11°59.30'	W061°46.00'	Prickly Bay (entrance)
WGDA08	N11°58.60'	W061°45.90'	0.25 miles W of Porpoises rocks
WGDA09	N11°59.00'	W061°45.10'	Approach for Mt Hartman Bay
WGDA10	N11°59.00'	W061°44.20'	Approach for Hog Island
WGDA11	N11°59.10'	W061°43.50'	Approach for Clarkes Court Bay
WGDAPB	N11°59.30'	W061°42.90'	Approach for Phare Bleu Marina
WGDA12	N11°59.30'	W061°42.70'	Approach for Port Egmont
WGDA13	N12°00.00'	W061°42.10'	Approach for Calivigny habour
WGDA14	N12°00.60'	W061°41.30'	Approach P. Bacaye/Bacelot Bay
WGDA15	N12°00.60'	W061°40.70'	St. David's Harbour (entrance)

Britannia Bay, Mustique

reflection

Chartering

Whether you want to go bareboat, fully crewed, one way, multihull, or monohull, you can find something to suit in the Windwards. I give a list of charter companies in the directory, and links to them on doyleguides.com.

For bareboaters without much experience, the easiest sail is from St. Vincent to Union or Grenada. Most charter companies will be happy to arrange one-way charters for an extra fee, and most skippered yachts will pick up and drop off at ports of your choice for no extra charge.

The sail from St. Lucia to St. Vincent is a long, hard day's sail. The return trip is often worse. If you are starting a charter in St. Lucia or Martinique, it makes a lot of sense to sail one way and finish in Union Island or Grenada. This is especially true if you only have a week or so.

Bareboating

I had the pleasure to run one of the first Caribbean bareboats ~ a little 31-footer called Rustler. When we said "bareboat," we meant it. Rustler came with a hand-start diesel that would barely push her out of the anchorage, a small icebox full of ice and 40 gallons of water, which were pumped up by hand. Mechanical complexities consisted of a massive British marine toilet, with endless valves and pumps. This antiquity was almost impossible to clog, but at the same time, however much you worked on the packing gland, within a couple of days it tended to squirt you in the eye. The outboard was a close relative ~ all chrome and stainless with no cover. You had to wind the cord round the flywheel for every start and go through an elaborate system of switching valves and vents and bleeding for exactly the right number of seconds. The only thing to be said in its favor was that even the roughest of mechanics could do a major overhaul with a screwdriver, a big hammer, and a pair of pliers.

When I look at some of the bareboat ads these days it seems that people want to take it all with them when they get away from it all. Freezers, fridges, hair dryers, microwave ovens, TV, telephones and DVD players are all available.

One thing that years of sailing has taught me is that anything mechanical, electrical, or electronic, when installed on a well-used yacht, will eventually go wrong. Bareboats are particularly susceptible because of all the different people using the gear. In practical terms, this means that breakdowns are part and parcel of a modern sophisticated yacht, and not necessarily a reflection on the efficiency and ability of the charter company. The charter people realize this, so they all help each other's yachts and do their best to have a breakdown and backup service, despite the problems posed by the Windwards, which are well spread out. But it is important that bareboaters appreciate the essentially adventurous nature of a bareboat holiday and not let it be ruined by a malfunctioning hair dryer.

I still have the log book from Rustler and there is an entry I am specially fond of. At the beginning it is written in the hand of the group's self-appointed leader, Dr. Smith, who was not the least bit happy. Each day was another disaster. He couldn't make the outboard start, he couldn't find the boat hook, one of the navigation lights malfunctioned, he was "very disappointed" in the condition of the boat. Then the handwriting changed and the new entry said: "Dr. Smith had to return home for pressing personal reasons. Rustler is now a fine yacht, the weather is perfect, the sailing fantastic. We are having a marvelous time."

A good thing about chartering is that those occasions that are terrible at the time make great stories later. A while ago a bareboat was on a reef in the middle of nowhere and on the radio to the company's local representative who was trying to assess the situation.

"We are hard aground, the rudder is broken and we cannot steer," lamented the charterer.

"Ok. I've got that," said the rep. "Now tell me, are you taking on water?"

There was a pause of a few seconds, then back came a very definite answer, "Oh no, we did that yesterday in St. Vincent."

Crewed charters

Having spent years both running bareboats and skippering charters, I can attest without any question that skippered charters produce more glowing praise. A crewed charter is also a real holiday for everyone, with no galley and cleaning chores.

Many agents talk a lot about matching charterers to crew. In fact, most charterers

Day charter schooner, Friendship Rose

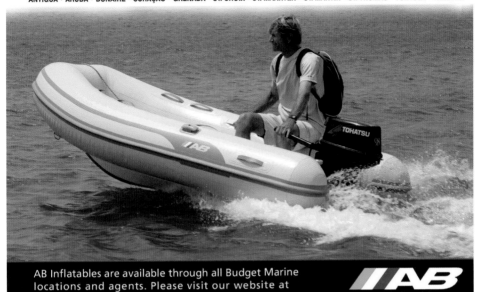

are happy, easy to please, and good company, and good professional skippers can adapt themselves to all kinds of people. Cooks develop a sensitivity to produce the right kind of food.

The modern large charter yachts that now make up the bulk of the fleet, have enough crew and separation of guests from the crew, that is it a bit like having your own mini-cruiseship, but with much better food and service.

Tipping is a big item for most crews as this makes up a large part of their income. Unless otherwise stated, 10 percent of the total charter fee is the norm and an appropriate figure for good service.

On smaller yachts with only a captain and cook, it is worth keeping in mind that, although yacht crews really enjoy what they are doing and genuinely like their guests, there is some strain to always being on one's best behavior and there are a few things that can make life a lot easier. It is a huge help if all the charterers go ashore for a couple of hours each day, either to shop, walk, or go to the beach. At this point the crew can put on their favorite music full blast and clean the boat with much banging and gay abandon. The charterers will return to a clean boat and a much-refreshed crew.

Cooks hate to be watched while they work. It makes them nervous and upsets their concentration. There is no way you would know this, because they are trained to smile and answer a string of questions; much better to leave them alone in the galley, and give them the attention they deserve when they produce that final work of art.

The cook usually works much harder than the skipper, so it is a great break if the guests decide to eat out, even if it is just a matter of having a sandwich ashore instead of returning for lunch. Unfairly, the best cooks get the fewest breaks, as no one can bear to miss a single meal.

It is a tradition on smaller yachts that, at some point, the guests take their crew out for dinner. For the crew the break is more important than the dinner, and if you are on a budget, they don't mind if it is somewhere quite simple.

Port Louis, Grenada

Professional Yachts

Most cruisers can quickly adjust to island time. If it doesn't get done today, tomorrow will suffice. This does not work for professional charter and superyachts on strict timetables, with guests arriving, chores to get done, and breakdowns to be coped with. I remember once many years ago arriving in Grenada with a charter turnaround on the eve of some holiday and not being able to get laundry done at any price.

Happily things are much better today. There are a number of good businesses that cater to professional yachts, and they will do what it takes to make things happen. I list these below.

Many of these agents have reasonable, standard fees for thing like clearing customs, and it would pay bareboaters or cruisers with short stops (one day to clear and out and tour the island for example) to take advantage of these services.

AGENTS

Martinique

Note: when dialing Martinique from over-seas dial + 596 596 + 6 digits, unless it is a mobile phone, in which case it is + 596 696 + 6 digits

You can base a superyacht in Martinique. It has all necessary support services, and if you are visiting the south, you will find Douglas Rapier (he is available 24/7) of Douglas Yacht Services to offer the very highest standard of professional service in everything a superyacht may want, from full provisioning and technical help to overseeing travel, private plane arrivals, restaurant and personal arrangements. English is his native tongue so you will have no communications problems. His office is in Marin Marina, but he keeps his mobile with him. Douglas Yacht Services, (0696) 45 89 75, (0596) 52 14 28, F: (0596) 52 07 36, VHF: 09, douglas.rapier@orange.com

St. Lucia

St. Lucia has dedicated agents to work with the large yachts. They can deal with customs, clear parts, arrange fuel, local provisions, and anything else. They will all work in any of St. Lucia's ports.

Ben Saltibus in Soufriere has been at it forever and is very professional. He works quite closely with Sam Taxi Service in St. Vincent and Henry Safari Tours in Grenada.

Benny Adjouda is the other accredited yacht agent. A big boat mooring is right off his Harmony restaurant in Soufriere. He works hard and quite a few superyacht clients would go nowhere else.

CJ Taxi Service in Rodney Bay Marina will also help with many things locally; you will be in good hands with any of them. With the new IGY Rodney Bay Marina, St. Lucia has become a good place to base a superyacht.

Ben's Taxi Service, (758) 459-5457, F: (758) 459-5719, Cell: (758) 484-0708, saltibus@slucia.cpm

Harmony Yacht Services (Benny), (758) 559 5050, cell: (758) 287 4261, F: (758) 458-5033, VHF: 16, harmonyiii@hotmail.com

CJ Taxi, (758) 584-3530, (758) 450-5981/ 458-4283, F: (758) 452-0185, VHF: 16

St. Vincent & the Grenadines

This archipelago offers ample support for a visiting superyacht. Sam of Sam Taxi Tours is an official ship agent and works with large yachts and some cruise ships. He has sub-agencies in Bequia and Union Island. He can clear your yacht in or out from most anchorages and handle all other needs. He has a good office up on a hill where he and his team keep an eye on arriving yachts.

Erika's Marine Services can handle yachts anywhere in St. Vincent and the Grenadines. They have agents in St. Vincent, Bequia, Canouan, and in Union Island, their main base.

Sam Taxi Tours, (784) 456-4338, F: (784) 456-4233, cell: (784) 528-2240 VHF: 68/16, sam-taxi-tours @caribsurf.com. In Bequia: RMS, (784) 458-3556, VHF: 68/16. rms@caribsurf.com In Union: (784) 494-4339, sam-taxi-tours @caribsurf.com.

Erika's Marine Services, (784) 458-8335, VHF: 68, info@ erikamarine.com

Grenada

Grenada makes a good superyacht base and has superyacht agents. They will handle anything you need, from checking in through customs to finding dock space, provisioning, and dealing with problems, and they will visit all Grenada's ports.

Dennis Henry of Henry Safari Tours has been at it the longest and he is professional, imaginative, and reliable, with a good back-up team. He owns two laundries and a large fleet of taxis and rather likes to be challenged on the odd occasion when he is thrown a problem he has not had to cope with before.

Roger and Claire Spronk run Spronk Ltd, a company based in True Blue. In addition to helping superyachts, they own both a gourmet store and a wholesale provisioning business, which handles a considerable quantity of the island's seafood, so they are particularly good at provisioning. Their base is at their restaurant, Bananas, in True Blue. They have started work on a waterfront base in Petite Calivigny.

Henry's Safari Tours, (473) 444-5313, F: (473) 444-4460, safari@caribsurf.com, VHF: 68

Spronk Mega Yacht Services, (473) 407-3688/439-4369/443-5663, Fax: (473) 444-4677, claire@spronksprovisioning.com

MARINAS AND FUELING

In Martinique, large yachts can fuel and dock in Marin Marina.

Marin Yacht Harbor, (SAEPP), (0596) 74 83 83, F: (0596) 74 92 20, VHF:09, info@portmarin.com

In St. Lucia, Rodney Bay Marina has fueling, but check the current depth into the lagoon.

Rodney Bay Marina, (758) 452-0324, F: (758) 452-0185, VHF: 16, rbm@igymarinas.com

Other fueling options include St. Lucia Yacht Services in Vigie, and Cool Breeze fuel station by the main town dock in Soufriere. Contact the agents to arrange tanker truck fueling in the main dock in Castries or Vieux Fort.

Cool Breeze Gas Station, (758) 459-7729, F: 459 5309

St. Lucia Yacht Services (758) 452-5057, VHF: 16

In St. Vincent, call Sam Taxi Tours. He will usually arrange for a tanker truck alongside the main docks in Kingstown.

Sam Taxi Tours, (784) 456-4338, F: (784) 456-4233, VHF: 68/16, sam-taxi-tours @vincysurf.com

An easy and good fuel dock in the Grenadines is B & C Fuels in Petit Martinique.

B&C Fuels, (473) 443-9110, F: (473) 443-9075, golfsierra@hotmail.com

You can also arrange fueling on the main dock in Tyrrel Bay through Bullens in Hillsborough.

Bullen's, (473) 443-7468/7469, F: (473) 443 8194 vbs@spiceisle.com

In St. George's, Grenada you can arrange fuel at the Grenada Yacht Club in St. George's. They can take boats about 160 feet long on their dock. You can get also fuel at the new Port Louis Marina, taking it from one of the superyacht berths, or you can arrange fuel on the main St. George's wharf through an agent,

Grenada Yacht Club, (473) 440-3050, F: (473) 440-6826, VHF: 16, gyc@ spiceisle.com

Port Louis Marina, (473) 435-7431, dockmaster: (473) 415-0820, VHF: 14, reservations@cnportlouismarina. com

Docking and fuel can be found at Prickly Bay Marina in Prickly Bay and Secret Harbour Marina in Mt. Hartman Bay. Take care to choose a channel suitable to your depth. Either marina can take almost any size of yacht that can make it into the bay.

Secret Harbour Marina (473) 444-4449, F: (473) 444-2090, VHF: 16 &71, secretharbour@spiceisle.com

Prickly Bay Marina, (473) 439-5265, VHF: 16, pricklybaymarina@ spiceisle.com

Marigot Bay, St. lucia

Frogfish, Polly Philipson at Dive Bequia

Scuba Diving

"It's fantastic. I could breathe under-water just like a fish, and fish swam up and looked at me. What an incredible feeling."

"It's the greatest sensation I've ever felt. When we swam back with the current it was just like gliding through a beautiful garden!"

These are typical comments from first-time divers who find that diving is the most exciting thing they have ever done. No wonder ~ it is the closest most of us will ever come to visiting a strange planet. Not only that, under water we are weightless and seem to fly. Like birds, we can soar, hover, and dive down to see anything of interest.

The underwater world is full of wonders: tall, soft waving "plants" that are really colonies of tiny animals, sponges that look like ancient urns, in colors ranging from yellow to a psychedelic luminous blue. Huge schools of fish swim by, unconcerned about our presence. Little squids move by jet propulsion, turtles and giant rays glide with elegant ease.

Yet many people are put off diving because they are under the impression it is complicated and difficult. Nothing could be farther from the truth. With modern equipment, diving is very simple and with one of the popular 'resort courses' you can be diving in half a day. In fact, the problem most divers have is to avoid boring their non-diving friends to distraction with tales of undersea adventure. The minimum age for most courses is 10.

Equipment

Experienced divers will want to bring their own masks, fins, and regulators. A really good comfortable B.C. (buoyancy compensator) is worth bringing, too. As for the rest, forget it. There is no point in humping tanks and weight belts; far better to rent them here. Those without any equip-

Ornate Elysia, Polly Philipson photo

Stoplight parrotfish

tary Blenny, Polly Philipson photo

Flying Gunard

ment don't need to worry. The dive shops will supply everything and it is usually excellent up-to-date gear. In many parts of the world you have to wear a protective wet suit against the cold, but in the Windwards the water is warm enough that for most of us this isn't necessary.

Courses for beginners

Anyone who just wants to give diving a go can do so very quickly with a 'resort course.' It will take one whole morning or afternoon. First you get a one-hour talk that tells you in simple language what diving is all about. Then you try out the equipment in shallow water and, lastly, you go for your first dive. A resort course only qualifies you to dive under the close supervision of an instructor at the same dive shop.

First dive

Wherever you take a resort course, the instructors will choose a site that is easy but interesting enough to attract aficionados. A typical example is Devil's Table in Bequia. The rocks and coral start at 12 feet and slope down to about 35 feet deep. You enter the water and feel a bit nervous, but you breathe out and gently sink. Soon your attention turns outwards. Large pillar corals rise from among the rocks. They look fuzzy, but if you swish your hand really close to them, the tentacles withdraw, leaving them looking like rocks. You stop to examine some pretty shells clinging to a waving sea fan and to your surprise a tiny damsel fish shoots up and tries to chase you away. He's protecting his patch, and you don't scare him; it's then you learn that you can even laugh through your regulator. There is a great deal more to see: brightly colored parrotfish and angelfish, moray eels staring from their holes, strange looking arrow crabs, and brightly banded coral shrimp. You enjoyed it? Good! Time to go to the next level.

Certification

If you've ever thought about getting certified, or if you try a dive and like it, then it makes sense to get certified on your holiday. If you get certified at home, chances are that it will be in a swimming pool, with nothing more interesting to look at than tiled walls. Your open water dives are likely to be in some frigid, grey lake. Furthermore, you will probably have to buy or rent equipment that is normally included in the course price down island. In the Caribbean, you can train at a cost not much greater than the dives alone. The course includes all equipment, you do everything in open water, the dives are fantastic, and you can take home a diving certificate as well as your memories. There are several diving associations that have accredited diving instructors who can train you and give you a certificate. These include Padi and Naui, which are equally good. The next step from the resort course is the new Padi Scuba Diver. This two-and-a-half day course certifies you to dive with any dive master at any shop to a depth of 40 feet. It is a good introduction and, being short, it is easy to do on holiday. You can complete your training on your next holiday, as this course counts as credit towards being an independent open water diver.

A full diving course in the islands takes about four or five days and includes a couple of hours of instruction each day, followed by a dive, during which you increase your practical skills.

For qualified divers

Some people, especially those chartering yachts, prefer to rent gear and go off diving by themselves. Others prefer to join a dive with professional instructors. At least for your first dives, I recommend going with the dive instructors. They know all the good sites, the hidden caves, the special ledge where angelfish live, and maybe they know where there is a tame octopus, seahorse, or frogfish. A good instructor is also a good guide and can point out many things that would otherwise be missed, which adds interest to your dive. Perhaps the most important reason is that many good dive sites are in places that can only be reached with a powerful dive boat rather than a dinghy. I have worked with many charterers who have tried it both ways and noticed that those who went with dive instructors had a much better time than those who went on their own.

The diving in the Windwards varies markedly from island to island and from one dive site to the next, so enthusiasts will want to try diving in several different spots. We will mention the good sites and their accessibility in the text under each anchorage section. Dive shops are listed in our directory.

Look for easy-to-visit dive and snorkel sites on our sketch charts. They are marked by flags.

Diving   Snorkeling

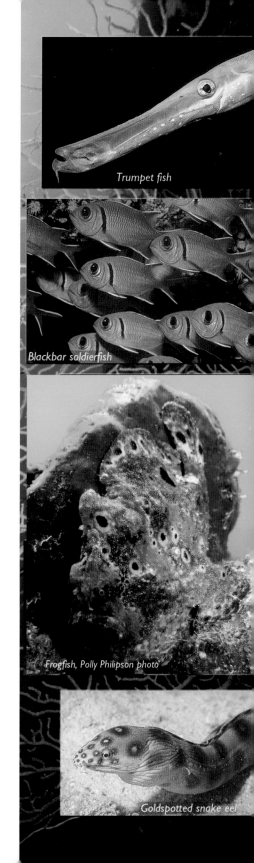

Trumpet fish

Blackbar soldierfish

Frogfish, Polly Philipson photo

Goldspotted snake eel

Anchorages in the
WINDWARD

**Martinique, St. Lucia, St. Vincent &
the Grenadines, Grenada,
Carriacou, & Petite
Martinique**

ISLANDS

Wallilabou falls

Grenada Sailing Festival, Jeff Fisher photo

Pigeon Island

Martinique

Yole racing, Marin

Regulations

Clear customs in Fort de France, Marin, Anse Mitan, Grand Anse D'Arlet or St. Pierre. Yachts present in Martinique waters for more than six months in one year are liable to import duty, with exemptions for storing your yacht while you fly abroad. Visas are not necessary for EU or US citizens. Other nationals should check. For places to clear, and opening hours, see our anchorage sections. Yachts pay no overtime fees or charges. Foreign yachts over 5 tons need national registration. (US state registration is not accepted.)

A 5-knot speed limit is in effect within 300 meters of all coastline.

Shopping hours

Shops often open 0800-1200 and 1500-1730, Monday through Saturday. Many offices close on Saturday. Supermarkets often stay open till 1900, and open on Sunday mornings.

Holidays

Jan 1 &2, New Year's Day & Recovery
Carnival Monday to Wednesday, 40 days before Easter. Feb 11-12, 2013 and March 3-4, 2014
Easter Friday through Monday, March 29-April 1, 2013 and April 18-21, 2014
May 1, Labor Day
May 8, Victory Day (1945)
Feb 22, Independence Day
May 1, Labor Day
Whit Monday, May 20, 2013 and June 9, 2014
May 22, Abolition of Slavery
Ascension Day, May 9, 2013 and May 29, 2014,
Corpus Christi, May 30, 2013 and June 19, 2014
July 14, Bastille Day
August 15, Virgin Mary Day
Nov 1, All Saints Day
Nov 11, Victory Day (1918)
Dec 25, Christmas Day

Telephones

Card telephones are widespread. Buy the cards at post offices, change houses, and most newspaper stands. You may need to insert a card for a reverse charge or telephone card call. Dial 00 to get out of the country and then the country code and number you want. Most Martinique call boxes have their number posted, so you can call your party and have them call you back. Martinique numbers are 10 digits, starting 0596, except cell phones, which are 0696. To call from the US, dial 011 596 then the whole number, excluding the first 0. It will start:
011 596 596... or 011 596 696....

Special inexpensive cards for overseas calls are sold in some shops. After putting in the number you are calling, you must finish with the "diez" (pound sign).

If you are roaming on a mobile phone, you will have to add a + to the beginning of the number. Local sims are available from Cart Orange and Digicel, as are prepaid USB ports for internet.

Transport

Martinique has a good system of buses or communal taxis (TC). These are reasonably priced, are found on most town squares, and run on fixed routes, mainly to and from Fort de France. There are also taxis. Typical taxi rates in Euros are:

Airport to Fort de France	25
Airport to Anse Mitan/Marin	60
Anse Mitan to golf course	10
Fort de France to Carrefour	8-10
St. Pierre to Fort de France	55
St. Pierre to Airport	63
Short ride	8
Full day tour	150
By the hour	40

Rental cars are available. You can use your own license. Drive on the right.

Yole sailing Marin

*T*he Caribs called Martinique *Madinina* ~ Island of Flowers. It is the largest of the Windwards and, apart from a few short spells under the British, has been French since it was colonized. It is a part of France and feels it, with excellent roads and a thriving economy. Nearly every bay has a wonderful government-built dock, ideal for leaving your dinghy. Fort de France is a busy city, bustling with shoppers and cars. The smaller towns are quieter and some look so clean they could have just been scrubbed. You will notice the smell of wonderful coffee and delicious cooking.

You can get almost anything done in Martinique ~ from galvanizing your boat to having stainless steel tanks made. The sailmakers are first rate, the chandleries magnificently stocked, and restaurants and boutiques abound. In short, when you have had enough deserted beaches and raw nature, Martinique is the place for a breath of civilization. And the island has enough excellent and varied anchorages for a week or two of exploring. Choose bays with fash-

ionable resorts, sleepy waterfront villages, or visit deserted bays with excellent snorkeling. Well-marked trails make hiking a delight.

The Empress Josephine grew up in Martinique on a 200-acre, 150-slave estate near Trois Ilets. A strange quirk of fate links Josephine and Martinique to the Battle of Trafalgar. In 1804, Napoleon was master of Europe, but the British still had naval supremacy and largely controlled Caribbean waters. However, ships were always scarce and some bright spark noticed that Diamond Rock on the south coast of Martinique was just about where the British would station another vessel if they had one, so they commissioned the rock as a ship. It was quite a feat to climb this steep, barren, snake-infested pinnacle and to equip it with cannons and enough supplies and water for a full crew of men. But they succeeded and for some 18 months H.M.S. Diamond Rock was a highly unpleasant surprise for unsuspecting ships sailing into Martinique. Napoleon was incensed; this was, after all, the birthplace of his beloved Josephine. Brilliant as he was on land, Napoleon never really understood

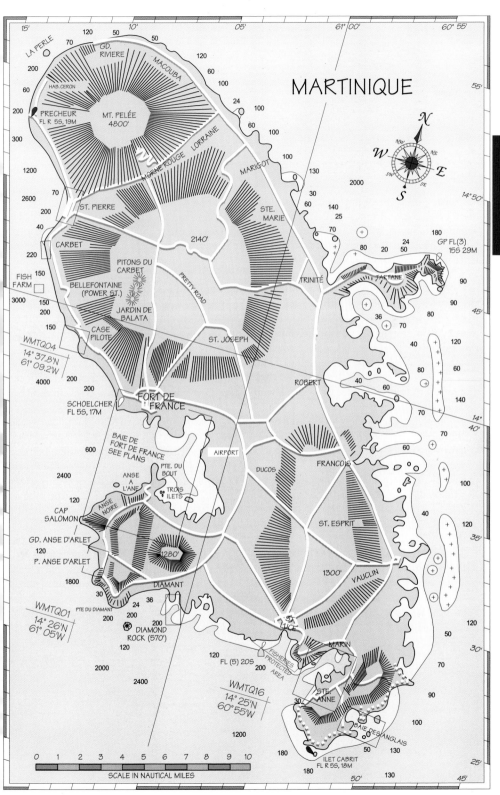

MARTINIQUE

LA PERLE
GD. RIVIERE
MACOUBA
HAB. CERON
PRECHEUR
FL R 5S, 19M
MT. PELÉE
4800'
MORNE ROUGE
LORRAINE
MARIGOT
ST. PIERRE
STE. MARIE
CARBET
2140'
PITONS DU CARBET
TRINITÉ
TARTANE
GP FL(3)
15S 29M
FISH FARM
BELLEFONTAINE
(POWER ST.)
JARDIN DE BALATA
CASE PILOTE
ST. JOSEPH
ROBERT
WMTQ04
14° 37.8'N
61° 09.2'W
SCHOELCHER
FL 5S, 17M
FORT DE FRANCE
BAIE DE FORT DE FRANCE
SEE PLANS
AIRPORT
PTE. DU BOUT
FRANCOIS
DUCOS
ANSE A L'ANE
TROIS ILETS
ANSE NOIRE
CAP SALOMON
ST. ESPRIT
GD. ANSE D'ARLET
1280'
P. ANSE D'ARLET
1300'
VAUCLIN
DIAMANT
PTE DU DIAMANT
WMTQ01
14° 26'N
61° 05'W
DIAMOND ROCK (570')
LUCE
MARIN
FISHERIES PROTECTED AREA
FL (5) 20S
WMTQ16
14° 25'N
60°55'W
STE ANNE
BAIE DES ANGLAIS
ILET CABRIT
FL R 5S, 18M
SCALE IN NAUTICAL MILES
0 1 2 3 4 5 6 7 8 9 10

Martinique

Diamond Rock

speak English and they are generally helpful. If you want the help of a good phrase book, check out Kathy Parsons *French for Cruisers*.

Numerous ATM machines will keep you in cash and most restaurants and businesses accept Visa and MasterCard. However, one or two only accept French cards. Ask before that seven-course meal or you may spend many hours washing dishes.

Navigation

The west coast (excluding the Bay of Fort de France) up to St. Pierre is mainly steep-to, and a quarter of a mile offshore clears any natural dangers.

Fish farms pop up off the coast from time to time. These are not dangerous by day but can be at night. They usually have flashing lights marking the outer limits. Currently, there is one off Bellefontaine with a clear passage inside or outside, approximate position 14° 40.2, 61° 10.2

The Bay of Fort de France has many shoals, especially at its eastern end. Check the charts and instructions given under the appropriate section.

The south coast of Martinique between Ste. Anne and Diamond Rock has several shoals extending up to a half mile offshore. Fish traps are plentiful and two or three are often tied together. It is best to stay in several hundred feet of water, outside the heavily fished area. The beat to Marin, usually against the current, is in protected water and can be exhilarating. It generally pays to tack fairly close to shore. On the rising tide, when the current sets east, the south coast can occasionally turn into a washing machine.

his navy or its problems and considered his men to be shirkers. Consequently, he ordered them to sea under Admiral Villeneuve, to free the rock and destroy the British admiral Horatio Nelson while they were about it. Villeneuve slipped out under the British blockade of France and headed straight for Martinique. Lord Nelson, with his battle-ready fleet, smelled blood and bounty and hurtled off from England in hot pursuit. However, poor information sent him on a wild goose chase to Trinidad, so Villeneuve was able to liberate the rock and return to France, prudently keeping well clear of Nelson.

Napoleon was none too pleased with Villeneuve because the British fleet was still in control of the high seas, so he was ordered to report in disgrace. Villeneuve preferred death to dishonor, so he put his ill-prepared fleet to sea to fight Nelson at the Battle of Trafalgar. Ironically, Villeneuve, who wished to die, survived the battle, and Nelson died.

Today Martinique is very civilized and while it helps to speak French, it is not absolutely necessary. Many more locals now

Racing boats in Pointe du Bout

Anchorage at St. Pierre

ST. PIERRE

St. Pierre lies at the foot of the Mt. Pelée volcano, not far from where European settlers wiped out the last of the Carib residents in 1658. It is said that before the last ones died they uttered horrible curses, invoking the mountain to take its revenge. Mt. Pelée, in true Caribbean fashion, took its own sweet time, until Ascension Day, the 8th of May, in 1902.

At that time, St. Pierre, with a population of 30,000, was known as the Paris of the Caribbean and was the commercial, cultural, and social center of Martinique. The wealth of the island lay in the plantations and the richest of these surrounded St. Pierre. Ships would take on rum, sugar, coffee, and cocoa, and enough was sold to make several of the plantation owners multimillionaires. There were also enough cheap bars, brothels, and dancing girls to satisfy the sailors.

The volcano gave some warning. Minor rumblings began early in April, and on April 23 a sizeable eruption covered the town in ash. Refugees from outlying villages started pouring in. On the 2nd of May a major eruption covered the city with enough ash to kill some birds and animals. Later the same day, Pierre Laveniere, a planter with an estate to the south of St. Pierre, went to inspect his crops with a party of workers and they were swept away by a vast avalanche of boiling volcanic mud. On the 5th of May, it was the turn of the Guerin Estate, just a couple of miles north of St. Pierre and one of the richest in the area. A torrent of volcanic effluent, including mud, lava, boiling gasses, and rocks, estimated to be a quarter of a mile wide and 100 feet high, completely buried the estate, much of the family and many workers.

Even before Ascension Day, many people had been killed in and around St. Pierre. So why did people stay? Evacuation posed huge problems, the roads were primitive and rough, and the ferries, the main form of transport, did not have the capacity.

Governor Mouttet, on the island for less than a year, desperately wanted the problem to go away and was encouraged to sit tight by most of the planters and business leaders who would have suffered financial losses if the city were evacuated. If he had gone against them, and the volcano had not gone off, his career would be over. He formed a committee to assess the risk, led by the science teacher at the school, Professor Landes, and they concluded there was no danger, a premature conclusion, given the scant knowledge of volcanoes at the time.

Evacuation would also have affected the coming elections in which black voters were seriously challenging the status quo for the first time. The local paper, *Les Colonies*, also did its best to persuade people that there was no danger, despite the deaths. Several hundred individuals had the sense to leave, but for the rest the destruction of such an important city was unimaginable.

Many were eyewitnesses to the disaster. People were approaching from Fort de France for the Ascension Day church service when they saw heavy, red smoke from the volcano descend on St. Pierre. Rather than continue, they climbed the surrounding hills to see what would happen next. The end came at two minutes past eight in the morning. The side of the volcano facing St. Pierre glowed red and burst open, releasing a giant fireball of superheated gas that flowed down over the city, releasing more energy than an atomic bomb. All that remained were smoking ruins. An estimated 29,933 people burned to death, leaving only two survivors in the center of town: Leon Leandre, a cobbler, and the famous Cyparis, imprisoned for murder in a stone cell. Twelve ships in the bay were destroyed at anchor. One managed to limp away with a few survivors.

Many ruins still remain. Post-disaster buildings have been built onto old structures, so many new buildings share at least one wall with the past. Ruins also form garden walls, and some have been tidied up as historical icons. A museum in a modern building depicts that era and the tragedy. It stands on top of old walls that are artistically lit up at night, making an enchanting backdrop for those anchored below. (You can read a more detailed history on doyleguides.com under Martinique.)

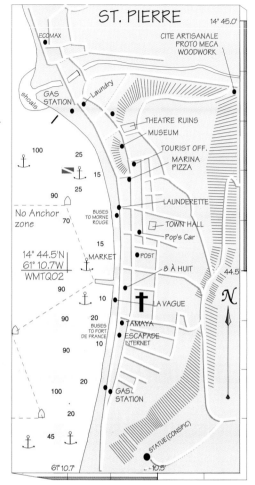

Navigation

St. Pierre makes a good overnight anchorage except when there are heavy northerly swells. There is an adequate shelf on which to anchor, about 25 feet deep, on either side of the town dock. The drop-off is very steep, so make sure you are well hooked. Occasionally, you have to move for local fishermen.

A series of yellow buoys with a cross on top designate a no-anchoring area to protect the dive site wrecks. This mainly affects large yachts anchoring in deep water. The dive sites now have moorings for dive boats. Yacht moorings are planned.

A conspicuous statue on the hill at the southern end of town is lit at night.

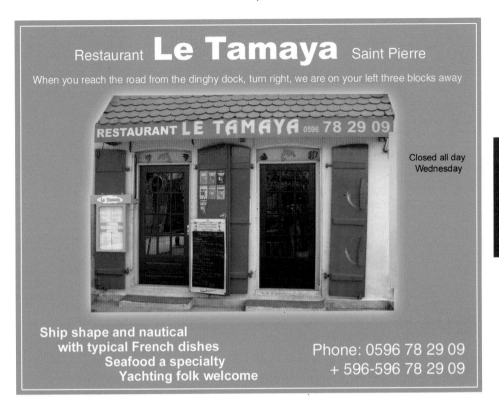

Restaurant **Le Tamaya** Saint Pierre

When you reach the road from the dinghy dock, turn right, we are on your left three blocks away

RESTAURANT LE TAMAYA 0596 78 29 09

Closed all day
Wednesday

Ship shape and nautical
with typical French dishes
Seafood a specialty
Yachting folk welcome

Phone: 0596 78 29 09
+ 596-596 78 29 09

Regulations/Communication

St. Pierre is a port of entry. The customs computer check-in is at the tourist office, on the east hand side of the road just south of the museum. They open weekdays 0900-1400. If you arrive on a weekend, you can wait till Monday to clear in. If you are leaving on a weekend, clear out in advance.

For internet, L'Escapade [$D] has both computers and wifi. They have a fabulous upstairs room overlooking the harbor: an ideal hangout while you sample their book swap and their drinks or coffee. They also offer quite a variety of food and snacks for lunch and dinner.

General yacht services

If you get permission from the town hall, you may be able to come alongside the town dock to take on water. It is also a good place to tie your dinghy. You can do your own wash at the automatic machines near the waterfront or L'auxiliaire, near the river mouth, will do it for you.

Technical yacht services

Proto Meca can be found in the Cité Artisanale on the edge of town. Proto Meca is owned and run by Jean-Michel Trébeau, who trained as an aviation machinist in France and now has a first rate shop. Anything you can break, he can fix, be it in stainless, aluminum, or bronze. He welds these metals and does all kinds of machining. He can rebuild your engine and resurface the block.

In the same compound you will find a carpenter and, if you are having a really bad day, a coffin maker.

Provisioning/shopping

The waterfront area has been renovated and includes an elegant replica of the old financial center. There are a couple of banks, several ATMs (the one at the post office is reliable), pharmacies, and a convenient 8 à Huit supermarket that closes for lunch and half an hour earlier than its name suggests. It also opens Sunday mornings. This is a good and quite large supermarket, but half of it is upstairs, so make sure you visit both floors.

Two other supermarkets, Nord Cash near the cathedral, and Ecomax, over the bridge at the north end of town, offer a more limited range, but are inexpensive. The market is good in the early morning and best on Saturday morning. St. Pierre now has clothing boutiques, souvenir shops, and places selling local fabrics.

Restaurants

St. Pierre has lots of restaurants, several open for both lunch and dinner. Le Tamaya [$C, closed Wednesday] is run by Jean and Jeanne Teissier who arrived in Martinique by yacht. This excellent little restaurant is smart and clean, with nautical decor, and both the food and presentation rank considerably higher than the very reasonable prices charged. (Tamaya won the silver medal given by the Antilles Gastronomic Academy in 2002.) Seafood is always available, as are tasty desserts. The owners do not speak English, but they do have a lot of English-speaking clients, and the menu has an English translation. They open for lunch and reopen for dinner at 1900.

Le Caraibes is popular come sunset, with its tables right out on the street. They serve meals and sometimes have entertainment. Next door is Tai Loong, a Chinese snack bar. On the west side of the road, La Vague [$B-C] has an impressive waterfront location and you can enjoy a Creole meal here.

On the road up the hill, Marina Pizza, [$C-D] is a pizza/pasta place and an ice cream parlor.

More restaurants open for lunch. L'Escapade [$D] is a good choice, with a lovely upstairs dining room, see *Communications*. Chez Marie-Claire [$C] and Le Guerin [$C] are upstairs in the restored market and both serve good local Créole food. There are a couple more restaurants at the south end of town.

Ashore

St. Pierre sits amid the most magnificent scenery in Martinique, so if you are thinking of sightseeing, this is an excellent place to begin. Rental cars are available from Eugene Garage and Pop's Car. Visit the tourist office and get the map of St. Pierre which shows most of the historical monuments; you can make your own walking tour. Get also their hiking map for Martinique, and ask for details of particular hikes you plan. Their map will get you to the start of the hiking trails and more detailed maps of the trails are posted by the trail parking areas.

The museum on the hill is dedicated to the 1902 eruption. It opens daily 0900-1200 and 1500-1700. There is a small admission charge. Two of the most interesting places to visit are the theater ruins beyond the museum and the prison where Cyparis was jailed, which is just below the theater (no charge).

For the energetic, there is a great walk (about an hour round trip) up to the statue of the Virgin Mary, which has the best view of St. Pierre. Our map shows the way.

It is a half-hour walk to Distillerie Depaz, and those used to hiking can make it, or you can take a taxi. The distillery is in lovely grounds with a waterfall, fields, and trees, set against Mt. Pelée as a backdrop. There is no charge to visit. The machinery is run by a steam engine and this is a perfect place to learn why that French white rum makes such distinctive Petit Punch. You can spend a long time wandering around here and stay for lunch [$B-C] at the Le Moulin a Cannes, perfectly situated on a hill overlooking cane fields to the sea beyond.

In the mountains to the south of St. Pierre, there is an extraordinary walk along the Canal de Beauregard. Built by slaves in 1760, this canal brought water around a steep mountain to supply the distilleries of St. Pierre. It is most interesting to start at the bottom end of the canal and walk towards the source. The canal is fairly level, often shady, and easy, but you must have a head for heights, for you walk along the outer canal wall, which is about 18 inches wide, and the panoramic views are often dizzyingly precipitous.

Plantation Ceron, north of Precheur, escaped the volcanic eruption and is a fine example of what the plantations were like before 1902. The gardens are a welcome antidote to boats, and you can spend as long as you like wandering around the shady estate gardens built along a river. There is an entry charge and it can be crowded. Afterwards, you can return to the road and head north. When the road ends, a footpath continues to Grand Rivière on the north coast.

If the weather is clear, ambitious hikers can head up Mt. Pelée. A road takes you within a mile and a half of the summit. Turn right just at the entrance to Precheur on the Chameuse Road. Non-hikers can enjoy the view from the top of the road.

For a scenic drive, the rainforest starts behind St. Pierre and the road up to the conspicuous volcanic observatory is impressive. You can continue from here to the main road that runs through the rainforest. When you reach this road, turn south and look for a tiny road, barely the width of a car, which goes to St. Joseph. It may be marked "impassable," but venture down it as far as possible.

Gorges de la Falaise are dramatic waterfalls in a narrow canyon on the east side of Mt. Pelée. The hike takes about an hour and a half from the entrance and it is closed in heavy rains.

St. Pierre has a big new science museum on the road north; I have not visited yet.

Water sports

Twelve wrecks of ships that sank in the tragedy of 1902 are nearby, most within dinghy range of the anchorage, and at depths from 30 to 150 feet. The best way to find them is to dive with a local dive shop. Otherwise, watch the local dive boats, which visit them frequently (most of them are now buoyed). In addition, the north coast has the best diving in Martinique, with dramatic walls, canyons, and reefs, and many more fish than you find farther south.

If you are diving on your own, there is an easy dive right off the beach in front of the big wall under the museum. It is a good reef, dropping from 40 to 90 feet, decorated with old anchors, a huge old chain draped

over the coral, and plenty of fish.

Papa D'Lo, a dive shop, is on the front street north of the main dock.

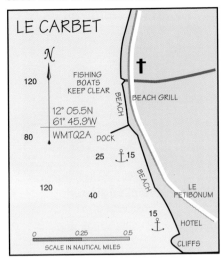

LE CARBET

Carbet is a small town on the headland just south of the bay of St. Peirre. You do not want to be here in northerly swells, but otherwise it makes an excellent lunch stop, and in suitable conditions you could overnight. Edge quite close to the beach south of the dock ~ some people like to anchor all the way down off the hotel in the south. Use the dock for your dinghy with a stern anchor to keep you clear, or beach it.

The attraction is a lovely beach on which there are several restaurants. Two of these are worth special mention.

Just north of the dock, Beach Grill [$B-C] is right on the beach (the floor is sand) and open to the sea. The food is good, and the generous portions are artistically presented. They open for lunch Tuesday to Sunday and for dinner Wednesday to Saturday.

Right down at the south end, Lepetibonum [$B] is famous for excellent food, more gourmet style, served right on the beach, and they open every day for lunch and dinner. Either can be crowded, so reservations are a good idea.

Art lovers should see the museum about Gauguin on the road towards St. Pierre. It includes letters, documents, artifacts, and a show of reproductions of Gauguin paintings.

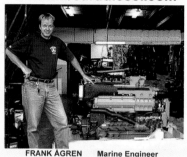

CASE PILOTE

Case Pilote is a delightful small town whose pretty church is one of the oldest in Martinique. It is a picturesque little fishing port, both charming and unspoiled. An extension to the port in the form of a sturdy, big ferry dock and other waterfront renovations have been completed. No ferry service is planned, so you can tie up on either side. Some swell can reach the dock, and inside is calmer. The dock has big rubber fenders that will mark your topsides; a fender-board will prevent that. Plans for a marina are being considered, but that is years away.

Anchorage outside the port is limited by the needs of the active fishing fleet, and when the fishermen put out seine nets at about 0600, hours they will wake anyone they feel is in their way and ask them to move. To avoid this, anchor well inshore on the northwest side of the bay (see our sketch chart). Go in as close as you dare, drop your hook, then back down and use a second anchor to keep your stern to any swells and to stop you from riding up on the beach. Or anchor just round the headland off the next small bay to the northwest in about 25 feet of water and use your dinghy to go to the port. Do move willingly, and right away, if asked.

Case Pilote

Regulations/Services

There are no customs in Case Pilote; clear elsewhere. You can leave your dinghy in the port. You will find garbage bins around the port or the village, and a small gas station in the marina sells fishing gear and ice, but they cannot supply yachts with fuel. For that and for diesel, you will have to jug it from the gas station.

Just over the main road, sandwiched between a pharmacy and a boulangerie, is Brunette Moustin's Lav' Express: a good laundry that opens weekdays 0730-1200 and 1330-1700.

People come here to visit Frank Ågren's Inboard Diesel, which is right at the entrance to the port. Frank is the regional headquarters for Volvo Penta for much of the Eastern Caribbean and does Volvo surveys and diagnostics up and down the islands. He also does warranty work. His big shop has a whole floor devoted to spares and he has the largest stock in the Windwards. He can supply spares at somewhat lower prices than you might pay elsewhere and shipping parts to other Caribbean islands is no problem. Beatrice in his office takes care of this. Frank has a hot line to the factory and, being Swedish, he speaks the same language as the engine, so anyone having Volvo Penta problems should give him a call. Frank and his team are now also a fully qualified sales and service agency for Northern Lights Generators and MTU engines, which should help the large yachts. Those visiting Frank can come inside the port where he has about three reserved spaces. Frank speaks perfect English. A large supply of new and secondhand spares is kept in stock, as well as new engines and generators. Inboard Diesel Service has a fast service boat and can, if necessary, visit other ports and islands. Frank has a team of Volvo associates in most other islands and he works closely with them.

Ashore

Case Pilote is charming and quiet. The church is worth a visit and it is pleasant to stroll around the town. For topping up provisions, visit 8 à Huit, whose name gives you their Monday-Saturday hours. They also open Sundays and holidays in the morning.

Snack Bar de La Plage [$D] is right on the waterfront and Chantal, the owner, is very pleasant. She opens about 0900 and stays open all day as a bar. For lunch she offers a variety of local dishes, all simple and delicious.

Water sports

Diving and snorkeling off the headland just south of the marina are very good. Huge rocks rise from 70 feet and the whole area is filled with brightly colored sponges, corals, and fish. If you don't have your own gear, contact the Case Pilote Diving Club. For those interested in wildlife, there is a bat cave in the cliffs behind the snorkeling area.

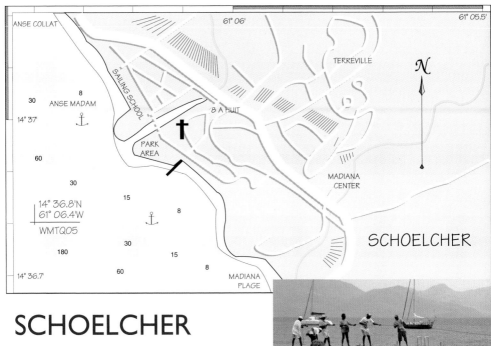

SCHOELCHER

Originally Case Navire, this town was famous for the water provided by its two rivers, making it a vital rest stop for ships of old. It was renamed after Victor Schoelcher, the anti-slavery advocate, and now covers a large area, bisected by the main west coast highway. The waterfront part is easily accessible to yachts and has the atmosphere of a tiny town on its own. It is an alternative, less urban anchorage to Fort de France, with pleasant beaches. Buses run to Fort de France frequently; it takes 15 minutes.

Good anchoring shelves are in front of the town or off Anse Madam. You can tie your dinghy to the town dock, though you will need a dinghy anchor. The waterfront adjoining the dock is a park area. Anse Madam has a long beach and is home to one of the largest and best sailing schools in the area.

Ashore

Within easy walking distance of the dock, you will find an 8 à Huit supermarket. Opposite is Oops, an ice creamery and creperie. Turn right along the waterfront for Balade de Neige, another ice cream place with a pizzeria and saladerie next door.

The Madiana Center is also within walking distance for the reasonably energetic. This popular conference and entertainment center has the best cinema in Martinique. (On Thursdays they show movies in their original language.) Cap Solomon in the center, will delight pub aficionados. They have a microbrewery on site so their beers are good and they serve a variety of food, including many "flammes." These are akin to pizza but with a much thinner crust. There is also a hair stylist.

For a major provisioning, you will need a cab or a car to visit the huge malls on the road to Fort de France. You can also use the Leader Price at Terreville. Go out of town and straight up the hill on the road to L'Enclos.

Le Deux Gros lies in a bay half way between the town of Shoelcher and Case Pilote. There is no problem anchoring there, but forget landing on the little concrete wall or the beach if there are any swells. However, if you do make it (a big tender can do so from either port) it is one the fancier restaurants in Martinique. They close Sunday evening and all day Monday.

Fort de France

FORT DE FRANCE

Fort de France, the capital of Martinique, is the largest and liveliest city in the Windwards. It is a great place for shops, restaurants, and people-watching. It has one of the nicest city anchorages in a pleasant area under Fort St. Louis, opposite the park and close by the public beach, which is well used in the early mornings. The new waterfront is a huge boardwalk where bouncing waves whistle below. This is also the dinghy dock and it leads onto a great playground for kids. In the late afternoon kids come to play, people come to hang out, and vendors set up on the roadside with snack foods and drinks. If you are puzzled by the turnstiles to get out, they prevent obnoxious kids from zooming up and down the boardwalk on scooters.

In town, the central Rue de la République has been converted into a delightful pedestrian street, and the large Cours Perinon Mall is right in town. Those wanting to explore Martinique can take advantage of the many buses that use the capital as their hub. You are close to chandleries and many yacht services.

Navigation

When approaching Fort de France from Cap Salomon, it is hard to see at a glance exactly where the harbor is as the surrounding area is built up, including a huge hotel and some apartment blocks at Schoelcher, a couple of miles west of Fort de France. As you approach, you can identify the main yacht anchorage by the prominent slab-sided fort wall, the big new circular apartment block that from afar looks like a giant water tank, and by the yachts at anchor.

The yacht anchorage is on the east side of the bay between Fort St. Louis and a line between the red and yellow buoys in the center of the bay. Leave the red buoy to starboard to avoid the isolated rocky shoal to its southeast. Charts show only about 5 feet on this shoal. I could not find any depths much less than 7 feet, but there may be shallower rocks (see chart p.79).

The water is shallow and rocky if you get close to Fort St. Louis, but level in many areas, once the depth reaches about nine feet. The anchorage is deeper (25-40 feet) towards the center of the bay for deep-draft

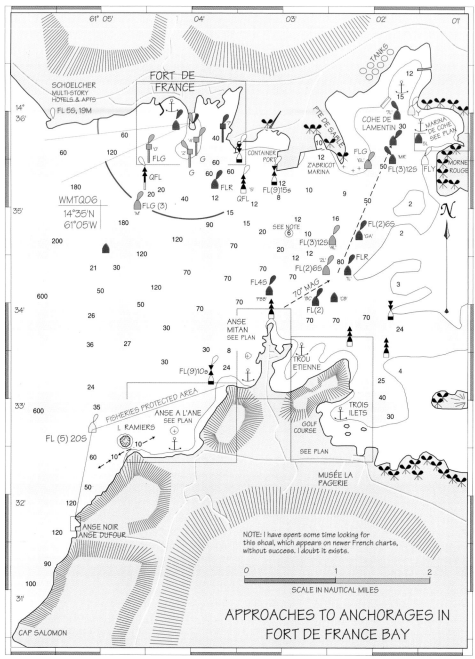

APPROACHES TO ANCHORAGES IN FORT DE FRANCE BAY

NOTE: I have spent some time looking for this shoal, which appears on newer French charts, without success. I doubt it exists.

SCALE IN NAUTICAL MILES

yachts. Holding in the bay is good when you hit clay-like sand; variable in soft mud. Fort de France is connected to Anse Mitan, Anse à L'Ane, and Trois Ilets by frequent ferries, which make the anchorage rolly from time to time.

If you need work done, you can find a work berth in the Baie des Tourelles. (Make

arrangements in advance and give cruise ships wide clearance.) If you are heading east to get there or southeast toward Anse Mitan, keep well clear of the shoals off the fort. It is possible to cut somewhat inside the green buoys, but to be on the safe side, go around them.

A new Fort de France marina is being

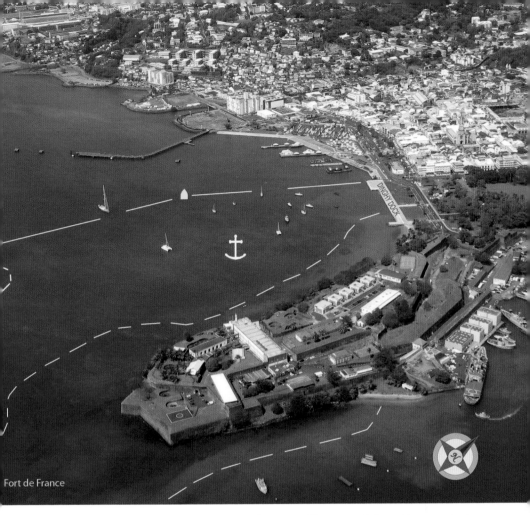

Fort de France

built down by Pte. du Sable. See our section on *The Industrial Zones*. If you visit Fort de France by car, the easiest pay parking is one of the many Vinci-parkings. There is one in the block next to Sea Services.

Regulations

Clearing in and out is easy in the hallway at Sea Services. Fill the form out on the customs computer, print your clearance, and have one of the staff stamp it. You can peruse the chandlery at the same time. (Open weekdays from 0830-1700; Saturdays from 0830-1200.) Or you can dinghy to the DCML fuel dock, open 0800-1900, except Sundays and holidays; open 0800-1230.

Communications

Cyber Deliss, just beyond Sea Services, is a classy cyber cafe and restaurant run by Francois-Xavier and Jean-Raymond. Art deco in style, it is shining and modern. They have a full boulangerie/patisserie, and they also do a variety of French style dishes. The menu changes daily and they open Monday-Saturday 0600-2200. If you bring your computer in and are eating or drinking, the wifi connection is free, otherwise the charges on their computers are 2 Eu for 15 minutes, 3 Eu for 30 minutes, or 5 Eu an hour, but they only have a couple of stations and they are often in use.

Cybercafe Pizzeria Palnet is upstairs, close by Cours Perinon. They open 0800-1700, selling coffee, pizzas, and more with free wifi for customers. Go up one more floor and they also have a big bank of internet computers starting at 2 Eu for 20 minutes, up to 5 Eu for an hour. Pay in the restaurant before you go up.

General yacht services

A good dinghy dock lies all along La Savanne. Small litterbins line the dock. Bigger tips are back on Rue Déproge, but since they have wheels, check out the location before carting in garbage.

DCML is a good fuel dock in Baie des Tourelles. They offer fuel, water, oils, beer, coffee, and both cube and chipped ice, as well as lunch sandwiches and sundry items. This is the easiest place to get ice in Fort de France. They open 0730-1900 weekdays, 0800-1900 Saturdays and 0800-1245, Sundays and holidays. Charter yachts qualify for duty-free when they have cleared out. Take the boat down or, for small things, dinghy down.

Ever since an employee, filling a visitor's cooking gas tank, died when it exploded, filling gas tanks is not possible. In an emergency, buy a small new French butane tank at a snack store beside the fire station on Blvd. Admiral Gueydon. Continue along the canal to see Fontaine Gueydon, once part of the water system and now a monument.

Barnacles bugging you? Need a new stainless fuel tank? The yacht services compound in Baie des Tourelles should solve your problems. You can dinghy there, bring the yacht, or check it out on foot. The walk to Quai des Tourelles is about 15 minutes from town. Head past Quai Ouest on the main road out of town heading east. Turn right immediately after the big, new buildings on the right side of the road. Follow the road and turn left when you come to a junction. This leads you to the new basin. At the heart of this compound is a haul out run by CarenAntilles, who have a larger facility in Marin. The shallow parts of the canal on the southeast side have been dredged to about 11 feet. The haul out has a 35-ton marine hoist that can haul boats about 2 meters deep. Artisans and engineers can do everything you need. Small boats can be stored on racks. Language is not a problem as most people speak some English.

If you are too long, wide, heavy, or ugly to haul elsewhere, you can arrange to be slipped alongside a ship in the huge Martinique dry dock, which will take anything up to a cruise ship (see also *Marin services*).

Chandlery

Sea Services, on Rue Déproge, is one of Martinique's largest chandleries. It is owned by Christophe Sirodot who worked for some years in the US. He is helped by Stephane and Valeire plus other employees who are attentive and all speak English.

Sea Services is really two adjoining stores. The western store sells yacht gear, including International Paints, 3-M products, 316 stainless fasteners, tenders, liferafts, stoves, anchors, barbecues, charts, and guides. They stock a good range of electrical equipment, from wire and connectors to solar panels, windlasses, and Aerogen wind generators, as well as a good stock of yacht electronics. They are big on Matt Chem cleaners in both yacht and commercial sizes, also Aquasale biodegradable products, including soaps. They have a full rigging service, run by Stephane from a dinghy locking line upwards. Their on-the-spot swaging works for up to 12mm wire and they do larger

diameters by order. Sea Services regularly delivers antifouling paint to all Martinique haul-out facilities, and can arrange haul-out quantities duty-free for visiting yachts for use in Martinique or to take away.

The eastern part of Sea Services features decorative nautical objets d'art, tablewear, and linens, but most of all a wide selection of good nautical casual and sportswear, including St. James, Fleur de Sel, and TBS. Many superyachts come by here to outfit the crew with shorts and shirts. They also have goodies for kids, microfibre products, elegant soft towels, non-skid molded shoes with removable soles, and all kinds of carri-ers, from back packs to wallets.

If you are down island and need something, give them a call or email: seaservices972@orange.fr. They can take your order, arrange credit card payment by fax, and Fedex it to you.

You will find two other chandleries in the Baie de Tourelles Caren-Antilles, an easy dinghy ride away.

Max and Cedric's Polymar is a good sized chandlery with a stock of ropes, fittings, fishing gear, and general accessories. They sell and service Lacomble Schmitt hydraulics. This is a good place to look at electrics and electronics, gauges and bilge pumps.

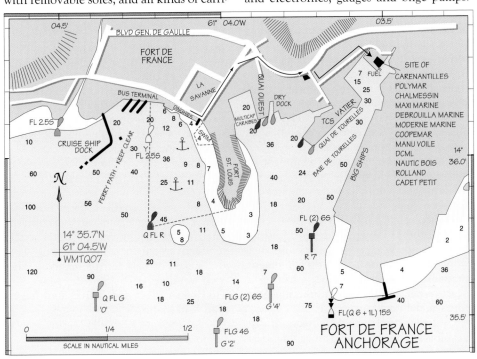

FORT DE FRANCE
ANCHORAGE

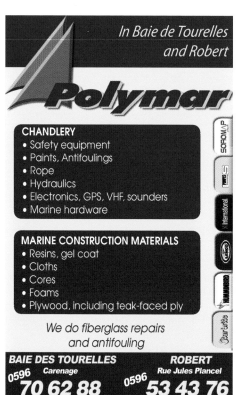

Baie des Tourelles

Polymar sells many products for projects, including marine and teak ply, which can be bought cut to size, resins, gel coat, cores, foams, cloths, and paints (including the International line). Polymar is also the place to get your scuba tanks filled. You can talk to them about glass repair and painting, which was once their main work. They currently do this, but if they stop, they should still be able to make a good recommendation. They have a second store in Robert.

M. Josepha's Coopemar is a fishing store, but it also has electronics, jerry jugs, some hardware and paints, as well as oilskins and shoes.

Littoral, at 32-34 Blvd. Allègre, lies next to the canal where the local fishing boats tie up. Wander in and peruse their wonderful selection of fishing equipment, probably the largest for sports fishing in Martinique, along with snorkeling gear, ropes, and diving knives.

Anyone need personal protection? Visit Levalois Racing on Rue Déproge for CS gas or foam and stun guns.

Technical yacht services

Most yachts services are to be found at the CarenAntilles compound in Baie des Tourelles.

Jean Pierre and François Chalmessin can work wonders with titanium (one of the few places that can weld it), stainless and aluminum, including welding, bending, building, and machining. Whether you have a broken winch or want a new pulpit or water tank, they can do it. They can also fix most marine cooking stoves and it is worth talking to them if you have a simple refrigeration problem. They can replace most parts and recharge systems.

Also into metal work is Jean-Michel Rolland who has TIG and MIG welders and can fabricate in aluminum and stainless. He speaks English and has built fancy, big aluminum yachts.

Manu Voile is a sailmaking shop owned by Emmanuel Resin who has over 25 years of experience. He has a young, keen team and will tackle anything from new sails (any size) to repairs, biminis, and cushions. Their location right on the waterfront is very convenient for unloading sails. They also make lazy bags for the mainsail. They open weekdays 0800-1300 and 1430-1800. They can collect and deliver and have a branch in Marin.

Bellance at Debrouilla Marine specializes in marine electronic and electric work and he has a good selection of lights and other electrical equipment for sale.

Maxi Marine has a magnificent and very clean showroom and workshop where they sell and repair Mercury outboards, for whom they are the agent in Martinique. They are also sales and repair agents for Cummins Diesel.

Moderne Marine repairs Mercruiser motors. Cadet Electrical will fix your broken starters and alternators and you can check them for anything electrical. Dupin, at Nautic Bois, is a carpenter who also works with epoxy.

S.A.V. des Moteurs, run by Joseph Féré, is on the road as you approach the compound. He services OMC outboards.

Marc Eugene at Renovboats is in the general area and does good fiberglass repair and spray painting. It is easiest to contact him by phone (0696-25-01-92).

Injectors or injection pumps need servicing? Check out our section on the Industrial Zones.

Provisioning

(See plans pages 83 and 88-89)

Changing money in Fort de France is now easy at the best rates, thanks to efficient little change places like Change Caraibes, which is at the Savanne end of Rue Ernest Déproge and opens weekdays 0800-1730, Saturdays 0800-1230. Another money changing shop, Martinique Change, is at the Blvd. Allègre end of Rue Victor Hugo, and yet another is at La Savanne end of the same road. Cash machines are everywhere, most intimidatingly public. Just beyond Sea Services, outside the car park, is an enclosed room where you can get you cash without being right on the street. The bank in the Cours Perinon is also somewhat discreet.

Provisioning in Martinique is a pleasure. There are giant supermarkets and good distributors for stocking up on wine and beer. Martinique customs deem that you can only buy duty-free fuel and liquor if you are a charter boat. The definition of a charter boat is rather left up to the business. It certainly helps if you have a brochure, and you must mark charter yacht on your customs form. But even if you do not qualify, the purveyors offer good wholesale prices on cases of beer and wine. Vatier has retired, but his company still sells wines and drinks, including to the yachting industry. You will find TCS nearby, another wholesaler, and they also

Approaches to Baie des Tourelles

The new boardwalk makes a good perch for viewing Fort Josephine and the beach

have a retail jewelry store.

The place for fresh produce and spices is the main market, best in the mornings and especially on Saturday.

Supermarkets in the town of Fort de France are more than adequate if you don't have time to get to the big ones. The best market may well be the new Carrefour Market in the Cours Perinon. Match, on Rue de la République, is good, and Casino is the largest town store and has good cheese, meat, and produce sections. The open market out front offers a good selection of fruits and vegetables. Leader Price, opposite Sea Services, is close. It is a popular market, with bargain prices on canned and dry goods, beer, and more. They also have reasonable frozen and produce sections. It can be crowded and slow. None of these stores currently delivers.

Friandises des Isles, with outlets on Rue Victor Hugo and Rue République, is a great little bakery with a good variety of breads, including whole wheat and baked delights that are a cut above most. You can buy a coffee here; also salad to go with your bread.

For the fun of shopping in a really big supermarket, you need to visit the out-of-town malls, where small shops surround gargantuan, modern supermarkets, called hyper-marchés. Buses go to all these places from the big bus and TC station in Point Simon, right beside the dinghy dock. Two of the best supermarkets, Carrefour and La Galleria, are described in our section on the industrial zones.

The others are towards Schoelcher and the closest is HyperU at Le Rond Point. It can be reached via the Schoelcher communal taxi, which leaves from the big communal taxi stand in front of the anchorage. The energetic may prefer to walk. It is rather uphill, but half an hour will get you there at an easy pace. En route, you may want to check out Weldom, a really giant hardware store with a vast range of household and project-related stock. Baobab is a garden store with lots of hose fittings and Christmas lights, and Sport 2000 is a giant sports store that includes kayaks and water sports. Farther along (next roundabout, we are no longer walking) is a Casino Géant, which has good frozen fish and many Chinese fixings.

Fun shopping

Visit the tourist office in La Savanne or the one on Rue Lazare Carnot. They will give you a good Fort de France map as well as a Martinique one, and they will answer

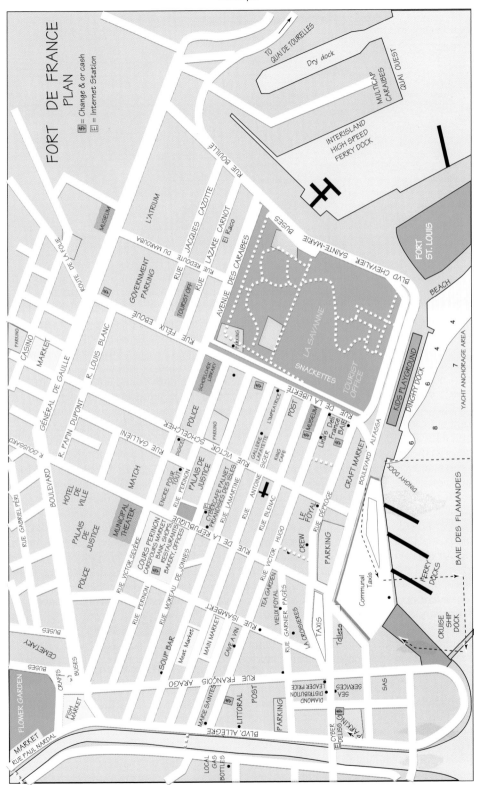

Martinique

FORT DE FRANCE PLAN

$ = Change & or cash
E = Internet Station

The main market, where you can get a good lunch.

your questions. Make sure you ask for their dining guide.

Cours Perinon is a big mall right in the middle of town, open 0800-1900. With two floors, it has glass-fronted elevators, escalators, and lots of shops, restaurants, and a really large bookshop (opposite the supermarket) with computers, stationary, and more.

On the first floor you will find the Caribbean Center with a combined gym, health, and beauty spa. Their Salon Franck Provost is the place to get a hair stylist for men and women. If you work out in the gym you can take a shower afterwards. All their charges are posted at: caribbeanbodycenter.com

If you need printer inks or special paper, check Encre Pour Tous, a block down Rue Perinon.

Right opposite Sea Services, Diamond Distribution is a good hardware shop with lots of tools and household stuff. La Foire Fouille, just before Sea Services, is a giant household store, generally cheap and junky, but it always has something you need. SAS, behind Sea Services, is a good windsurfing shop run by Remi Vila, a French champion.

Fort de France is the place for both fashionable shopping and souvenir hunting. The biggest handicraft market is on Boulevard Alfassa and another is near the fish market. You will find everything from jewelry to handbags, paintings, and varnished palm fruits. Half the artists and carvers in Haiti must be kept busy whipping out an overwhelming number of coconut trees, banana plants, fruits, and models in balsa wood. These are available all over town. The biggest congregation of souvenir shops is on Rue Déproge towards La Savanne.

Fort de France is the only place in the Windwards for Paris fashions and stylish clothing shops. Start by wandering down Rue Victor Hugo from La Savanne. As you cross other roads, turn now and again when tempted. Enjoy the pedestrian Rue de La République; return by Rue LaMartine. Gallerie Lafayette, which takes up the corner between Rue Antoine Siger and Rue Schoelcher, is a department store where everything is laid out so that it is easy to see. When you need a break, you can have a coffee at Lina's. Don't forget to check out the St. James line at Sea Services (see *Chandlery*) or visit the local market.

Restaurants

Restaurants are plentiful, geared to the local market, and for the most part, prices are moderate and the food is straightforward and correctly prepared. A few are really upmarket with prices and sophistication to match. Lunch is the best value for money, as restaurants compete to attract the workers.

Fort de France also has a pleasant atmosphere in the evening, with outside seating in several places.

For a Continental breakfast or coffee try L'Impeatrice [$D]. They have wicker chairs, outside seating, and it is inexpensive. Deli France is an alternative.

A pleasant place to take lunch is in the main market, between Rue Victor Hugo and Rue Antoine Siger, amid the bustle of people selling fruits, tropical flowers, exotic alcoholic drinks, souvenirs of all kinds, and straw goods. Tables are set out both at one end of the market and upstairs. About half a dozen small restaurateurs [$D] offer typical Créole meals at bargain prices. There is a fresh fruit juice stand where you choose your fruit and watch it being juiced. Close by, Marie Saintes is another small local restaurant, good for lunch.

Le Foyal [$B-C] is new, modern, and efficient with a pleasant outside seating area. They open 0730 and close after midnight; you can eat any time, and the food can be good. Before you choose from the menu, go inside and look at the daily specials on the board. They also have a gourmet restaurant and menu upstairs [$A], and an ice cream parlor adjoining.

La Baie [$B-C], owned by Jocelyne Guiout, is a very pleasant upstairs restaurant overlooking the anchorage and park. You can sit inside in air conditioning or outside on the balcony. They serve Créole dishes, and the food is generally good.

In the evening for something cheap, try the Soup Bar [$D, opens at 1700]. It has an old-fashioned atmosphere, with seats inside and out on the street. The food is good and reasonably priced as they concentrate on soups, salads, lasagnas, and few other things.

Aux Vieux Foyal [$A-B], is another atmospheric restaurant in an old house with green umbrellas outside. They serve lunch and dinner and have live jazz on Saturday at midday. Neujo Mejico [$C] (opposite Sea Services) is upstairs and good, with reasonable lunch time specials, and while you can eat Mexican, you don't have to.

La Croisière [$B-C, closed Sunday], is a pleasant upstairs restaurant with a great balcony for watching life on the street below. It is informal, relatively inexpensive, and serves both French and Créole dishes for lunch or dinner. Owner Alex Zizi has good local jazz groups on Friday and Saturday nights.

The Crew [$B-C, closed Saturday and Sunday evenings] is reliable and moderately priced. They serve good French food. It is easy to find room at dinner, though it is packed with businessmen for lunch.

Fancy a smoked salmon sandwich? Then Lina's [$D] on Rue Victor Hugo is just the ticket, with elegant sandwiches and salads and wine by the glass, all in a pleasant air-conditioned building with seating on two floors. Leave some room for dessert and excellent coffee. Lina is open till 2200.

At the fancy end, El Raco [$A-B], is on Rue Lazare Carnot north of La Savanne. This is a very quiet spot, but rest assured you will find it, and Hugues Balcaen, who is very pleasant, will welcome you into his restaurant. Two intimate, cave-like dining areas make for a delightful atmosphere, with some very contemporary arty decoration. El Raco is open for lunch from Monday to Friday and for dinner from Tuesday to Saturday. This is a good choice for a special night out; dress reasonably well and enjoy excellent food and a great wine list.

La Cave a Vin [$A], owned by M. Grouvel, is both a fine restaurant and a gourmet food store. Their collection of wines, which you can buy by the bottle or case, may be of interest. The restaurant serves excellent French food and is quite pricey. They expect you to dress well. If you are in CarenAntilles, Le Grand Voile and Kenny's open for lunch.

Wherever you eat, beware of those little green peppers. They are often put beside the food as decoration, and they are the hottest of hot.

Transport

Fort de France is a convenient starting point to see the island as there are buses and communal taxis that go to all major towns and villages. Currently, most of them start right outside the new ferry docks. If you are going to the airport, take the "Ducos" car. The charge is less than five Euros. Most of the suburban buses go from the west end of Blvd.

Ashore

Général de Gaulle. These include buses to Dillon, Balata, and Didier. Buses to Lamentin go from the east side of La Savanne. Taxis are in a new block just over the road. Marc Pharose is a good English speaking taxi driver who knows where everything is (0696 45 09 56). He does not work on Sundays.

History buffs should visit the little pre-Columbian museum on Rue de la Liberté [closed Sunday] and the Ethnic History Museum on Blvd. Général de Gaule. Architecture buffs should see the Schoelcher Library, a very elaborate metal building designed by Gustav Eifel, made in France, and shipped here.

The playground behind the boardwalk

THE INDUSTRIAL ZONES

With coastal regions collecting top dollar for rentals, it is not surprising that more and more businesses are now found in the industrial zones, which run from Fort de France, past the airport, to Rivière Salée. If you are renting a car, drive to Carrefour and take the airport road. Most businesses are reached from one of the following major exits: the first is Rivière Roche; the second, Jambette; the third, Californie; and the fourth, which is easily identifiable by La Galleria, is Les Mangles. Note also the turn off to Le Lamentin or La Lezarde. Lareinty is a zone right opposite the airport. Continue on for Rivière Salée, using the same exit as for Trois Ilets. Taxis can be of help. Buses go to Carrefour from the western end of Blvd. Général de Gaulle, by the cemetery.

Provisioning

Carrefour at Dillon is the first large and well-laid-out supermarket you come to on the airport road and it is excellent for a major provisioning. Some prefer to go a little farther, to the even larger La Galleria, which is a mall to end all malls, with two floors, over a hundred shops, lots of restaurants, and glass-fronted lifts and escalators, making it a favorite hangout for many Martiniquais. The huge Hyper U supermarket has everything.

Price differences exist between this market and Carrefour, but neither is consistently higher. If you are coming from Marin, Euromarche at Genipa is the market of choice, between Riviere Salée and the airport.

Chandlery and services

Inter Sport is across the major highway from Carrefour. It is a vast general sports shop that includes fishing, boating, kayaking, windsurfing, surf-kiting gear, and more. You might not find what you are looking for, but you will certainly find something you want. Mer et Sport in La Jambette is a large general sports store.

Turn off at Calafornie for Atelier Sylvestre, the hydraulic hose specialists. They can remake any hose. They also stock many special hoses and you can buy fuel-resistant hoses or very heavy-duty hoses. Fittings are available in stainless or aluminum and the owners speak English.

Of interest at La Lezarde is Antilles Miroiterrie. They stock glass, mirrors (in glass and plastic), acrylic sheet in various thicknesses and quality, and PVC. They will cut all materials to shape. Martinique Diesel is also at La Lezarde and they service all kinds of injectors and fuel pumps except Caterpillar and Cummins and have a vast stock of filters.

The Fedex office is near the airport, in the original airport block. Continental Marine in Lementin is the Yamaha agent, has spares, and can sort out Yamaha outboard problems.

Rivière Salée is the home of West Indies Nautic Distribution (WIND), run by Bruno Marmousez. This is a big store with a brand new showroom. They specialize in everything you need for any kind of boat job, and they sell wholesale and retail. Their technical knowledge about all their products is more than excellent, and they know everything about compatibility between paints, how to make a two part-polyurethane flexible, which resins to use, and more.

They sell paints, epoxy, and polyester resins, fiberglass materials, and the latest cores, including the ultra-light hollow polypropylene cores, as well as the best structural foams. They have teak and holly laminated ply. They can match any boat color with high quality polyurethane, and they sell sandpaper, masks, gloves, brushes, and all the application tools. On big jobs you can negotiate wholesale prices. They also sell Jotun and Seajet antifouling, and a wide variety of marine batteries at good prices.

Wherever possible, Bruno stocks the most environmentally friendly products available.

WIND is also the best flag outlet in the Eastern Caribbean. They have or can quickly get any kind of courtesy flag or ensign. They also wholesale flags. You can check out flags of all nations on their web page (www.wind-flag.com), plus meet the staff and see some products.

It is worth visiting the store, but if you cannot make it personally, email or call Bruno (he speaks excellent English) and he will happily deliver to your boat.

While here and with a car, if you are

in too much of a hurry to make the giant stores, you can shop at Leader Price, which has easy parking.

Port de Plaisance de L'Etang Z'Abricots is a partly constructed, new, municipal marina whose name is rather longer than the marina itself. The marina area has been dredged (now about 10 feet deep) and two floating docks serve as outer walls. Berthing docks have now been ordered; when completed it will be for local yachts. You can take a look and, if it is still in limbo, anchor here in the wilderness amid the mosquitoes.

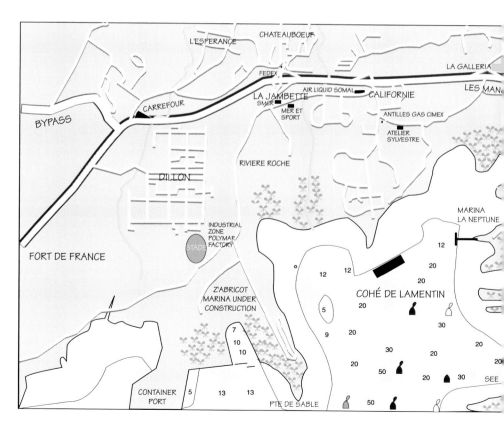

Martinique

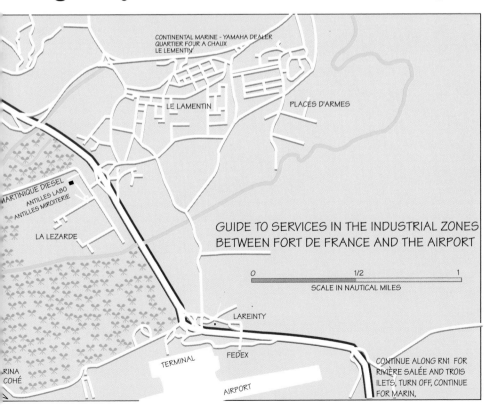

CONTINENTAL MARINE - YAMAHA DEALER
QUARTIER FOUR A CHAUX
LE LEMENTIN

LE LAMENTIN

PLACES D'ARMES

MARTINIQUE DIESEL
ANTILLES LABO
ANTILLES MIROITERIE

LA LEZARDE

GUIDE TO SERVICES IN THE INDUSTRIAL ZONES
BETWEEN FORT DE FRANCE AND THE AIRPORT

0   1/2   1
SCALE IN NAUTICAL MILES

LAREINTY

RINA
COHÉ

TERMINAL

FEDEX

CONTINUE ALONG RN1 FOR
RIVIÈRE SALÉE AND TROIS
ILETS, TURN OFF, CONTINUE
FOR MARIN,

AIRPORT

COHE DE LAMENTIN

(See also our "Approaches to Anchorages in Fort de France Bay," page 76)

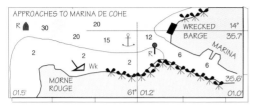

APPROACHES TO MARINA DE COHE

This murky backwater is only of interest if you need to get close to the airport, are hiding from a hurricane or an ex-wife, or need a place to leave your boat while you go away.

To approach from Anse Mitan, start by the black and yellow buoy just off Pte. du Bout and head about 70 degrees magnetic, which will join you to the main channel. Leave all the red buoys to starboard and the green ones to port. From Fort de France, head east, going outside the green buoys marking the shoals off the fort, then head about 130 degrees magnetic until you join the main channel from Anse Mitan to Cohé de Lamentin. The troublesome shoal is the one extending from Pte. de Sable. The water on this route is mainly 10 to 12 feet deep, but watch for unmarked obstructions.

Marina de Cohé is in a somewhat strange, quiet, hot creek tucked in the mangroves. As you approach, be sure to leave the red buoy off Morne Rouge to starboard. The entrance to the marina is hidden down a small creek that is marked by a wrecked barge. Stay center channel and do not cut the corner on the southern shore, which is where most people go aground. Yachts of around 6-foot draft can get in.

There is another dock, usually full of local boats, tucked up in the northeastern corner of Cohé de Lamentin.

POINTE DU BOUT

Trois Ilets, showing the approaches

channel no anchoring

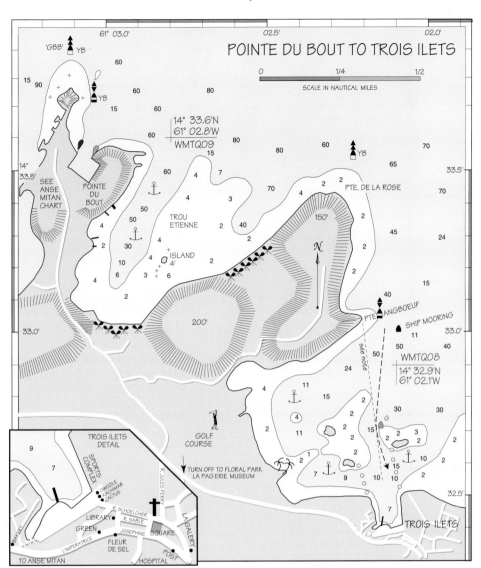

POINTE DU BOUT TO TROIS ILETS

SCALE IN NAUTICAL MILES

TROIS ILETS DETAIL

TROIS ILETS

Trois Ilets is a photogenic town, not overrun with visitors. Some of the old houses are built of wood or stone, and capped with fish-scale tile roofs. A handsome square lies between the church and the town hall. This pleasant area offers several scenic, quiet, and secure places to anchor, some of which are protected enough to ride out a hurricane. You land on the fancy new waterfront walkway and head towards the church.

Approach from Anse Mitan by leav-ing the black and yellow buoys off Pte. du Bout, Pte. de la Rose, and Pte. Angboeuf to starboard. The easiest anchorage is found by following the coast in from Pte. Angboeuf and anchoring off the golf course. There is one 4-foot shoal, but otherwise the approach is easy. The approach to town is between the islands: Steer for the eastern island till you see the green buoy and leave it to port. After rounding the buoy, turn a little east again to avoid the shoals off the island to the west. Do not anchor in the main channel marked by yellow buoys.

Typical old houses, Trois Ilets

Communications

For internet, visit Cyber-base des Trois Ilets above the library. Open Tuesday 1000-1400, Wednesday to Saturday 0830-1300.

Otherwise try La Galery shop which is part of the Quincaillery and it is in Quincaillery; you will find a computer. Open Monday to Friday 0800-1300 and 1600-1800, and at least Saturday morning.

Restaurants

For dinner try the fine old Fleur de Sel [$A-B], run by M. & Mme Fischer. They open for dinner, Monday to Saturday 1930-2230; the food is excellent, the atmosphere quaint and artistic.

Three other restaurants are on the same road and they also serve lunch. Dadou et Andrea [$B, closed Sunday] offers Créole cuisine. Green [$C-D] has both Créole food and entertainment, and Sole et Luna [$C, closed Wednesdays] is an Italian restaurant. Down on the waterfront, some small snack bars offer a great location for a drink.

Ashore

More yachts use this port now that there is a ferry to Fort de France that runs about every half hour. Garbage bins are at either end of the waterfront. There are mangrove tours that are reputed to be good.

In town you will find a local market (open every day), a post office, a butcher, a wonderful boulangerie/patisserie/ice creamery, a pharmacy, a couple of general stores, and a hospital. A tourist office is stationed in the market square and, should you wish to rent a car, the woman at the tourist office will send you in the right direction.

There are plenty of attractions a fair walk away. Trois Ilets is one of the few places in the islands where you can play golf overlooking your yacht in the bay below. Opposite the 18-hole golf course is an ancient distillery, a floral park (usually closed), and La Pagerie Museum, the original home of Empress Josephine. Our guide explained that most of the old estate house burned down when Josephine was three years old, and her father was such a gambler and womanizer that he could not afford to rebuild. They lived in part of the factory, where she stayed until she left for France for an arranged marriage at the age of 16. Her first husband was killed in the French revolution, but she escaped thanks to a lover (of which our guide said she had plenty). When she married Napoleon he was 27 and she was 33. Since this was an unthinkable age difference, it was published that they were both 28.

About one and half nautical miles to the east are some potteries, one of which produces the lovely fish-scale roof tiles used both in Trois Ilets and in St. George's, Grenada. Around these is the Village de la Potterie, a visitor attraction with numerous boutiques, restaurants, and a place to rent kayaks for mucking in the mangroves. The adventurous can dinghy there, tide permitting. It is opposite Gros Ilet and obvious because of the big industrial-looking brick warehouse and red roofs. Head east from Trois Ilets, follow the coast till you get past the first shoal on your port, then head towards Gros Ilet about half way before heading into the pottery. Tie up amid the bricks before you come to the tiny kayak dock. You might be able to make use of a couple of makeshift wooden landing platforms. Take care in the shallows.

TROU ETIENNE

Just occasionally, the weather goes crazy and storms from afar create huge swells that make both Fort de France and Anse Mitan untenable. If this happens, it is possible to pop round to the other side of Pte. du Bout and anchor in Trou Etienne. As you come from the west, leave both yellow and black buoys to starboard, and as you enter the bay, do not go too close to shore. There are many private moorings and the water is either rather deep or too shallow for easy anchoring. Docks and roads are private, but there is a small public access path just north of the hotel. The hotel is quite conspicuous.

Village Creole

ANSE MITAN

Anse Mitan is part of the Trois Ilets district, and the head of the peninsula is called Pte. du Bout. Originally a super-chic tourist area, it is now a tad seedy round the edges, with the abandonment of the giant hotel (originally the Meridien), the destruction of the Ponton du Bakoua, and some buildings, roads and pavements needing upkeep. It still has a lot to offer, including beaches, boutiques, and restaurants, and it is fun for people-watching. Two ferry services run to Fort de France and Anse à L'Ane: one out of the marina at Pte. du Bout, the other from the Langouste Dock at Anse Mitan. Ferries start at around 0600 and finish at about 2300. Check times on the notice boards on the docks.

Anse Mitan is attractive, but not generally overcrowded with yachts. Since the last and possibly final demise of the Ponton du Bakoua in hurricane swells, there are few yacht services.

When approaching Anse Mitan, the main danger is the reef lying 200 yards west of Le Ponton. Yachts are often anchored all around this reef, which is marked by a red and black buoy. Anchor anywhere among the other yachts. Holding is good in sand, but poor on patches of dead coral. Leave a couple of hundred feet in front of the beach clear for swimmers and leave the channel clear for the ferry. The no-anchoring areas are sometimes marked by yellow buoys.

On those very rare occasions when there is a bad northwesterly swell, go to Trou Etienne, on the other side of Pte. du Bout, or better, to Trois Ilets.

Regulations

You can clear customs via a computer in Somatras Marina office. Opening hours are 0900-1230 and 1500-1800 weekdays, 0900-1230 Saturday.

Communications

Laverie Prolavnet, the laundry by Village Créole has single internet station, open 0830-1200, Monday to Saturday, (see *General yacht services* below). Several bars including L'Explorateur offer wifi.

General yacht services

You can tie your dinghy on the inside of the ferry dock. Most people use one of the old docks from the abandoned hotel (see our sketch chart), but there are no guarantees this will continue. You can find garbage dumpsters all though town.

Somatras Marina (Marina Pte. du Bout) [VHF: 9] is a small marina offering stern-to berthing with water and electricity (no fuel). Short and long-term berths are sometimes available for yachts up to 50 feet long and with less than 8-foot draft.

Laverie Prolavnet by Village Créole is a fast laundry and internet station, open 0830-1200, closed Sundays. Owner Mme. Lamarthee, from Mauritius, speaks excellent English. She will iron if you wish, as well as arrange dry cleaning. Your laundry is done the same day; she stays till the work is finished.

Technical yacht services

Hervé Lepault has a Voilerie Caraibes Martinique loft in the Village Créole, on the north side facing out. This small branch of the much bigger Marin loft may not be here for too long.

Provisioning

The 8 à Huit supermarket is compact but complete. It is the cheapest place to have a cold beer.

Stock up on baked goodies in La Baguette. They have an excellent variety of breads, including pain complet and poppy seed baguette. Vegetable sellers sometimes set up on the roadside. Consider renting a car to drive to the giant Carrefour at Genipa.

Turn left towards Fort de France, pass two roundabouts, then take the tiny turn off with a very small Genipa sign. Go under the highway and it is on your left.

Fun shopping

Like ice-cream? Well, you will find lots of it here, and all of it good. Italian Cocco Bello is on the outer part of Créole Village; more glaceries are inside, and more are on the road to the marina.

Pointe du Bout is a shopper's dream of trendy little boutiques. Try starting at the Créole Village, beside the entrance to the Bakoua. It is built in Caribbean style, just Disneyfied enough to make it theatrically enticing. It is chock-a-block with shops that sell elegant clothing, kids clothes, jewelry, handicrafts, and objets d'art. Continue down the street towards the marina for more of the same, plus more casual clothing, souvenirs, magazines, and books. There are also a pharmacy, massage parlor/beauty salon, and several hairdressers.

Restaurants

One of the delights of Anse Mitan is to stroll over to La Baguette and have a breakfast of French coffee, fresh croissants, and pain au chocolat. Dozens of restaurants line the streets. I mention a few reliable ones that are not too touristy.

For fine food, go to La Manureva [$A-B closed Tuesday and Wednesday]. It is one of the fancier and more appealing restaurants. Owners Viviane and Oliver pay attention to detail, creating a pleasant ambience with good art on the walls and a bar built like a boat. The food is French with one or two Créole dishes and it is properly prepared and served like a work of art.

La Poisson D'Or [$B] has been around forever. It is on the back street, but has a pleasant atmosphere, is reasonably priced and serves good Créole seafood. Part of their building is now a mini market.

Copacabana [A-C] is both a Brazilian restaurant and a pizzeria. Go when you feel in need of stoking up on some really good meat, properly prepared the Brazilian way. On Friday and Saturday, they often have live Latin music.

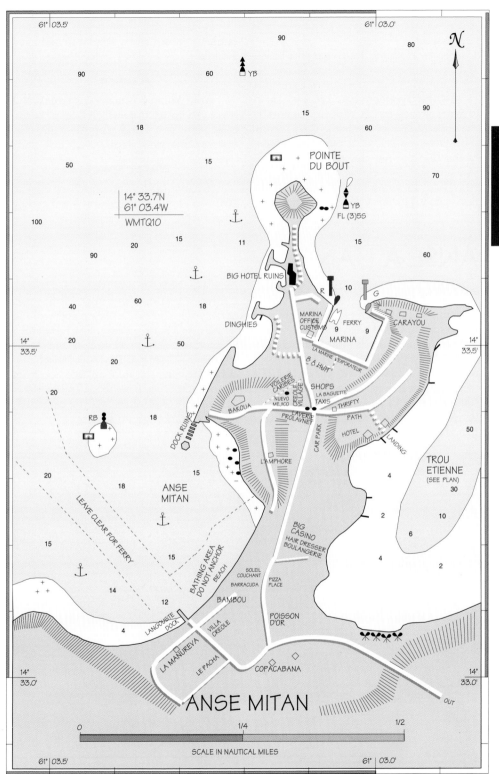

La Villa Créole [$B] is touristy but fine if you want entertainment along with a Créole meal.

For the pleasure of sitting on the beach and watching scantily-clad beautiful people, check out Au Soleil Couchant or Barracuda [$C-D]. If you prefer to watch people clad in designer clothes, try one of the restaurants by the marina. The most reliable is La Marine [$B]. Here you get to sit out in the open, facing the marina, the surroundings are pleasant, and the food fair value.

There are seven restaurants in La Village Créole. Havana Café is the place to sip a drink and watch people pass.

Le Bambou on the beach has entertainment most nights; wander in and have a drink.

Ashore

Anse Mitan has many car rentals and it is a good place from which to explore the island. The taxi stand is on the main road opposite Somatras Marina.

Water sports

If you want to go diving, check out the Attitude Plongée in Somatras Marina; they have people who speak English.

ANSE A L'ANE

Just around the corner from Anse Mitan is Anse à l'Ane, a sweet little bay with a charming beach. It is a pleasant anchorage in good conditions, though you may roll each time the regular Fort de France ferry runs.

Right in the middle of the bay, about one-third of a mile offshore, is a hard-to-spot reef about 4-feet deep. You can pass on either side to anchor in about 12 feet, on a sand bottom. Make sure your anchor is well dug in and leave the ferry channel clear (some-

times buoyed). Anse à l'Ane is open to the northwest and should be avoided in times of heavy ground swells. When approaching from Anse Mitan, give the first headland a wide clearance as it is all rocky and shoals stick out 270 yards at Pte. Alet (see chart). When heading toward Cap Salomon from Anse à L'Ane, you have about 9 feet of water between Ilet à Ramiers and the mainland, enough for most yachts to pass.

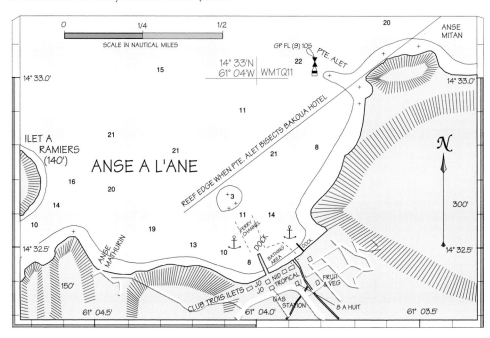

Trou Etienne

Beach at Anse a l'Ane

Services/ shopping

Anse à l'Ane is a holiday area, though much less built up than Anse Mitan. The beach has some shade, provided by seagrapes and palm trees. Leave your dinghy on the dinghy dock (swells permitting) or on the very inner end of the ferry dock.

Garbage bins are at either end of the car park and a gas station that sells ice can be found on the main road. A good 8 à Huit supermarket is open 0800-2000 except Sunday when it closes at 1300. Opposite is a hair stylist, and to the side is Blu Coco, a big gift/beach shop. Pomme Canelle is a greengrocer that also sells tropical flowers and smoked chicken, open 0830-1300, 1630-1900.

Restaurants

Ready for a meal out? For lunch La Case a Glace [$D], Nid Tropical [$B-D] and Kaza Pipo have the best locations right on the beach. Kaza Pipo [$B-D] also has wifi and serves Créole food, very inexpensive lunches, and set dinner menus.

Pignon sur Mer [$A-B] serves fine Créole food. The restaurant at the Club Trois Ilets [$A-B] offers both lunch and dinner, with entertainment many nights. Chez Jo Jo [$C], is an inexpensive restaurant and the local hot spot, with live Zouk music most nights. It is informal and shorts are fine.

Water sports

The dive shop Corail Club Caraibes, at Club Trois Ilets, has several instructors who speak English. There is also the new Calypso Plongée behind Kaza Pipo.

Anse a L'Ane anchorage showing the reef

Anse Noire

Anse Dufours

ANSE NOIRE

(map)
ANSE NOIRE
N
31.9'
0   1/8
SCALE IN N.M.
60
WMTQ12
14° 31.8'N
61° 05.4'W
GOOD SNORKELING
14°
31.8'
40
30
20   26   26
GOOD SNORKELING
18   11
12   6
STEPS
TO ROAD
61° 05.4'
05.2'
31.7'

ANSE NOIRE

Anse Noire and Anse Dufours lie about halfway between Ilet à Ramiers and Cap Salomon; two bays, one white sand, the other black. They should be avoided in northerly swells, but are otherwise well protected. Anse Noir is the better anchorage, as you will not be in the way of fishermen and there is an excellent dinghy dock. Small, colorful cliffs rise on the southern headland and there is a steep hill on the northern one. Palms line the black sand beach at the head of the bay and a large fancy dock juts out from the beach. Behind the beach, a steep jungly valley rises into the mountains. Popular as a daytime anchorage, Anse Noire is usually deserted and peaceful at night. The wind swings in all directions. Moorings are planned for this bay.

People occasionally anchor in Anse Dufours, a small fishing village with a white sand beach. If you do, be prepared to move for the fishermen any time of day or night.

Ashore

It is pleasant just to sit in Anse Noir and watch the kingfishers and other birds on the cliffs. An interesting trail follows the shady strip of riverine forest up the seasonal river behind the beach to the main road. Domaine de Robinson behind the beach sometimes has rooms to rent.

You probably won't get dinner, but for lunch climb the steps up the cliff, follow the road, on your left Desir's Sable D'Or [$C-D, closed Tuesday] specializes in fresh seafood and Créole meat dishes at reasonable prices. Or take the bougainvillea-lined road down to Chez Marie Jo [$C-D, closed Sunday] Maga Most [$D], and Snack Chez Nini [$D], on the beach.

Water sports

The snorkeling around the headland into Anse Dufours is superb: walls, crevices, and rocks decorated with sponges, tubeworms, and anemones, which attract a large variety of small fish. A particularly lovely deep grotto is halfway in Anse Dufours (you can see it in the aerial photo).

Grand Anse D'Arlet

Map labels:
GRANDE ANSE D'ARLET
14° 30.5'
CAP SALOMON
RESTAURANTS / TI BATEAU
100
70
50
30
25
18
10
120
40
20
12
30
25
LEAVE MIDDLE OF BAY CLEAR FOR FISHERMEN WHEN POSSIBLE
100
30
8
14° 30'N 61° 06'W
120
70
15
10
WMTQ13
120
50
10
100
35
25
15
10
15
10
WK
30'
N
0   1/4   1/2
SCALE IN N.M.
61° 06'
05'

GRANDE ANSE D'ARLET

Grande Anse D'Arlet is a little village set on a white sand beach with magnificent mountains towering behind. In the right light, when the hills are lush green, it is spectacular. Once a fishing village, a few dugout fishing pirogues remain, though for the most part it is now geared to tourism and the northern corner has a touch of the Riviera, with brightly colored beach umbrellas. A fancy new walkway runs behind the beach. Avoid sailing too close to the center of the village as a shoal area extends seaward several hundred feet. The holding is variable with weed and some broken coral, as well as good sand.

Regulations

Le P'Ti Bateau, a restaurant right at the head of the dock, has a customs computer and you can clear in and out when they are open; about 1030-1800 daily.

European funds have been granted for ecological moorings that will be placed throughout the area, from Anse Noir to Anse D'Arlet. I suspect they will be compulsory for yachts up to 25 meters and that there will be charges. I will post updates on doyleguides.com.

General yacht services

Le P'Ti Bateau has wifi and they can also provide water via a long hose that reaches down the dock.

Isabel's Kay Zaza is a boutique and laundry. Bring laundry at 1000 when it opens and get it back the same afternoon. Or bring it later and get it the next day. Isabel does wash, or wash, dry, and fold by the 5 kg load. She plans to bring back an internet computer

Grande Anse D'Arlet

Martinique

and fax machine. Kay Zaza is an artistic shop with gifts, ornaments, casual clothing, hats, art, and jewelry. They sell stamps and postcards and will mail them for you.

Ashore

Grand Anse D'Arlet wakes late and is fully ready for the day by about 1100. Earlier risers wander down to L'Abre Pain for coffee at their beach bar in the form of a boat, which can be quite a gathering place from 0900.

Several small food stores sell groceries and ice. When you get to the dock, go up to the main road, and whichever direction you turn, and you will come to one. These open at 0800. For more, you will have to visit Anse D'Arlet.

Le P'Ti Bateau [$B-C], right at the head of the dock, is a very pleasant, clean, reasonably priced restaurant, ideal for lunch ashore. They also open for a barbecue dinner on Friday and Saturday nights, starting at about 1900.

Otherwise Bidjoul [$B-C], Les Arcades [$B-C], L'Abre Pain [$B-C], and Le Payot [$B-C] are all Créole restaurants along the pathway behind the beach. They set tables and chairs on the beach to create an en-chanting place to have dinner right on the waterfront. Bidjoul is popular, their cooking is simple, well done, nicely presented, and they have a live lobster tank. Just beyond Ti Payot is a restaurant owned by Plongée Passion. They do a very good local lunch on the beach.

At the northern end of the beach, behind all the fancy Mediterranean style sunshades, is Ti Sable [$B-C], a slightly fancier establishment. Chez Evelyne and Chez Nita open for lunch at the southern end of the beach.

Cars can be rented from the beach area, and the coast road from Anse D'Arlet, which winds over the hills to Diamant, offers spectacular views. Anse D'Arlet is within easy walking distance.

An excellent trail follows the headland round to Anse D'Arlet. From the dinghy dock turn right on the road and look for the sign on your right hand side.

Water sports

Snorkeling is interesting all along the southern shore and between Grande Anse D'Arlet and Anse D'Arlet. Divers can join Plongée Passion or Alpha Dive, both along the waterfront.

FISH FARM

KEEP CLEAR

ANSE
CHAUDIERE

Anse D'Arlet

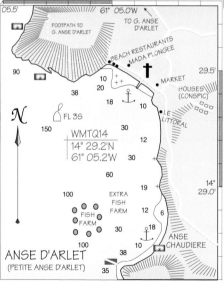

05.5' 61° 05.0'W

FOOTPATH TO
G. ANSE D'ARLET

TO G. ANSE
D'ARLET

BEACH RESTAURANTS
MADA PLONGEE

90

29.5'

10
20
18

MARKET

HOUSES
(CONSPIC)

38

10

LE
LITTORAL

FL 3S

WMTQ14
14° 29.2'N
61° 05.2'W

150

30

12

30

60

14°
29.0'

100

19

EXTRA
FISH
FARM

12   6

FISH
FARM

30

18

10

ANSE
CHAUDIERE

100

38

ANSE D'ARLET
(PETITE ANSE D'ARLET)

35

Scrawled filefish

ANSE D'ARLET

The photogenic village of Anse D'Arlet (called Petite Anse D'Arlet on most charts) has a few lovely old houses and a picturesque church. Everything is well painted and maintained. A handsome promenade follows the waterfront. Anse D'Arlet makes a good overnight anchorage unless the wind is too far in the south.

When approaching town, look out for the rocks to the west of the dock. Some are visible but others extend some yards seaward. Anchor in one of the sand patches off the town dock. A fish farm is in the southern part of the bay. Parts of it are marked by unlit green buoys; other parts are unmarked. Avoid this area at night and keep a good lookout by day.

Anchorage may also be found at Anse Chaudière in the southeastern corner of the bay, which is a great hideaway anchorage and good for snorkeling. Approach with caution, as isolated rocks extend about 100 feet offshore. Anchor on the sand bottom in 10 to 12 feet.

Services/ashore

The Europe Union is funding moorings in this bay. I will give updates on doyle-guides.com. Ashore you will find a couple of minimarkets, a post office, gift shops, and a pharmacy. If you need cash, an ATM is in the little market where you get fresh produce in the mornings.

Alain's L'Oasis boutique is connected to Zaza's in Grand Anse D'Arlet and Alain should be able to arrange to take laundry there for you. He also sells casual clothing, hammocks, pareos, and many colorful gifts.

For lunch, gravitate to the plastic chairs set out on the beach northwest of the river. Sandwiches and local meals are available from many small restaurants. This area has been carefully renovated with a pleasant walkway along the waterfront. Some of these restaurants also open in the evening.

Otherwise, Le Littoral [$B-C] is a good Créole restaurant a short walk away on the road leading south out of town. They have a great view overlooking the bay and open every day from 1100-1500 and 1900-2200.

You can hike from here, over the headland to Grand Anse D'Arlet and return by

the road, which is shorter.

Water sports

Mada Plongée will be happy to take you diving, and David, the owner, speaks English. They sometimes have exhibitions of local art next to the dive shop. Snorkeling is good in Anse Chaudière. It may be worth giving scuba a go here as well. If you are anchored in town, try the rocks off the dock. Everyone else does.

Anse D'Arlet; photo above, the library building

THE SOUTH COAST OF MARTINIQUE

There are no good anchorages along Martinique's south coast until you get to the eastern end. Several shoals along this coast extend up to half a mile offshore. There is deep water (over 100 feet) outside these shoals. It is best to stay in this deep water to avoid the numerous fish traps at lesser depths.

As long as you don't get too far offshore, the sail east to Ste. Anne is usually a brisk beat to windward in protected water, and it can be a great sail. Sometimes on a rising tide, when the current reverses to the east, it can become a bit like being in a washing machine. If it gets really rough, you can head well offshore till you are away from the tidal influence.

BAIE DU MARIGOT

Having said there are no good anchorages along this coast, there *is* an anchorage. It is not good, in that it often rolls (though this should be no problem for multihulls), and entry is extremely tricky and should only be attempted by those with years of Caribbean and reef navigation experience. The reefs are not at all easy to see and they are very dangerous, with swells often building as you go in. Once inside, it is a delightful bay with the large Novotel on one side and a deserted headland on the other. The view is great.

Navigation

Baie du Marigot lies to the east of the town of Diamant. When coming from the west, you see a conspicuous peaky hill behind. A building with a red roof stands on the western headland, and the Novotel buildings are to the west of this, though partially hidden by trees. A reef, Caye de Obian, lies almost on a direct line between Pte. du Diamant and the entrance. It is about a mile offshore.

The approach is down a very narrow channel, 30 feet deep, with shallow banks and reefs on either side, up to half a mile offshore. While there is just enough water to stray onto the banks in some places, you want to stay in the deep water. Swells usually roll into the shore, making the approach dangerous if you make a mistake. The channel includes a curve. The approach should only be made in calm, sunny conditions, with good light for spotting the shallows, which are often hard to pick out. It is strictly a matter of eyeball navigation.

Once inside, there is ample room for anchoring; the prettiest area is towards the eastern headland. If you are on a monohull, you will probably need to use a stern anchor to make life bearable.

Ashore

The large Novotel on the western shore has boutiques and restaurants.

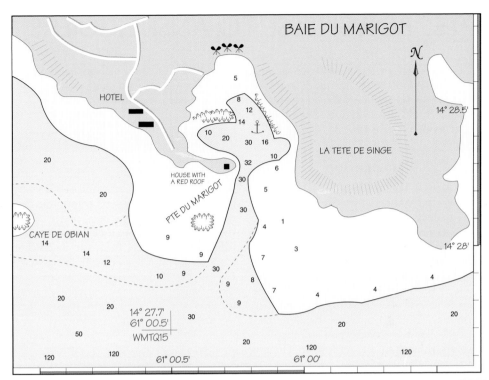

BAIE DU MARIGOT

HOTEL

LA TETE DE SINGE

HOUSE WITH
A RED ROOF

PTE DU MARIGOT

CAYE DE OBIAN

14° 28.5'

14° 28'

14° 27.7'
61° 00.5'
WMTQ15

61° 00.5'

61° 00'

Baie du Marigot
Note the long passage between shoals
that are hard to see.

CAYE DE OBIAN

PTE. BORGNESSE TO ANSE FIGUIERS

Pte. Borgnesse is the western headland as you enter Cul de Sac Marin. A couple of pleasant anchoring areas lie between this headland and Anse Figuiers, with some quiet hidden beaches.

Navigation

A wide shelf, about 9-14 feet deep, follows this coast. Off the shelf, the depth drops rapidly to 200 feet. There are some large shallow areas on the shelf that must be avoided. You can find your way inside them to anchor. A mile to the northwest, Anse Figuiers is a delightful bay and a popular holiday beach behind which you can see the eco-museum building with its conspicuous chimney. To get into Anse Figuiers, pass outside the shelf in deep water and approach Anse Figuiers from the southwest. There is a good shelf off the beach in 10-25 feet of water. If you have a fast dinghy, you can visit that way from St. Anne.

Ashore

Snorkeling is fair all around the headlands.

There is ample water to dinghy up the Rivière Pilote for a couple miles to the town of Rivière Pilote. This is an entertaining exercise and the scenery is quite pretty. Along the eastern shore is an area with numerous junked railway cars from the days when sugar cane was moved by rail. Entry to the river is close to shore between the coast and a man-made causeway. You will see many fishing boats and even a mini-marina along the first part of the trip.

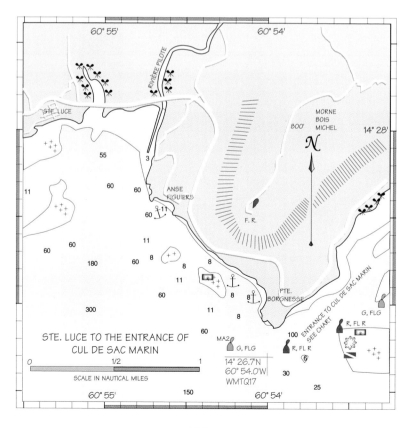

STE. ANNE

STE. ANNE

The white buildings of Ste. Anne stand out clearly against the surrounding green hills. Above the prominent historic church, a walled path leads up to a shrine. Ste. Anne is a delightful seaside town, with a sleepy holiday atmosphere. The town is tiny, but it has an adjoining beach that is magnificent and popular. The surrounding countryside is attractive with shore walks to even better beaches.

Navigation/regulations

Yellow buoys delineate a no-anchoring area off the beach and town, which seems to vary in size (from 2010 till now you could anchor right up to town); the anchoring area outside this is huge. You can also eyeball your way south and anchor off the Caritan Hotel. The water depth is 10 to 20 feet, sand bottom. Most is good holding, though there are some patches where the sand is too hard to get the anchor down. Shoals lie close to shore between Ste. Anne and Anse Caritan and off the southern part of Anse Caritan. If you are arriving here from abroad, you must first go to Marin and clear customs.

Weather permitting, you can visit pretty daytime anchorages south of Ste. Anne off Anse Meunier and Grande Anse

STE. ANNE AND
CUL-DE-SAC DU MARIN

des Salines. Approach Anse Meunier with caution as the bay is quite shoal. Avoid the rocky shallows between Pointe Catherine and Pointe Pie. Grande Anse des Salines is spectacular and popular.

Services

The town dock is good for dinghies. Garbage bins are just beyond the dock. But if these move, there are more down by Rendezvous Restaurant and these have special bins for recycling glass and plastic bottles. Ice is available at the Rendezvous Restaurant and the supermarket adjoining the market.

Communications

Snack Boubou, next to Les Tamariniers, has an internet cafe with computers and wifi.

They open about 0730-2000, but sometimes close on Wednesdays. It is a good place for breakfast. Cyber Base is an inexpensive, government-run internet center in the tourist office. It is upstairs at the back of the building (take the side street). Opening hours are Monday and Friday, 0800-1300, other weekdays 0800-1600, subject to change. Croque Pain, a boulangerie snack bar, sells Ben and Jerry's ice cream and has an internet room; open daily 0800-1800.

La Dunette and Paille Coco have wifi. Take your computer in and have a coffee to get the password. It might work from anchor.

Provisioning/shopping

Both the bank and post office have ATMs. Step off the dock and turn right and you will find the 8 à Huit supermarket to be adequate for topping up your stores. Check also Salines Services; they have a store and change bureau.

Opposite is L'Epi Soleil, a boulangerie/patisserie good for coffee, sandwiches, and snacks. Walk through the store to a pleasant sitting area right on the waterfront where they have a restaurant.

Farther down the street on the right is the fish and general market, with fresh meat, fruits, vegetables, and handicrafts.

Fun shoppers will enjoy the little craft stores and boutiques on every street.

Restaurants

Restaurants abound, both in town and on the beach that stretches from Ste. Anne to the Club Med.

Check out the little street opposite La Dunette. Chez La Martine, a shop, puts out tables in the evening, and serves delicious accras, along with very inexpensive beer.

Le Coco Neg is an intriguing tiny back street restaurant that has a pleasant atmosphere and serves traditional Créole meals. La Dunette [$B] has a perfect location and a dinghy dock. This is the happening place with live music and it is a perfect place to stop for a beer or ice cream.

Les Tamariniers [$B-C], has a cute exterior, and Le Rendezvous, which is inexpensive, has a good waterfront location, as does Paille Coco in front of Epi Solliel.

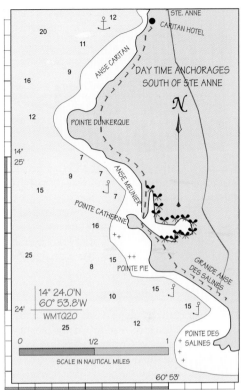

Pizza Don Amillo is next door.

The whole of the long beach is lined with restaurants. Touloulou specializes in seafood; their adjoining snack Tiloulou serves simple, tasty food and the daily special is excellent value for lunch.

Maryse (ex Le Sud) tells me Madi's

Grande Anse Des Salines

Marin Yacht Harbour

Delices Caraibe is one of the better beach restaurants, and how could I resist a restaurant with a snack called Ti Kano?

Le Filet Bleu has been around since I have been coming here and is quite popular.

Out at the other end of town, Gianna and Isabella's Al Casanova, has a good reputation for Italian food.

Ashore

The church square leads to two main streets, one along the waterfront and a parallel one at the back. Coming from the dock, turn left along the front street to climb over the hill to the popular beach that stretches all the way to Club Med. (A just-completed coastal walkway avoids the hill.)

Behind the church a curious leads up to the shrine on the top of the hill.

The coastal area from St. Anne, right round to the south and back up to the east to Anse Trabaud is a park with a trail. Hikers and bikers should take the road toward Anse Caritan and then follow the trail that goes all the way along, or just behind, the shore to Anse des Salines. Anse des Salines is one of Martinique's finest palm-backed beaches and very popular; ideal for people watching.

Those who prefer a more private setting will pass several smaller beaches along the way. Bikers can continue on to Anse Trabaud and back over the middle. (The trail is such that you will push quite a lot.) It takes about three and half hours at a leisurely pace.

Communal taxis run to Fort de France.

Water sports

A good place to start snorkeling or diving is at the second red buoy in the channel toward Marin. Snorkelers can follow the shallow part of the reef and divers can head south into deeper water where they will find a large collection of sponges, including some unusual shapes. This is a good place to see corallimorphs, pencil urchins, and small, colorful reef fish.

Kalinargo, the local dive shop, is at the Ste. Anne end of the beach that leads to Club Med. They dive twice daily, at 0830 and 1330. They will also fill tanks.

Another dive shop, Natiyabel, is at the fishing port, and rents kayaks.

Small sailing catamarans and sailboards are available for rent on the beach.

Cul-de-sac du Marin

MARIN

Marin, a pleasant small town, is one of the Caribbean's largest yacht centers, with the huge Marin Yacht Harbour Marina, a haul-out facility, and a vast array of yacht services and technicians. Where else in the Windwards can you walk into a mechanic's shops and view a row of marine engines on show and ready to install? You can find technicians of all stripes and they are gener-ally helpful and good at what they do ~ and there is not much that cannot be done. This is the main base for the Martinique charter industry: Star Voyage, Outremer Concept, Croisiere Caraibes, Dream Yacht Caribbean, Kiriacoulis, Liberty Sail, Sparkling Charter, Punch Croisieres, VPM Dufour, Corail Caraibes, Turquoise Yachting, Chimere Yachting, Regis Guillemot Charter, and Petit Breton all have bases here.

Navigation

Cul-de-Sac du Marin is a vast, deeply indented bay, surrounded by hills and lined with mangroves. It is full of shoals that are often visible in good light. The whole area is a gunkholer's dream and the best place to be in Martinique during a hurricane. The entrance channel is well marked by buoys and beacons. After you pass Club Med, head for the apartment buildings behind the forest of masts until you see the big red and green buoys in the middle of the bay. Pass between them, leaving the red one to starboard and the green one to port. Follow the channel in, leaving the red buoys to starboard. Shoals lie in the "no anchoring" area off Marin Beach, so avoid navigating through it.

Small yachts going between Marin and Ste. Anne can take a short cut between the outer two red buoys. Avoid the 6-foot shoal that lies east of the outer red buoy (see our sketch chart).

Regulations

Marin is a port of entry and a customs officer is available at his office in the marina every morning; usually arriving about 0700 and leaving at 1230. They use the new do-it-yourself system on computers. Customs may eventually cut out this office and just have computers in the marina, which would make clearance available in the afternoon.

Douglas Yacht Services can pre-clear large yachts via the internet.

Anchoring is forbidden in the swimming area marked by yellow buoys in front of the beach.

Communications

Marin Yacht Harbour has bay-wide wifi access if you have a booster aerial. You need to buy a card; minimum 3 Eu for 2 hours.

Both Cart Orange and Digicel sell USB wifi ports (3-G) that use prepaid cards. These are good for all the French islands, and some other islands with roaming. For SIMS and phone time, there is a store in Artimer, one just past Ti Toques, and two for Digicel in the Anette Mall.

The shore email facilities are good, with high-speed access. Many people take their computers into Mango Bay or Quai 13 which have free wifi for customers.

Cyber Marin has a good bank of computers and reasonable rates. It is at the head of the bay a few steps from Ti Toques. You can get copies made here. They also sell Haagen Dazs ice cream and some good bread: both baguettes and longer lasting whole-wheat loaves for yachts. They open weekdays 0630-2000 and Saturdays 0830-1300.

You can send emails upstairs in the marina in Balade et Mer, and those on the hard, use the email over at Cyber Carene in the CarenAntilles main office.

General yacht services

Services, shops and restaurants in Marin are in several locations, easy to reach by dinghy. Some are close around the marina; others are over by CarenAntilles, the large slipway, or at Artimer. All have dinghy docks.

Artimer is a big development, designed to include the boating trade. It has been cleverly designed to use the river and you can dinghy right up; the dinghy ride is novel. You pass the anchored yachts off CarenAntilles staying quite well inshore until you see the channel which is marked by flags. Pass down the channel, leaving red (orange) right returning, then enter the river. For a short while you get this nice river ride among the mangroves, in the middle of nowhere. Suddenly you arrive in a giant shopping mall with dinghy tie up in a little basin. You need to be able to climb a ladder, but the ladders are very large and secure. CarenAntilles and Artimer are also close by for easy walking.

You will find garbage disposal both at the marina and the haul-out, with oil and battery recycling. You can get water and fuel at both.

Marin Yacht Harbour [VHF: 09], (Marina du Marin), is the only large marina in Martinique. Owned by Eric and Glen Jean-Joseph and managed by Eric, it is good, friendly, and inexpensive and some people in the office speak English. They have been awarded the blue flag as an environmentally friendly marina. Dinghy docks are in front of the nautical block (Mango Bay) and down at the new Yacht Harbour Center (port office). With 750 berths, there is normally plenty of

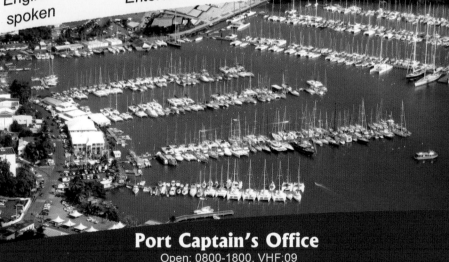
Martinique

room for visitors who are placed on the most accessible berths (see sketch chart). You can get diesel, gasoline, and water on the fuel dock daily: 0730-1730. Dockage is available with 220-volt/50-cycle electricity; 110-volt transformers are also available. (The 220-volt does not work with two lines of 110.) They have 100 moorings, but most are on permanent rental. You can often get one for a few nights. Call on the VHF: 09 to get help coming in. The marina is huge, but most of it is connected with a waterfront walkway. The marina facilities are in two blocks. The original nautical block is where you have customs, chandleries, and many services. The Port Office is in the huge new Yacht Harbour Center at the head of the bay. This giant marina mall has restaurants, charter companies, shops, and nautical services.

Some berths are suitable for mega yachts of any length and up to 4.5 meters draft. At Douglas Yacht Services, Douglas Rapier and his team, including Nadege and Stephanie in the office and Celine in provisioning, are there to ensure that big yachts have everything they need. They can pre-clear your yacht before arrival and do full provisioning and refueling, as well as technical support, travel, private jet arrival, medical, and other personal arrangements. Douglas is available 24/7 and keeps his phone at his side. For smaller yachts, he does project management (see *Technical yacht services*).

Blanc Marine is a convenient modern laundrette in the new Yacht Harbor Center. It has a central computerised system that takes both coins and notes. If you have a big load they have a 14 kilo machine as well as several at 7 kilos, and the driers are large. Soap is available, and for those big party nights, so is a dishwasher; open daily 0700-1930.

Bichik (VHF :69), the fuel and camping gaz dock at CarenAntilles, is a good establishment run by Gabriel and Laupa. They open 0700 to 1900; 1700-1900 on Sunday. If you bring your laundry, you can have it washed, washed and dried, or washed dried and carefully folded, which works well if you have 5 kilos or less. They put the laundry right in the machines, so bring it before 1600 and never on a Sunday. This is also an active

social spot and meeting place. People come to the Bichik store to drink a beer or coffee, have a lunchtime sandwich, watch some sports on TV, and use the book swap, which includes an English section.

Lav@net laundrette in the Anette Mall, opens 0600 to 2300, with wifi access.

Cyber Marin also has a laundrette, open 0600-2000. If you want to wash and dry, Sylvie, who runs it will move it over for you.

CarenAntilles [VHF: 16/73] is a large haul-out facility with many support services. We show their location on our sketch chart. You can easily visit by dinghy, though you have to brave the run-down dinghy dock. CarenAntilles can take boats with up to 23-foot beam with their 65-ton travel lift, and catamarans any width up to 60 feet long on their new hydraulic trailer. For the most part there is plenty of water in the bay for the approach. If you start at the outer buoy and head towards the dock, you should have 12 feet. The shallowest part is out by the buoy. While CarenAntilles are happy to store boats, they concentrate more on boats undergoing work. Rates depend on both how long you need to be ashore and the current exchange rate for the euro. Fax them for a rate sheet. You can do your own work on the slip or, if you prefer, there are workshops that can do it for you. Facilities include toilets, showers, and a restaurant. The yard manager, Jocelyne, speaks good English.

Dock Cleaner Ecologique is a floating dry dock run by Croisieres Caraibe Charters (office in Artimer). They can take anything up to 70 tons, 13 meters wide, and 1.8 meters deep. This is especially good for big catamarans. It is ecologically friendly, with all run-off being held in tanks. Their rates vary by the season. Call Philippe: 0696 77 45 87 or the office: 0596 74-64-58.

If you want to sell your yacht or buy one, Caraibes Yachts, managed by Jean Collin, is part of a larger company with offices in Guadeloupe, St. Martin, the Dominican Republic and Panama, and is an excellent place to start. They are in the new Yacht Harbour Center.

Try also Eric Vasse at Punch Croisieres charter company, Veronique at Petit Breton (used yachts or new Lagoon and Jeanneau), or A&C brokers. All are in the original nautical block. Other charter companies also sometimes sell used yachts.

If you need a survey, Jacques Scharwatt is a surveyor and his office is next to Diginav.

Medical problems can be fixed according severity and need. If you walk up the hill from the market you will find a doctors' office at the top. (If you have walked up the hill do you really need a doctor?) Here you will find Dr. Jean Louis Deloge and Dr. Veronique

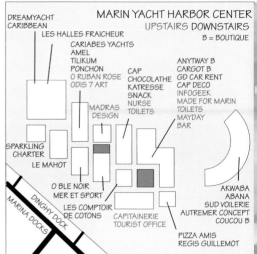

MARIN YACHT HARBOR CENTER
UPSTAIRS DOWNSTAIRS

DREAMYACHT CARIBBEAN
LES HALLES FRAICHEUR
CARIABES YACHTS
AMEL
TILIKUM
PONCHON
O RUBAN ROSE
ODIS 7 ART
CAP CHOCOLATHE
KATRESSE
SNACK
NURSE
TOILETS
MADRAS DESIGN
SPARKLING CHARTER
LE MAHOT
O BLE NOIR
MER ET SPORT
MARINA DOCKS
DINGHY DOCK
LES COMPTOIR DE COTONS
CAPITAINERIE TOURIST OFFICE

B = BOUTIQUE
ANYTWAY B
CARGOT B
GD CAR RENT
CAP DECO
INFOGEEK
MADE FOR MARIN
TOILETS
MAYDAY BAR
AKWABA
ABANA
SUD VOILERIE
AUTREMER CONCEPT
COUCOU B
PIZZA AMIS
REGIS GUILLEMOT

Claisse (office 0596 74 98 24). Both are GPs, and in addition, Dr. Claisse specializes in sports medicine, perfect for tortured muscles and joints. Alternatively, behind Leader Price, is the big Alizes Medical Center. In general, you can walk in, but will probably have to wait quite a while.

If you need serious and immediate attention, or don't like to wait, get Douglas at Douglas Yacht Services to help you. Otherwise, the emergency number is 115.

Chandlery

If you like boat stuff, you will love all the great chandleries around Marin.

Over in CarenAntilles, Carene Shop, owned by Hervé Ferrari, is right in the Caren-Antilles compound and is a good technical chandlery for everything you might need on the slip. Paints, antifoulings, epoxies, polyesters, and cloths are carried, as well as zincs, through-hulls, and lots of plumbing, hoses, and marine batteries, including Trojan and Optima. You will also find a full range of 3-M cleaning and polishing products to get your boat looking like new. They are direct importers of International Paints and have their technical booklets. They can match any paint color using two-part Spralac paints. They have a neat way to help you touch up paint with Spraylac. They have a machine that will fill a spray can, matching any color. It contains a special hardener activated in the air, so it

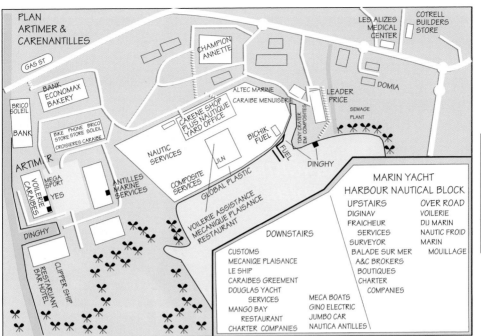

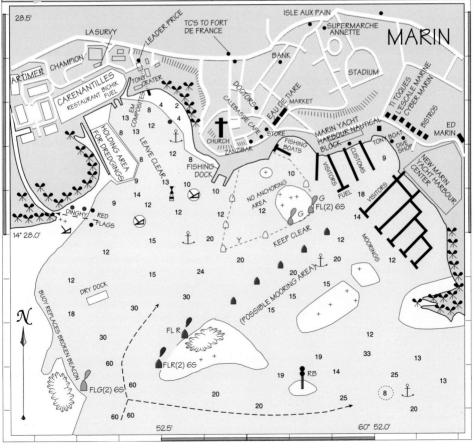

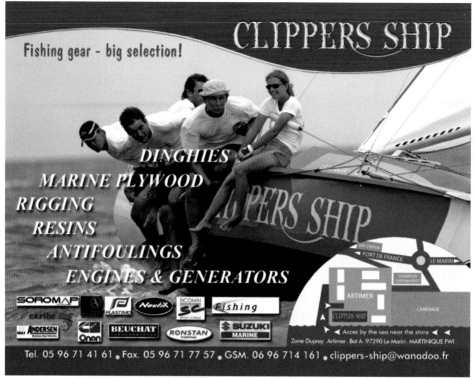
comes as a single can and you do not have to use it all at once, and it is not that much more expensive than regular spray cans. Upstairs, they are expanding to include more general chandlery and electrical items, plus second hand things.

In the marina (nautical block) Le Ship, owned by Viviane Caillot, is a great chandlery with a big stock. You will find stoves, Jabsco heads, anchors (Le Ship is Caribbean distributor for Brake spade anchors), chain, rope, charts, pumps, stoves, a great collection of LED bulbs, electronics, cruising guides, charts, and all kinds of yacht hardware. They sell the Plastimo range of inflatable dinghies. This is also the place for good acrylic wine glasses, linens, and some fun and fancy nautical decorations.

Caraibe Marine is an excellent chandlery, combined with numerous technical services. Owner Philippe Leconte started as a rigger, he then expanded into electrics and built a chandlery. He now has workshops that cover rigging (Caraibes Gréement), electrics, refrigeration, and water makers (Caraibes Energie), electronics (Caraibes electronique), and woodworking (Caraibes Menuisiere). For details see *Technical yacht services*. This expansion is reflected back in the chandlery, which is the largest in Martinique on the technical side. It also means if you buy something that needs installation, they can do if for you, and if it later needs service, they can do that, too. Need some new hatches? Caraibes Marine will have them in all shapes and sizes, as well as all the seals when you need a replacement. I am impressed because they stock things like the little plastic inserts for track cars that wear out and are hard to come by.

You will find a wide range of general chandlery, including safety gear and general hardware, as well as cooking stoves, charts, ropes, paints, and electronics ~ everything down to a kettle. Ask Philippe about solar panels. He advises 24-volt panels for a 12-volt system with a converter, because this gives a higher input over a longer time.

Caraibe Marine is also the Caribbean service center for Fountaine Pajot, Jeanneau, Catana, and Alliaura Marine.

Dinghy over to Artimer to visit Clip-

Tel: + 596 596 74 80 33 (in FWI) 0596 74 80 33
Fax: + 596 596 74 66 98, Mob: 0696 27 66 05
email: contact@caraibe-greement.fr
Special order dept: isabelle@caraibe-greement.fr

Caribbean service center for:
FOUNTAINE PAJOT - JEANNEAU
CATANA - ALLIAURA MARINE

The Eastern Caribbean's Biggest combined chandlery and workshops

We are the Caribbean's most impressive chandlery with hatches of every size, tracks, cars, winches, electrics, and electronics plus all the spares for everything we sell. We have of course ropes, chain, and anchors. In fact everything you could want including the kitchen sink and kettle!

Official agents for the world's best mast & rigging companies
LEWMAR, HARKEN, Z-SPAR, NAVTEC, FACNOR, PROFURL, BAMAR, SPARCRAFT, MARECHAL, SELDEN
Swaging 2.5-26mm, Rod rigging for BSI AND NAVTEC
Hydraulic systems.
We do onboard repairs

We sell, install and repair major refrigeration, electrical and watermaker companies, including:
GENERATORS: ONAN, KOHLER, FISCHER PANDA
WINDMILLS: AEROGEN, DUOGEN D 400
REFRIGERATION: VITRIFIGO, CRUISAIR, AIR MARINE
WATERMAKERS: SEA RECOVERY, AQUA BASE

We sell, install and service:
RAYMARINE
NKE, FURUNO, ICOM,
MC TECHNOLOGIES,
NEXUS

Full wordworking shop from replacing a plank to installing a new cabinet for a fridge.

WW   e.fr

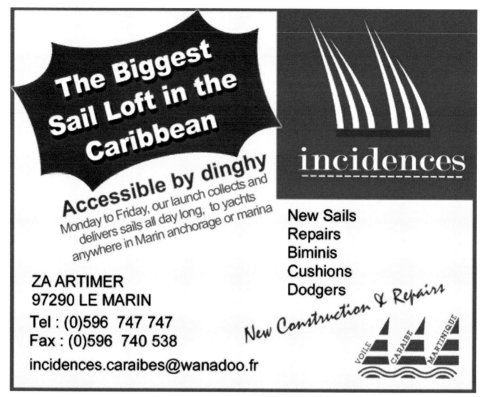
pers Ship, a giant chandlery that takes up two floors. It is owned by Jocelyne and her son Gillet, sometimes helped by Emmanuel. They are all helpful and speak good English. They have a broad selection of materials and fittings, including sheets of marine ply, resins, cloth, Andersen and Fredericksen winches, electrical panels, solar panels, electronics, anchor winches, Morse cables, hatches, and light fittings. They stock stainless and aluminum pipe, icemakers, windmills, Caribe and Apex inflatable dinghies, Onan generators and Suzuki outboards, which they also repair and service. They carry Zhik racing clothes and nautical shoes. This is probably the best place to get your fishing gear: they have a great selection and reels are reasonable. Clippers Ship carries a big range of fasteners including rivets, which can be hard to find in some other shops.

Gillet and Emmanuel also own Alizes Composites. They do all kinds of fiberglass repairs and construction. See *Technical yacht services/glass and paintwork.*

A few steps away, YES also has a technical chandlery mainly devoted to electricity and plumbing, but there are fastenings and other items worth checking out. They have great electrical fittings, and the best range of modern, third generation, super-bright LED lights and bulbs that I have seen in the Windwards. They carry a good stock of Sinemaster portable generators, light enough to carry back to your dinghy. They have solar panels, Mastervolt components, and batteries. On the plumbing side, they stock new water-makers, including eco-tech, and lots of plumbing. They sell cleaners and boat chemicals. They also fix electrics and watermakers (see *Technical yacht services*).

Over in the new marina block, Mer et Sport has a branch of its marine oriented sports shop, about half chandlery, the rest clothing and sports stuff.

Technical yacht services
Sailmakers/Canvas/Cushions

Technical yacht services are found in Marin Marina, in CarenAntilles and in Artimer. In Artimer, the Incidences (Voilerie

Caraibes) sail loft, some 6000 square feet of state-of-the-art design, is the largest in the Caribbean, and a giant by international standards. Hervé Lepault, the owner, and his team can tackle any job from windsurfer to superyacht. Sails may be brought in by launch or truck and hoisted straight up into the loft on a giant traveler system. Their launch collects and delivers sails on board anywhere in the Marin anchorage or Marin Yacht Harbour at any time during working hours from Monday to Friday, with no extra charge; call on VHF: 16.

This is a huge, efficient loft, so turn-around time on repairs is fast. Hervé also has an upholstery department for boat cushions and will bring in any color fabric to suit your job. New sails are by Incidence, the well-known French sailmaker, and carry their guarantee. They are computer-designed in France and sewn here. They make many cruising sails in woven Spectra, which has a life and weight similar to Dacron, but will hold its shape significantly better. With this giant loft, there is plenty of capacity for making new sails fast. Hervé, who also has a loft in St. Martin, speaks excellent English.

Voile Assistance in CarenAntilles is a small, friendly, and personal sail repair and canvas shop owned and run by Didier and Maria, who do the work. They build awnings, biminis, cushions, and covers, including fancy inflatable covers. They also sell sailcloth and canvas by the yard.

Voilerie du Marin, run by Daniel Karner, is in a cute local wooden house on the main road opposite the marina. Dan is the agent for Doyle Sails. He can measure your boat for a new set and get a quote. He also repairs lots of sails, whatever the make. He also does all kind of canvas work.

Manu Voile, a good sailmaker with a loft in Fort de France, has now opened Sud Voilerie in the new marina block. This is a convenient location and Manuel, the owner, works here, which ensures you get a good job.

Technical yacht services
Electrics, Electronics & Watermakers

Artimer is the home base of Thierry's Yachting Engineering Services (YES). This is both a technical shop (see *chandlery*) and

a service point. On the service side they fix all electrical problems as well installing any kind of electrical equipment. They sell, service, and install watermakers, and fix all makes. They have a van and can make visits to other harbors.

Upstairs in the main marina building is Jacques Fauquet's Diginav electronics showroom and workshop. Jacques has been in this business for over 30 years and knows more about marine electronics than anyone else in Martinique. He works on all makes and knows what goes wrong with many of them so when a repair becomes due, he can work efficiently, repairing if possible, only replacing when necessary. Jacques speaks English, and is pleasant to deal with.

Diginav's showroom has a good display of Raymarine, Furuno, Brookes and Gatehouse, and Garmin electronics in stock, as well as many spares for them. They can set you up with a satellite communication system, and safety gear such as Epirbs. They do a lot of sales and installation work for American and European yachts, and are agents for

Aquabase water-makers, for Kohler, Fischer-Panda and Onan generators, Danforth and Vitrifrigo refrigeration, and Cruisair and Air Marine air conditioning. They stock batteries, solar panels, and wind generators, and you will find all kinds of electrical components, including Link and Blue Sea, as well as electrical parts, water filters, and more.

Caraibe Electronique, also in the Caraibe Marine stable, sell, install, and service Raymarine, NKE, Furuno, Icom, MC technologies, and Nexus. Since they are together with Caraibe Gréement, it is a convenience when you are getting a new mast or taking the old one out for service, that they can install most of the electronics at the same time without having to deal with a third party. (See them at Caraibe Marine, see *Chandlery*.)

Gino is an electrician who shares an office with Meca Boats in the New Marina Block. Whatever your electrical problems ~ motor, generator, charging, or general work in any voltage ~ Gino can help. He does the electrical work for Douglas Yacht Services.

See also for Tilikum under *Refrigeration* for Victron systems and charging.

Technical yacht services
Rigging

In the marina, Caraibe Gréement (part of Caraibe Marine) is a full rigging service run by Philippe Leconte. Philippe can handle any rigging problem you may have, from replacing stays to a complete re-rig of your yacht, even including a new mast. This is probably the best rigging shop in the Windwards. They can swage up to 26 mm and have equipment for some rod rigging and hydraulic hoses. Difficult splices, including rope to wire, are a breeze. Caraibe Gréement are agents for Profurl, Facnor, Lewmar, Navtec, Gioit, Z-spar, Spectra, Selden Harken, and many other brands. They always keep spare booms, poles, and all kinds of battens in stock. Anything they do not have can be shipped in on short order by Isabelle LeConte, the special order specialist. They are happy to work on your yacht and make repairs aloft. They fix and sell hydraulics, including Le Comble. They will also reglaze and seal your worn-out, leaky hatches.

Superwind and Silentwind windmills.

Jacques is technically excellent, and can handle the most complex systems, including superyacht electronics. This has made him very much in demand. He manages to keep up, but it is still helpful if you contact him in advance (email is fine).

Pochon Marine, in the new marina block, is a new branch of a large French electronics company. They sell Furuno, Icom, Garmin, Lowrance, Simrad, Magellen, B&G, MC Technologies, Raymarine, Cobra, NKE, Sharp, Hummingbird, and are agents for Kannad and other Epirbs. They have Thrane and Thrane Sailor communications, and Schenker water makers. They also carry televisions for yachts, windmills, and hydro-generators. It is run by Willy Bulteau, who handles any installation and service that might be necessary and his wife, Rachel. They open weekdays 0830-1230, 1400-1700, plus Saturday mornings in high season.

Caraibe Energie, part of Caraibe Marine, sells, installs, and repairs electrics, refrigeration, and water-makers. They are agents for Sea Recovery, HRO, and

Their new website allows you to estimate the cost and order rigging and other items online. Visit them at Caraibe Marine (see *Chandlery*).

Bernard Blaineau and his son Sylvan run Antilles Gréement, a general rigging shop. They work cheerfully and well on all kinds of masts, including carbon fiber and all kinds of rigging except rod. They can swage up to 16mm wire. They will make visits anywhere in Martinique and are happy to climb up the mast. They do smaller work such as lifelines and do their own aluminum and stainless welding for rigging parts. Bernard races and has experience of high tech boats. Sylvan speaks good English, and you can call him at (0696) 40 91 07.

Technical yacht services
Refrigeration

Frederic Moser at Tilikum has an office in the new Yacht Harbour Center. He is an excellent man for refrigeration and air conditioning, and also electrics. He speaks English and does new installations as well as repairs on either air- or water-cooled units, and he can figure out the best system for you. He is agent for Danfoss and ACC compressors. Charter companies pay him to replace their standard compressors for his water-cooled system, which uses half the power. It is a really neat unit. For bigger systems, he puts several smaller units together. On the electrical side, Fred is agent for Victron, carries a big stock of their products, and is good at all charging systems, inverters, and problem solving.

Patrice Fougerouse at Fraicheur Service is another first-rate refrigeration man. He is agent for Webasto, Danfoss, U-Line, Crui-sair, Climma, and Frigoboat. He will fix any make of refrigeration and air-conditioning and he can sell you a new unit and do full installation. You will find him upstairs in the Marina nautical block, above Douglas Yacht Services.

Nautic Froid is a small refrigeration shop next to Voilerie du Marin. The owner is not often in so it is best to call.

See also Caraibes Energie under *electrics*. They sell, service, and repair refrigeration.

Technical yacht services
Mechanics/Welding/Fabrication

A branch of Patrice Caillot's Mecanique Plaisance is in the marina. Their shop is new and shiny, with many new Perkins, Volvo, Westerbeke, and Yanmar engines and generators, as well as outboards, in stock at competitive prices. The diesel engines can be sold to overseas yachts tax-free. The shop also sells a full range of spares for most things mechanical, including all kinds of filters for fuel and oil. They have inverters, batteries, fasteners, and isotherm fridge units (no service on these). They have a big repair shop over in CarenAntilles and are the main repair shop for all the brands of motors they sell, and they help out with other makes of engine when they have time. They guarantee their work. There is easy access to come alongside to remove an engine.

You will be in excellent hands with Yvon Icare at Antilles Marine Services: he speaks English and is an excellent diesel specialist. He has a wonderful new, clean workshop in Artimer and is agent for Nannidiesel, Caterpillar, and Man engines and keeps some in stock, from 10 h.p. upwards. For larger engines, he also stocks Iveco. He is an agent for Hurth and ZF drives and Dessalator water-makers. He has been so successful that he now generally only works on these brands. He is happy to sell new engines and water-makers, which he keeps in stock. His shop is in the new Artimer complex, not too far from the dinghy landing. You can buy engine parts here and spares such as filters.

Yvon often flies to other islands to work on superyacht engines and gearboxes. He also works in collaboration with Christophe Domon of Navy Techniques in St. Barts. If Yvon is out on a job, his wife Patricia will look after you.

It is very nice to see a new enterprise, Meca Boats, open up in the nautical block of the marina. It is run by Rubin Martial who used to be a BMW mechanic, and he fixes both inboards and outboards. At the moment he is a one man show, so try to give him a little notice, especially for a big job.

Tony Boat is an outboard shop in a container near Sparkling Charter. Owner Tony Cavalier can fix your outboard whatever the

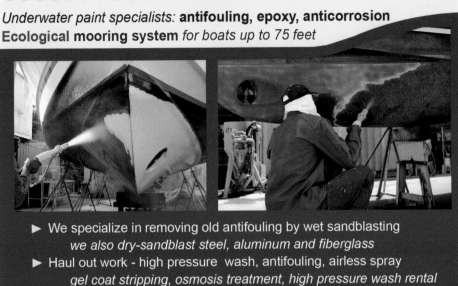
brand and whatever the size.

As you come off the dock in CarenAntilles, Altec Marine is in a big building in the corner of the yard, ahead and to the right. This is a machine and fabrication shop run by Margiotta Luigi. He has a huge amount of equipment here and can do any kind of fabrication or repair, including turning shafts up to 80 mm. They are normally busy, so now-for-now may not be possible.

Tony Crater works in a container in back of EM Composites outside CarenAntilles. He does tig and plasma welding and fabricates, welds, and polishes stainless and aluminum and makes many bimini frames.

See Clippers Ship for sales and service of Suzuki outboards.

Technical yacht services
Glass and Paintwork

Talba Gaston's Nautic Services in the CarenAntilles compound is the best place to get your boat's antifouling, epoxy, or coal tar priming done. He is a specialist at various coatings and has over 20 years of experience. He is an authorized antifouling applicator for International, Sea Hawk, and many other brands, and he works with brush, roller or spray. Gaston has a giant new high-tech sandblaster, and one of his major specialties is removing old antifouling by judicious and careful wet sandblasting. He can bring your boat right back to gel coat so it looks like new. He is the man for dry sandblasting which he does on steel, aluminum, and polyester. He will also polish your topsides so you are ready for the season. If you prefer to do things yourself, he rents some equipment, including a high-pressure washer.

Gaston has a new company, GT Global Horizon, which imports silicone-based antifouling. This is an interesting antifouling, completely free of toxins that makes the surface so slippery that marine organisms cannot get a grip. If you move a lot they drop off. If you are a harbor hugger, then the lightest wipe should take them off. I am eager to test out.

MARIN ANCHORAGE & MARINA

NO ANCHORING

DINGHY CHANNEL TO ARTIMER

In addition, Gaston makes cradles for shipping yachts long-distance.

Alizes Composites is owned and run by Gillet and Emmanuel. Their young and energetic team has a mobile workshop in a large van and can work on site. They do all kinds of fiberglass repairs and construction, including composites, they match gel coat, spray topsides, and treat osmosis. They can also construct and repair wood-epoxy. You can ask at Clippers Ship with which they are closely associated. (See *Chandlery*.)

Also in CarenAntilles, Global Plastic is run by Pascal Gruet. He is a fiberglass specialist and makes many new centerboards for cats. He can build and repair in polyester or epoxy. He also repairs gel coat and can match color. In addition, he can respray in gel coat as an alternative to paint.

A few steps away, Composite Service, run by Nicolas Vigneron, repairs and fabricates in either polyester or epoxy. He does gel coat repair and resurfacing and can match any color. He does two-part polyurethane spray painting and he likes to create art out of polyester.

EM Composites is on the other side of the river from CarenAntilles; just walk out of the gate and keep turning right. Etienne Maran does fiberglass construction: fishing boats, dinghies, tanks, and two-part polyurethane spray painting. He has waterside access for large runabouts or very small yachts.

Technical yacht services
Woodwork

Serge Pivan runs a woodworking shop in CareneAntilles called Caraibe Menuiserie, which is part of Caraibe Marine. He is a good man to see for all your woodwork, from planks to joinery. His shop is just north of Bichik.

Otherwise there is a house carpenter, Menuisiere Ebenisterie, near Leader Price.

Technical yacht services
Liferafts & Inflatables

Those with inflatables will be glad to know that La Survy (just outside the CarenAntilles gates) offers a repair service. The Phillias family has over 32 years of experience. Their modern shop is temperature and humidity controlled and they will fix any kind of inflatable. They repair and are warranty agents for Zodiac, Avon, Bombard, BFA, and Plastimo. Several tenders and liferafts are on show, with more in stock. They have flares and other safety gear. (You may have to ask to see it.)

Technical yacht services
Project Management and Other Services

If you are going to leave your boat in Martinique and have work done while you are away, it makes a lot of sense to have a project manager. Douglas Rapier of Douglas Yacht Services will act for you in this capacity. English is his first language, he has all the right contacts, and will make sure you get a good job on time. He has a good team, including Nadege in the office and Gino on the docks. He can help out if you are in a hurry and need someone to organize repairs for you.

Frank has a lovely computer shop called Infogeek in the new Yacht Harbour Center. He has fair prices on laptops and accessories and he can fix your laptop and sort out computer problems. He works on integrated marine computer systems of the kind found on fancy yachts. He does much of this work in association with Douglas Yacht Services.

For boat signs, visit JLN in CarenAntilles.

If you have a Lagoon that needs help, Corail Caraibes Charter is the Caribbean agent. If you have a Jeanneau, Catana, Fountaine Pajot or Alliaura, contact Caraibes Gréement.

If you have an Amel that needs help, the agent is in the Yacht Harbour Center.

Transport

We give the location of the TCs on our map, and it is easy to get to Fort de France. There are also numerous car rental agencies, including GD location in the new Yacht Harbour Center.

Taxis stand by just outside the marina on the town side. If you want to call one, try Thierry Belon. He is personable and reliable, and he speaks a little English (0696 25 88 52). If you need someone more fluent in

English, call Max Lamon (0696-26-03-94).

Don't want to sail home? Check Dockwise Yacht Transport (yacht-transport.com).

Provisioning

Appro Zagaya is an excellent provisioning service run by Cathy and Pascal. Their office is a little hard to find, so best work by phone, fax, or email. This is a professional and friendly operation where they enjoy their work. You can go onto their web site (www.appro-zagaya.fr) and shop or download their lists and order by email or fax. They will deliver right to your dock, in specially designed plastic bins. They need three days' notice and this is a full provisioning service, so your order needs to be over 200 Eu. This is perfect for people coming down on charter, short of time, or who hate shopping.

Douglas Yacht Services does full provisioning for the superyachts. This is a fully professional service, and items not available in Martinique are flown in from France.

If you prefer to shop yourself, you have a choice of supermarkets. The Champion Supermarket in the Centre Commercial Annette, just behind CarenAntilles, is in a mall whose other stores include a bookshop, a photo store, mobile store, beauty shops, gift shops, a boulangerie/patisserie, and rotisserie. It will probably have the widest selection and it is ample for a regular provisioning, with good packaged cold cuts, frozen meat, frozen seafood, cheese, and wine sections. It is an easy walk from the CarenAntilles dinghy dock.

Leader Price has the best location, with their own dinghy dock for your use. This is a reasonably priced market that is popular with locals and often has good fresh produce, frozen meats, fish, and shrimp. Many things they sell, like Real Cola, are their own brand. Mix it with enough rhum and lime, and no one will ever know. The Economax, at Artimer, is inexpensive but very limited.

Ed Marin is the most spacious market, very modern with big, wide aisles. You will not feel claustrophobic here. They have a good selection, and are just behind the Yacht Harbour Center, within easy walking distance through the car park. They open 0800-1930 except Sunday, when they close at 1300. Delivery is possible for a fee.

Caribizz in the Yacht Harbour Center mainly sells wine, beer, beverages, and tobacco products. It is duty free to any non-EC boat that has cleared out. If you are in the marina, they will deliver right to your boat.

Le Halles Fraicheur, is a new green grocer and high-end store with good wines and specialty foods in the Yacht Harbour Center. They are closed Sunday and Monday.

Check out Chocolathe under *Fun shopping*. In the Annette Mall, Anette's Nature A is a health and specialty food store.

For a giant, modern, really good supermarket, Carrefour at Genipa is the closest and avoids the heavy traffic near Fort de France. Drive past the Rivière Salée exit, pass two roundabouts, and look for a tiny right turn with a small Genipa sign (blink and you've missed it). Pass under the highway; it is right ahead.

The local market is good for produce, spices, local drinks, and souvenirs.

Aux P'tis Delices is a super boulange-rie/patisserie a few steps from the marina nautical block towards town. You can also have a great sandwich lunch here, or coffee and something delicious. Or check out La Farandale in the Artimer complex. Isle aux Pain, in the back of Marin, is even bigger.

For party, picnic and all kinds of fancy disposable wear check out Miguel de Laval's Cap Deco in the new marina block.

Fun shopping

The new Yacht Harbour Center is a fascinating structure with lots of levels, cor-ners, steps, and even a spiral staircase. It is a natural for kids and in the afternoon parents let their kids explore while they check out all the boutiques in this block. These include Made for Marin, Mylene, Cargot, Anyway, Cap Chocolathe, Madras design, Odis 7 Art, and Les Comptois do Cotton. Look for Frank's computer shop called Infogeek.

Cap Chocolathe is an ultra-fine food store run by Jean-Francois Guillet that fea-tures wonderful chocolate products, sweets, elegant teas and accessories, and very fine preparations that will add zest to your cooking. I made my start here with bottle of "Fruit de la Passion", a combination of passion fruit pulp and vinegar, which has both a great color and flavor and livens up salad dressings, works well in a marinade, and creates a delicious fried fish if you just add a little before you cook. I followed it up with a similar product but made with poivrons au piment d'Espelette ~ equally zesty and delicious. I shall be back to try other things. This is also a perfect shop for little presents of bon-bons or even big ones. If you know a chocolate lover, they have a life-sized cocoa pods that are made of chocolate colored to be realistic. Hollow inside, they are packed with other chocolate delights. They have a Facebook page where you can see some of their products.

Fishing enthusiasts can get their hooks into shopping at Akwaba, in the Yacht Harbour Center. This is a giant fishing store, with rows of rods and hooks, lines, and sink-ers. They have nautical clothing, snorkeling gear, lots of good tackle boxes, and any kind of fishing gadget you might want. Next door,

their Abana sells marine batteries, diving gear, and oils.

Clippers Ship in Artimer Mall (see *Chandlery*) also has excellent fishing gear.

Brico Soleil is a good general hardware store in Artimer, with a separate gardening section in another building. Cotrill is a big builder's supplier if you need lumber or plumbing. Oye Oye is a mixed bag store near Leader price ~ from power tools to exercise machines.

Souvenir hunters will find numerous shops to choose from, especially in the Yacht Harbour Center and the road opposite. If you need sportswear, Mega Sport is in the Artimer complex.

Caribbean Imports, below the Anette Mall, has a selection of household gear. If you cannot find it here check the giant Domia, next to McDonalds, which is behind Leader Price.

Restaurants

Gone are the days when it was hard to find a restaurant here. I mention only a few or the many.

Mango Bay [$B-D] is right in the marina, with a great view over the yachts. You will be welcome in shorts. This is an excellent place to come for breakfast, lunch, or dinner. They have a deli with excellent sandwiches, croissants, pain au chocolat, and ice cream. Their bar is a gathering place in the evenings for many yacht crews. Daily specials, pizza and pasta, and a menu that changes every few months are available for both lunch and dinner; you cannot beat the location. They cook both French and Italian

New Yacht Harbour Center

specialties and it is one of the better and more reliable restaurants in Marin. If you like the daily special: go for it, it is usually excellent. You can bring your computer and use the free wifi (no computers after 1830, Friday to Sunday).

Le Mahot [$D], owned by Evelyne Murat, is a pleasant, inexpensive new restaurant in the just finished Marin Yacht Harbour Center. Seating is traditionally French; on the pavement under a giant awning with a view over the boats. Monday to Friday they offer a very generous 12 Eu 3-course menu. The food is simple but very good with fresh seafood, chicken curry, ribs and more. They open every day from 0800 till the last person leaves. Dinner offers a lot of barbecued food especially on Friday and Saturday nights when they have live entertainment, which often takes the form of traditional Créole dancing.

Marin Mouillage [$D] is right behind the marina. They do a brisk lunch trade, with tasty local specials, and are open as a bar in the evenings. On Friday and Saturday evenings they barbecue spare ribs. They are very busy, as the food is good and reasonably priced.

L'Escale Marine and Ti Toques are two restaurants close to each other. L'Escale Marine [$C-D] has a traditional area with tables out onto the pavement, where you sit in the shade of the awning and trees and watch passers-by. Service is relaxed and friendly. They serve mainly crepes and quiche-type tarts, along with some raw specialties, with ice cream to follow.

Ti Toques [$B-C] is a smart, modern, street-side establishment open to the breeze, with fast, snappy service. Their food is generally good. They post old favorites and daily specials on a blackboard. While mainly French cuisine, they also do pizza and ice cream. Eat there or take away.

Indigo [$B-C] is the floating restaurant, just outside the new Yacht Harbour Center, with an unbeatable location for hanging out over the water in a nautical atmosphere. It is owned by the Annette family and serves Créole food at a reasonable price.

Zanzibar [$B] is upstairs and open to the breeze. Their food is very acceptable, and their fondant choclolat and creme brulée are superb.

The new Yacht Harbour Center has quite a few entertaining restaurants and bars. Katress is a fine little cafe for smoothies, breakfast and morning coffee, or a lunch sandwich and specials.

O ble Noir [$D, closed Mondays] is a creperie and ice cream place with ample space for hanging out. Pizza Amis is a popular pizza place where many come to hang out when work is over.

Le Mayday [$B] takes up much of the top floor near the marina office, with comfortable easy chairs, open to the breeze. This is a great spot for a coffee or drink and they serve good food.

Le Sextant (closed Sunday and Mon-

day) is the CarenAntilles restaurant with a large dining area overlooking the work area, and the bay beyond. They serve generous daily lunch specials which are great value and geared to hungry workers. In the evening it is a bar and hangout with live music, usually a couple of times a week. You can bring your computer for the wifi.

Restaurant La Paillote Cayali [$C-D] is for those who want to eat right on the beach. Sit out next to the waves and eat a variety of local specialties at reasonable prices. Open all day every day.

Calebasse Café, has interesting musical groups some evenings.

A little hotel in Artimer is by the dinghy dock. It sometimes has a restaurant.

If you have a car, Paradisio [$B-C] is a wonderful lunchtime restaurant behind the beach at Cap Chevalier (take the road to Cap Chevalier, then follow the signs). It has a pleasant, light and lively garden atmosphere, and serves inventive French and Créole food, which is usually excellent. It is so popular that it is advisable to book in advance.

Ashore

One of the better shore treats is to visit Eau de Tiaré, a complete beauty and health spa run by Kathy and Carina. Kathy is a Vincentian who grew up in Mustique, so English is her first language. She is full of fun and will make you feel immediately at home For some years they have been operating outside of town, but by the time this comes out they should be in their splendid new

facility upstairs in the historic old building just west of the market (door on the road leading up the hill). They offer all kinds of beauty treatments, including manicure, pedicure, facials, waxing, and more, as well as a variety of massages. Hairdressing is available. Prices vary from about 40 to 80 Eu. The new location will include a steam bath and other improvements.

If you cannot find it, or for some reason the move is not complete, just call Kathy (0696 37 47 50 or 0596 74 33 57).

If you rent a car or hike, make an effort to climb the hill on the west side of Marin for the spectacular view, not only across the bay but all the way to Baie des Anglais. As you leave Marin and head for Fort de France, there is a roundabout just opposite Ilet Dupres. Follow the signposts for Morne Glommier and enjoy the ridge.

Marin is a good area to shake the rust off your old bike and give it a run. The road up to Le Cap and over to Macouba is pleasant and from here trails lead south along the coast.

Water sports

Nautica Antilles is an excellent diving equipment shop in the marina. You can buy or rent gear here, including compressors. If you want something you do not see, ask, as Nautica Antilles is linked to a larger retail outlet near the airport.

If you want to go diving, check out Christophe at Immersion Caraibes. He speaks English and will make it easy. You will find him in a little house near Tony Boat.

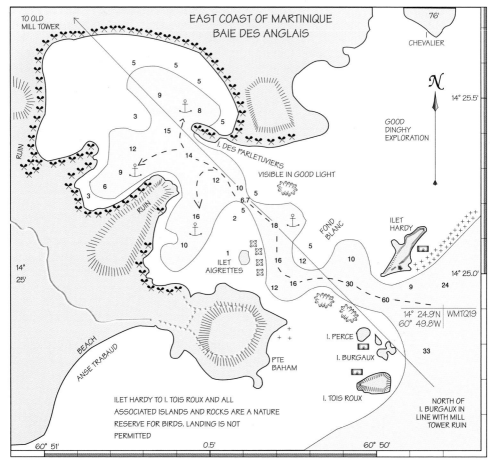

EAST COAST OF MARTINIQUE
BAIE DES ANGLAIS

TO OLD MILL TOWER

CHEVALIER

76'

14° 25.5'

GOOD DINGHY EXPLORATION

I. DES PARLETUVIERS
VISIBLE IN GOOD LIGHT

RUIN

RUIN

FOND BLANC

ILET HARDY

14° 25.0'

1
ILET AIGRETTES

ILET HARDY TO I. TOIS ROUX AND ALL ASSOCIATED ISLANDS AND ROCKS ARE A NATURE RESERVE FOR BIRDS. LANDING IS NOT PERMITTED

BEACH

ANSE TRABAUD

PTE BAHAM

I. PERCE

I. BURGAUX

I. TOIS ROUX

14° 24.9'N
60° 49.8'W WMTQ19

NORTH OF I. BURGAUX IN LINE WITH MILL TOWER RUIN

14° 25'

60° 51'   0.5'   60° 50'

THE EAST COAST OF MARTINIQUE

This guide covers all the most frequently used anchorages, but does not include most of Martinique's east coast. This area is pleasant and interesting, but it is also tricky, with many reefs and shoals in water that is often difficult to read. The charts that are available are short on details where it matters, and over the years it has claimed more than its fair share of hulls. Adventurous cruisers who wish to visit should buy the Trois Rivières guide to Martinique by Jerome Nouel. It is in French and English, with excellent color photographs, and is the only guide that covers this area well. We do include Baie des Anglais, the closest east coast anchorage.

BAIE DES ANGLAIS

The wine locker is full, you are stuffed on restaurant meals, you have seen enough elegant boutiques to last a lifetime. What next? Consider a few days of quiet recovery in Baie des Anglais. Baie des Anglais is less than 3 miles up Martinique's east coast. It is a large mangrove-lined bay, with some small beaches and several little islands for dinghy exploration. There are no restaurants, no shops, and while there may be another boat or two, you are likely to have it to yourself.

Regulations

The islands at the entrance to Baie des Anglais, including Ilet Hardy, Ilet Perce, Ilet Burgaux, and Ilet Tois Roux, are bird sanctuaries and going ashore is not permitted.

Navigation

The navigation is tricky and Baie des Anglais should only be visited in relatively light trade winds (<15 knots). The entrance is downwind and down sea. Enter between Ilet Hardy and the group of islands that include Ilet Perce, Ilet Burgaux, and Ilet Tois Roux. Ilet Hardy has a distinctive rock knoll on its southeastern shore. Once past Ilet Hardy, look for the two reefs to the northwest of Ilet Perce and pass fairly close to them. (You will see Fond Blanc to starboard.) Note that there are quite a few isolated rocks just to the east of Ilet Aigrettes. By now the seas should be relatively calm and you will find there is a large daytime anchoring area about 20 feet deep to the west of Fond Blanc, between Ilet Aigrettes and the visible reef on the other side of the channel.

Your strategy from here on in depends on your draft, the size of your engine, the strength of the wind, and whether your insurance premium is up to date. You have to cross a bar of soft mud in unreadable water with the wind right behind you. For boats of less than 6-foot draft, there will probably be little problem. For boats of 6.5-foot or 7-foot draft, the width of the deepest channel is very narrow, and at low tide sounds out at about 7 feet. The seamanlike thing to do is to anchor in the deep water and sound out the channel with a lead line in your dinghy. As you look at Ilet des Parletuviers, you will see an old mill tower just behind it, a little to its left. A range I found helpful is to be on a line between the northern edge of Ilet Burgaux and this old mill tower. The deepest water is probably a hair to the southwest of this line. Once over the bar, you have plenty of water and many perfectly protected anchoring spots; inside Ilet des Parletuviers is the most popular. If you dinghy over to the shore near Ilet Aigrettes, you can find a way through to Anse Trabaud, a lovely but fairly popular beach. Dinghy exploration is also good up to Ilet Chevalier.

Go to Baie des Anglais well provisioned because, should the wind and sea get up while you are there, seas break across the entrance and you may have to wait a while to get out.

For an adventure, dinghy up behind Islet Chevalier, carry on to the beach with the kite-surfing, and land the dinghy. Take the short walk to the Paradisio for lunch, but book in advance on your mobile phone (see Marin restaurant section). A coastal footpath takes you round to Ste. Anne in the south and Anses Macabou in the north.

Baie des Anglais

PASSAGE BETWEEN MARTINIQUE AND ST. LUCIA

Northbound

The passage from St. Lucia to Fort de France is usually a fast reach. A course of due north from Rodney Bay gets you close to the lee coast. It doesn't hurt to be a little offshore when you arrive, as the wind tends to follow along the coast and is fluky close in. If Martinique is visible at the outset, it will appear as two islands, because the low-lying land in the center is not visible from St. Lucia. As you approach Martinique, Diamond Rock stands out as a clear landmark.

If you are heading for Ste. Anne, you can often make it in one tack, but be sure to head up a bit to allow for current as you cross.

Southbound

The southerly passage from Anse D'Arlet is sometimes a pleasant reach. At other times it can be hard on the wind. As the wind flows round the land, you will be pointing high as you follow the coast. It often pays to motor sail to stay reasonably close to shore before setting off across the channel. If sailing, it may pay to sail fast on the southerly tack and hope to play lifts later. When you see St. Lucia, head for the highest (rather rounded) mountain in the north end of the

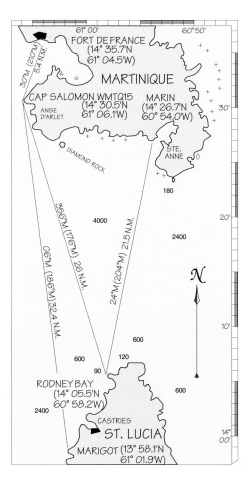

island until you make out the distinctive shape of Pigeon Island, a clear double peak joined by a slope. The higher twin mounds of Mt. Pimard and Mt. Flambeau (see Rodney Bay chart) also sometimes stand out.

The sail from Ste. Anne to St. Lucia is usually an easy reach.

St. Lucia

Anne Purvis views Pigeon Island from its highest point

Regulations

Ports of entry are Rodney Bay, Castries, Marigot Bay, Soufriere, and Vieux Fort. Entry charges in $EC are as follows: $15 navigational aids, $10 practique (up to 100 tons), and clearance fees of $5 for under 40 feet and $15 for over 40 feet. In addition, charter yachts less than 40 feet pay $20; between 40 and 70 feet, $30; and over 70 feet, $40. Charter yachts also pay $15 per passenger. Three day in-and-out clearance is available with the same crew. You may do the paperwork in advance on eseaclear.com. Immigration usually gives six months when entering on a yacht.

Normal office hours are weekdays 0800-1200 and 1330-1615. Those clearing outside these hours pay a reasonable overtime fee. Customs may ask you where you want to visit. If you include Rodney Bay, Marigot, Soufriere, and Vieux Fort, that covers most anchorages.

Spearfishing, damaging corals, and buying coral, turtle shell, or out-of-season lobsters (lobster season changes annually usually August to February or later) are forbidden. Sailing yachts are generally allowed to troll a single line or handline for pleasure, others need a fishing license. No scuba diving (except for underwater work on your yacht) may be done without a qualified guide. Pets are not allowed ashore. Personal watercraft need a license from the ministry of tourism.

Holidays

Jan 1 and 2
Easter Friday through Monday, March 29-April 1, 2013 and April 18-21, 2014
Feb 22, Independence Day
May 1, Labor Day
Whit Monday, May 20, 2013 and June 9, 2014
Corpus Christi, May 30, 2013 and June 19, 2014
Carnival (varies) – Monday and Tuesday, around the middle of July
First Friday in August, Emancipation Day
Thanksgiving, October (variable)
1-2 November, All Saints' Day
22 November, St. Cecilia Day
December 13, National Day
Dec 25 and Dec 26, Christmas

Shopping hours

Most shops open 0830-1230, then 1330-1600. Saturday is a half-day. Banks close by 1500 except Fridays, when they are open till 1700. Supermarkets open longer.

Telephones

Cell phones are the easiest way to go; Lime or Digicel. For the USA & NANP countries, dial 1 + 10 digits (see p.19). For other overseas calls, dial 011 + country code + number. When dialing from overseas, the area code is 758 followed by a 7-digit number.

Transport

Buses ($1.50-$7 EC) run to most towns and villages. If you are going a long way, check on the time of the last returning bus. Taxis are plentiful. The sample taxi rates below (for 1-3) may increase soon:

	$EC
Rodney Bay to Vigie	66
Rodney Bay to Castries	66
Rodney Bay to Hewanorra	220
Castries to Hewanorra	180
Rodney Bay to Marigot	130
Short ride	20
Day tour	500

Extra charges after 2200, before 0600, and for more than three people.

There are plenty of rental cars. You need to get a temporary local license at $54 EC.

The airport departure tax is $68 EC, usually included in your ticket.

The Marina at Marigot Bay St. Lucia

Pitons View from La Haut

*S*t. Lucia, the largest of the English speaking Windwards, is mountainous and lush, with many beautiful white sand beaches. Tropical rainforest covers the steep slopes of the center and gives way to cultivated agricultural land around the more moderately sloping coastal fringe. Bananas are the principal crop. For sheer physical beauty, the area around Soufriere and the Pitons is outstanding.

St. Lucia offers excellent sightseeing and hiking. You can see most of it by taxi, bus, or rental car. Adventurous travelers willing to combine driving with hiking will want to rent a four-wheel drive vehicle and explore some faraway corners such as Grand Anse or Anse Louvet on the windward shore. Any taxi driver will be delighted to take you on a tour. Popular tours include; round the island, plantation tours, and rainforest tours. St. Lucia now has a rainforest aerial tram that will take you in the canopy. There are also ziplines on which you can fly through it yourself.

Those interested in nature should contact the National Trust, which runs tours to Frigate Island and the Maria Islands as well as turtle watching tours. It is worth calling the forestry department about rainforest tours. They can supply knowledgeable guides.

When planning your tour, consider Mamiku Gardens. They lie on the east coast at Mon Repos, between Dennery and Micoud (about halfway between Castries and Vieux Fort). These 15-acre gardens have been beautifully planned, with open spaces, winding, narrow paths, and several hidden surprises, including some ruins and hideaway seats.

There are many marked trails in St. Lucia that you can follow on your own, including rainforest hikes at the height of land as you drive across the island on the main road to the airport.

St. Lucia offers an excellent, full-service marina with a haul-out in Rodney Bay, and a smaller marina in Marigot. The choice of restaurants and shoreside activities is vast. St. Lucia is a charter center, with charter companies in Rodney Bay and Marigot Bay.

138

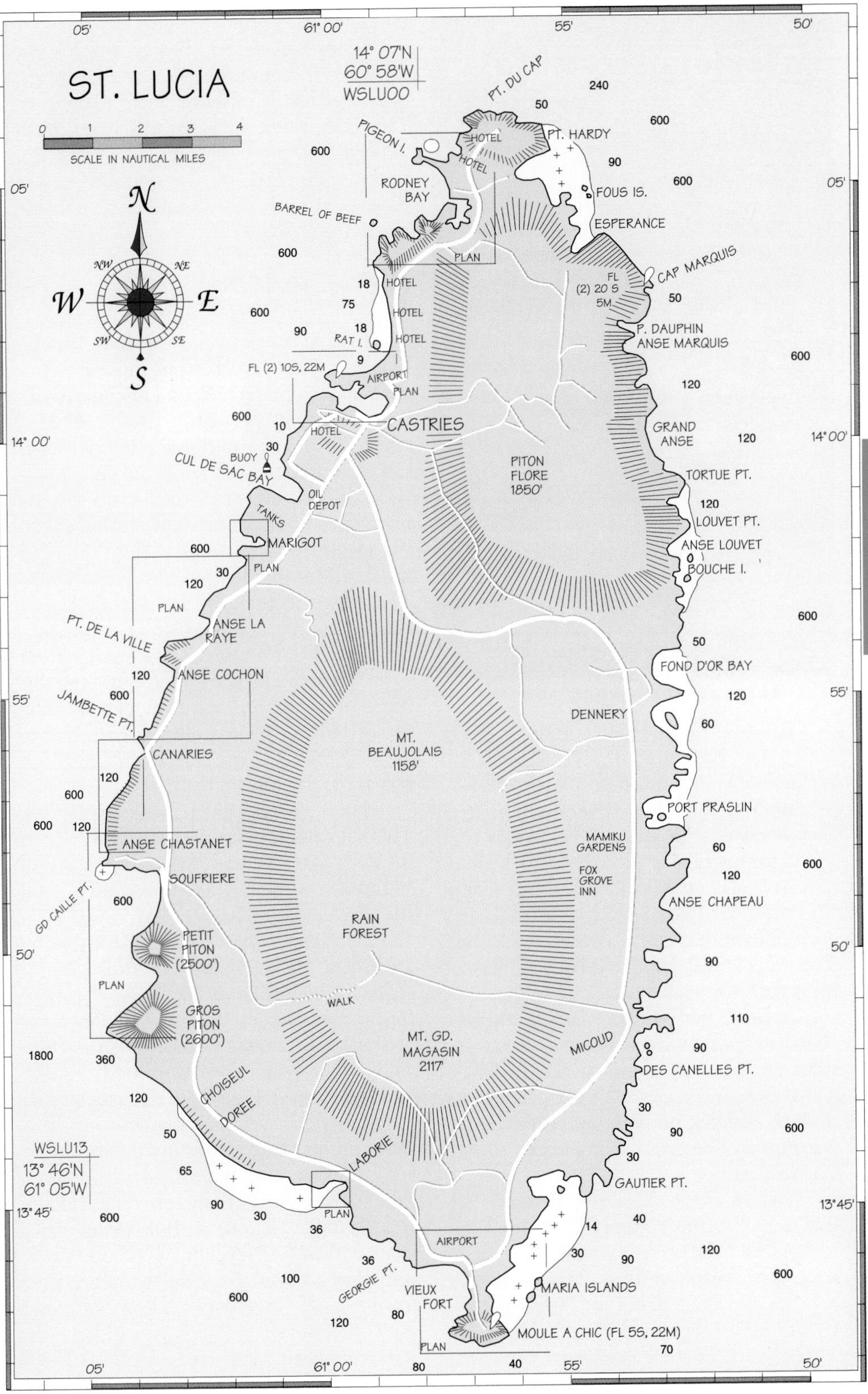

ST. LUCIA

14° 07'N
60° 58'W
WSLU00

0   1   2   3   4
SCALE IN NAUTICAL MILES

N
NW   NE
W   E
SW   SE
S

PT. DU CAP
240
50
600
PT. HARDY
PIGEON I.
HOTEL
90
600
HOTEL
FOUS IS.
RODNEY BAY
600
ESPERANCE
BARREL OF BEEF
CAP MARQUIS
600
PLAN
FL (2) 20 S
5M
50
18
HOTEL
75
P. DAUPHIN
600
18
HOTEL
ANSE MARQUIS
90
HOTEL
600
RAT I.
9
FL (2) 10S, 22M
AIRPORT
120
PLAN
GRAND
600
HOTEL
CASTRIES
ANSE
120
10
14° 00'
PITON
FLORE
1850'
TORTUE PT.
BUOY
30
120
CUL DE SAC BAY
LOUVET PT.
OIL DEPOT
ANSE LOUVET
TANKS
BOUCHE I.
600
MARIGOT
600
120
30
PLAN
50
120
FOND D'OR BAY
PLAN
ANSE LA RAYE
120
PT. DE LA VILLE
ANSE COCHON
DENNERY
60
55'
600
JAMBETTE PT.
MT.
BEAUJOLAIS
1158'
120
CANARIES
PORT PRASLIN
600
120
60
600
MAMIKU GARDENS
120
ANSE CHASTANET
FOX GROVE INN
ANSE CHAPEAU
GD CAILLE PT.
SQUFRIERE
RAIN FOREST
90
600
PETIT PITON (2500')
PLAN
110
WALK
90
GROS PITON (2600')
MT. GD. MAGASIN
2117'
MICOUD
90
1800   360
DES CANELLES PT.
120
CHOISEUL
30
DOREE
90
50
600
LABORIE
30
65
WSLU13
13° 46'N
61° 05'W
GAUTIER PT.
13° 45'
600
90
30
PLAN
40
36
PLAN
AIRPORT
14
36
30
120
GEORGIE PT.
90
100
VIEUX FORT
MARIA ISLANDS
600
80
600
120
MOULE A CHIC (FL 5S, 22M)
PLAN
70
80   40

Navigation, west coast

Between the northern tip of St. Lucia and Rodney Bay, there are several shoals and no anchorages, so it is best to keep clear.

Rodney Bay offers several anchorages that are dealt with in detail below.

Barrel of Beef is a low-lying rock about a quarter of a mile off the southern side of the entrance to Rodney Bay. It is marked by a white light that flashes every five seconds. The water is deep enough (about 18 feet) for most yachts to pass inside it.

Between Barrel of Beef and Castries, the coast sweeps back in a large bay containing Rat Island. The northern part of this bay is full of reefs and is best avoided. On leaving Rodney Bay, the normal route is to pass inside Barrel of Beef and head directly toward Castries Harbor.

Tapion Rock forms the southern entrance to Castries Harbor. There are some rocks close by, so give it a reasonable clearance. Two miles south of Castries, Cul de Sac Bay is a huge depot for Hess Oil. It is well lit and makes an obvious landmark by day or night. There is a flashing buoy in the middle of the entrance to this bay.

From Cul de Sac Bay to the Pitons, St. Lucia is mainly steep-to, and keeping a quarter of a mile offshore clears all dangers. There are a few rock hazards lying up to 100 yards or more offshore. The worst is a sizable rock patch off the southern end of Anse Chastanet that should be given wide clearance.

RODNEY BAY

Rodney Bay is over a mile long. On the northern shore, an artificial causeway connects Pigeon Island to the mainland, providing the bay with protection. In the old days, when Europeans entertained themselves by sailing around in wooden boats taking pot-shots at each other, Pigeon Island was the main base for the British navy in this area. It was ideally situated, being in sight (on most days) of Martinique, the main French base. There used to be a fort, hospital buildings, barracks, and storerooms. Now the St. Lucia National Trust conserves it as a delightful park. There are shady gardens, and the fort has been partly restored. The climb to the top of both peaks is well rewarded by the views. Strategically placed signboards tell you about the history.

There is a small entry charge to the park. This helps finance the National Trust, which works to preserve the environment as well as historic sites. The anchorage off Pigeon Island is delightful and breezy.

Near the Pigeon Island Park dinghy dock, you will find Jambe de Bois [$C-D], a delightful restaurant/bar and art gallery run by Barbara Tipson, an active member of the local animal-welfare organization, which often helps place unwanted animals. Jambe de Bois is slightly offbeat with an arty atmosphere. You can relax in an easy chair, catch up on email on their wifi, check the bookswap, and enjoy local art. It makes a great hangout, with comfy corners and breezy spots outside. Jambe de Bois opens daily from 0900-2100, except Mondays, when they close at 1700. On Sunday nights, they feature good jazz groups and on Saturdays they often have a group playing oldies, You have to pay the park entry fee until 1700.

:: RODNEY BAY MARINA
BOATYARD

LOCATED IN ST. LUCIA AT IGY RODNEY BAY MARINA, THE RODNEY BAY MARINA BOATYARD HAS ALL THE NECESSARY AND CRUCIAL CAPABILITIES TO CARE FOR YOUR VESSEL INSIDE AND OUT.

BOATYARD SERVICES
- Fuel, oil, water and ice services
- Portable and fixed pump-out facilities
- Boat repair management
- Vessel caretaking
- Antifouling & detailing
- Fiberglass repairs & spray painting
- Sail, rigging and osmosis Repairs
- Fabrication and welding services
- Teak deck installations
- Electrical services
- Mechanical services
- Water maker services
- Propeller and shaft repairs
- Selden mast repairs

BOATYARD CAPABILITIES
- 75-ton Marine Travelift
- 40-ton Transporter
- Carpentry
- Electronics
- Yamaha and Mercury Outboard dealers
- Yanmar dealership
- Volvo Penta dealership
- North Sails representatives
- Chandlery
- Hurricane storage

RODNEY BAY MARINA BOATYARD
CONTACT: EDWIN CHAVEZ
T 758-452-8215 • F 758-452-9725
ECHAVEZ@IGYMARINAS.COM • WWW.IGY-RODNEYBAY.COM

The restaurant does a late breakfast, as well as lunch and dinner. Fresh fruit juice is available, along with many daily specials and snacks.

On the causeway, Sandals, a conspicuous, all-inclusive hotel with bright red roofs, makes a good landmark.

A little farther down, The Landings is a large and fancy new condo development built around canals where owners keep their yachts. You can dinghy up to their Beach Club [$B], an informal restaurant set between the beach and the canal. It is open all day, offering everything from sandwiches and burgers to full meals and daily specials. Fancier food is to be had at Palms [$A], a gourmet restaurant near reception.

Outside the lagoon, on the north side is Gros Islet Village, which is occasionally a hotbed of crime. Marine patrols have made things way better and there have been no recent problems, but take care if anchored close to the village.

To the south of the channel entrance is Reduit Beach, one of St. Lucia's finest beaches and the home of many hotels and the St. Lucia Yacht Club. This is a popular anchorage with mainly good holding. Watch out for a poor holding spot close to the southern entry into the lagoon.

Navigation

Rodney Bay Lagoon is a large and completely protected inner lagoon that is entered via a dredged channel between Reduit Beach and Gros Islet village. This is lit by port and starboard lights at the entrance and at the inside end of the channel. Approach the channel in the center. IGY Rodney Bay Marina has dredged the entrance and marina area so there is sufficient depth for yachts of 13 feet draft to come in and tie up. Yachts of 15 feet draft have made it with care and attention to tides. The shallowest water is just outside the entrance so if you can make it into the channel, you should be good to the big boat dock.

Many yachts tie up at the marina. It is also possible to take an IGY marina mooring in the inner lagoon, where depths are 7-9 feet. You may anchor in the outer bay to the southeast of Pigeon Island right round the causeway to Gros Islet, and off Reduit Beach.

Pigeon Island anchorage

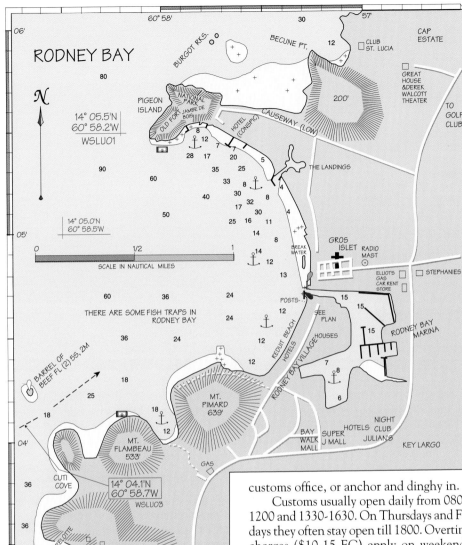

RODNEY BAY

The outside beach anchorages occasionally become untenable in extreme northerly swells. Anywhere within acoustic range of Gros Islet beach can be noisy (more so out in Rodney Bay than in the lagoon).

Rodney Bay is a major hub of tourist activities, with many hotels, malls, restaurants, and an 18-hole golf course nearby.

Regulations

IGY Rodney Bay Marina is a good place to clear in. If you plan to stay in the marina, go into a berth (see below) and walk to the customs office, or anchor and dinghy in.

Customs usually open daily from 0800-1200 and 1330-1630. On Thursdays and Fridays they often stay open till 1800. Overtime charges ($10-15 EC) apply on weekends, during lunch, or after 1615. Entry charges are $30-40 EC, depending on the size of the boat, with extra fees if you are on charter. Details of fees are given at the beginning of this chapter. Only the skipper should come ashore to clear; other crew should stay on the yacht till clearance is complete. If you have internet access, you can save time and effort by pre-clearing the entry on eseaclear.com.

If you need emergency clearance when everything is closed, the customs guardroom in Castries can arrange it at: (758) 468-4859.

Do not exceed the 4-knot speed limit in Rodney Bay Lagoon. This applies to all vessels including inflatables and dinghies.

LAGOON ENTRANCE

Anchoring is not allowed in the lagoon, but IGY moorings are usually available.

Shipping in parts? Invoices and shipping papers must be marked "for transshipment." Many items are duty free, there are charges for documentation, and you need to use one of the agents. Ian Dezouzay (Reliant Brokerage), knows the local customs officers well. Lisa Kessel, the wife of Chris, the surveyor, also specializes in clearance for yachts.

Communications

A cruisers net operates on VHF:68 at 0830, Monday to Saturday. You can use Rodney Bay Marina as a postal drop and for sending faxes. USA-direct telephones and several public card and coin phones make communications easy.

If you have a marina berth or mooring, the marina wifi should cover you.

In the marina, Rent A Ride offers an excellent email and fax service and they send Fedexes. In addition, you can use their copier. You can rent one of their cars and they are used to dealing with yachts. They open weekdays 0800-1700, Saturdays from 0800-1300, Sundays from 0900-1200.

Digicel and Lime have sales outlets in the Baywalk Mall. All the marina restaurants and bars have free wifi, as do Pizza Pizza, Jambe de Bois, and many others.

General yacht services

IGY Rodney Bay Marina [VHF: 16] is an excellent marina with a large, solid dock that can take 32 megayachts up to a maximum of 250 feet. Fancy floating docks accommodate 221 regular yachts. They have 30 moorings in the inner lagoon (0.35 cents per foot per night).

Rodney Bay Marina is a pleasant place to stay, well protected from the elements amid lawns and coconut palms, dockside restaurants, and cafes. It is home to a business community that includes a bank, marine services, a food store, boutiques, massage therapists, and many taxi drivers as well as a well-stocked, duty-free chandlery. A few charter companies are based here. The businesses are friendly and for many yachting folk Rodney Bay Marina has become their home-away-from-home in the Caribbean, creating a sense of community.

The manager, Adam, is open, accessible, helpful and popular with his customers. You will usually get a spot in the Marina, though it can be packed when the Arc arrives in mid-December. Call for a dock space and the staff will help you in.

Dock I, the big, new concrete dock is available for yachts up to 250 feet long and has 110, 220, and 380 volts up to three phase and both 50 and 60 cycle electricity. This dock also has high-speed fueling.

Docks A through E have 220 volt, 50 cycle electricity. Docks F, G and J have 110 volt, 60 cycle electricity. All docks have water and wifi is available on all docks and if you have a suitable aerial, on the moorings.

Hot showers are a pleasant feature, and the garbage disposal includes a special place for used engine oil. The management offers double docks for the hurricane season: ask in the office.

If you need a technician or help with varnishing, the main desk will have a list of registered independent contractors. You can get your laundry done and fill all kinds of LPG gas tanks at Suds Laundry. If you need to get boat parts cleared in, ask at the front desk.

A convenient bus to town runs from outside the marina, and a plethora of restaurants and a golf course are close by. Within the marina, day trips to Martinique or along the coast are available.

Rodney Bay Marina Boatyard [VHF: 16] is part of the marina and is St. Lucia's only haul-out facility. It is well organized by Edwin Chavez. The travel lift is 75 tons and can take up to a 28-foot beam. For most boats it will not be necessary to remove a stay. They have room for about 120 yachts in long-term storage and another 20 undergoing work. If you are leaving your yacht here in the summer months, the yard has cradles and tie-downs.

The marina boatyard will either handle all jobs on the slip, however large or small, or they will put you in touch with the correct contractor. There are options for working on the boat yourself, but otherwise, the marina organizes and is responsible for all work on the slip.

The fuel and work dock is alongside, to the east of the travel lift, making lifting and working on engines and masts easy. A gelcoat-stripper is available for osmosis work, and they have two big under-cover paint sheds.

Duty-free fuel is available for anyone who has cleared out, on the fuel dock, or high-speed fueling on Dock I. The fuel dock also sells water, ice, and lubricants.

John and Verniel Leo can give a helping hand. They have a modern, air-conditioned mini-bus taxi, and are happy to run you around. Verniel does laundry (she collects and delivers, and it is done well), and she also does interior boat cleaning. John does detailed cleaning or polishing inside or out, and can generally lend a hand. Call 721-0817/486-9481/725-6730. You might also see Sparkle, another laundry.

Island-wide mega-yacht services are offered both by Ben Taxi, who has self-contained rooms to rent overlooking Rodney Bay, and who offers jeep rentals, and by Benny (Harmony Beach). Both live in Soufriere, but come north frequently. CJ Taxi is the main man in the north for yacht services for all sizes of yachts (see *Transport*).

Kennedy Joseph is well practiced at varnishing, cleaning, polishing, and more (716-0383).

For medical problems, The Rodney Bay Medical Center is a block east from the JQ Mall. You can walk in and they have several GPs as well as a dermatologist, ear nose and throat specialist, a pediatrician, and testing services. GP Tanya Beaubraun is good. Prices vary, so ask. Tapion Hospital in Castries has many medical services and lab facilities, call for details and appointments.

You won't find a better place for dental work in the Caribbean (and beyond) than Kent Glace and Associates, just few steps from the dinghy dock by JQ Mall. Pass the Baywalk Mall towards the main road and look on your right behind Caribbean Smiles. Kent Glace is excellent and he does all the surgical work: implants, complex extractions, crowns, cosmetics, root canals, and fixing root canals that have gone bad, as well as regular dentistry. He is aided by two other dentists, Dr. Barnard and Dr. Michel,

plus they have two qualified hygienists, a rarity in the Caribbean. You will get top quality care here at less expense than in the USA. If you happen to have kids, Desma at Caribbean Smiles next door is an orthodontist. Kent Glace and Associates is open weekdays 0800-1700, Saturdays 0900-1200. Kent himself works in town on Thursdays, but the other staff are still there.

Chandlery

Island Water World is a large, duty-free chandlery managed by Ian Cowan, one of St. Lucia's most knowledgeable yachtsmen, and his wife, Rosemary, aided by an excellent team, including Sophie, who has been answering questions from those on yachts for many years. This well-stocked store is part of the Caribbean-wide chain, and draws a lot of yachts into Rodney Bay. You can get just about anything here, from electronics to toilets and fridge units, plus cores, ply, and Burma teak. If you don't see what you want, ask Ian. If it cannot be had in St. Lucia, he can order, ship, clear, and deliver the item direct to your boat, whether it is a main

engine or a small part. Island Water World stocks Johnson and Mercury outboards and is an agent for Yamaha. They sell Caribe and Walker Bay inflatables. Ian is the person to source your Yanmar parts.

Johnson's Marine Center is a large marine and hardware store just opposite Rodney Bay Marina. They keep a good stock of basic equipment at reasonable prices. This includes deck gear, rope, chain, anchors, fenders, fastenings, electrical fittings, lights, wiring and fuses, paint and sandpaper, fishing and snorkeling gear, fuel and oil filters, and Mariner outboards and accessories. They can special-order any marine hardware you might want, duty free. In addition, they keep a big selection of plumbing, wood, electrical, and household hardware, including power tools.

Technical yacht services
Project Management & Maintenance

Ulrich at Destination St. Lucia (DSL) is very helpful, straightforward, and knowledgeable about boats and local technicians. His crew can get your boat repaired, your refrigeration cooling, and your engine back working. If there is something they cannot handle, they will recommend the right technician. DSL will look after your yacht while you go away, and will undertake all kinds of yacht management, and will put suitable yachts in their large charter fleet. This is a long-established company you can rely on. Ulrich's wife, Sandra, started a German-language book swap in their reception area.

Charles Beausoliel (aka Blough) at BBC Yachting has a charter company and looks after and fixes boats when the owners go away. It makes sense as the team that fixes the charter yachts can also work on yours. They can do varnish and maintenance jobs, and bring in the right people when they need it for other work. They can have your boat hauled and painted and ready when you return.

On the charter side, BBC has Beneteaus, a cruising cat, and speedboats. Chartering can be day or term and bareboat or skippered. They also offer deep sea fishing. Blough has worked with yachts from way back when he and I worked for Steven's

Yachts under Ian Cowan, and he will do yacht deliveries and supply captains.

Technical yacht services
Sails/Rigging/Cushions

Rodney Bay Sails is the sail loft and rigging shop in the marina. Kenny Abernaty is the man to see. He has worked as a sailmaker for over 30 years, is very good, and now owns the loft. Rodney Bay Sails do any form of sail or canvas repair and will create you new biminis, awnings, and covers. They build many bimini and awning frames and are set up to work and bend 1-inch stainless tube. Talk to the Kenny about cushions and drapes. He can either do it himself or recommend the best person for it. New sails come from Doyle Sails in Barbados.

Rodney Bay Sails are also riggers and can handle anything from replacing a shroud to ordering and installing a complete new rig. (They do not do swaging, however.) In this they work closely with Ian Cowan who is the agent for Selden masts, Furlex, and Profurl.

Technical yacht services
Electrics/Electronics/Watermakers

You will be in good hands at MarinTek, run by Egbert Charles, who speaks French and Spanish as well as English and has many years' experience working with yachts. His company handles both electrical and watermaker installation and repairs, along with any associated mechanics. Egbert is the Volvo dealer and can sell you a new engine, and do repairs or warranty work. He is factory-qualified for all Volvo engines, including electronic diagnosis. He sells the Walker Air-sep high performance air filters for them. MarinTek is also the dealer for Northern Lights and Kohler generators. In addition, they can fix any electrical problems on a yacht and have a department for rewiring starters and alternators. They are worth approaching if you have problems with other generators. They will try to help if they have time. MarinTek are the agent for Dessalator water makers, and repair and service all water maker brands. MarinTek polishes fuel and cleans tanks, and if you are tired of getting this done, they do stock the

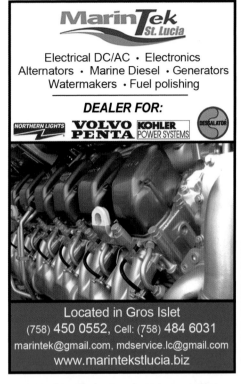
St. Lucia

AlgaeX and Micfil continuous fuel polishing systems. It is easiest to call them, but if you want the shop, it is north of the boatyard on our map of Rodney Bay Lagoon.

Regis Electronics is the St. Lucian branch of the Greenham Regis chain, which has many stores in the UK. Jon White, the owner, offers sales, installation, and service for all your Marine Electronic Equipment, Air Conditioning, Charging systems, Refrigeration and Watermakers. They are agents for most brands of electronic gear and keep both new equipment and many spare parts in stock, which makes them the best people for your electronic requirements, whether you are buying a whole new system or upgrading or repairing your present one.

Regis are the factory authorized dealers for all the major manufacturers including Amptech, Balmar, B&G, Cruisair, Furuno, Fischer Panda, Garmin, HRO, Icom, Marine Air, Mastervolt, Raymarine, Spectra Watermakers, Seafresh, Simrad, Schenker, Victron, Waeco and Westerbeke Generators. You can also start from scratch here and order new gear from the catalogue. Regis

will install it on your boat and Jon will have some good ideas on what to buy and have it shipped duty free.

Lakshman Persaud's Calidad Communications are IT and computer specialists. Lakshman can fix your computer (hardware or software) or superyacht communication systems; they work with all satellite systems including KVG, Iridium, and Immarsat. They sell a variety of wifi aerials that will extend your range. It is best to call them as the shop (behind Baywalk Mall, see our chart), is poorly signposted and may be empty.

Technical yacht services
Mechanical/Metalwork

Quick and Reliable Mechanical Services is run by Alwin Augustin, who lives up to the company's name. He works on all diesel engines, from Caterpillars on superyachts to Yanmars on cruisers, including Perkins. He does mechanical work on generators, including Onan, Fischer Panda, and Northern Lights, and he has an excellent reputation for efficiency, service, and skill. It is easiest to contact him via his mobile (758) 520-5544/584-6544. For parts, he works with Ian Cowan at Island Water World, who can bring in all parts fast and is hooked into the Yanmar computerized system.

Tony's Engineering is run by Tony George, a good general mechanic who can weld and repair diesel engines of all makes including Caterpillar, Detroit, and Perkins. He can come to the yard to sort out your alignment and shaft problems. It is easiest to call him (452-8575/715-8719).

In the boatyard compound, Lawrence (Chinaman) runs the metalworking shop. He can weld and fabricate in any metal.

Heading down the channel, Rory MacNamara's Mac's Marine sells Mariner and Evinrude Ecotec outboards and fixes all brands. They have a dock where you can bring your engine in for repair, and a big waterfront showroom where they sell outboards, Caribe and other inflatables, cleaning products, boating accessories, and toys.

Island Marine Supplies, run by Pinkley, is next to Mac's Marine. It is the sales and service agent for Mercury and Mercruiser. They keep a good range of engines in stock for all sizes of boats and fix all makes of outboard.

For Volvo diesels, Northern Lights, and Kohler, see MarineTek under *Electrics*.

Technical yacht services
Glass/Woodwork

In the boatyard compound, Elvis (Mermaid Repair), and does a good job for all glass repairs, painting, and general on-the-slip work.

Richard Cox of Cox Enterprises is a good general man with years of fiberglass, woodworking, and other maintenance experience. He can sometimes be found around Mac's Marine, where he helps build boats.

Kelly Charles is another good paint and glass man (715-3369), and there is a contractor in the boatyard known as Fiber who does first class gel-coat matching.

Several good guys can handle your carpentry, whether decking, joinery, or planking. You generally have to call them, as their shops are not close to the marina.

They include: Pride (284-7948), Tyson (487-5641), Robin Unwin (485-1101), and Simon Edwards (458-0213). Remy (450-2000) fixes electrical gadgets: TVs, FM radios, and CD and DVD players.

Technical yacht services
Inflatable Repair

Francis and Debra's Liferaft and Inflatable Center is on the left side of the channel as you enter the lagoon. They have an 80-foot customer dock with about 10 feet alongside, making it easy to drop off and collect dinghies. They are happy to help out their clients with water.

They are working on a specialized shop to sell small craft accessories and they work with Budget Marine to sell Tohatsu outboards.

One of their companies: International Inflatable Ltd., is a major inflatable tender store, with a bonded warehouse and many models available, including Zodiac, Apex, and AB.

Liferaft and Inflatable Center can test, fix, and vacuum-bag all makes of liferafts. You are invited to watch them unpack and examine the contents and decide what gear should go back in. They have one of the few Caribbean stations that can test and fill liferaft cylinders. They repair all makes of inflatables, do some of the best work in the islands, and guarantee their work for a year. If you have an expensive aging RIB, they can retube it. They can apply dinghy names along the fabric on both sides. They also offer repair and renovation for solid fiberglass and RIB boats up to 30 feet.

When you take an inflatable in for repair, be there when they give it a good check over, so you can decide if it is better to replace it; they take old dinghies and dinghy/outboards in trade. This makes buying the new one more affordable and means they often have guaranteed, beautifully restored, secondhand inflatables for sale. Apart from liferafts, you can bring your fire extinguishers, lifejackets, and M.O.B modules for testing and servicing.

Technical yacht services
Refrigeration

Prudent of Prudent Repairs is the best refrigeration man, or you can try Wayne of Quick Fix refrigeration.

Technical yacht services
Other Services

Chris Kessell (Kessel Marine) is the local yacht surveyor; his prices are reasonable, and you can arrange for him to come and visit anywhere in St. Lucia.

Jo Boxall has Scribble, a design studio upstairs in the marina. She will design boat names and signs and arrange for the transfers to be cut and placed. She can also design fancy yacht brochures, and she has contact for helicopter photos.

Windward Island Gases, just beyond Glace Motors, tests scuba tanks and can fill most kinds of gas bottles, including CO_2, argon, helium, and nitrogen.

Ask Tony George, MarinTek or any of the project managers about hydraulics. Some hydraulics can be fixed, but if the job is complex and requires high pressure, Martinique is probably the nearest place to get complex issues solved.

Transport

When you want to get out and about, you will find a taxi stand by the gate and buses on the main road. All the registered Marina taxi drivers wear uniforms and are reliable and good. They are used to dealing with yachts, and you know where to find you when you return to your yacht and find that you forget your camera or handbag on their seat. JQ Mall has another stand.

Chris Joseph (C.J. Taxi, VHF: 16) is a good and reliable driver who is part of the Rodney Bay taxi crew, and he usually listens to his VHF radio. Chris also rents cars and jeeps, can arrange limousines, and owns some rental apartments. Chris runs good tours and is always on time for that early airport departure. In addition to cruisers, Chris Joseph connects well with the superyachts, and he has the know-how to arrange fuel bunkering, clear in parts, and bring customs to your yacht. He will help with flowers and provisioning and will make

St. Lucia

any arrangements you need.

If you need a water taxi, there are several around. Marley can be reached at 486-2874 and he charges about $15 EC per person one way to the Reduit Beach anchorage and up to $26 EC per person to Pigeon Island.

You can arrange bike rentals through All Round Adventure run by Mark. They offer one hour to long-term rentals and will deliver to the marina.

Provisioning

In the marina, Flower Shack, a great little flower shop, is close by the dinghy dock. Deirdre, the owner, cuts flowers either the day they sell or the day before, so flowers and foliage are really fresh and long lasting. Her business has its own greenhouses for anthuriums and orchids, and she also sells potted plants. Deidre does flower arrangements and can handle all the demands of the mega yachts. She has an outlet in Baywalk Mall and will deliver anywhere in St. Lucia.

G's Marina Mart is a good minimart that can take care of topping up your stores, especially liquor and beer. They open 0700-2100 except Sundays when they open 0800-1400. It is part of the bigger Glace Supermarket, which is across the road beyond Johnson's Hardware. They also sell phone top up cards.

Starfish is a restaurant and deli. On the deli side they have good bread, cold cuts, fish, cheeses, and specialty items. They sell top quality frozen meats as well as pre-packaged vacuum packed cooked foods, ready for you to bring to life. They offer a full provisioning service: Call Stina or Deslyn, 452-0100 out of hours: 716-2109.

Duncan and Michelle at Delirius (see *Restaurants*) also do full yacht provisioning.

The Bread Basket (BB's) sells fresh bread, croissants, cakes, Danishes, and other baked goods. For really large quantities, contact them in advance.

For large supermarkets and more shopping, dinghy over to the malls in the southern part of Rodney Bay, in the general area known as Rodney Bay Village. There is a dinghy dock close by. Super J is in the JQ Mall; Food Market is in the Baywalk Mall.

Neither has a big variety of local produce but both are otherwise excellent. Food Market is fancier, more spacious, with more upmarket items, and opens 0700-2200 Monday to Saturday, 0700-1800 Sundays. Super J opens 0700-2200 Monday to Thursday, 0700 to 2400 Friday and Saturday, and 0700-1600 Sundays and holidays.

Fun shopping

Right in the marina, Drop Anchor is a branch of the famous Sea Island Cotton Shop, with a wide range of casual wear and attractive handicrafts.

Rodney Bay has giant malls with cash machines, pharmacies, clothes shops, household goods, even computers and more. The JQ Mall has 60 stores and businesses, including a stationery store, and a bookstore. The inside shops in JQ are generally quite small and adjoining, which makes for easy browsing. On the top floor, check out Caribbean Perfumes, where local tropical aromas from trees, plants, and flowers are made into perfumes and colognes ~ an unusual gift or souvenir. They sell some local pottery, arts, crafts, and jewelry.

Across the road, the even bigger Baywalk Mall has endless shops, banks, restaurants, and vendors stands. The shops here tend to be larger, with lots of clothing.

Walk out of the JQ Mall and turn left and you will find a big new pharmacy that sells a lot of household things. Continue to the next supermarket (also good) and a few paces to the left of that is Valmonts Hardware store with household items, hardware, and clothing. If you cannot find the perfect gift in the marina or Rodney Bay Village, check out the boutiques in the big beach hotels.

Restaurants

Rodney Bay has the best collection of restaurants in the Windwards, with many of St. Lucia's top chefs in attendance. They are excellent and plentiful, with seven in the marina alone. Nowhere else has such a choice of really fine places to eat out.

One place to start the day in the marina is the Taylor family's BB's [$C-D] any time after 0730 for coffee with a full cooked breakfast, or a plate of fresh croissants. Nick, Carmen, and family have turned this into a delightful marina restaurant. The inexpensive local lunch specials are as good a bargain as you will find and locals come her to eat or take away. Their snack menu, which includes rotis and sandwiches, is available from morning through the evening

In the evening BB's changes character; the bar comes alive, the decorative lights turn on, and it becomes a pleasant place for a reasonably priced dinner [$C], or pizza in an informal atmosphere. Come in shorts if you want. The food is straightforward, carefully cooked, and very tasty. The menu includes lots of fish and shrimp dishes, as well as steak and ribs. Arrive in time for happy hour 1700-1900, with two for one beers, wines, and rum punches; sit at the long bar, or in the outside seats. They do a big Sunday lunch with roast beef, turkey, or fish, and have a big TV for important games.

Café Olé is a charming cafe with a delightful eating space outside facing the

St. Lucia

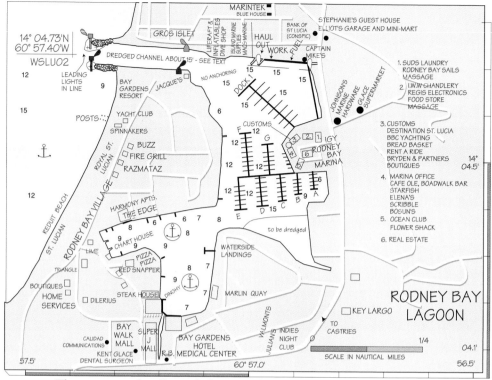

marina. They serve good coffee and always have a selection of delicious baked goodies to choose from. This is a great place for lunchtime sandwiches and salads. To ensure a seat for lunch, go early. Charlotte (Charlie) and Ben, who own it, are welcoming and helpful. Café Olé opens at 0700 for breakfast and stays open through the evening. Meals and snacks are always available. Ben and Charlie also have the adjoining Boardwalk Bar, which is the marina's most popular meeting spot. It opens about 1230, has a popular happy hour from 1700-1800, and keeps going till midnight. You can get food from Café Olé.

Next door, Starfish Noodles bar and restaurant [$B-D], serves great food. They specialize in wok noodles dishes, which are excellent. It is owned by Chef Bobo who also owns the Edge, so you can also get sushi, and many other dishes, along with totally delicious and decadent desserts. They open late morning and stay open until after dinner. Starfish is also a delicatessen and provisioning service and sells get great nut bread (see *Provisioning*).

Next in the block is Elena's [$C-D].

Elena, who is Italian, runs a great coffee shop with all kinds of coffee, an ice creamery, and a giant pizza oven. They open for breakfast (cooked or continental) and stay open till dinner. The pizza oven (closed Mondays) is fired up from 1200-1500 and from 1800 on. The thin crust genuine Italian pizzas are delicious. They make fresh fruit juices, crepes, sandwiches, and salads; available any time during the day.

Upstairs, Bosun's [$C-D] has a comfy, pub-like atmosphere where tables are set out on the balcony with a view of the marina. They open every day till late at night and have a wide-ranging menu. Being upstairs, it has a quiet atmosphere, and during the ARC you can often get service here when the others are forming queues.

Ocean Club [$B-C] is the largest and liveliest restaurant in the marina, open to the breeze, with a swimming pool and seating both in and outside. This restaurant has come alive under the new ownership of Martin and Phil from Boston. They open daily from breakfast through dinner and happy hour is 1700-1900 nightly. There is nearly always something going on, with live

entertainment at least four nights a week. You might want to check their facebook page for the latest program, but they always do parties during big events, like OC Jazz line during jazz festival, lots of activities during Arc, and they have been running a Thursday night Latin Fiesta with tapas, salsa dancing, and other entertainment.

They have good food and a wide-ranging menu with a nightly special bargain meal for two for the price of one. Their bundled Heineken beer, five for the price of four is popular.

Bruce Hasckwhaw's Captain Mike's [$C-D], is also in the marina, but way over by the haul out. You can walk there on the easternmost dock. Bruce belongs to St. Lucia's best known sports fishing family, so the fish is always fresh and usually comes in about 1800, from the sports fishing trips. This is the most informal and least expensive place in the marina. The beers start at $4EC, and you can get a giant plate of local food for lunch and a beer for $20EC. Dinner is baby back ribs, steak, and fish, mainly mahi mahi and kingfish. You eat well here, can come in

shorts and flip flops, and it won't break the bank. If you are mainly drinking, try a snack of fish cakes or fish strips.

Other restaurants are all around the lagoon, in Rodney Bay Village, opposite the St. Lucian and on the small roads near Super J. Dinghy tie-up is available at Super J and The Edge.

The Edge [$A] hangs out over the water, so you can tie your dinghy to your table leg. It is one of St. Lucia's top restaurants, perfect for a special night out or for showing off to your friends. The owner, Chef Bobo is from Sweden. He led the St. Lucian culinary team to a gold medal and was awarded chef of the year, and he has evolved a fusion of Caribbean and European flavors he calls Eurobbean. His trio of ceviches is so excellent, you will want to come back to make sure it was really as good as you remembered. A full sushi bar at one end of the restaurant has its own seating. Their cuisine is excellent, original, and artistic. Tuesday night is sushi night with specials on sushi and live music. They serve breakfast (continental, St. Lucian, and full), and a first-rate businessman's lunch.

IGY Rodney Bay Marina

Fire Grill and Lounge Bar [$A-B], a new venture for Chef Bobo, is a short walk down the road. This big, open building has a massive open kitchen, which leads into a coffee area and then a bar, which together make up the central hub. This leads out to numerous areas and corners. You can get perfectly barbecued meat and fish cooked right in front of you and artistically garnished. Their lounge bar is perfect for cocktails, after-dinner drinks, and scrumptious desserts. They sometimes have live music. They have a kind of eating happy hour with early food and drink specials from 1700-1900.

On the waterfront, with its own dinghy dock, Indira Ashworth's Charthouse [$B-C] has a cheerful decor with lots of jungly plants. This restaurant was one of the first in Rodney Bay. The service is prompt and the food consistently good. Specialties are steak, seafood, and ribs. The Charthouse is very popular, so reservations are advisable.

Indira also runs Pizza Pizza [$D], close by. Kids and families love Pizza Pizza because of the playground, which has a trampoline, climbing frames, and lots more. You can sit outside on park-like seats. They serve pizza, pasta, and salads. Their pizzas are American style, with plenty of cheese and toppings, and judging by the popularity of the place, they are rated very highly. Pizza Pizza has free wifi.

Above Pizza Pizza, Indira has another restaurant spot which she plans to have open by the time this book comes out; possibly serving Cuban food. The entrance is on the far side of the building to Pizza Pizza.

Rodney Bay now has two excellent Indian restaurants to enjoy. The flavors and style of each is different, so if you are into Indian food, try both.

Razmataz [$B-C, evening only, closed Tuesdays] is a first-rate Indian restaurant. Try to make the 1700-1900 happy hour, which is very popular. Razmataz is managed by Suzie Wright, who has Indian connections, and her partners in the venture are Dependra and Bipendra Bahadur, brothers from Kathmandu in Nepal, who cook like angels.

Since many fruits and vegetables from India were introduced to the Caribbean long ago, fresh ingredients are no problem. A tandoori oven is kept going 24 hours a

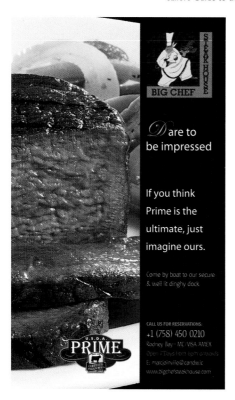

day, and the food is reasonably priced and excellent. Nepalese, Tibetan, or Chinese specialties are often added to the menu. It is best to reserve in advance. Ask for a table on the patio.

Spice of India (closed Mondays) is in Baywalk Mall. Owner Adil Pervez Shwerwani is from Deli and spent some years as executive chef in some of Grenada's best hotels. He brings his chefs from north India and obviously knows how to keep people happy as in 2012 he rated top restaurant in Rodney Bay on Trip Advisor. Cool out for lunch in their air-conditioned dining room [$C-D], when they offer a big tasting menu with a large selection of dishes that change every day. This will satisfy the hungriest sailor, or for lesser mortals, two can share. Dinner [$B-C] starts at 1800, when Adil brings his experience as executive chef to serve not only excellent food, but presented with artistry and flair; fine dining, Indian style. It is not a bad idea to book, especially if you have a big group.

Walk into Big Chef Steak House [$A], on any night of the week and you'll find the appetizing aroma of steaks on the grill and the cheerful buzz of happy patrons, many of them regulars. Owners Rose and Marc serve excellent seafood. Rose has been both a teacher at the English Cordon Bleu and a yachtswoman who completed the Sydney-Hobart Race. They run a super operation, with first-rate service and top-quality ingredients. You will not get better steaks. They start with the best certified Angus beef, they cook it exactly the way you want, and present it artistically. (If you eat one of their largest [32 oz.] steaks, you can return for a free steak another night.) But, leave room for dessert; their crème brulée is divine.

TheBig Chef Steak House opens every night at 1800. On Saturday nights from 2030-2230, Bo Hinkson plays music and on Wednesday and Friday nights David Elwin entertains. They also run Chef-2-U, which sells frozen cooked meals vacuum-bagged for your boat's freezer.

Big Chef also owns Tapas on the Bay which will open in October 2012. Their dinghy dock adjoins the JQ dock, this will create a well-lit secure hub, a wonderful

meeting place for shopping, a cool lunch spot, and an evening tapas bar and restaurant, opening at 1100.

Tapas on the Bay offers delectable bites of food accompanied by fine wines, sherry, or local rum. Expect everything from authentic Spanish to a Caribbean twist on tapas, along with paella, fresh fish and homemade rustic bread. Enjoy a drink with a dish of olives at the cool stone fronted bar or take a table on the deck in the breeze. The dinghy dock makes for easy access from Rodney Bay Marina for Tapas on the Bay and Big Chef.

Pat Bowden has a golden touch when it comes to restaurants, and she has proved this at Buzz [$A-B], her newest creation, located opposite the Royal St. Lucian. The garden setting is pleasant, the service impeccable, and the cuisine inventive. Vegetarians will find they get equal treatment here in their choice of dishes. The menu has a wide selection of seafood, including perfectly grilled fish, lobster, and crab cakes. Meat lovers will enjoy charbroiled steaks, baby back ribs, Moroccan lamb, and West Indian pepperpot. Try to leave room for some of their chocolate

brandy ginger cheesecake or other temptations. The restaurant is often humming, so booking is advisable. Buzz is open for dinner every night (closed Mondays April to November). Buzz is a short ride from Rodney Bay Marina and if transport is a problem, give Pat a call.

Another of St. Lucia's top restaurants for fine dining and simple elegance is Jacques [$A-B, open for lunch and dinner]. They have a superb location on the waterfront overlooking the lagoon and marina, next to the channel. You can tie your dinghy right outside.

You will be charmed by owner Jacques and his wife, Kathy. Jacques has worked in the best hotels, Kathy is a professional restaurant manager. Jacques brings his training and experience as a skilled chef from the Loire Valley. He has adapted this to local ingredients to produce what Kathy calls "an exciting blend of flavors, herbs, and spices of France and the Caribbean." Jacques provides a lot of different flavors which will delight and surprise. His cooking is inventive and he is very much into seafood. Try his excellent

St. Lucia

Mediterranean fish and seafood soup. You will eat well here and enjoy the ambience. Come relax on Sundays when they offer a wonderful jazz brunch from 1130-1500.

Chef Xavier [$A-B] is upstairs in the Bayshore Mall. Xavier is one of St. Lucia's top chefs and he makes everything taste wonderful. In this restaurant his partner is Bruno, a wine specialist. In the dining room you can choose to sit outside on the balcony or inside. Both share a view of brightly painted Caribbean buildings and a glimpse of Rodney Bay behind. The more elaborate fine dining is in the evening, but lunch is delicious, with great salads and pastas and it is reasonably priced.

Delirius [$B-D] is a bar, restaurant, and yacht provisioning center, which opens from 1100 to late at night weekdays, from 1700 Saturdays (closed Sundays). It is owned and run by Duncan and Michelle, who are popular enough that it has quickly become not only a great restaurant, but also the happening bar. The atmosphere is informal and open, and it is among the most popular drinking spots in the area, from a dedicated early crowd to a late night hangout crowd. On the deck, you can get an excellent meal at a reasonable price. Delirius serves good coffee, snacks, lunch, and dinner.

If you would like to meet some of the local yachting community, the best place to do so is at the St. Lucia Yacht Club [$D]. They have an upstairs bar right on the beach, which opens Tuesday to Friday 1500-2030. Weekends and holidays are special, when they open 1100-2030 and serve inexpensive, simple, and good lunches. Although it is a members' club, visiting yachtspeople are always very welcome, and the atmosphere is pleasant and friendly. The club has an interesting bookswap, a TV for sports events, and world-class squash courts. You can pull your dinghy up on the beach outside, or walk from one of the dinghy docks. This is the place to find out about local sailing events and they run a first-rate program to teach children how to sail. Consider becoming a member. Overseas membership is very reasonable, supports local youth sailing, and gives you discounts on the bar in the club and food at Spinnakers next door.

Bay Gardens Beach Resort {$B-C] is open and very friendly. They have wifi, a great pool and jacuzzi, and a first rate restaurant. They sometimes host the regular, open, get-together women's lunch on Wednesdays (listen to the morning net VHF: 68, 0830 for details, or call Marsha on the same channel). They have an excellent beach buffet with live music and other entertainment on Saturday nights. You can watch them launch a series of "fire balloons".

Other restaurants worth a mention include Key Largo [$C-D], for excellent pizza

view from yacht Club

and a great gym, Memories of Hong Kong [$C-D] for fine Chinese food, La Terrace [$A, evenings only] for good French food and also a convenient guest house, Spinnaker's [$B-D] with a great location on the beach by the yacht club and Whiskey in the Jar, a genuine family-run Irish pub in the middle of Rodney Bay Village. Go for happy hour; 1800-1900, and meet Irish Mike and Madeline and Johanna.

The best bargain for cheap food is to eat at one of the restaurants on the top floor of the JQ Mall for a cafeteria style lunch.

Ashore

A great way to relax is to try a Swedish massage, get a facial, hot waxing, or whatever. Two places do this, both right in the marina. Debra Nichols's Soothing Touch Massage is next to the sail loft, and offers everything from full body massage to pedicure. Debra will make boat visits. The other is L'Essence Massage, upstairs over the supermarket. Pick up a brochure in either.

Cas-en-bas is a lovely beach on the east coast, a couple of miles from Rodney Bay (main road north, turn right at the Gros Islet turn-off). The road is rough but walkable, with good hiking north or south from Cas-en-bas. Marjorie Lambert, along with friends and relatives, does an inexpensive local lunch on the beach. They also have an all-night beach party every full moon. They can organize horse riding for you, or you can do it with Trims. Marjorie will also organize a beach party for groups (T: 520-0001 or 450-0491). If you have a mountain bike, this east coast area, from Cap Estate to

Esperance Harbour, is perfect. You will also find kite surfing here.

It is not unusual for yachtspeople to sail into Rodney Bay, check out the protected anchorage, and say, "This is it, I am going to buy property." If having your boat close to your house is important, then look at some of the available properties in Rodney Bay lagoon. The new Admiral Quay, with waterfront and garden apartments, all with docking facilities, and the similar Rodney

St. Lucia

Gun emplacement at Point du Cap

Quay both have enough units that some are usually on the market.

An agent who handles these and properties all over the island is fellow yachtsman Jonathan Everett. You will find him at Home Services, an office in Rodney Bay Village.

The small town of Gros Islet is picturesque and very local, with lots of small restaurants. On Friday night the village is closed to traffic and everyone dances in the streets or wanders from bar to bar. All along the street, stalls sell such goodies as barbecued conch on a skewer and barbecued fish and chicken. If you like to eat sitting down, the lovely old Scottie's Bar, right in the center of town, puts chairs out on the street. Security was a problem here for a while. It seems better now, but to be safe, go in a group or by cab or bus and return the same way. Stay in well-lit areas.

Water sports

The water in front of the St. Lucian Hotel is completely flat and is good for beginner windsurfing. Boards are available for rent at the hotel.

There is passable snorkeling around Pigeon Island. New scuba sites are being found in the north. If there is not too much surge, Burgott Rocks is a place you often see eagle rays. Barrel of Beef has boulders,

sponges, and colorful reef fish, including sergeant majors. Fisheries regulations require that visiting scuba divers must go with an approved dive shop.

Scuba Steve's Diving is a Padi 5-star Golden Palm Resort owned by Stephen and Shirley Smith. They are highly qualified and can do nitrox, as Steve is a gas blender and EFR instructor. They will be happy to teach you (up to instructor level) or take you on a dive. They are well equipped, with two fast dive boats with bimini protection. You will find them in the entrance to the lagoon, next to the inflatable workshop. They can pick you up from your yacht and will fill in-date tanks if you have a card. They also repair Scubapro gear and do visual tank inspections.

FROM CAP ESTATE TO VIGIE

Outside Rodney Bay, from Cap Estate to Vigie, are more attractions, just a walk, bus ride, or taxi-hop away.

Transport

Travel World is owned and run by Jocelyn helped by her delightful staff. Her office is in Lanse Road near Castries. But

St. Lucia

you don't have to go near the office; just call Jocelyn on the phone and tell her what you want ~ tickets, car rentals, or tours ~ and she will arrange everything and deliver your tickets (or car) to you. They are more than a regular travel agent, and they also deal in real estate sales and rentals, and will run errands like shopping, getting things together for a party, or anything else that would save you time and effort.

Jocelyn and her team work hard to get you the best rates, which has earned them many dedicated customers. They now have a service charge of $20 US, but it is well worth it, because their service is good.

Ashore

If you cannot find what you want at Johnson's, Sunbilt is another big hardware store about a mile and half towards Castries. A little farther is KL Marine, the local Yamaha Agent, then Computer World, a giant computer store, where you can buy computers, or get yours fixed. Another mile or so brings you to the first roundabout and Mega J, a giant store selling everything from foods (bulk or retail) to plumbing, with auto accessories, electrical, household, and pharmacy items thrown in.

The Gablewoods Shopping Center is about halfway between Rodney Bay Marina and Castries. As you approach Vigie, American Drywall is on your left, (includes a bike shop) and opposite is Home Depot, a good household store. At the next roundabout is Fedex.

Cap Estate, a luxury development, is set in green, rolling hills to the north of Gros Islet. Golfers will be happy to know that this is the place to play golf. The National Trust has a nice little park at Pt. du Cap (Morne Pavillon) which makes a good walk from Rodney Bay (see doyleguides.com).

Windjammer Landings is an upmarket villa development just south of Rodney Bay. The anchorage is tricky, so those who want to go there by boat should contact the managers and they will provide a guide. They have restaurants and boutiques.

VIGIE CREEK

VIGIE

TAPION ROCK

CASTRIES HARBOUR

CASTRIES AND VIGIE

Castries is a reasonable anchorage, so when you are ready to visit town, by yacht is a fine way to do it. Half a mile away is the quiet Vigie Cove, also a good, if small, anchorage. When cruise ships are in town these two are linked by numerous little ferries that tour around the harbor, stopping at the Coal Pot, Pointe Seraphine, and the craft market.

CASTRIES TOWN

Castries lacks a unifying architectural style but has plenty of variety. Some effort has been made to retain the Caribbean character of the buildings that face Derek Walcott Square along Brazil Street. The area between Peynier Street and Chausee Road, along Brazil, Micoud, Chisel, and Coral Streets has an interesting Creole atmosphere, with balconies, gingerbread, and old and new buildings. Happily, many smaller new buildings are now being designed in keeping with the old architecture.

The new buildings on the north side of the waterfront are of a more recent style, and these, plus other new blocks in town, look modern and clean. The big market, with food, handicrafts, and clothes is fascinating. For fresh food, Fridays and Saturdays are better than earlier in the week.

Regulations

Castries is a port of entry, though it is much easier to clear

Orchids at Pink Plantation

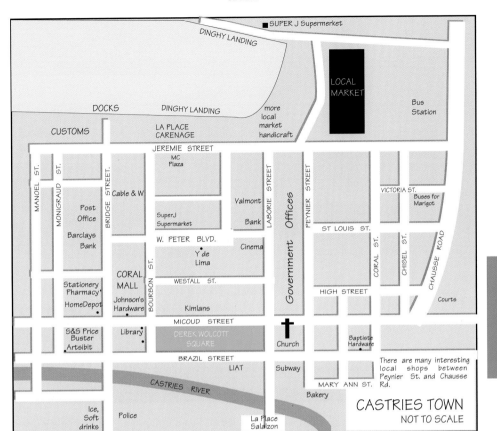

SUPER J Supermerket

DINGHY LANDING

LOCAL MARKET

DOCKS   DINGHY LANDING

Bus Station

CUSTOMS

LA PLACE CARENAGE

more local market handicraft

JEREMIE STREET

MC Plaza

VICTORIA ST.

Buses for Marigot

Cable & W

MANOEL ST.

MONIGRAUD ST.

BRIDGE STREET.

Post Office

Valmont

SuperJ Supermarket

Bank

LABORIE STREET

PEYNIER STREET

Government Offices

ST LOUIS ST.

Barclays Bank

W. PETER BLVD.

Cinema

Y de Lima

CORAL ST.

CHISEL ST.

CHAUSSE ROAD

CORAL MALL

Stationery Pharmacy

HomeDepot

BOURBON ST.

WESTALL ST.

HIGH STREET

Courts

Johnson's Hardware

Kimlans

MICOUD STREET

S&S Price Buster

Library

DEREK WOLCOTT SQUARE

Church

Baptiste Hardware

Arteibit

BRAZIL STREET

LIAT

Subway

MARY ANN ST.

There are many interesting local shops between Peynier St. and Chausse Rd.

CASTRIES RIVER

Bakery

Ice, Soft drinks

Police

La Place Salaizon

CASTRIES TOWN

NOT TO SCALE

St. Lucia

in Rodney Bay or Marigot. The officials insist that entering yachts come straight to the customs dock, or if there is no room, to the anchorage right beside it.

Give the cruise ships a wide berth when entering and leaving so you don't make the port police anxious.

Communications

Netcom in La Place Carenage has internet and is open weekdays 0800-1630, mornings only on Saturday.

Transport/Services

The big bus station is behind the local produce market. All routes are numbered. 1A is Gros Islet, 2H is Vieux Fort, 3D is Soufriere. The Marigot and Canaries buses go from Victoria Street.

You can find somewhere to leave your dinghy between the craft market and La Place Carenage. Although you need to make sure it does not interfere with the ferries. Entry is through La Place Carenage, which makes it pretty safe, but it closes at night, so ask what time. You can also leave it on the north shore, which is always open and unguarded. You can find a sign or tree to lock to.

Provisioning

The easiest supermarket is Super J, close to the market. You can tie your dinghy close by. Pharmacy and stationery stores are on Bridge Street.

You will find general hardware and computer accessories at Home Depot or Valmont. If you need acrylic sheet or synthetic canvas, then J. N. Baptiste is the specialist. For auto, electrical, and other household items, try Johnson's. Bandag sells auto parts.

La Place Carenage has duty-free liquor stores, well situated for stocking up on small or large quantities of wine, liquor, and Cuban

cigars. It is right on the main wharf in town, so you can load up your dinghy.

Fun shopping

St. Lucia's local market ranks among the best in the islands. It occupies several buildings as well as outdoor areas and spreads to both sides of the road. It is a riot of color and excitement as hundreds of local vendors sell their wares. Spend an hour or two here enjoying the scene and take the opportunity to stock up on local foods, t-shirts, coal pots, straw work, and handicrafts. The market includes a street of tiny food stalls, each owning a single outside table. Here you will find the cheapest and tastiest local food on the island. A ferry links the market with Pointe Seraphine, the duty-free shopping mall where you will find about 50 pleasantly laid out tourist shops. Take your passport for the duty free.

Just down the road, La Place Carenage is another place for tourist shops ~ lots of them, all pleasantly laid out and well air-conditioned, with everything from international jewelry to handicrafts. They have a theater where they run Our Planet, an interactive light and sound production.

Coral Mall has a good selection of local shops.

Restaurants

The Pink Plantation House [$B-C], is a special restaurant that I highly recommend for lunch, whether you are anchored in Castries or in Rodney Bay. It is on Chef Harry Drive, just outside Castries (a short taxi ride), set high on the Morne with a spectacular view over Castries. It belongs to Michelle, one of St. Lucia's best local artists and potters. She has shops in Pointe Seraphine, Marigot and JQ Mall and is a partner in the Coal Pot (see Vigie). Michelle has taken this historic estate house with beautiful gardens and created a super restaurant on the generous balcony. The food is traditional Caribbean and excellent. You can wander in the garden, which has an extensive collection of orchids, and you can see Michelle's work in the house, both

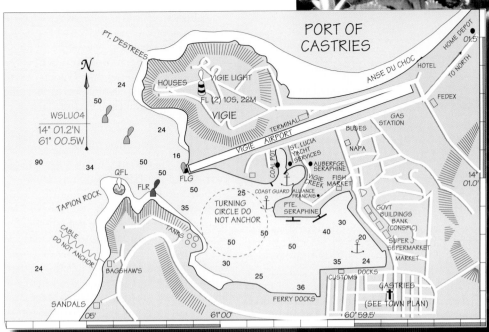

PORT OF CASTRIES

WSLU04
14° 01.2'N
61° 00.5W

PT. D'ESTREES

HOUSES
VIGIE LIGHT
FL (2) 10S, 22M
VIGIE
VIGIE AIRPORT
TERMINAL
TANS
COAL POT
ST. LUCIA YACHT SERVICES
AUBERGE SERAPHINE
VIGIE CREEK
FISH MARKET
COAST GUARD
ALLIANCE FRANCAIS
PTE. SERAPHINE
CUSTOMS
FERRY DOCKS
DOCKS
BAGSHAW'S
SANDALS
TAPION ROCK
CABLE DO NOT ANCHOR
QFL
FLR
FLG
TURNING CIRCLE DO NOT ANCHOR

ANSE DU CHOC
HOME DEPOT
TO NORTH
HOTEL
FEDEX
GAS STATION
BUSES
NAPA
GOVT BUILDINGS
BANK (CONSFIC)
SUPER J SUPERMARKET
MARKET
CASTRIES
(SEE TOWN PLAN)

14° 01.0'
01.5'

24 50 24 90 34 50 16 50 50 35 50 25 50 50 30 25 36 40 30 20 35 24 24 30

05' 61°00' 60°59.5'

---

pottery and paintings. While doing so you will soak in the atmosphere of the lovely old Caribbean estate house, which will give you a feeling of the Caribbean from years ago. The Plantation house is open for lunch Mondays to Fridays and some nights for dinner.

If you need something right in town, probably your best bet is Rituals [$D] in Coral Mall.

VIGIE

A light on Vigie Hill (flashing 2 every 10 seconds) is helpful in identifying Castries Harbor at night.

Vigie is a good overnight stop on your way up or down; take dinner at the Coal Pot and maybe a quick trip to town. It is handy for Vigie Airport as well. You can anchor either inside or outside Vigie Creek. Although generally well protected, Vigie Cove does suffer from a surge in a really bad northwesterly swell.

Anchoring in the creek can be tight but there is more room outside. Carnival Cruises have several moorings; the outer two are white and used when swells come in. If there are no swells you can often use them for a small fee if you talk to the crew on their catamarans. On cruise ship days, Vigie bustles with ferries and day-charter boats. There is easy access to Pointe Seraphine.

Services/provisioning

St. Lucia Yacht Services (SLYS) has a fuel dock and they sell water and fuel weekdays 0800-1600,

Lily pond, Auberge Serphine

weekends 0800-1400.

There is no public dinghy dock, but you can use the SLYS dock after hours, and some of the surrounding waterfront at other times. If you are visiting the Coal Pot you can tie your dinghy up by their waterfront shed, or dock your yacht on their big dock just beyond the restaurant. Pointe Seraphine has its own dock, but you must stay clear of the ferries and be off when day-charter cats come in.

A short walk on the road to town gets you to a big NAPA agency, which stocks filters, parts, sprays, seals, polishes, and tools. They are agents for OMC outboards, with full sales and service. In addition, they stock inflatables, ropes, and some marine hardware.

If you need a taxi, give Theresa a call. She is a good and reliable and stationed in Vigie Airport (384-9197/458-4444). The main Fedex office is a mile away, opposite the bottom of the runway.

Also in Vigie (in the white pyramid opposite Pointe Seraphine entrance) is the Alliance Francais. They offer French lessons and an internet cafe, and it is worth checking out their coming cultural events. Dinghy to town to provision.

Restaurants

A good reason to come to Vigie is to eat at the Coal Pot [$B, closed Saturday lunch and all Sunday]. It has a romantic setting right on the waterfront. It also has a romantic history. Many years ago, Bob Elliot sailed across the Atlantic and into this cove. He fell in love and married Sonia, whose family owned the land, and they built this as their house. Michelle, their daughter, spent her first few years growing up here. Later, Bob converted the house to a storehouse for his beloved day-charter brig, Unicorn, and then into a restaurant, keeping the suitably nautical decor. Michelle and her husband Xavier, who is French and a superb cook, now run the restaurant. Xavier has another excellent restaurant in the Baywalk Mall (see *Rodney Bay*). Mango Moon, a gym, is on the Coal Pot grounds.

While in Vigie, check out the amazing colony of egrets and other birds around the colorful lily pond in front of Auberge Seraphine. Auberge Seraphine is also a fine place for coffee or a meal and they have wifi and an internet station.

Navigation
Castries to Marigot Bay

As you leave Castries, give a reasonable clearance to Tapion Rock.

Marigot lies about a mile south of Hess Oil's huge tanker depot at Cul de Sac Bay. In the old days, it was so well tucked away that a British admiral is reputed to have hidden his fleet here, disguising the masts by tying coconut fronds in the rigging. Today you cannot miss it, with the prominent buildings of the Marina Village and all the yachts inside. Once you pass the Hess Oil depot, the wind tends to become light and contrary, not a bad place to start powering.

Heliconia

Marigot Bay

MARIGOT BAY

Marigot Bay is a completely sheltered, mangrove-lined bay, famous as a hurricane harbor. From inside, it affords a perfect backdrop for that sunset photo and rum punch, as you look across the beach spit with its lacy palms. While peaceful and quiet, it has an active community with lots of shore-side attractions; it is a great place to shop, eat out, take a stroll, and admire any superyachts that may be in.

Navigation

Enter through the buoyed channel, which favors the southern shore and avoids a shoal that extends way out from Marigot Beach Resort. The minimum depth in the channel and inner bay is 5 meters (16.5 feet). Costly and delicate underwater electric cables and water pipes cross right at the entrance to the inner harbor. Do not anchor!

You can anchor on either side of the channel where there is adequate depth, or inside if you can find room among the moorings, where the holding is passable in soft mud. The Marina at Marigot Bay, with the Soufriere Marine Management Association (SMMA), has 20 reliable moorings in the inner harbor, which are white with a blue stripe. They cost $30US a night, but you may raft up to three boats (combined maximum 60 tons) for this. Nash or Michael, who wear Marina t-shirts, help arriving yachts moor, can take the fee, and give you an official receipt. If you need any kind of help or recommendation, Nash is a good man to ask, as he knows everyone and is president of the local water taxi association.

Others will greet you offering unofficial moorings (mainly outside) that look just like the SMMA moorings. Some are poor and they can go adrift, so you are taking a chance. Get a receipt as you pay, and just say "no" to anyone who becomes persistent, pushy, or in any way objectionable. The SMMA may take over these moorings one day, and if so I will post it on doyleguides.com Outside is lovely, but you get more vendors and speeding dinghies than in the lagoon.

Regulations

There is a 4-knot speed limit in the harbor. Marigot Bay is an official port of entry, with customs and immigration. They usually open from 0800-1200 and 1300-1615. The office is upstairs in the Marina Village. Eseaclear works well. If you will arrive after closing and someone is leaving early the next morning, use eseaclear and call Bob at the marina for help well in advance (451-4275).

SLASPA (port authority), next to the marina office, collects the entry fees

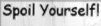
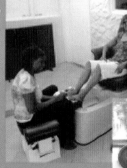

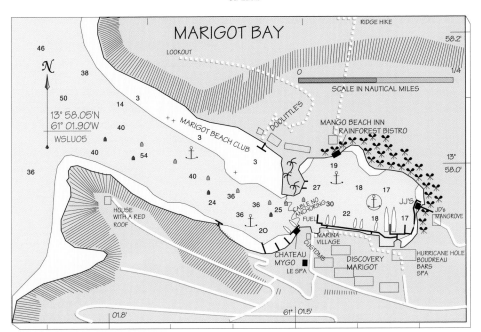

Yachts should use the garbage bins in the Marina (look for the signs). Or you may give it to Johnson, who comes by in an inflatable, for a fee. There is also a dump down the road.

The MBBA (Marigot Bay Business Association) works hard to keep the bay safe for cruisers.

Communications

You will get excellent wifi in much of the inner bay from Marigot Marina. Chateau Mygo also has wifi, as does Doolittles.

Sip and Surf (S&S) internet and coffee shop in the Marina Village is a full internet cafe and they offer cheap overseas calls. Marigot Beach Club also has computers.

General yacht services

Dinghy docks are at Chateau Mygo, in the Marina Village, by Hurricane Hole, at Doolittle's Restaurant, or over at JJ's. Dinghies must not be tied to the yacht docks.

The Marina at Marigot Bay is part of the Marigot Bay Development and has moorings and alongside and stern-to berths for yachts up to 250 feet. Contact Bob Hathaway in the office (451-4275, VHF:16/12). They will arrange berthing and can help organize day labor.

The superyacht berths have high-speed, sealed fueling. Small yachts can get diesel and gasoline on the fuel dock next to the customs dock. Duty free is available. Electricity, 110 and 220 volt, 50 and 60 cycle, is available as is 410 volt, 3-phase for superyachts. They provide holding tank pump-out. A full and self-service laundry is upstairs in the Marina Village. The marina office is a good place to buy our guides. Ask the marina about special rates on hotel nights ashore.

The marina also sells phone cards, has local information, arranges taxis or reservations and the staff are generally helpful.

Chateau Mygo [VHF: 16] has half a dozen stern-to berths and can supply water and electricity. They occasionally have moorings available. If you are having dinner, they usually do not charge. They have a laundry with next-day service.

The superyacht agents, Ben Taxi and Harmony Benny, come on a regular basis (see *Soufriere*).

Chandlery/technical yacht services

Chateau Mygo has a small surf/chandlery shop, with boating accessories, cleaners, safety gear, and fishing equipment. They have an arrangement with Island Water

World and can bring anything in that store quickly.

Shaid has a team to repair and fix his charter fleet, and he offers this service to visiting yachts. If anything goes wrong, from the motor to the mast, this is a good place to start.

On the other side of the bay, Complete Marine Services has a work barge with a crane. Their main line of work is marine construction. They also do yacht surveys, excellent underwater and salvage work. They watch boats when people are away, undertake project management, install new equipment, and fix things. If it is not something they like to do, they will point you in the right direction.

Provisioning/fun shopping

Mari Gourmet, behind the Marina Village, is a good, small supermarket. They open 0730-1830, except Sundays and holidays 0800-1300. They can sell duty free cigarettes and liquor. Next door is St. Lucia National Bank and an ATM machine.

In the marina village, the Baguette Shop sells good bread and baked goodies. You will also find a collection of souvenir, jewelry, and art shops. Tired of standard "made in China souvenirs with the island name stuck on?" In Melinda's little store, Fe Sent Lisi, everything is made in St. Lucia

MARIGOT BAY

The Marina Village

This colourful Caribbean style village is built around an attractive courtyard garden overlooking the Marina at Marigot Bay and the tranquil waters of the inner bay.

The Marina Village has a raft of facilities and services to satisfy the most discerning yacht-based visitors.

The St Lucia Customs and Immigration Yacht Reception Office is based in the Village making clearing into and out of St Lucia easy and convenient for Marina users.

Other facilities include a well stocked chandlery, doctor's office, laundry and excellent provisioning services provided by the Marigourmet supermarket and wine shop—you can pre-order to ensure you get everything you need.

Fresh bread, baguettes, paninis and cappuccinos can be found dockside at the French bakery and café.

There are also duty-free gift shops, a jewellery store, designer clothing boutique and an art gallery.

Coupled with excellent at-berth facilities in the Marina, the Marina Village is an ideal one-stop shop for superyachts and Caribbean cruisers.

For more information and provisioning lists, contact **The Marina Village**.
Email: **info@themarinavillage.com** / Website: **www.themarinavillage.com**
Telephone: **1 (758) 451 4275** / Fax: **1 (758) 451 4276**

For Marina bookings use the numbers above or email marina@marigotbay.com . Berths from 30ft to 250ft available.

COME STAY IN THE BAY
Marigot Bay , St Lucia

and artistically crafted.

Clear Blue is owned by local artist Michelle who has some of her own pottery and paintings, as well as those of other local artists. At Fired Up, you can decorate pottery yourself, and Nautique has fancy casual wear. The Marina Village has a doctor's office, and you can rent a car.

For more provisioning, take a taxi to the Promise Supermarket and Highway Liquor store on the main highway.

Transport

Numerous ferries and water taxis are available to go anywhere in the bay or to and from your yacht. Chateau Mygo [VHF: 16] has several water-taxis available for hire, along with a land taxi.

Taxi Service Marigot [VHF: 16] are the local taxi drivers who wait near customs.

Kieran has a classy 30-foot Intrepid for taxi work, fishing, and tours.

Restaurants/ashore

In the marina village, the Baguette Shop has pleasant seating and sells wonderful sandwiches, coffee, pizza, soups, salads and burgers; great for breakfast or lunch.

Chateau Mygo [$B-D, VHF: 16] is a large enterprise run by the Rambally family. Years ago, Mama Sheila started it as a no-frills food shack. Now a waterfront restaurant, guest houses, Le Spa, and boutiques, are in tropical gardens that go from the road to the beach.

The Ramballys are a Caribbean/East Indian family who have many ties to yachting. Doreen runs it with her son Shaid and they both like cruising, so whichever one is not off sailing runs the restaurant. Shaid speaks English like a Californian and Spanish like a Costa Rican, which is where Andrea, his wife, is from. Among them the family speaks English, Spanish, Italian, French, Norwegian, Patois, and Hindu. Chateau Mygo restaurant stands on legs out over the water and has both a main menu and thin-crust Italian pizzas.

Their food is a fusion of East Indian and Creole, spiced by ideas garnered from around the world. Local seafood is a specialty, including lobster, shrimp, conch chowder, and fish.

The seafood combo is great. Baby-back ribs and USDA black Angus steaks are popular with many sailors. In season, Tuesday night is steak blow-out night, and Thursday night is Indian night, with traditional curries. Both nights have music. Saturday is Creole food, and Wednesday night is barbecue. Rotis and burritos with homemade salsa are popular for lunch.

Gloria, another Rambally, runs Le Spa Marigot here. She has you covered head to toe: the best barber in St. Lucia, a good hair stylist, manicure, pedicure, nails, massage, and even make up. She is popular locally for doing complete make-overs for brides, and will even arrange the wedding. Her team will do on-boat treatments. Her prices are reasonable, and customers say it is great.

Shaid runs a charter company (Bateau Mygo) with both day- and term-charters available from his dock and with reasonably priced bare-boat charters to qualified people. He uses locally trained crew, including all-women crews. In addition, the Ramballys have very nice villas to rent and a small real-estate office.

Ready for a special night out? You have a delightful surprise awaiting you at the Rainforest Hideaway [$A, closed September], rated by Fodor's as St. Lucia's top restaurant. Approachable only by sea, it combines brilliant food with an absurdly romantic atmosphere in an intimate dining area where you eat amid the mangroves, perched out over the water. Brightly lit fish in the enclosed dinghy dock are the before-dinner cabaret. This restaurant was built by hand by Jim Verity and Chef Myron. Stephen Donally is the Maitre D.

It is a magical experience, so you want to don at least long pants and a sports shirt, and you need to reserve as long in advance as you can. The menu changes frequently. You usually choose between a two and three course menu. There is always fresh fish, shrimp, and meat on hand, cooked with flair and imagination and served with great artistry. A full moon makes for perfection. A couple of nights a week they have excellent jazz piano and other music. If you have a party of six or more wanting to come for dinner from Rodney Bay, they will arrange

complimentary transportation for you.

Above and connected, is the Marigot Beach Inn, bright and sunny with a lovely bay view, perfect for shore time. It is run by Judith Verity, and if you love it here, they are going to build 12 holiday residences above.

Marigot Bay Development has two restaurants. The open-air Hurricane Hole Bar [$B] has a view of the bay and is casual and friendly in style. They offer a good varied menu. Next door, the Boudreau Restaurant [$A], on a large deck overlooking the bay, is a fancy, up market restaurant. They have the fanciest spa in St. Lucia for all kinds of treatments for beauty and relaxation.

On the north shore by the entrance is Marigot Beach Club, owned by Dave from England. This is a delightful area, magnificently gardened and leading onto the beach. His Doolittle's restaurant [VHF: 16, $B] is comfortable and right on the waterfront. Nightly happy hour, two-for-one, is from 1700-1900. Live entertainment is frequent in season. They offer a wide variety of food, well prepared and decoratively served. This is also a great place for breakfast or lunch. Marigot Beach Club has rooms for nights ashore.

David and Justin run JD's Mangrove and JJ's Dock [$B-C, closed Sunday]. This is an informal bar/restaurant, built on the dock. Justin, once a chef for Marigot Bay Development, is good and his lunch menu is inexpensive and simple; dinners are more elaborate.

If you walk up the hill behind JJ's you come to Marigot village, which is local, friendly, and enjoyed by locals and visitors. At JJ's plaza [$D] you can drink in the Tipsy Bar, get a good local meal in Tropical Cuisine [$C-D]. They also have boutiques, and a hair salon. Just down the road is Julietta's Restaurant [$B], high on stilts with a magnificent view of Marigot. Do not come in a hurry, but come and enjoy; the food is good. Julietta opens daily for lunch and dinner.

The top of the hill on the north side of Marigot Bay is a national park with a good hike to the ridge. Dock at Rainforest Hideaway, walk up to Mango Beach Inn and ask them to show you the trail. For a small fee, you can ask for Jo Jo, their gardener, to guide you. Wear shoes with a grip. You can also hike to a different part from Dolittles; ask in the office and make sure you get back before sunset when they lock the gate. This whole area is a favorite with birders.

Walk about a mile to the main road to catch a bus to Castries. On the return journey, most bus drivers are willing to bring you all the way to the customs dock for a little extra.

Water sports

Dive Fair Helen operates from JJ's. Several excellent dives are just south of Marigot in the area of Anse Cochon.

Marigot to Soufriere regulations

Two marine management areas control this area. The northern part is the Canaries and Anse la Raye Marine Management Area (CAMMA), and the southern part is the Soufriere Marine Management Area (SMMA) [VHF: 16]. Both are administered by the SMMA. They regulate all anchoring, diving, and fishing. They have placed many yacht moorings for yachts up to 70 feet, which are white with a blue stripe. (Red or orange moorings are for dive boats or snorkeling dinghies.) Five moorings are available for yachts up to 120 feet. In some places you may also anchor (see section descriptions).

There are charges for taking a yacht in the Marine Management Areas, which includes use of the moorings. Currently for two days: $EC: $40 for a vessel up to 40 feet, $54 to 70 feet, Weekly rates are: $80 up to 40 feet, and $108 to 70 feet. Vessels over 70 feet pay $162 per day. A small daily per person fee is being considered ($2 US). If it comes into effect I will post it on doyleguides.com.

As in the rest of St. Lucia, spearfishing and damaging, taking, or buying coral or sponges are strictly forbidden, as is the dumping of garbage, oil, etc. Fishing is forbidden in the marine reserves. You can pick up any available mooring. Always put your mooring line through the loop on the mooring rope; do not put the loop on the mooring rope on your cleat. A park ranger will come by to collect the fees. Park rangers carry identification and give official receipts; make sure you get

Anse la Raye

one. The Marine Park staff are very helpful with finding taxis, giving weather alerts, and making yachts feel welcome.

MARIGOT TO ANSE LA RAYE

Trou l'Oranger is a small white sand beach occasionally used by day-charter boats. Anchoring off this beach is only permissible between 0900-1700 hours. In calm, pleasant weather, it can be worth a stop for a swim and a snorkel.

Anse La Raye is a picturesque fishing village and a fair overnight anchorage. It is good in settled conditions with no northerly swells (no fees currently collected). There is plenty of swinging room off the town in 15 to 20 feet of water. The northern part of the bay shoals quite rapidly. The night to go is Friday, when they have a fish fest. Tables and chairs are put right down the center of the front street, and vendors set up stalls on both sides of the road and cook seafood: fish, lobster, lambi, and floats to go with them. It is very popular locally and currently has an atmosphere of peace, goodwill, and good food. You can use the big new dock or pull your dinghy up on the beach, swells permitting.

River Rock Falls is a good 2-mile hike up a pretty road that starts on the northern edge of the village. It is well signposted, so you will not need a guide. Do not expect a wild, tropical falls; this is a gardened area where the fall and rock pool have been partially created with concrete. What you lose in immediate visual satisfaction you gain by the convenience of seats, tables, changing rooms, and a generous balcony overlooking the falls. The $5 EC entry fee is good value if you carry up lunch and spend a few hours relaxing, swimming in the pool, and exploring the surrounding area. With luck, you may have it to yourself.

The much wilder and more beautiful Bois de Nave fall is in the hills to the southeast of the village. You will probably need to hire a school kid to show you the way. The hiking in this area is excellent, with trails laid out by Jungle Tours. However, swimming in the falls is not encouraged, as it is a drinking water source. After hiking, you can cool off in the big pool to the left of the road on your way back to the village. This large pool by a cleft in the rocks is the most popular bathing place for locals.

Ask anyone the way to La Sikwee restaurant, which is set in lovely old sugar mill ruins that have been carefully gardened. It is not always open, so call before you go. Some town bars also sell snacks.

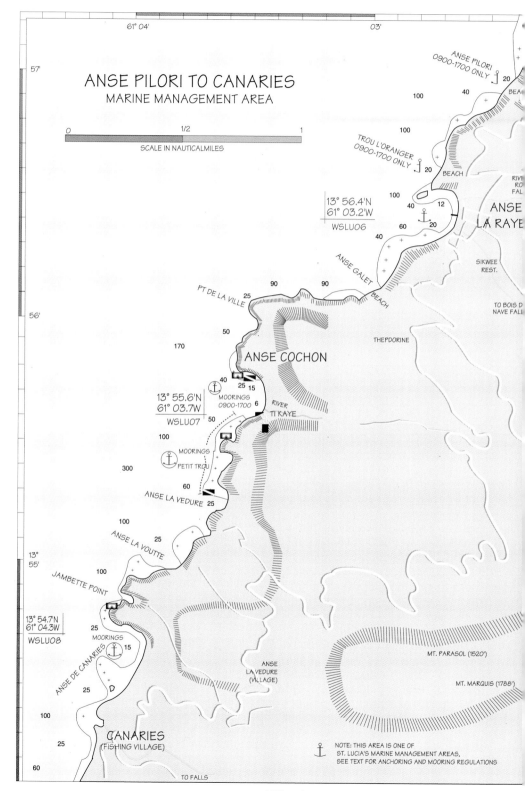

ANSE PILORI TO CANARIES
MARINE MANAGEMENT AREA

ANSE PILORI
0900-1700 ONLY

TROU L'ORANGER
0900-1700 ONLY

ANSE LA RAYE

SIKWEE REST.

TO BOIS D
NAVE FALL

RIVE
RO
FAL

BEACH

BEA

0   1/2   1
SCALE IN NAUTICALMILES

13° 56.4'N
61° 03.2'W
WSLU06

ANSE GALET BEACH

PT DE LA VILLE

THEPDORINE

ANSE COCHON

13° 55.6'N
61° 03.7W
WSLU07

MOORINGS
0900-1700

RIVER
TI KAYE

MOORINGS
PETIT TROU

ANSE LA VEDURE

ANSE LA VOUTTE

JAMBETTE POINT

13° 54.7'N
61° 04.3W
WSLU08

MOORINGS

ANSE DE CANARIES

ANSE
LA VEDURE
(VILLAGE)

MT. PARASOL (1520')

MT. MARQUIS (1788')

CANARIES
(FISHING VILLAGE)

TO FALLS

NOTE: THIS AREA IS ONE OF
ST. LUCIA'S MARINE MANAGEMENT AREAS,
SEE TEXT FOR ANCHORING AND MOORING REGULATIONS

St. Lucia

ANSE COCHON TO ANSE LA VEDURE

Anse Cochon is a beautiful little bay with an attractive beach. It lies about 3 miles south of Marigot. You pass Anse La Raye, after which is a rocky headland. Anse Cochon is tucked up in the corner just past this headland. Moorings have been placed in Anse Cochon. They are all white, but commercial boats have priority on the ones in the north side of the bay. Moorings continue about half a mile south to Anse La Vedure. One of these is specially designed to take the brig Unicorn, which does not stop for long, but if they ask you to move, you must. The coastline is attractive all the way along and usually comfortable enough for overnighting. If the moorings are taken in Anse Cochon, you may anchor right off the beach in sand, but you must move if asked to do so by fishermen.

Ti Kaye has a dock, but it is small and used by the dive boat by day, so it is best to beach your dinghy; you can tie it to the Ti Manje railings. At night you can use the dock for your dinghy. You will probably need a stern anchor. Take great care in swells.

Ashore

Ti Kaye [VHF: 16] is a charming cottage hotel perched on the southern headland of Anse Cochon. Nick, the owner, maintains a friendly atmosphere. On the beach, Ti Manje [$B-C], set on a big deck over the rocks, makes a perfect lunch stop; the view is perfect, the food good and reasonably priced. You can call Ti Manje at 456 8110 and they may be able to deliver lunch right to your boat.

Climb the scenic staircase up to the top of the hill. Here is a whole new world with lovely gardens, a pool, and fabulous views over the bay. Plan a trip to Kai Koko Spa, which is spectacularly beautiful, perched on the edge of the cliff, the precipitous view of the bay filling one side of each room.

ANSE LA RAYE

ANSE COCHON

Allow some relaxing time in the welcome room with a hot tub right by the open view. Enjoy many kinds of massage and beauty treatments.

Kai Manje [$A-B], with its panoramic view is the main restaurant. You get a perfect photo of your yacht below and the very best platform for viewing the green flash. Dinner is an imaginative blend of local, oriental, and other dishes, artistically presented with a daily changing menu that usually includes lots of fresh seafood and meat. (Vegetarians can be catered to.) You might prefer it for lunch if you want a break from the beach. Ti Cave (open from 1500) is an air-conditioned bar and hangout room built on the edge of the cliff with the whole of the west wall in glass looking over the bay.

Water sports

Island Divers make diving here really easy; the diving is in small groups and fun. They are a full Padi shop. Talk with Robert. Unless he is underwater you will get him on his cell, 285-3483. They keep their fast, comfortable dive boat in Castries so can easily pick up dive groups from yachts in Marigot, and meet up with yachts in Soufriere. Snorkeling and land/sea trips are available.

The diving is excellent. The water is 25-60 feet deep with a coral and rock slope descending onto sand. Isolated rock outcroppings out on the sand are covered in corals and sponges. These underwater fairy castles teem with small fish. Though there are not many large fish, the abundance and variety of small fish and reef creatures more than compensates. The wreck of the Lesleen-M is in the middle of the bay. It is a 165-foot freighter and lies in 67 feet of water. It was deliberately sunk in 1986 to make a dive site. The wreck has attracted an exceptional col-

Mooring area

JAMBETTE PT.

CANARIES courtesy SMMA

lection of invertebrates, many of which are uncommon elsewhere. Rosamond's Trench is another delightful dive in this area. It starts between two small canyon walls. There are many sponges, invertebrates, and colorful reef fish.

The snorkeling on the south side ranges from interesting to excellent, especially for more experienced snorkelers. Snorkeling off the rocky headland at the north end of Anse Cochon is fair, with brightly colored sponges, corals, and parrotfish.

ANSE DE CANARIES

Anse de Canaries is supposed to have several moorings about a third of a mile north of the village. They keep getting stolen, but you may anchor in the same spot in about 20 feet of water. Cliffs surround this pleasant, quiet area, and overnighting is permitted. The snorkeling is good, but move for fishermen if asked.

Canaries has great hiking, interesting bars, restaurants, a night club, and a famous street party. Unfortunately, the dock is pretty useless for a dinghy. You can beach it if swells permit. Canaries has some good local restaurants, including Del's, which has a great view and is on the edge of town going north. Check Zap International and, for drinking, visit Discipline Bar.

Every other Saturday is Canaries Creole: a festival of music and cooking that starts at 1500 and ends at midnight. The vendors wear traditional costumes, and the bands play local music of all types. It is special, but which Saturday will it be? Call and ask Margaret Edwards (459-4402/4701). Margaret also has La Maison Estate, with lovely gardens about a 10-minute-walk on the road to Castries (look for the flags). They open a bar for visitors and will cook you a great local meal if you let them know you are coming. They also have a special function place on the river called Moon River.

Enjoy excellent hiking to two waterfalls in the area. To find them, go to the main road and head south across the bridge. Take the road on your left just over the bridge.

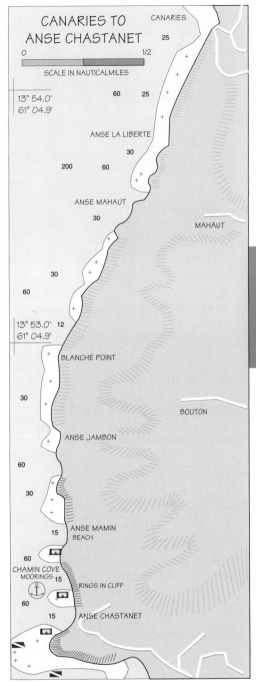

This soon leaves civilization as it winds back into the forest. After a couple of miles, you look at an amazingly verdant and broad valley surrounded by hills. Follow the well-marked road till it becomes a path and continue for another half-hour till you come to

Soufriere

an old bridge crossing the river. Keep straight (do not cross the bridge) and you come to the first falls; small, and dramatically set in a grotto with the water pouring through a hole in the rock. The lighting can be spectacular mid- to late morning, when the sun shines through the hole. A good pool for swimming lies below. If you have the energy, return to the bridge and continue another hour for the second, even prettier falls. Take $5 EC each to pay the owners of the land. You can get a trained guide who knows the history and the plants. Ask anyone for Dave Julien.

SOUFRIERE AND THE PITONS

Soufriere is a small, picturesque town set amidst a scenic wonderland dominated by the towering twin Pitons. Its exceptional beauty will enthrall hikers and photographers. The surrounding water is a magnificent marine park. There are many great things to see and do, the coastline is wonderful, there are lots of small restaurants, and those who like snorkeling, hiking, and diving could easily spend a week in the area.

When approaching Soufriere from the north, beware of the shoal that extends from the south side of Anse Chastanet, off Grand Caille Point. If you run aground, you will be fined for damaging the reef.

Ask one of the park rangers about the current security situation. There were no recent problems, but dinner time thefts have happened form time to time.

Harassment is mainly a thing of the past, but a few waterfront youths pester yachts, take drugs, and are best avoided. If they come on to you, just say "no." Should anyone annoy you, contact the SMMA [VHF: 16]. If you cannot reach them, call Benny [Harmony Beach, VHF: 16] as he is usually around and does help. Take a description of the person and the name of their craft. It is unwise to invite strangers on your yacht; a few might check out the yacht with an eye to returning when you are out. If vendors "bad mouth" a restaurant, avoid them; they plan to get you to go to some bad restaurant where you can be overcharged so they can get a kick-back.

The biggest danger is speeding pirogues and other craft. Stay alert, especially when swimming and snorkeling.

Regulations

The whole area shown on our sketch chart is part of the SMMA. Regulations and fees for using the management areas are given on page 175 (see *Marigot to Soufriere, Regulations*). The SMMA has an office in Soufriere on the waterfront where you can check up on your email and the latest weather. Everyone here is very friendly and welcoming.

The SMMA provides moorings and

anchoring is not allowed. SMMA check their moorings, which are generally reliable, though occasionally fail in big swells. There are five large yacht moorings for yachts up to 120 feet. Larger yachts will be helped with anchoring; call the SMMA.

Soufriere is a port of clearance for pleasure yachts. Customs is in the SMMA building and immigration is in the police station. Customs are on eseaclear and their hours are Monday-Thursday 0800-1630, Friday 0800-1800, Saturday and Sunday 0800-1630. You will pay $10-$15 EC overtime after 1630 on Fridays and on weekends. There are also port fees to pay; we give these in *St. Lucia at a Glance* page 136.

Don't give garbage to vendors, as they may dump it in the water. Take bags into town and use the bins just north of the SMMA office.

Anyone scuba diving must be accompanied by an official dive guide. An SMMA diving fee applies to all dives. It is only $40 EC for a year, though if you are just passing through, you can pay $13.50 EC for one day. Snorkeling fees are included in your SMMA mooring fee, and you can snorkel anywhere. If you are an accredited diver and have your own equipment, the SMMA can put you in contact with a guide. Several yacht-friendly dive shops will help you. Action Adventure Divers provide all levels of service, including guides and yacht pick-ups, (see *Hummingbird Anchorage*). Hawksbill Tours offer personal dive trips (see *Soufriere Town*), Island Divers do rendezvous pickups (See *Anse Cochon*).

If you have a problem, Tapion Hospital has a hyperbaric chamber.

Services

Many people with boats will offer to help run you to town or take you for a tour or longer ride to Castries or Vigie (it is faster by boat than car). The best are members of the Soufriere Taxi Association or the Watercraft Association [VHF: 16], professional groups of properly equipped and insured water taxis; the only ones to use for longer trips. Benny, at Harmony, is good, has a seaworthy pirogue, and stands by on VHF: 16 (Harmony Beach). He wants to encourage more yachts and will tie up your lines for free if you give him a call.

Mango, captain of Hawksbill Adventure's yellow pirogue, is good for all trips, including long ones to places like Vieux Fort and Marigot, as is Mystic Man Tours (see Soufriere, *Services*).

The registered Soufriere water taxis are often too busy for small trips, like a run ashore, but there are other unregistered pirogue owners who are happy to do such short runs. These include Captain Bob, Malcolm's Water taxi (722-5048/286-2277), Marcellus, and Francis (Welcome Taxi). They are nearly always on the water.

St. Lucia

Moorings

ANSE CHASTANET

Anse Chastanet is an attractive cottage hotel built on a hill that slopes to the sea. Several yacht moorings are available off the cliffs north of the beach in Chamin Cove. Underwater rocks lie just south and north of the moorings, so approach with caution. While often reasonably peaceful, this area can be untenable in times of a northerly swell. The snorkeling right from your boat is superb.

The Anse Chastanet beach bar is a congenial lunch spot, with two boutiques in the same area. For dinner, they have a very fancy restaurant up the hill. They rent bikes on cruise ship days and have shady, scenic mountain bike trails behind the next beach north.

Water sports

Scuba St. Lucia at Anse Chastanet [VHF: 16] is one of the largest dive operations in the Windwards, with two resort courses and four dives daily. They do not fill tanks. Scuba St. Lucia takes divers on the Anse Chastanet Reef for their first dive at 1100. It is best to turn up half an hour early and remember to bring your diving card.

If you are not certified, resort courses are available, and these usually start at around 0900.

Anse Chastanet reef extends seaward from the beach and is still in reasonably good condition. The shallower parts are fair for snorkeling, but avoid cruise ship days. Diving is excellent along the length of the reef, which slopes from about 30 to 80 feet. Sheet corals, solitary corals, and brain corals are abundant, as are a delightful variety of sponges, from the azure vase sponge to large barrel sponges. The water is clear and reef fish abound, with clouds of brown and blue chromis, along with sergeant majors, brilliantly colored parrotfish, and goatfish. All kinds of jacks and snappers cruise just off the reef. Currents are fierce on the outer part of the reef.

Snorkeling is excellent along much of this coast.

Navigation

When you go from Anse Chastanet toward Soufriere, be very careful of the reef off Grand Caille Point. Not only might you damage your boat, but you will also be liable for hefty fines (up to $5,000 US) for damaging the reef.

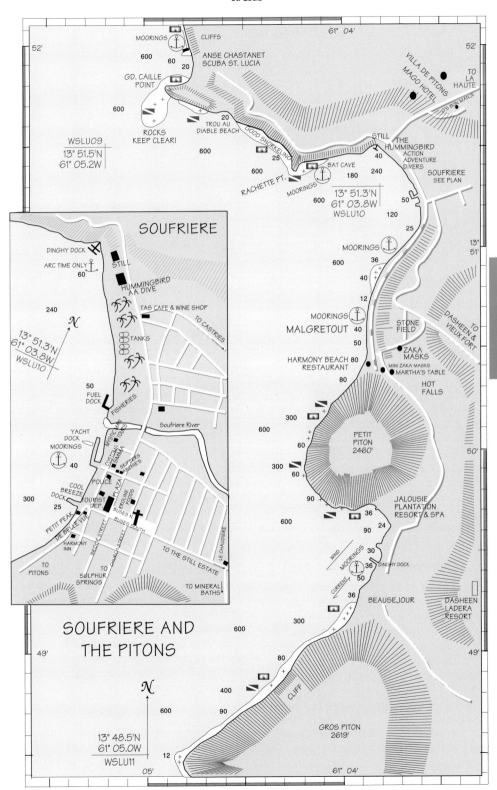

SOUFRIERE

WSLU09
13° 51.5'N
61° 05.2W

MOORINGS
CLIFFS
600
60
20
GD. CAILLE
POINT
600
ROCKS
KEEP CLEAR!

ANSE CHASTANET
SCUBA ST. LUCIA

20
TROU AU
DIABLE BEACH
GOOD SNORKELING
25
600
RACHETTE PT.
MOORINGS
BAT CAVE
180
600

13° 51.3'N
61° 03.8W
WSLU10

61° 04'

52'

VILLA DE PITONS
MAGO HOTEL
TO LA HAUTE
LES BON MANJE

STILL
THE
HUMMINGBIRD
ACTION
ADVENTURE
DIVERS
40
240
SOUFRIERE
SEE PLAN
50
120
25

13°
51'

MOORINGS
600
36
40
12
MOORINGS
MALGRETOUT
40
50
HARMONY BEACH
RESTAURANT
80
80
600
300
60
300
60
600
90
600

STONE
FIELD
ZAKA
MASKS
MINI ZAKA MASKS
MARTHA'S TABLE
HOT
FALLS

PETIT
PITON
2460'

DASHEEN &
VIEUX FORT

JALOUSIE
PLANTATION
RESORT & SPA

36
90
24
WIND
MOORINGS
30
36
50
DINGHY DOCK
CURRENT
36
BEAUSEJOUR
DASHEEN
LADERA
RESORT

50'

49'

600
300
80
400
90
600
12

CLIFF

GROS PITON
2619'

61° 04'

SOUFRIERE

DINGHY DOCK
ARC TIME ONLY
STILL
60
HUMMINGBIRD
AA DIVE
TAS CAFE & WINE SHOP
240
TO CASTRIES
N
13° 51.3'N
61° 03.8W
WSLU10
TANKS
50
FUEL
DOCK
FISHERIES
Soufriere River
YACHT
DOCK
MOORINGS
40
MYSTIC INN
GEMMA'S
CUSTOMS
SKIPPER'S
BOWIE'S
300
COOL
BREEZE
DOCK
25
POLICE
PLAZA
BEROLINE FOODS
TOURIST
DEP.
BUSES NORTH
BUSES SOUTH
PETIT PEAK
DE BELLE VUE
BRIDGE STREET
CHURCH STREET
HARMONY
INN
LE CHAUDIERE
TO
PITONS
TO
SULPHUR
SPRINGS
TO THE STILL ESTATE
TO MINERAL
BATHS

SOUFRIERE AND
THE PITONS

N

13° 48.5'N
61° 05.0W
WSLU11

52'

49'

05'

St. Lucia

TROU AU DIABLE

This beach lies between Gd. Caille Point and Rachette Point. Sand covers the middle of the bay, but there are lovely coral gardens, ideal for snorkeling and diving, to both the east and west. The snorkeling is better to the east; the diving to the west. It is a reasonable dinghy ride from Soufriere or the Hummingbird, and you can tie to an orange dive buoy, if available, or to one of the SMMA marker buoys if not.

HUMMINGBIRD ANCHORAGE

This is a fishing priority area. Use one of the seven yacht moorings in the area of the bat cave. It has an attractive, remote feel, and the snorkeling is good right off your boat. Around the time of the ARC (ask the SMMA), you can anchor in the northern part of the beach off the Hummingbird. Take a line and tie stern-to the shore. Previously, you could anchor here from 1800-0600, but some yachts overstayed and interfered with the fishing, so this is now banned.

A dinghy dock in the corner of the bay makes getting ashore easy. Use a stern anchor for swells. Be prepared to deal with dinghy watchers.

Timothy Joseph, who has a boat called Surprise, occasionally works for the Hummingbird. He is reliable and you can give your garbage to him.

Communications/services

The Hummingbird offers free customer wifi and the staff will help customers with telephone calls or faxes during normal office hours. You can check your email here. Wifi from other sources may reach the moorings.

Owner Joyce, who has run the Hummingbird for over 30 years and recently was awarded an M.B.E for her services to St. Lucia's tourism, gets much of her business from yachts and welcomes them warmly. Dinner guests from yachts are welcome to a free shower, 12 gallons of fresh water if they bring containers, and a bag or two of free ice to take back on board.

Ashore

The Hummingbird Restaurant [VHF: 16, $A-B] is the most elegant and charming of Soufriere's waterfront restaurants, featuring a wall made of pottery coal pots, wonderful hand carvings, and an exquisite view across the pool to the Pitons beyond. The food is excellent ~ a blend of French and Creole cuisine, with seafood a specialty.

A skipper bringing in a party of five or more gets a meal selected by the house for free. Meal guests are also welcome to use the pool. They have live music most Wednesday nights in season. If you are leaving your dinghy on the dock, tell security (Benji, Gabriel, or Thomas), and they will keep an eye on it for you.

Joyce also has the Hummingbird's Bamboo Beach Bar, which is popular for sunset or moonlight cocktails. Happy hour is from 1700-1900 and they keep going till the last person leaves.

Hummingbird is a great daytime hangout and lunch is excellent. You can get lighter fare: try their delicious chicken and mushroom sandwich in white wine sauce. You can always finish with Joyce's famous vintage fruitcake.

The office is very helpful with advice and will answer any questions you may have. They will arrange taxis and tours at a fair local rate. Batiks, handmade on the premises, are featured in their boutique, and Joyce offers a 10 percent discount on batiks to yachts (but not other items). Rooms are available, with a 15 percent discount in the summer, 20 percent in winter.

The Still Beach Restaurant [$B-C] is next to the Hummingbird and, with the associated Ruby Estate, which lies just out of town, is run by David Dubolais. This restaurant has a big balcony overlooking the anchorage, and serves good local food. The staff are welcoming and friendly and you can ask them about Ruby Estate and the tours that are available there.

Water sports

Snorkeling is good all the way between the anchorage and Trou au Diable Beach. If you snorkel in shallow water off the beach in front of the Still Beach Restaurant, you are

186

welcome to the

HUMMINGBIRD RESORT

Batik Studio
10% discount to yachts on batiks!

Live Music
Wednesday
"Kweyol night"
in season

Bamboo Beach Bar
Happy hour
1700-1900
open until..

free customer
Wi Fi

Yacht
discounts on rooms, Ask!

JOYCE (YOUR HOSTESS)

Gourmet Restaurant
With a perfect Pitons view
Open breakfast, lunch and dinner
(breakfast 7-10 am)

Hot and cold showers
Overnight Accommodation
email: hbr@candw.lc
www.istlucia.co.uk

The Yachtsman's Favorite Bar
Our guards will watch your
dinghy and your yacht.

Image labels: BAT CAVE, STILL, HUMMI, BAT CAVE MOORINGS, DINGHY DOCK, TOWN MOORINGS, SOUFRIERE BAY (WESTERN PART)

likely to see streams of bubbles rising to the surface. They are from a minor underwater volcanic vent.

Action Adventure Divers, in the Hummingbird, work with yachtspeople wanting to dive in the SMMA. It is run by two brothers from a fishing family in the area: Chester (an advanced Padi instructor) and Vincent (a dive master). They know all the good spots. You can contact them through VHF: 16 or phone. They will be happy to come by your yacht and pick you up. They offer a variety of services, from resort courses to full certification, and if you have all your own gear and boat, their charges can be as low as $15 US per person, the standard rate for a guide. They use a pirogue with a bimini for sun cover, are flexible and helpful, and are delighted to work with those on yachts, who they see as their main customer base. You can ask them about underwater hull cleaning.

SOUFRIERE TOWN

The town of Soufriere was the set of the movie *Water*, starring Michael Caine, and it has many charming old Creole buildings with balconies and gingerbread. Much has been done recently to upgrade the town and waterfront.

There is a yacht and general-purpose dock just off the SMMA. You can use this for your dinghy. Guards on duty from 0800-1600 are not completely successful in preventing would-be dinghy watchers, but if you tell the watchers that the guards are going to watch it for you, they lose interest and disappear.

Moorings start to the south of town and continue right round into Malgretout. You swing on these moorings so do not need a stern line. Security in the SMMA has been generally good recently, but if you are going out to dinner, ask the rangers about the current status.

Communications

The SMMA has an email station and a bookswap. Sonia, who is often in the office, is very helpful. You can also use Lcheapo internet cafe in the Excelsior Plaza. Valencia on the desk tells me they open 0900-1800, Monday to Friday. You might pick up a wifi signal on a mooring.

Services

Water, fuel (gas and diesel), and chipped ice are available alongside the fishing port dock, open 0630-1800 every day. You can also buy fish here. Otherwise, you can use the Cool Breeze gas station right at

Labels on image: HUMMINGBIRD · FISHERIES FUEL DOCK · DINGHY DOCK · SMMA OFFICE · MAIN DOCK · SOUFRIERE BAY (EASTERN PART)

the head of the town dock. Come alongside after the day-charter boats have left.

St. Lucia's two main yacht agencies are based in Soufriere. They have very similar names which can cause confusion, but both have a good reputation.

Ben's Yacht Services offers fueling, provisioning, taxis, car rentals, finding parts, getting technicians, on board, customs clearance, laundry and getting visas.

Benny [VHF: 16: Harmony Yacht Services] has a laundry and will pick up from your yacht anywhere in the SMMA. He has a water taxi if you need one, and if you want a guard on board when you go out to dinner, he will post one for $30 EC. He also offers the full array of super yacht services (see: *Malgretout*).

Hawksbill Adventures have a powerful yellow Pirogue with a sunshade, run by Terry "Mango" Joseph. Mango is a good and often busy skipper. He offers a quick way to get to Marigot and farther north, as well as to Vieux Fort, so picking people up from either airport is no problem. He offers coastal and land tours, including a half day that features ziplining, visiting the volcano, and other local attractions.

Charles Richards (Mystic Man Tours) operates a professional water taxi service and he is easy to reach, with an office next to the SMMA. He is well worth knowing for a number of reasons: he will reliably take you to a restaurant in the evening, he has good success rate if you want to go sports fishing, he runs great whale-watching tours, and he is good for longer trips (getting to Castries, for example). In addition, he fixes most of the local outboards in the area (his workshop is in the fishing complex) and he can get yours running again if you have a problem.

Soufriere Foundation, down the street from the SMMA, acts as a general help and information center. They will get you a car rental, find you a tour, fix up a hike with the forestry department, make a booking for dinner, and tell you about all the local attractions.

Transport

Ben's Yacht Services stands by on VHF: 16. Ben is a knowledgeable taxi driver and guide who will happily take you on a tour of the area, help you provision, find fresh flowers or fruits, get your guests to the airport, make you restaurant reservations, take you there, and be your general help in Soufriere. He has a fleet of taxis and good drivers. Call him on the phone. Ben also offers full superyacht services (see *Services*)

Harmony Yacht Services, run by Benny, has both good water taxis and several land taxis for different demands. (See also *Malgretout*).

Provisioning/fun shopping

In town, Eroline's Foods is a great little supermarket. It is clean, with an ample array of foods to provision your boat. I was pleased to see they had local frozen fish for sale. It is connected to Fond Doux Estate, which supplies much of their produce. It opens 0800-2000 Monday to Saturday, and 0900-2100 on Sundays and holidays. If you buy more than you can carry, they will deliver it to your nearest dock. Soufriere has a couple of banks and pharmacies.

Debbie's Image Tree is a nice souvenir shop set in a gorgeous old gingerbread building on the main square.

Restaurants

Many delightful restaurants can be found in this area.

Skipper's and Archie's [$D], side by side, a few steps from the SMMA, are the best cheap-and-cheerful joints in town; probably cheaper than cooking for yourself. The cooking is local and good, and they serve food all day long. Archie's has a big TV and shows the latest sports events. Skipper's is open to the street and has some outside tables.

De Belle Vue Restaurant [$C-D] is in a cute room upstairs looking out over the water, and they cook good local food. Opposite, Petit Peak [$C-D] is in the building that served as the town courthouse back in 1898.

Way in the back of town, a long walk or a short ride, Le Chaudiere [$D] is just beyond and opposite Still Estate. Mekeje, the owner, used to work with the SMMA. Her cooking is excellent. Lunch time she often caters to visiting tour buses with a big bargain buffet. For atmosphere come in the evening or on a non-tour day

Some of the more exciting and memorable restaurants are outside town. Some you can hike to, others are a short taxi ride away; negotiate first. Unfortunately, there are no set rates for short rides and ripping off tourists is second nature to most of the Soufriere taxis who approach you. Based on other island rates, the one way taxi fare to Dasheen or Morne Fond Doux heading south, or La Haute heading north should be $25-30 EC. If you get a ridiculous quote ($20 US is not unusual), take a bus. The buses all line up on the main square, one lot heads north to Castries and the other south towards Vieux Fort. Everything is uphill from Soufriere, so riding one way then walking back downhill is a good option.

The Dasheen Restaurant at Ladera Resort [$A] has the most awesome view of any bar in the Caribbean; just to walk in is unforgettable. The original owner/designer made the most of the location, keeping the buildings small and interesting and completely open to the view. He was called back as architect when they expanded, and under his hand the restaurant and bar are exotically designed as a series of three completely open rooms climbing the ridge line. They are perched on the edge of a giant precipice looking straight down the valley between the Pitons. It is hard not to exclaim, "Wow!" when you first see it. From the top

Dasheen

room you can look down through both the second room and the bar to the bright blue swimming pool set in a flower garden below. It gives a spectacular 3-D effect within the hotel and beyond to a dramatic Pitons view. Ladera Resort is ably managed by M. Botlois, whose staff will welcome you for lunch, dinner, or just a drink.

Lunch is, of course, a great time for the view, though if you arrive for an early cocktail, dinner offers you both a day and night perspective, with the chance of a dramatic sunset. Nights are spectacular when the moon is full. Gourmets will prefer evenings, when the gold-medal-winning chef creates a dinner that is a fitting accompaniment to the view. In addition to the restaurant, ample snacks and sandwiches are available in the bar for lunch. Sunday buffet brunch is an excellent choice, but come reasonably early. While there, do not miss their new boutique, which stocks local crafts, pottery, books, and essentials.

By day, the energetic can walk up to Dasheen from Malgretout. (Walk up the

Jalousie road away from Petit Piton, turn right on the main road, and keep going; it is a good long hike.) It is a long but pleasant walk back down.

Opposite Dasheen is Hotel Chocolat, originally Rabot Estate, owned by an English chocolate maker. They cultivate cocoa for their chocolate (made in England), have plantation tours and rooms for rent along with a tall spidery restaurant [$A]. The restaurant is okay on the inside, as probably are the rooms, but from the outside it looks and feels like an architectural bad hair day. The buildings don't fit the beautiful countryside and are a stark contrast to the old estate house, still standing, which is gorgeous.

Much more pleasant in appearance is Morne Fond Doux, another old estate with a nice restaurant. It has some lovely, authentic Caribbean buildings. They have added rooms by buying pretty traditional buildings from various part of the island and rebuilding them on the estate. Their restaurant is open for both lunch and dinner [$B] and you can take a half-hour estate tour

on delightful trails.

In the other direction, many restaurants lie on the road between Soufriere and the top of the hill on the way towards Castries. All have great views over Soufriere.

La Haut Resort [$B-D] has a spectacular panoramic view of the Pitons, which is greatly enhanced by a brilliant display of bougainvillea planted in the foreground, making a perfect photograph. The grounds have been artfully gardened and include little fishponds, and many people find them rewarding for bird-watching. Owner Stephanie Allain, from Canada, offers a variety of dishes using local ingredients enhanced by ideas from the outside. Come for a lunch or dinner. If you come for dinner, arrive before sunset, and in any case bring your swim suit and plan to spend some time hanging out in the pool with its spectacular Pitons view. La Haut is a mile and a half uphill from Soufriere on the main road to Castries. Get a bus or taxi up (negotiate a taxi fee of about $25 EC). Walk back down: just keep sticking one foot in front of the other and gravity takes care of the rest.

Gee's Bon Manje is owned by Ryan and Ginette, who cook excellent local food, especially prawns and fresh fish. It is a seven-minute walk up the hill on the main road to Castries. Turn right at their sign. You head a bit downhill on this road till you see it up on your left hand side. The restaurant is on two floors and has a pleasant open feel with a view over Soufriere. They open from breakfast to dinner. Lunch is downstairs, lighter fare, and inexpensive [$C-D]. You can also hang out downstairs in the evening where they have a bar and snack type food. Dinner upstairs is fancy and good [$A-B].

Mago Estate Hotel [$A] is an upmarket, elegant establishment. You can dress up if you want to. They have one of the world's more impressive fireplaces hewn out of a giant boulder left in place during building. The pool, the view, and lots of tropical foliage evoke a feeling of romance. The food is first-rate.

Villa de Pitons [$C-D] has a rather quaint atmosphere, with lots of rooms linked by many steps around a central swimming pool with a fountain, and murals and batiks all over the walls. Dora and Michael offer a fairly eclectic menu, with interesting-looking dishes from the Caribbean and other countries. They open from breakfast to dinner, with a lighter lunch menu.

The Beacon is even farther uphill than La Haut. They have a big open platform restaurant with a good view over Soufriere and as well as being a regular restaurant, often do functions.

Water sports

Snorkeling and diving are good throughout the area. Hawksbill Tours have a very powerful yellow pirogue with a sun shade. They have a dive instructor and offer private diving trips to those on yachts. It is reasonably priced for two couples or more. Make the arrangements with Captain Mango, discuss the gear you need, and they will pick you up from your yacht and deliver you back after the dive. A complete dive shop, where you can join a dive, is planned.

Ashore

The Sulphur Springs, between Ladera

Diamond falls

Resort and Soufriere, look like a scene straight from hell, with barren, brightly colored earth, bubbling pools, and huge spurts of steam. They have an area here where you can take a mud bath.

Much more scenic and pleasant are the naturally hot Diamond Baths, built by Louis the 16th. They are a 20 minute walk out the back of town. Pass the Soufriere Estate and look for a road on your right. It is posted, but only if you look back. The baths are combined with a beautiful tropical garden.

Take a few dollars and your towel, and you can luxuriate in these baths set amid a well-tended tropical garden. My favorite are the big private baths at the top, where piping hot water comes straight from the volcano into two huge tubs ($10 EC per person to enter the gardens, $15 EC per person for the private baths, or $10 for the tepid outdoor pools. Pay as you go in). They have a snack bar and shop on the river.

As you head up hill to the south, Morne Coubaril is right opposite the road that goes to Jalousie (about a mile). It is a delightful old estate with a restaurant, and they offer half-hour estate tours and ziplining. Their zipline trail is pleasant and scenic. Many of the lines start on platforms up big old banyan and mango trees. The guides are entertaining, tell you about your surroundings, and are also very safety conscious.

The rainforest area near Morne Fond St. Jacques has exquisite views for walking or hiking. You are required to have a guide and pay a fee when hiking in the rainforest reserve ($10 US per person), but walking on the road leading to it, amid the lush

vegetation with hidden glimpses of the Pitons below, is also beautiful. For hikes into the rainforest, ask the Soufriere Foundation to call the forestry department. They have knowledgeable guides in the Soufriere area who can arrange to come and take you on a rainforest tour. (They can provide transportation from the nearest dock.) One of the most interesting is a 2.5-hour loop tour to the Maho waterfalls. Take your bathing things for a shower in the fall and a swim in the pool above it.

Marshall Simon (459-7390) is a hiking guide who will take you on a variety of hikes including the rain forest. He does birding hikes and can take you to waterfalls. Moray (459-5496) is another guide who specializes in rainforest hikes, usually half a day. He mentioned a new hike that follows trails from the movie Superman 2.

Nearby roadside attractions on the road to Fond St. Jacques include several waterfalls, New Jerusalem, and Toraille (in a lovely little garden); take your swim things.

MALGRETOUT

This is a lovely place to moor, along a beautiful beach. The Marine Park has put in moorings and for some, you will need to take a line ashore. Agree on a price in advance ($15 EC is fair). If you would prefer to moor yourself, say so. There are several deeper moorings where you can swing free, including at least two that take yachts up to 120 feet. One is right in front of Benny's, one is farther north. Small yachts can use them if no big boats are booked in. If you are moored

St. Lucia

stern to over sand, you can put out a second anchor as security, as occasionally moorings pull loose here in big swells.

A pretty old road (now a trail) runs from the waterfront in Soufriere to the far end of Malgretout beach and this makes walking to town easy.

Communications/Services

At the southern end of the beach, under a blue roof, is Benny and Marcelene's Harmony Beach Restaurant and Bar [VHF: 16, $C-D]. Benny is well aware of the needs of yachts and is most helpful. He keeps a 24-hour radio watch and responds to calls from anyone having a problem. He sometimes has wifi that covers the area from Malgretout over to the bat cave. You have to call for a password. It is free for his customers. You can sometimes get other wifi signals.

Benny does laundry (collection and delivery to your yacht), has an internet cafe, and runs a water taxi. He is a registered ship's agent and does customs clearance, local provisions, and full support for large yachts anywhere from Rodney Bay to Vieux Fort.

Restaurants/Ashore

Harmony Beach Restaurant, Bar and Apartments [$B-C] is tucked right under Petit Piton. The family land continues up the hill for about 100 acres. One of the great things about eating at Harmony Beach is that you don't need to launch your dinghy. Benny will send Benny Junior in a giant pirogue to pick you up anywhere in the Soufriere area, and he will post a guard on your yacht while you are at the restaurant at no charge. Marcelene is an excellent cook. You will love the Creole fish, and you eat with a great view of Malgretout and Soufriere Bay. Everything is cooked from scratch, they use all fresh ingredients, and the prices are reasonable.

They have some nice apartments to rent behind the restaurant. If you want to go hiking or climb the Pitons, one of Benny's relatives will act as a guide and they own taxis. You can visit Benny's little rum shop in town, called Harmony Inn, which is usually manned by his son, Benny Jr.

Benny's sister Martha runs Martha's

SOUFRIERE AND THE PITONS

SOUFRIERE

St. Lucia

Tables [$C-D], a few hundred yards towards Jalousie from the main road above Harmony. She cooks excellent local food for a reasonable price, has a glimpse of the sea, and is open for lunch and dinner. Keep going uphill beyond Martha and you come to the little hotfalls set in a pleasant garden. $7.50 EC gets you in, and you can enjoy the hot pools below.

Just above the anchorage you can see Stonefield Estate [$B-C]. This elegant family hotel has a lovely restaurant area with a swimming pool and a view over the yachts. Trails lead to some excellent examples of Carib petroglyphs. If you walk uphill to the concrete Jalousie road and keep going uphill (away from the Pitons), the estate is to the left and is marked. They serve elegant Creole food.

If you turn left on the upper concrete road (heading toward the main road), you will pass Zaka Masks, an art studio selling the best and most brightly colored hand-painted masks in St. Lucia. They also build Piton meditation chairs, which are elegant looking, collapsible, and comfortable. Hikers can turn right on the main road and walk to the sulfur springs and Ladera. Zaka also has a mini outlet opposite Matha's Tables.

Diving and snorkeling are excellent around Petit Piton, though there is current. Drift-snorkel with your dinghy from Malgretout.

BETWEEN THE PITONS

Moorings are available in the area shown from Jalousie Plantation to south of Bang. If your maneuvering skills are insufficient to pick up a mooring, you will have offers of help from local water taxis. Do not feel obliged to accept such offers. Note that the wind and current can be strong in this area, and that the current is sometimes against the wind. This area is sometimes calm, sometimes rolly, and it can change with the tides. It is also popular, so when busy, it is best to arrive by late morning. The three outer moorings are suitable for yachts up to 120 feet.

The beach between the Pitons is part of Jalousie Plantation, one of the Windward's most elegant resorts, which is in a spectacular setting. You can pull your dinghy up on the beach by the fishing boats.

Ashore

The Jalousie Plantation [$A] is open to the public, with two restaurants: The Great Room, for fine dining in the main building, and Bayside on the beach for breakfast, lunch and dinner. They have an excellent spa with a massage center, facials, hairdressers, saunas, and hot tubs. If you need essentials or casual wear, check the boutique near the reception. Wherever you want to go in the resort, you can get a ride. Just look out for the shuttles and wave one down. To find a taxi, take the shuttle to the main gate. All kinds of tours and rental cars can be arranged at the hotel desk.

If you wish to climb Gros Piton, (about 4 hours round trip), guides are available from the trail head. The cost from the trailhead is $30 US per person. You can call them at (286-0382). To get in shape, take the road past Bang to the height of land, it has to be one of the steepest roads in the world.

Water sports

The dive around the base of Petit Piton is excellent. Start from close to the beach and explore at whatever depth you feel comfortable. There are wonderful sponges, good coral formations, and an extraordinary variety of fish. Sometimes huge schools of fish make magical patterns in the sunlight. Apart from reef fish, such as angelfish, blue chromis, parrotfish, scorpionfish, and damselfish, there are lots of hunters out there: jacks and snappers swim in fair-sized schools, and occasionally one sees a monster fish. Another good site for both snorkeling and scuba is under Gros Piton, just below the prominent cliff. A sloping dropoff with plenty of fish and coral goes down to great depths. There are sometimes currents in this area.

Navigation
South coast: Pitons to Vieux Fort

The trip from the Pitons to Vieux Fort

is against both wind and current, but it is only about 11 miles and is usually somewhat protected. Keep clear of the reefs that extend about half a mile offshore between Choiseul and Laborie. Laborie, about three miles before Vieux Fort, is a delightful little harbor.

LABORIE

Laborie is an authentic small fishing village on the south coast, about three miles west of Vieux Fort. It is easily identified by the big quarry just to its west. If you are tired of tourist spots, visit Laborie: The locals are friendly and not intrusive, the pace of life is easy-going, and yachts occasionally visit.

Navigation

Approach from the south or southeast to avoid Laborie Reef, which lies up to half a mile offshore on the west side of the bay. The approach is easy in good light, and if the sun is in your eyes, you can anchor in Petit Trou. The best anchorage is right off the end of the town dock in about 15 feet of water.

Or you can find your way in towards the beach on the other side of the center reef, and you might even explore the broken reef farther up the beach for an anchoring spot. (Best to do this with a dinghy first as it is tricky.)

Laborie is well protected in most conditions, but it is exposed in southerly winds, and rolly in southeasterly swells.

Ashore

Ashore, turn left down High Street. An internet cafe on your right opens at 1000 and closes at 1830 Monday to Saturday.

A little farther down the big community center and post office is conspicuous, and then comes a small local market, a supermarket, and an active fish market. It is hard to walk more than a half a block without passing a bar or two.

The restaurants in town are inexpensive and local. Captain Kent's Big Bamboo Cafe and Wine Bar [$C-D, closed Monday] opens for lunch and dinner and has an outside bar and barbecue at the back, and tables out on the pavement.

Market Place Restaurant [$C-D] is good and almost opposite. Farther west, over the bridge, you can get a great roti at Ann Marie's A & A. It is a tiny building marked only by a Piton sign. Farther west on the left with an excellent view over the playing field is Zoe's [$C-D closed Mondays]. This is an excellent place for a local meal, but give Zoe a little notice. Way down the road, Linda's Sea Breeze has a great beach view, but you have to book.

For fancier fare, take any bus heading to Soufriere and get off a mile or two down the road at Debbie's Home Cooking [$B-D]. This is a large restaurant that is reasonably priced and quite famous for its first-rate local food. On Sundays they do a giant buffet.

Walk the spectacular long beach. Behind Laborie, way up in the hills is Morne le Blanc (aka The Top of the South). The GSM aerials on the hill will show you where it is. They have a picnic spot and a viewing platform with a panoramic view towards Vieux Fort.

In Laborie, plans for the future include a craft market near the playing field, a beachside fisherman's restaurant, and some hiking trails.

VIEUX FORT

Tired of sharing the Caribbean with too many other visitors? Vieux Fort does not have a tourist bone in its body. You can enjoy this thriving local town with some great old wooden houses and two active ports: commercial and fishing. The people are generally friendly and welcoming, and you will find supermarkets and hardware stores in shopping malls. The fishing port makes it amenable for visiting yachts, though if you are used to the tourist scene, you may suffer from culture shock.

The anchorage is well protected and a long walk (or short ride) away is one of the Caribbean's most magnificent windward beaches, a beach so long that you are guaranteed half a mile or so to yourself. It is an obvious pickup or drop-off point for those arriving or leaving from Hewanorra, St. Lucia's largest airport.

Navigation

The sail to Vieux Fort from the Pitons is 11 miles, usually to windward. It may be protected, but if the current is running to the east, it can be rough. Keep well clear of the reef that extend about half a mile offshore between Choiseul and Laborie.

The most convenient anchorage for getting ashore is west of the new fishing port. Leave the green marker to port as you approach. Anchor between the marker and the western wall in 10-20 feet of water, or outside the green marker in 25 feet of water. Avoid the shoal along the northern wall of the fishing harbor that extends both north and west. Here you are close to town and can leave your dinghy in the fishing port. The holding varies between good and poor, so make sure you are well dug-in before going ashore (see also *Services*).

You can also anchor in either of the bays southwest of the large ship harbor marked on our chart. Anchor south of all the beacons. Shoals extend from the shore, so approach cautiously. To enter the first bay, pass to the west of the big, rusty post just outside the bay, as there is a shoal inside this post toward the shore. The second bay is far more scenic, with some passable snorkeling. A shoal comes out from the middle of the bay but you can anchor either side of it, or outside it. Several wrecks in both bays manage to snag anchors. If you are worried, have someone snorkel to help pick the spot.

The large ship port is run by St. Lucia Marine Terminals. They are not geared for yachts but have been quite helpful. You can often leave your dinghy alongside the roll-on dock to the north of the main pier. You cannot leave it here when the dock is in use. For town, use the fishing port.

Regulations

Vieux Fort is a port of entry and customs is at the head of the large ship dock. You may have to travel two miles to the airport to clear immigration. In compensation, no port fees are being collected at the moment. A bus will take you close to the airport, or you can call Bayne, a reliable taxi in Vieux Fort (cell: 720-8425). Keep him in mind when you need to come back with shopping.

Communications

The closest place for internet is Jemann, a cute local craft shop and internet cafe run by Peter and Bribiane Morgan. The Document Center, a good office store with internet and Fedex, is in the big building

Vieux Fort

where Clarke St. joins the highway. They open weekdays 0830-1630, Saturday, 0900-1300. Wegosite.com is an internet cafe at the Courtyard Mall (next building from the big Singer sign), open Monday to Saturday 0830-1800. Kimatri, The Old Plantation Yard, and The Reef all have wifi.

Services

Ice and outboard fuel are available in the fishing port on the eastern dock. You could stay overnight in the fishing harbor stern-to on the northwest wall if there is room. You may be charged $20 EC. There are no dockside services; ask first. Depths in the fishing harbor are about 6 feet close to the eastern dock, and about 7-8 feet farther out, where you can stay the night.

Filling with water is possible alongside the roll-on dock in the commercial port (when free). Talk to someone in the operations department; as you will have to arrange it with the water department. Big yachts can have fuel trucked to the commercial port. There is no water for filling a yacht in the fishing port, but you can probably arrange to fill a couple of jerry jugs in the port for

a small fee if you ask security. Cooking gas is available at the gas depot just outside the commercial port.

Fletcher's Laundry and Dry Cleaning is on New Dock Road. Virginia Fletcher charges $30 EC for a load to wash and dry and can turn it round in a day if you get it in early enough, otherwise 24 hours. Open approximately 0800 to 1600.

The fishing port is the obvious place to leave your dinghy. Put it in the northwest corner on the dock. Lock it up and, if leaving it at night, ask the security guard to keep an eye on it for you and tip him when you come back. On holidays and weekends, school kids can be pestiferous. Bribing one to guard the dinghy works, but it would still be smart to take the red kill switch with you. If you have a problem, there is a good chance you can leave it on the roll-on dock at the secure Commercial Port, where they are very helpful, though ingenuity is necessary for tying up, as there are no rings.

Hippolyte, right outside the dock area, is the DHL agent and can clear parts through customs. Francis Raymond, of St. Lucia Refrigeration on New Dock Drive, has lots

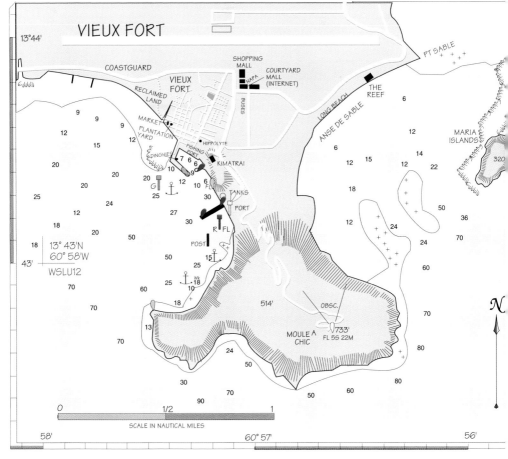

of refrigeration and stove parts, but he does not make repairs.

The Liferaft and Inflatable Center at Rodney Bay has their big duty-free warehouse near the airport, so call them if you need a new dinghy.

Vieux Fort is an excellent place to deal with boat linens and mattresses at Lubeco bedding factory, which is owned by Stephanie Allain, who also has La Haute in Soufriere. They supply both fitted and flat sheets for any size bunk (take a pattern) and have really nice fabrics in many designs, including 100 percent cotton and organic cotton. The also sell towels and they produce good-quality, high-density foam mattresses. They can make these to any shape. You get a mattress properly finished with a quilted cover, which adds comfort. Lubeco is in the industrial estate, just off the road to Laborie.

Provisioning

Shopping is good and most banks have ATMs. One large supermarket is in the mall by the roundabout. The even bigger Gablewoods South is a few miles down the main road heading towards Laborie. Fruits and vegetables in town are good and are less expensive than in Castries. The fish market in the fishing harbor has great buys on fresh fish.

Napa has batteries and tools and there are other hardware stores.

Restaurants

Several restaurants make Vieux Fort a pleasant destination.

The Kimatrai [$C] stands on the hill overlooking the yacht anchorage. It is an old-fashioned hotel, cool and breezy, with a marvelous view of the harbor. It is open all day and is a great place to hang out, relax, write postcards, play pool, use the wifi, catch up on your diary, or watch cable TV. It has the perfect location for sunset. This is also an excellent place to eat. They cook very well - try their rack of lamb or fresh fish.

Old Plantation Yard [$D], run by Conrad Simon and Choix Mechiour on Commercial Street, is a wonderful lunch place full of character and very special. You eat in a big courtyard shaded by breadfruit trees and decorated with a big old pirogue. They serve local stews and dishes and it is inexpensive and fun. They have quite a few historical artifacts in the main room.

Patrick and Linda's Pat's Bar [$C-D] is quiet and relaxing. They open from 1000 till the last person leaves. Stop by for lunch or dinner. They will cook anytime, but only start when you order, so it takes about half an hour. They specialize in seafood and various meats, but don't have chicken. Chicken you can get at Sabi's Restaurant, a very popular lunch place close to the port.

When you are ready for some beach time, hang out at The Reef [$C-D, closed Monday evenings], on the eastern shore. The owner, Cecile Wiltshire, is a software engineer and runs slucia.com (not stlucia), and she has wifi. The Reef is open for breakfast, lunch, and dinner, serving local dishes at very reasonable prices. Seamoss and coconut water, saltfish bakes, lambi, and squid are on the menu, as are pizzas. The Reef collects interesting people, makes a great hangout, and is an excellent place to spend a few hours. It is also good for a simple overnight stay (they have four rooms)

Cecile is also a windsurfing instructor, and next to her restaurant is her Reef Kite 'n Surf Center, which has international instructors and all the latest kitesurfing and sailboard gear. It normally opens from November to June. This is a good place to buy secondhand gear, as they replace their equipment every year.

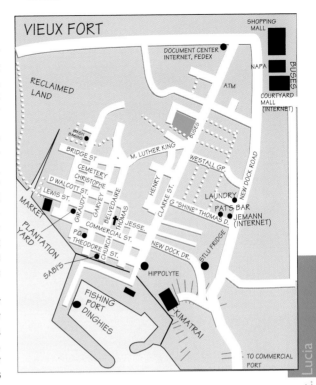

Next door, Island Breeze [$C-D], is another cheap and cheerful bar/restaurant right on the beach, open every day for lunch and dinner, serving beach bites, burgers and grilled food, and the food is good.

Just a short way to the south, along the same beach, is Sandy Beach Inn [$B-D, closed Mondays], a new restaurant under French management serving French Creole food, especially fresh fish. They open for lunch; for dinner you will need to reserve.

East of Vieux Fort the Maria Islands are a nature reserve and home to a species of lizard and a snake unknown anywhere else in the world. The National Trust building is right beside The Reef, and you can arrange for a guided trip. The energetic should hike up to the Moule a Chic lighthouse for the view.

Crafty Creations and the Art-and-Craft center are at Choiseul, a fair taxi ride away. You will find baskets, carvings, seed jewelry, pottery, and household items made from natural local materials.

PASSAGES BETWEEN ST. LUCIA & ST. VINCENT

Northbound

The northbound passage between St. Vincent and St. Lucia can be hard on the wind and hard on the body. The north end of St. Vincent is unbelievably gusty on occasion and more than a little bumpy. It is not unusual to have gusts of 30 to 40 knots for a few miles, so it pays to be prepared. I often do this trip single-handed and am not overly fond of it, but find the easiest way to do it is as follows: motor-sail close to the coast under reefed main and engine and wait until the full force of the wind hits before deciding what to do. If you are comfortable under main and engine, keep going that way until the wind steadies down. Otherwise, if you have roller furling, just unroll a little of the jib until it gets calmer. The main thing is not to arrive at the north end with too much canvas, where reducing sail can degenerate into hanging onto flailing Dacron as the boat bucks about and tries to throw you over. Once you get about five miles north of St. Vincent, wind and seas generally become more constant and you can adjust sail accordingly. The current will set you to the west, so head up if possible. It is going to be a long day, so plan to leave early from Cumberland Bay or Wallilabou, as that will make it seem shorter.

You may be able to avoid some wind and sea by heading offshore from Wallilabou, but in that case you are likely to have a hard beat to St. Lucia.

If heading north from Blue Lagoon in reasonable weather, the passage up the windward side of St. Vincent is shorter and you get the windward part over early, leaving a good sail to the Pitons. The trick is to tack about 4 miles to the east of St. Vincent to stay well off any bad seas close to shore. If the wind is in the north, you may have to make more than one tack. There is a windward lee under the Soufriere volcano (back pressure). When you reach this, if you tack out a few miles, you will get better wind and a better angle for crossing the channel.

Southbound

The southbound trip is usually a lovely broad reach. If you cannot see St. Vincent from St. Lucia, a course of 208° magnetic should start you in the right direction. If you plan to stop in St. Vincent, nature lovers will favor Cumberland or Wallilabou and those who like waterfront bars can clear customs in Wallilabou or Chateaubelair and continue on to Young Island Cut. If you plan to go all the way to Bequia, make sure you allow plenty of time.

In reasonable conditions, you may prefer to go windward of St. Vincent when sailing from Vieux Fort or Soufriere to Bequia.

PASSAGES BETWEEN ST. LUCIA AND ST. VINCENT

PITONS AT 13° 48'N 61° 05'W

SOUFRIERE

ST. LUCIA

VIEUX FORT 13° 43.'N 60° 58'W

211° (37°) MAG. 30 MILES

230°(50°) MAG. 24 MILES

6000

13° 23'N 61° 13'W

SOUFRIERE VOLCANO

CHATEAUBELAIR

ST. VINCENT

203

Pinky captures Bequia on canvas as seen in *Island Life Boutique*

St. Vincent & the Grenadines

Regulations

St. Vincent and the Grenadines together make up one country. The main customs stations are in Chateaubelair, Wallilabou, Kingstown, Bequia, and Union Island. With a little effort you can find customs in Mustique and Canouan.

The entry charge is $35 EC per person per month, unless you leave within that month, in which case you pay again when you reenter. In addition, charter yachts based outside St. Vincent are charged $5 EC per foot per month, with a $125 occasional license fee. You can cruise here as long as you wish. You will normally be stamped in for a month, and then return for extensions, which are in the same office and easy to obtain. Those clearing outside normal office hours (weekdays 0800-1200, 1300-1600) will pay overtime.

Overtime fees are Sundays/holidays customs: $63 EC, immigration $50 EC, other days: customs: $45 EC, immigration $35 EC.

No jet skis or similar craft are allowed anywhere in St. Vincent and the Grenadines. Spearfishing is strictly forbidden to all visitors.

You are welcome to fish, but only for your own consumption. You can troll when sailing, or hand-line at anchor or from the shore, except in any marine park, where no fishing is allowed. Buying lobster out of season (the lobstering season is October 1 to April 30) is illegal, as is buying a female lobster with eggs (easily seen as red "caviar" under the tail), or any lobster less than 9" in length. Corals must not be damaged. Fines run at around $5,000 EC.

Holidays

Jan 1, New Year's Day
Jan 2, Recovery Day
Jan 22, Discovery Day
Easter Friday through Monday. March 29-April 1, 2013 and April 18-21, 2014
First Monday in May, Labor Day
Whit Monday, May 20, 2013 and June 9, 2014
Carnival, 2nd Monday and Tuesday in July
August bank holiday; 1st Monday in August
October 27, Independence Day
Dec 25, Christmas
Dec 26, Boxing Day

Shopping hours

Most shops open 0800-1200 and 1300-1600. Saturday is a half day and most places are closed by noon. Banks normally open Monday through Thursday 0800-1200, and 1300-1500, and on Fridays 0800-1200, and 1500-1700.

Telephones

Card and coin phones may be found all over the island. You can buy phone cards in selected shops. For calls to USA and other NANP countries, dial 1 plus the full number. For other overseas calls, dial 0 + country code + number. Dial 115 for an overseas operator. When dialing from overseas, the area code is 784, followed by a 7-digit number.

Transport

There are inexpensive ($1.50-$6 EC) buses running to most villages. If you are going a long way, check on the time of the last returning bus. Taxis are plentiful. Sample taxi rates for up to four are:

	$EC
Blue Lagoon to Airport	35
Kingstown to Young Island	35
Airport to Young Island	25
Kingstown to Blue Lagoon	50
Short ride	20
By the hour	50

Rental cars and motorbikes are available (see our directory). You will need to buy a local license, which costs $65 EC.

Airport departure tax is $40 EC

Cumberland Bay

St. Vincent

S t. Vincent is an island of towering mountains, craggy peaks, and dramatic precipices. Everything is dressed in a tangle of dense green forest. St. Vincent's steep and wild terrain was among the last to be settled by Europeans. At the time Columbus sailed through the islands, St. Vincent was inhabited by the Kalinargo who had migrated from South America and had a more poetic name for the island Hairoun, which means "home of the blessed." They were a fierce tribe who had wrested the land from the Arawak people who preceded them. Columbus called them Caribs.

While the newly-arrived Europeans exploited nearby islands, a slave ship was wrecked off Bequia and the Caribs took the slaves as their own. However, these slaves were fierce and warlike and proved to be a problem. To control this, the Caribs decided to kill all the young male black children.

This caused a revolt among the slaves, who killed all the Caribs they could, stole their women, and ran into the hills. They kept the names the Caribs had given them, followed some Carib customs, and became known as the Black Caribs. Over the years they took control of much of the land from the original Caribs and put up intense resistance to British settlement. Finally, in the late 18th century, the Black Caribs were defeated by a superior British force and shipped en masse to Honduras.

The northern end of the island is dominated by Soufriere, a 3,000-foot volcano. A friend of mine was anchored under the volcano in April 1979 with an amateur geologist on board. Together they scaled the volcano and peered into the depths. The geologist declared it safely dormant. That night, which happened to be both Friday the 13th and Good Friday, there was a rumbling

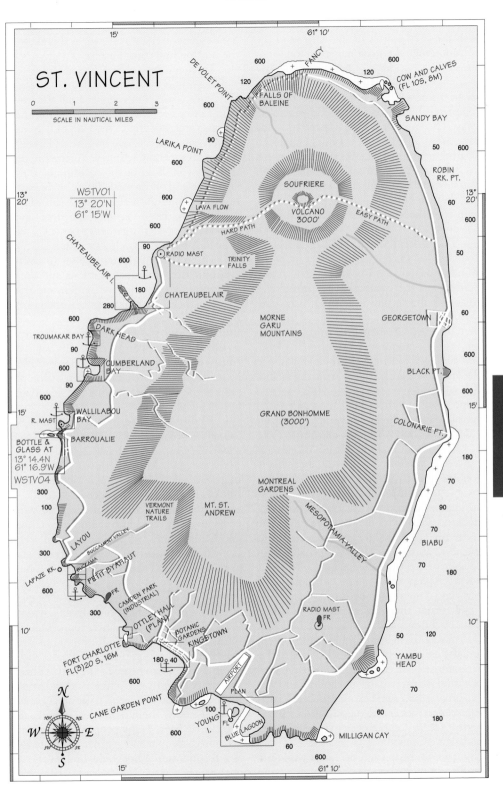

ST. VINCENT

0   1   2   3
SCALE IN NAUTICAL MILES

15'   61° 10'

600   FANCY   600

DE VOLET POINT   120   120   COW AND CALVES
(FL 10S, 8M)

FALLS OF
BALEINE   SANDY BAY

600   600

LARIKA POINT   50   600

90   ROBIN
RK. PT.

600

WSTV01
13° 20'N
61° 15'W   600   SOUFRIERE   13°
20'   60

600

13°   LAVA FLOW   VOLCANO   EASY PATH   600
20'   3000'

HARD PATH   50

CHATEAUBELAIR I.   90   RADIO MAST   TRINITY
FALLS

600   180   CHATEAUBELAIR

280

600   DARK HEAD   MORNE   GEORGETOWN   60
GARU
TROUMAKAR BAY   MOUNTAINS

90   CUMBERLAND   BLACK PT.   600
BAY

600   90

600   GRAND BONHOMME   600
(3000')   15'
15'   WALLILABOU
BAY   COLONARIE PT.

R. MAST   BARROUALIE   180

BOTTLE &
GLASS AT   MONTREAL   70
13° 14.4N   GARDENS
61° 16.9'W
WSTV04   VERMONT   90
NATURE   MT. ST.
300   TRAILS   ANDREW   70

100   BIABU

LAYOU   BUCCAMENT VALLEY   70   180

300   BUCCAMA   PETIT BYAHAUT   RADIO MAST
LAPAZE RK.   FR   FR   10'
600   CAMDEN PARK
(INDUSTRIAL)   50   120
300   OTTLEY HALL
(PLAN)   BOTANIC   YAMBU
GARDENS   HEAD
FORT CHARLOTTE   KINGSTOWN
FL (3)20 S, 16M   180   40   70

600   AIRPORT
PLAN
N   60
NW   NE   CANE GARDEN POINT   100   180
W   E   600   YOUNG   FL
SW   SE   I.   BLUE LAGOON   MILLIGAN CAY
S   60
600

from the very bowels of the earth and the volcano erupted with a massive cloud that landed dust hundreds of miles away. It created murk in the area so thick they couldn't see to the bow of the boat and had to leave completely blind, steering by compass to get away. The eruptions, which lasted for some days, were Soufriere's second since 1902. The other was in 1973. As you sail by, you can see some rivers of dark volcanic matter that flowed down from the summit. Despite the absence of any warning, everyone left soon after the first eruption and there were no casualties.

The enthusiastic should hike up Soufriere, as it is unquestionably one of the Windwards' best and most exciting hikes. Starting on the windward side, there is a clear trail that begins in farmland and goes through rainforest, montane forest, and then into an area where only tiny plants can survive. The mountain top is often in cloud, and you need a little luck to see down into the crater or get the views over the island. The wind often blows hard and it is cool and damp, so take a rain jacket. Be careful not to get blown into the crater, which is a sheer 1,000-foot drop with no guardrail. Take lunch with you and eat it near the top, as the longer you spend there, the more likely you are to get windows in the clouds and be able to see into the crater. The crater is an impressive cone, with a huge, growing, smoking volcanic dome in the middle. The crater rim is at 3,000 feet; the mountains to the north attain 3,800 feet. The volcano can be approached from the leeward side, but it is a much longer hike (about four hours each way) and a reliable guide is essential.

It seems that neither nature nor man was sure they wanted tourism in St. Vincent, for it lacks the acres of white sand beach, and the convenient, easy anchorages of the Grenadines. In compensation, this very beautiful island remains unspoiled, and you can drive or hike amid exotic, almost theatrical, scenery. Its fierce, rugged terrain is the perfect scenic complement to the appealing and gentle Grenadines farther south. Those doing a round trip from St. Lucia who only wish to stop one way are better off visiting St. Vincent on the way north, as this makes the northbound trip shorter.

Try to see some of St. Vincent's interior, which is totally wild. Roads run up both of St. Vincent's coasts, but none goes all the way round or crosses the middle. Climbing the volcano or a boat trip to the Falls of Baleine are recommended. I love Montreal Gardens in the Mesopotamia Valley. Perched upon the very threshold of the mountains, they are at the end of the road. Tim Vaughn and his team maintain these gardens beautifully. Little paths, dense vegetation, a river, and broad views make the gardens a perfect place to spend an hour or two away from it all.

Those who like things closer to town can tour the Botanical Gardens and Fort Charlotte. The Botanical Gardens are the oldest in the western hemisphere, and it was here that Captain Bligh brought the breadfruit tree after the mutiny on the Bounty fiasco. A direct descendant from his original tree is on display. You will find many youths to guide you through the gardens. One or two are good and entertaining, but negotiate fees in advance.

While many places are good for wandering off on your own, a guide is essential for some hikes, especially the western approach to the volcano. Bad robberies have occurred in this area, which has also become the smokebasket of the ganga generation.

Good guides are available who will cover everything mentioned above. Clint and Millie Hazel, who run Hazeco Tours, come from Vincentian families dating back to the 1700s, and they have an exceptional and intimate view of the island's history, politics, and society. They know local people at every stop and are knowledgeable about local plants and crops. Their tours include food, snacks, and refreshments and are reasonably priced on a per head basis with a minimum of two people. They are willing to arrange tours from Cumberland and Wallilabou, but you will need to contact them in advance, as their radio does not reach these little bays. Many people also contact them from Bequia and get met on the ferry. We also mention other guides under various anchorages.

Chateaubelair: Chateaubelair Island is in the foreground

St. Vincent & the Grenadines

Navigation, west coast: north to south

Navigation along this section of the coast is straightforward, as the land is steep-to except for the clearly visible Bottle and Glass rocks near Barrouallie. A quarter of a mile offshore clears all other dangers.

CHATEAUBELAIR

Chateaubelair lies at the southern foot of Soufriere, St. Vincent's volcano. The coast here is rugged and photogenic, with dramatic hill and mountain outlines, cliffs, and beach. In settled weather it can be a dream. However, in times of northerly swells, Chateaubelair can be untenable, so great caution must be used during the winter months, when dangerous northerly swells often arrive without warning. A steep cliffy slope covered in palm trees lies along the eastern half of the bay. This is the calmest and most scenic place to anchor. There is an ample anchoring shelf, 20-40 feet deep. Don't anchor too close to shore as rocky patches extend in places. The bottom is sand but some of the boulders you see tumbling into the sea along the water's edge have made it onto the sand, so if you anchor on rope, snorkel on your anchor. There is also a good sandy anchoring shelf with excellent holding in front of the Beach Front Restaurant, though just to the northeast of the restaurant is a deep hole.

A rock lies in the middle of the channel between Chateaubelair Island and the mainland. A navigable passage, some 35 feet deep, runs just south of this rock (between the rock and the mainland). There are rocks around, so only attempt this in good light.

Be prepared to move for fishermen if they ask. You can dock your dinghy at the town dock, swells permitting.

There were serious security concerns here for some years. I have been told the men responsible are now in jail, and people are staying here without a problem. If you want to be really safe and if swells permit, anchor in front of the Beach Front Restaurant, but the eastern hill anchorage has been fine, too. If you want to check with the local police, their number is 458-2229.

Regulations

Chateaubelair is a port of clearance and you can clear in here. Turn right and walk along the beach from the dock and customs is a couple of hundred feet along, in the house where a path leads back. Immigration is in the police station. Head up the road from the dock, take the uphill left turn, and it is on your right. Whenever I have cleared in here it has been a wonderful, friendly experience. Customs is open weekdays 0800-1600; Saturday 0800-1200. If you plan to clear out here and want to be sure it is open, the customs phone is 485-7907.

Ashore

Most people in the north of St. Vincent are naturally friendly in the nicest way. Try to keep it that way. Treat people with friendly respect. It is good to buy produce if vendors come out and offer it to you, but beware of giving anyone money to go buy fruits or run errands in the village. Don't give to beggars unless they have real handicaps.

Esron Thompson's Beach Front Restaurant [$D] is a conspicuous building on the beach. He and his wife Gail will cook you the most wonderful fresh fish at very reasonable prices that are geared to the local market. For preference, eat upstairs under a shelter with a panoramic view of the bay. But watch out as you get towards the top of the stairs ~ the third one from the top is a little higher than the rest and tries to trip you up. If you are not overnighting, this makes a great lunch spot when heading south; anchor right off the restaurant. They do sometimes have very loud, late-night music on weekends.

Chateaubelair lies in the heart of some of St. Vincent's best hiking. The volcano is a full day's hike. Trinity Falls is a four-hour round trip, but you can get a taxi some of the way. The Darveo Falls are a pleasant 40-minute hike, with a second falls higher up. Take your bathing things, for you can swim at Trinity Falls and take a good shower at the Darveo Falls. Ask about the ancient carved stones. Wherever you go, it will be in beautiful scenery. Taxi tours and walking guides are available through the Beach Front Restaurant.

Water sports

The whole of Chateaubelair Bay is an invitation to snorkel. Interesting boulders and rocks abound. For divers, Chateaubelair Island is magnificent and you can find a good dive almost anywhere around it. On the west side, a steep wall has been sculpted by the sea into ravines, hollows, and tiny caves, that are home to eels, soapfish, and other creatures. It is decorated by a variety of black corals, including wire coral. Giant gray angelfish often gather over the sand at about 90 feet. You will find a reef 40 feet deep where huge structures, covered with a colorful mixture of corals, rise from the sand like fairy castles. Pufferfish swim by with what look like broad smiles on their faces. Huge schools of tiny silver fish catch the sun in a brilliant display. You will see a good variety of brightly colored reef fish and creatures such as Christmas tree worms, snake eels, and maybe an octopus. On the north end of the eastern side, a dramatic wall plunges to about 130 feet, with elegant soft coral formations. Farther south, diving is not as deep but is equally pretty. You might be lucky and find the dive mooring just off-island in the passage between the island and the mainland.

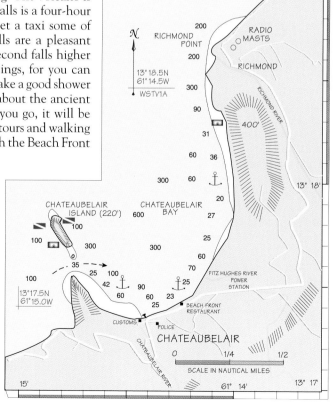

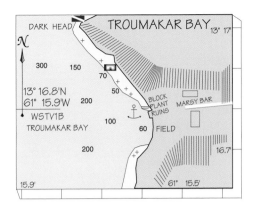

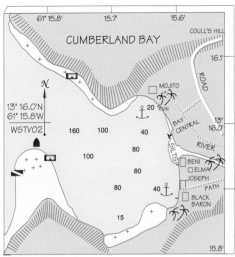

TROUMAKAR BAY

This small bay has room for only a handful of yachts. It is well protected, except in bad northerly swells. Steep hills ashore afford panoramic views for energetic walkers. There is good snorkeling all along the northern shore. The water here is deep ~ you begin to think the bottom does not exist as you approach the beach. Anchor bow or stern to the old block plant ruins, at the northern end of the beach, or tie to a palm tree.

Ashore

Troumaker is at the end of the road, but a good end. Perched on the slope near some massive ruined foundations is Marsy's Bar and Restaurant [$C- D, VHF:16], owned by Alstar Mars and Yvonne who also own much of the hillside. You can drink here all day long at regular prices, which are lower than most happy hours, and Yvonne will be delighted to cook you a local meal at a very reasonable price, given an hour or two notice. There have been no security problems here, but as added security their number is 458-2879.

CUMBERLAND BAY

This deep and enchanting bay is part of an estate in the heart of St. Vincent's wildest and richest land. A forest of coconut trees and bananas flows down the valley to the beach. At dusk cattle egrets roost together in nearby trees and at night the tree frogs set up a rich chorus. Sometimes the bay becomes a boiling mass of jumping tuna and fishermen can often be seen with their seine nets, waiting patiently. Cumberland is unspoiled by tourism. There are many here happy to take you on a tour or feed you, but it is all so unsophisticated that it has the charm of an untouched settlement. The land around is steep and dramatic with excellent hiking. Enter toward the north of the bay to avoid the large rocky shoal that extends from the southwestern headland. Cumberland is very deep and you will need to anchor bow or stern to a palm tree. There will be many eager to help. Do not tow any helpers into the bay; wait till you get right in and choose one of the people inside the bay itself. You can anchor to the north or south of Bay Central. The water on the north side is shallower.

Regulations/services

Cumberland Bay has no customs; clear in or out at Wallilabou or Chateaubelair.
Bay Central (Cumberland Beach and

St. Vincent & the Grenadines

Cumberland Bay

Recreation Park) is a government-built facility with a dock selling water ($50 EC to fill), ice, a launderette, showers (for $5EC they even supply a towel), bar and restaurant, and a welcome center. You can come alongside for water (up to about 2 meters draft), and deeper boats can come stern-to; the depth drops off fast. The staff, Matthews, Althea, and Grenville, are very helpful.

Restaurants

The restaurants serve good food, are reasonably priced and fun.

Bennett [$C-D] has the bar/restaurant called Beni in the middle of the beach. He has been here for a long time. It is an amusing place to hang out. Beni can cook a good local meal, especially seafood, and serve fresh local juice. Bennett is also a good man to talk to about hiking. The new Cumberland Nature Trial (about three hours) is in the rain forest high above spring village near the water source for the hydro-electric piping, which brings it at speed to several small generators in series. You need a taxi to take you there. Beni can also take you to other hikes, including Darkview Falls. Beni has a great package, which includes a tour and full dinner with a drink afterwards. If you are eating in his restaurant, he will give you free water and ice.

Joseph is a fisherman who has been here for as long as I can remember. He has restaurant right on the beach. Joseph's Place [$C] is perfect for a real local style barbecue of fresh fish or chicken, but give him a little notice if you can; he needs time to catch the fish. You can ask Joseph about steel pan. He knows a band he can hire. Joseph is also out and about in the bay fishing, taking yacht lines, and helping however he can.

Two cousins, Julian and Lloyd, rent the old Stevens place at the north end of the beach and have created Mojito [$C-D]. It has a great view over the rest of the bay and a varied menu, which includes rack of lamb with coffee rum barbecue sauce and pineapple and lemon grass seafood curry. The captain eats free with five or more guests. Once when I anchored off the restaurant with guests on board I shouted out "Are you open for lunch?" Within a few minutes someone swam out to my boat with a waterproof menu. The food was excellent.

The Black Baron [$B-C], a tavern run by Jean-Louis and Corinne from France, has the most character, with a pirate's den, complete with a treasure chest. They open every day in season and serve French and Creole food made with fresh local ingredients. This was the first to offer, on two-day's notice, a whole roasted suckling pig for dinner; now several restaurants offer it. They have a good sized menu, and for lunch you can get lighter soups and salads. They have a dinghy dock, but you will need a stern line. Being French, they attract many French boats.

Bay Central [$D] has a little restaurant open from 0800 until the last customer leaves. This is the cheapest place to eat and you get things like chicken and chips and fish broth. On the last Friday of the month they hold a fund-raising barbecue starting about 1400 for about $15EC a head

Thelma has the smallest place, a colorful little shack called Rough and Roggade Bar [$D], which also sells produce du jour. Thelma cooks good food at some of the best prices along the beach. She is often helped by Carlos, the water taxi driver.

Mama Elma [$C-D] is the newest beach bar, near Joseph. She is open for lunch and dinner every day and you can get everything from goat water to lobster, with plenty of fish and chicken.

Ashore

Although some of the locals look like bad guys in a spaghetti western, for the most part they couldn't be nicer and more helpful. Joseph can sell you fish, Ricky will bring round a crate of fruits on his windsurfer,

Carlos and Brother have water taxis, help with lines, and arrange trips and hikes. Suzanne Stapleton does the same, and she is fully qualified as a guide by the tourist department. Kenny also does lines and guides. Marsden and Abbey will enjoy taking you hiking. Blackman has a water taxi.

You might meet Ashi, the artist who makes handicrafts and paints most of the signs. James works at Black Baron, but also sells handicrafts, Carolyne sells jewelry next to Thelma. Others will take your lines and be generally helpful. You will have to be their judge. Try not to do business with anyone you find aggressive or objectionable in any way.

Shamara Pierre braids hair and does manicure and pedicure under a palm tree and will give you an artistic nail-art job. Give her a call (531-3336) or ask for her at Mojito's.

You should definitely take a walk here. An easy one is up Coull's Hill to the north, which rewards you with a great view of the anchorage. Walk back to the road, turn left and keep going. (If you land on the south side of the bay, you must ford a small river, but that is part of the fun.) There is a rum shop in the village, just at the point when you are dying for a drink.

Better yet, arrange with one of the guys to take you on the Cumberland Nature Trail in the rain forest. You need transport to get you to the start which is up above Spring Village.

WALLILABOU

Wallilabou, a picturesque bay surrounded by dramatic hills, is about a mile south of Cumberland. Here you are in the heart of St. Vincent, among charming and delightful people. A picturesque tropical waterfall lies just a mile down the road. In 2003, Wallilabou became famous as the main location for the movie "Pirates of the Caribbean," starring Johnny Depp. Wallilabou Anchorage, a pleasant restaurant/hotel makes part of the waterfront. They maintain a room full of artifacts from the movie, and have some of the props; it is fun to visit.

Enter in the middle of the bay and pick up the moorings put down by the Wallilabou Anchorage Restaurant, or anchor where there are no moorings, and tie bow or stern to the wall, or to a tree. In times of northerly swells, the northern corner of the bay is more protected. However, it also has a reputation for occasional thievery, which happens less often off the Wallilaboiu Anchorage.

Men in rowing boats occasionally approach you from as far as three miles away, asking to take your stern line ashore. Refuse all such offers; there are always plenty of line helpers in Wallilabou itself. If you want someone reliable to deal with, try Joel Browne (431-5248/497-2354) or Alex (Kirk Grant, 526-4793). They are good, but not always around as they are sometimes away on boats. Joel skippers for some charter companies. Other guys who are okay to take lines include Ron and Ronnie (the twins) Speedy, and Bagga. You will have to figure out who

you want to deal with, though things seemed much more relaxed the last time I visited. The going rate for someone to help you with your lines is $15 EC. Most line handlers are good these days.

You may enjoy buying fruits and vegetables on display by vendors, but beware of the offer to "go fetch you nice produce" The quality of the product rarely matches the description and if you give money in advance, you may never see the vendor again.

You can also anchor in Keartons Bay, one bay south. Rock Side Cafe has five moorings, which they keep for dinner guests. Call them before you come in and get instructions as they are bow and stern moorings. If Kensley is around, he will help you tie up and book him to take you ashore for dinner in big swells; as it could be dangerous in your own dinghy. If he is not around, Orlando will help.

Regulations

Customs clearance is available daily between 1700 and 1800. Moderate overtime is usually charged.

Communications

Wallilabou Anchorage Restaurant has wifi for which you need a password. This is good for a year and costs about $5US. You may be able to get wifi from your yacht, otherwise in the bar.

Services

Steve and Jane Russell, who run the Wallilabou Anchorage Restaurant [VHF: 68], are keen to attract yachting customers. They have a good dinghy dock and offer moorings ($20 EC, refundable when you eat ashore), free showers, and inexpensive water via a long hose from the dock. Phone, fax, and email communications are available, as are block and cube ice and overnight accommodation. Do not give garbage to the boat vendors. Most stick it in the rocks. Wrap it well and take it ashore to the restaurant and they will show where to put it (no charge).

In Keartons, Rock Side Cafe has internet, wifi, laundry, and showers and can provide water to the moorings via a long hose. These are mainly provided for their dinner guests.

For a professional mechanic, or other service, ask Steve. You can also ask Joel Browne (431-5248/497-2354) who helps a lot of the bareboats in the area. If you have any problem with any vendor, call the coastguard: 457-5445.

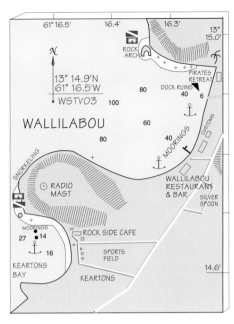

Restaurants

Rock Side Cafe [VHF 16/68, $B] in Keartons, away from the bustle of Wallilabou, is a magical tiny garden oasis overlooking the bay. Orlando from St. Vincent and Rosi from Germany are the owners. They keep moorings for their dinner guests (call and book), and Orlando or Kensley will help you tie up if necessary. You can also dinghy round (swells permitting) or ask Orlando to get Kensley to bring you over in his water taxi. The small size of this place is part of its charm. You eat outside under a thatched roof. You need to call them to get ashore (they will bring you in or show you the way), as a reef lies along much of the beach. Rosi and Orlando are wonderfully welcoming and treat you as friends. They can also provide water, internet, wifi, showers, fresh produce, and laundry. The food is usually fresh fish and really excellent; visiting is a special experience. Give them at least a couple of hour's notice, if possible.

Orlando has Orlando Adventure Tours, based at Rock Side Cafe. He is a scuba diver, so can take qualified people diving and anyone snorkeling. He can also arrange hiking, driving and boat tours and, for German guests, Rosi often guides.

The Wallilabou Anchorage Hotel, Restaurant and Boutique [VHF: 68, $B-C] has a delightful location where you can eat looking out over your yacht, in a "Pirates of the Caribbean" ambience. Owners Steve, who is from St. Vincent, and his wife Jane, from England, are very pleasant and sometimes are in the bar in the evenings. The restaurant is great for seafood. It serves generous portions of very well-prepared local food, particularly fish, shrimp, and lobster in season. Happy hour with cheaper drinks is 1700-1800. They have a small museum, with some magnificent Carib stone head carvings, plus ancient telephones, whalebones, a room of "Pirates" movie artifacts, and lots of tortoises. They will provide a lively little band by special request.

Ron and Ronnie, the twins, have the Golden Spoon Bar and Restaurant [VHF: 68, $B], in the village, a short walk away. an interesting place for a drink if you want a local experience.

Behind the ruins of the big dock in the north of the bay is the Pirates Retreat. This is a rough and ready bar. Come here and have a good rum punch hand-made by the owner

St. Vincent & the Grenadines

215

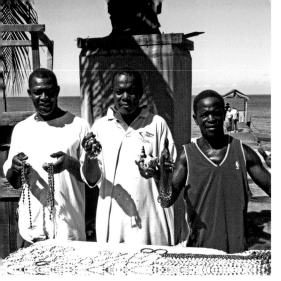

Anthony (The Shadow) Edwards. Anthony is probably the most entertaining character in the bay and he likes music. Be careful if you anchor in the shadow of The Shadow as several yachts have been visited by petty thieves in this area.

Ashore

A little waterfall garden lies about a mile up the road from Wallilabou, with a perfect swimming hole. It is a mini park with a bar, changing rooms, and toilets. Gardens with pretty walkways surround the falls and show the old dam ruins at their best. Bring a towel for a beautiful and refreshing swim, you will feel far from the sea and it is worth going just to see the magnificent old fig tree that has become part of the wall on the far side of the old dam. Entry is $2 EC per person, and while the park officially closes at 1700, the guard will usually let you in later. The walk here, through lush countryside, is delightful. Go to the main road and turn left; look for the falls on your right. Along the road you will pass Morna's Craft Shop. Here, Berthold does impressive machinery sculptures, and weaves great baskets and bowls. He also sells brightly colored t-shirts and his own guava liqueur, from the guava tree outside.

Wallilabou also makes a good base for exploring St. Vincent. The Soufriere volcano, the rainforest, Trinity Falls and the Vermont Nature Trails are not too far away. The approach to the volcano from this side passes rather close to the center of the

Marijuana Growers Association land. This is not a smart place to venture on your own. Take a guide and stay with him. Arrange a guide through the Wallilabou Anchorage Restaurant.

Rather than buy from the floating vendors who can be too numerous, visit the jewelry sellers who have stands at the head of the dock: Reynold Simmons, Joel Garden, and Cedric Davis.

Water sports

The diving in this area is excellent. For those who like to go on their own, a fair dive can be made right off the rock arch on the northern side of the bay (the snorkeling is good here also). You will find a pleasant reef at 30-40 feet, with lots of colorful sponges and soft corals inhabited by many reef fish, including angelfish.

For other dives you will need a seaworthy dinghy or local pirogue and guide. Castle Cove is off the headland just north of Troumakar Bay. This dive has a fabulous terrain of steep slopes and cliffs full of crevices, holes, and tunnels. The sponges are brightly colored and plenty of hiding places usually harbor lots of fish. The return trip along the top of the cliff makes for some great views, with schools of brown chromis hovering on the edge. We saw spotted drums, angelfish, and slipper lobsters. Seahorses and frogfish are not uncommon here.

Rock Pile is off Mount Wayne (the second long, black sand beach south of Barrouallie). This unusual dive is along a massive pile of rocks about 20-30 feet deep. The outer edge of the rocks is shaped much like the bow of a boat, and the presence of an old anchor here makes one wonder whether there may be a wreck buried among the rocks. Rock Pile is very colorful, with many sponges and soft corals. Schools of barracudas are the norm and lots of moray eels live here. You have a good chance of seeing frogfish.

Peter's Hope is off the old factory south of Barrouallie. This is a colorful shallow reef, from 20 to 60 feet, where you find a lot of king crabs and have a good chance of seeing turtles.

BARROUALLIE

You can easily identify Barrouallie by the conspicuous Bottle and Glass rocks. It is a picturesque local town with a few quaint buildings. People used to stop here to clear customs. That no longer happens, but if you want to experience a laid-back local village; this is it.

Navigation

If you are coming from the north, give a reasonable clearance to the last visible rock in Bottle and Glass as there is an underwater rock that extends seaward a few hundred feet. Anchor between the town dock and Pint Rock. There is an adequate anchoring shelf for a quick stop in about 25 feet of water. For overnighting, it is advisable to get one anchor hooked in the shallow water, drop back and set another in the deeper water, holding the boat bow to the beach. You can tie your dinghy to the town dock. You do not need any line handlers here.

BUCCAMENT BAY

Buccament Bay lies at the base of the Buccament Valley, one of the longest, deepest and most scenic valleys on the leeward coast. The hills attract showers that often hang there without reaching the coast; in the afternoon it is not unusual to see an ever-changing rainbow over the valley for

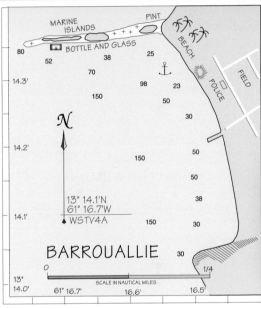

up to half an hour at a time.

The bay is well-protected and very calm, though like any west coast anchorage, it would be susceptible to exceptionally bad northerly swells. It is well protected from the southerly surge that can affect other south coast anchorages farther east. The easiest place to anchor is close to the beach from the north corner to the river. The water is very deep off the shelf, so make sure you are well hooked.

Ashore

Buccament Bay Beach Resort is a high-density waterfront resort. As you sail by, it sticks out like a badly fitting toupee: a glowing white beach of imported sand for tourists

Buccament Bay

Bat

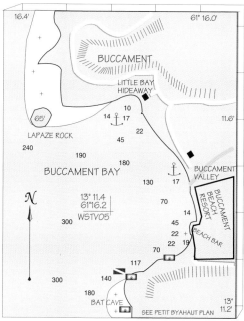

16.4'   61° 16.0'

BUCCAMENT

LITTLE BAY
HIDEAWAY

10
14   17   11.6'
22
65'   45
LAPAZE ROCK
240
190
180
BUCCAMENT BAY   BUCCAMENT
130   17   VALLEY

N   13° 11.4
61°16.2
300   WSTV05   70
14
45
22 +
22   19
70
117
300   140
180   +
BAT CAVE   13°
+   11.2'
SEE PETIT BYAHAUT PLAN

Water sports

The snorkeling from this bay round to Petit Byahaut is exceptionally good, with lots of brightly colored sponges, small healthy corals, many reef fish, octopuses, and more. Tow your dinghy; anchor it here and there in spots you like, and use it to return when you are tired.

PETIT BYAHAUT

This small and beautiful little bay has a little beach backed by hills, with several conspicuous peaky outcroppings of rock. It is a perfect hideaway anchorage with excellent snorkeling. Usually a good overnight anchorage, it is occasionally uncomfortable in southerly swells, when a stern anchor will help cut the roll.

If you are coming from the north, you pass the village of Layou, then Buccament Bay with the big new development. The next major bay is Petit Byahaut. Byahaut Point is a distinctive rounded headland. Pass the headland, head into the bay and anchor. The seabed is mainly weed so make sure you are holding. If you are coming from Kingstown, Byahaut Point is the farthest headland you see after you leave Kingstown Bay, after Camden Park, Questelles, and Clare Valley. Ashore, Petit Byahaut looks private; you may see a small green roofs poking out of the vegetation.

along this coast of lovely black sand beaches. This does not stop it being a very pleasant place to stop ashore for a meal, though there is rather too much security to make it yacht friendly. (Over time, this may moderate.) You will be stopped and questioned. You can go to one of the restaurants but you will probably have to contact them and have them come escort you in. The Bay is the main beach bar overlooking the pools and the bay. They also offer the Safran, the Bamboo, and a sushi bar.

Bat Cave

Petit Byahaut

Ashore

Petit Byahaut, approachable only by sea, is a charming, edge-of-the-world spot. It used to be a mini tent hotel, which is closed and the bay is for sale.

Water sports

Snorkeling is super in Petit Byahaut Bay and there is excellent snorkeling and diving easily accessible by dinghy right along the coast to Buccament Bay. However, currents can be strong. The bat cave is a short dinghy ride away and can be done as a dive or a snorkel in calm conditions. There is about three feet of water at the cave entrance. You can find somewhere to anchor your dinghy outside and there is good snorkeling in this area. Inside the cave it is quite dark, but you can see the bats, which cling by the hundreds to the cave walls and roof. Crabs climb up among the bats. You catch a glimpse of a tunnel that leads off to the left because you can see a hint of light at the end of it. This tunnel is about 30 feet long and about 4 feet wide. You rise and fall on the swells and if the swells are large it can be dangerous. The tunnel leads out into a fissure about 30 feet high and 40 feet deep. Below, the water is a brilliant blue. You swim out through the fissure and divers go down to two huge rocks at 80 and 130 feet

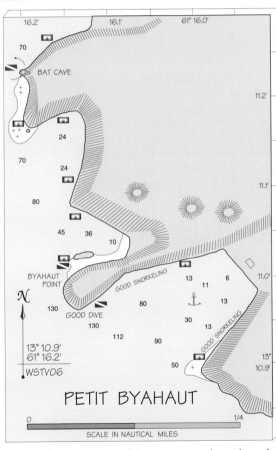

that are covered in sponges and corals and teeming with all kinds of fish. The ascent is up a wall textured with nooks and crannies. If you do the bat cave, it is most important not to disturb the bats. Two species live here: fishing bats (*Noctilio leporinus*), which eat fish

Wallilabou Falls

and insects, and the St. Vincent fruit-eating bat (*Brachyphylia cavernarum*), which was thought to be extirpated and is endangered. So swim quietly through the cave, without talking or splashing, and don't use flashlights or take flash photographs.

Dinosaur Head is the face of Byahaut Point that faces the anchorage. Below is a 120-foot wall covered in coral, sponges, and seafans. You swim through large schools of tangs and see queen angelfish, eels, snappers, and spotted drums.

OTTLEY HALL

Ottley Hall lies just to the west of Kingstown, on the far side of Fort Charlotte. It is a yachting facility.

Services

This yard has a 35-ton travel lift, a 200-ton ship lift, and a dry-dock for anything up to 65 meters long, 15 meters wide, and 6 meters deep. Special covered sheds on rails can be rolled over yachts on the hard or in

OTTLEY HALL

the dry-dock so that respraying and repainting can be done out of the rain. There is a fuel dock and long-term storage for smaller yachts. A marina area in front of the workspace is passable under many conditions, but when swells come in it can be untenable.

Ashore

The boatyard runs in a very low-key mode. The storage and haul-out parts are fully operational, but the labor force tends to be minimal. Check it out for yourself and see if it suits. The marina is a short taxi ride from Kingstown.

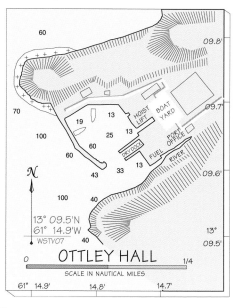
OTTLEY HALL
SCALE IN NAUTICAL MILES
13° 09.5'N
61° 14.9'W
WSTV07

220

Kingstown Harbour, with the cruise ship dock on the right

KINGSTOWN

Kingstown, St. Vincent's capital, is an interesting local town, for those who want to see the authentic, rough edges and all. It has some charming corners with old stone buildings, cobblestone sidewalks, and handsome arches. The older buildings date back to the late 1700s. An unusual feature of the architecture is that many buildings have pillars on the outside of the pavement supporting floors above, leaving a covered walkway underneath. The new market is a fascinating place to shop, despite the building being architecturally challenged, with a gloomy interior. (Designed by a foreigner, it seems to me a strong argument for governments to have more faith in their own people.) It has four floors of stalls and small shops with excellent fresh fruits and vegetables on the ground floor, clothing and handicrafts upstairs.

Attraction in Kingstown include the botanical gardens (you can walk there) and Fort Charlotte for the great views, (take a taxi). Check out the lovely old National Trust building which has a permanent exhibit of Kalinargo pottery.

The new cruise ship facility has a yacht dock at its inner end where superyachts can tie up to clear customs and provision. Facilities for smaller yachts are poor. You can anchor west of the bus station and may find a space to tie up your dinghy at the cruise ship facility. Keep yacht and dinghy guarded. Most yachtspeople currently visit Kingstown by road or ferry. Taxis and buses are readily available from both Young Island Cut and Blue Lagoon, and ferries connect Kingstown with Bequia.

Regulations

Entry here can be longwinded. Customs are in the baggage hall and normally fast, but immigration, down the road at the police station, often has long lines of passport applicants. The system is not designed for yachts. Sam Taxi Service can do it all for you from any anchorage.

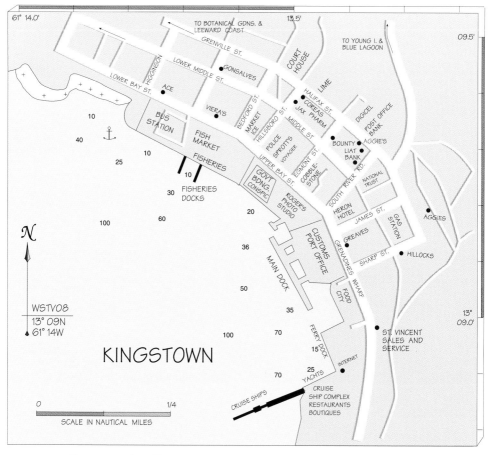

Communications

Internet stations are fast, air-conditioned, and inexpensive. Take your choice between the Port Authority Internet cafe just outside the cruise ship dock (open 0700-1900 daily), and Computec on Egmont Street.

Chandlery

For yacht chandlery, look at our section on Young Island Cut and Blue Lagoon. Of interest in Kingstown is St. Vincent Sales and Services, a modern shop conveniently placed opposite the ferry dock. They are a NAPA jobber, have excellent buys on filters, and make hydraulic hoses while you wait.

For more general hardware, try Ace or Viera, opposite the bus station. They have good buys on silicone seal, 5200, sandpaper, and tools. Sprotts has an excellent selection of tools and household hardware. Trottman's

has a good range of electrical supplies, and you can find several lumber yards, as well as plumbing and hardware stores.

Provisioning

There are many supermarkets to choose from. The biggest and best downtown is C.K. Greaves, which is open 0800 till 1700 Monday to Thursday; to 1900 on Fridays, and from 0700-1300 on Saturdays. Its subsidiary by the airport is open till 2000 nightly, except Thursdays and Fridays when it opens till 2100, and Sundays, when it opens 0800-1100. The Greaves in town gives a charter yacht discount (just tell the cashier) and delivery to Young Island Cut is negotiable for large orders (talk to a supervisor). Products include delicatessen meats, smoked fish, French cheeses, whipping cream, and a good selection of wines and liquors. You can contact them in advance for a full provisioning

Courthouse, Kingstown

service, and if you need anything they do not have, they will buy it for you.

For a more extensive choice of wines, the place to go is Gonsalves Liquor. This state-of-the-art wine and liquor shop is set in a lovely old historic building with a climate-controlled wine room. It is a pleasure to visit. They sell wholesale as well as retail and have a huge selection from all over the world. You can contact them in advance for a list of products. They will deliver to the nearest dock, and their staff can give good advice on their wines. They are open Monday to Friday 0800-1700, and Saturday till 1300.

The Marketing Board's Food City is a large supermarket with some good prices, especially on produce, and the widest selection of root vegetables you are likely to find. The local market is lively and colorful, with many vendors eager to offer you produce.

Aunt Jobe's Market is modern, large, very spaciously laid out, and a pleasant place to shop. It is just outside the downtown area, a ten minutes walk. Head down Grenville Street, turn right on the main road, then head north past the hospital. It is in a mall with plenty of parking. They have an excellent selection of most things, including good produce and delicatessen sections. Ask if you don't see something, because some items like brie cheese and some of the fish may be hard to find. They are open daily from 0700-2130, except Sunday 0700-1400. They also offer full provisioning.

Fun shopping

Shopping in Kingstown can be fun — the stores are all interesting and local. You sometimes find car batteries rubbing shoul-

ders with fabrics. Department stores include Laynes and Jax. Middle Street is quaint and like a local clothing market, with stalls down much of one side.

For boutiques geared to tourists, wander down to the cruise ship complex.

Restaurants

You can choose a lunch spot to suit your mood; we mention just a few. Clean and inexpensive, Bronte Wallace-Singh's Bounty [$D] is perfect for light snacks (rotis and small lunch plates). This little cafeteria-

St. Vincent & the Grenadines

223

WILKIE'S

YOUNG ISLAND

YOUNG ISLAND CUT

style restaurant has lots of charm and it is decorated with local art that is for sale. They also have a handicraft and boutique corner. The Bounty is upstairs on Egmont Street.

Basil's, in the Cobblestone Inn [$C-D], is cool, spacious, and sociable. Here you can get a first-rate lunch buffet, and this is where everyone meets.

Flow is an excellent wine bar with food. It opens weekdays at 1100 and Saturdays at 1800.

The Golden Apple on Halifax Street has good local food. Out on the cruise ship pier are several small lunch places [$D]. You can sit in the open overlooking the bay and take your choice. Mona's is usually open and good for local food.

Aggie's [$D] has two branches: one in town on Halifax Street. The other, just out of town on Town Hill Road, is a short walk away. This is a good home-style restaurant that opens at 0800 in the morning and keeps going till after dinner. They serve good and inexpensive local food and have a big lunch buffet on Wednesdays (town), and Fridays (Town Hill) for $25EC.

Grenadine House [$A-C] is a really nice upmarket restaurant with excellent food. It is part of a hotel and in the same group as Bequia Beach Hotel in Bequia. Take a short taxi ride there. You can walk back.

THE SOUTH COAST OF ST. VINCENT

Navigation

The current along this coast is predominantly westward, up to two knots. It reverses weakly to the east for a few hours on the rising tide, which can create choppy seas.

When leaving Kingstown for Young Island, give the headland good clearance, as there is a submerged rock about 200 feet south of its eastern end.

Two good anchorages lie close together: Young Island Cut and Blue Lagoon. Both are well served by buses and taxis to Kingstown, and are well placed for exploring St. Vincent. These anchorages are within dinghy reach of each other, so read about services and shore facilities for both.

This is the center of yachting in St. Vincent, and several bareboat companies are based here, including Barefoot Yacht Charters, TMM, and Sunsail.

The closest supermarkets and shopping area are near to the airport, a short taxi ride away. Cooking gas is in this area, at the filling station just before the airport.

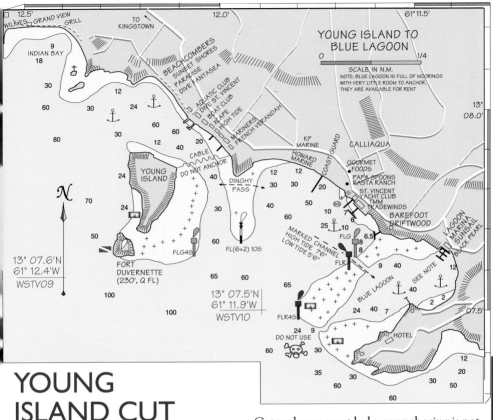

YOUNG ISLAND TO BLUE LAGOON

YOUNG ISLAND CUT

Young Island Cut lies in clear water between Young Island and the mainland. At night the lights of Young Island take on a fairy-tale look. Between here and Blue Lagoon you have a good choice of restaurants.

Young Island Cut is open and easily entered from the west. The channel to the east of Young Island is narrow, curves, and is best given a miss, even with the beacons.

You have to anchor with care. The current sweeps through both ways and the center of the cut goes as deep as 60 feet. There is good holding in the north or western parts of the anchorage, but it occasionally rolls. Anchoring bow and stern is essential or your boat will swing with the change of current and bang into someone else. Holding is poor close to Young Island. Young Island's electrical cable carries 11,000 volts, enough to make your whole boat glow, so anchor well clear or, better still, use a mooring.

Moorings are available in Young Island

Cut and are a great help, as anchoring is not easy. The present system of unauthorized moorings is managed by Sam Taxi Tours and Charlie Tango who both feel that if you rent one of their moorings, you should also take their taxi. To avoid two boats competing for your business when you arrive, call on the VHF and book your mooring in advance. Mooring rates for boats up to 80 feet are $20 US. Charlie charges the same for bigger boats. Sam charges $29 for larger boats. The moorings have proved secure and reliable and many were built to take large yachts.

Young Island Cut is close to Calliaqua and Blue Lagoon, the whole area is within walking or dinghy range, so read both sections.

Regulations

There are no customs in Young Island Cut, Calliaqua, or Blue Lagoon. It is probably worth paying Sam Taxi Tours to clear in for you, as is a major hassle to do it yourself in town.

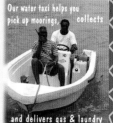
Communications

Sam Taxi Tours has an excellent wifi system that works both in Young Island Cut and Bequia. Beachcombers has internet during normal business hours.

General yacht services

Sam of Sam Taxi Tours [VHF: 68] is one of those who rents moorings. Sam is an agent for large yachts and even cruise ships. With agents in Mustique, Bequia, Canouan and Union, Sam can handle big yacht needs right through the islands. His customs clearance is very popular, and he can arrange it anywhere, even the Tobago Cays (through his agent in Union). Sam charges $80 US for yachts up 80 feet, up to $400 US for really large yachts with many people. (Extra transportation charges are applicable in some anchorages.)

His crew does laundry and fills gas bottles. Sam Taxi Service handles communications (including email) and many skippers get their spares sent here, which Sam will clear through customs. Sam Taxi

Tours also rents cars and has a fleet of taxis for scenic or shopping trips, and he arranges duty-free fuel bunkering for larger yachts. He will collect and dispose of well-wrapped garbage in Young Island ($5 EC a bag).

Charlie Tango [VHF: 68] is the other moorings man; Charlie runs a full taxi and tour service, he has apartments to rent, and will help in any way he can.

Erika's Marine Services is another mega-yacht agency based in Union Island. They, too, have agents in St. Vincent, Bequia, Mustique, and Canouan. (See *Union Island* for a full description.)

Provisioning

The road around the airport is becoming a major shopping area. Sunrise Supermarket, opposite the airport terminal, is the one of the biggest and best markets and is part of C.K. Greaves.

From Greaves, Aunt Jobe's supermarket is on the left heading toward Calliaqua. Next to Aunt Jobe's is a large Ace hardware store. Several more supermarkets are on the

At the Peak

Hiking the volcano

St. Vincent & the Grenadines

Young Island side of the airport. Delco has not only food, but quite a selection of hardware. Another new supermarket lies just round the corner. Trotmans's has a branch of their electrical store a little farther toward the airport on the right side of the road.

In Calliaqua, Gourmet Food has a fair selection, including lots of hard-to-find specialty foods, along with good frozen meat, shrimp, and fish. They offer a complete provisioning service and will work with yachts, though most of their work comes from hotels and restaurants in the Grenadines. They can give you a list of their stock and prices.

In Calliaqua you can sometimes buy fish from the fish market in the afternoon when the boats come in ~ try around 1600. See also *Blue Lagoon*.

Ashore

Young Island Cut has quite a few restaurants. Take your time, wander along, and peruse the menus till you find the one that suits you. Read also about *Blue lagoon*.

If you look west from the anchorage, you will see a large building at the end of the beach, to the west of Young Island Cut, in Indian Bay. This is the Grand View Beach Hotel, one of St. Vincent's grandest traditional hotels, owned by the Sardine family. By day you can walk there by going up the road at the end of the Young Island Cut beach, down the other side to the next beach, then follow the beach. There are a couple of reasons to visit. The Grand View Grill [$C-D closed Mondays], on the beach, is run by Caroline, the artist of the Sardine family. Her excellent paintings are all through Grand View and you can check out her little art gallery below the restaurant. The Grand View Grill opens daily at 1400 and the kitchen stays open till 2200. This is a great place to relax. They serve pizza, pasta, snacks, and grilled meals, including fish, shrimp, and steak. Try to make it on a Friday, when they serve genuine spicy Jamaican jerk food.

Up the hill, the hotel pool has one of St. Vincent's great views from atop a cactusy knoll. This is also the place for a more formal

228

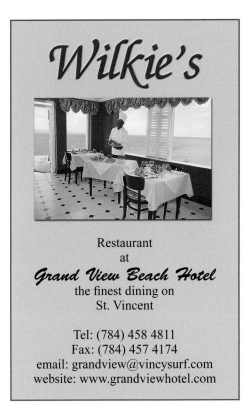

dinner at Wilkie's [$A-B], the hotel's main restaurant. They have a great chef who has an a la carte menu that changes daily. Grand View has squash courts, a gym, and tennis courts available to the public.

Beachcombers [VHF: 68, $B-D] is at the western end of the beach, opposite Young island. It is an intimate and pleasant restaurant: seating is on a deck and the view of the anchorage and sea beyond is framed by almond trees. Delightful flower gardens are in back. Seafood, local specialties, and snacks are available. They open all day every day. Beachcombers has rooms for rent and a popular health spa, with sauna, steam room, Turkish bath, aroma therapy, facials, and a gymnasium.

The French Verandah [$A] at the Mariners is upmarket and excellent: a good place for a special night out. The atmosphere is romantic, with candlelight and the sea. Owner Miguel is originally from France and her French cuisine is superb. You can also get good Indian food. They have a perfect location right on the waterfront and don't mind customers using their dinghy dock on a regular basis.

High Tide [$B-D, closed Monday] is a lovely restaurant with a good dinghy dock. It is owned by the Greaves family and managed by Desiree. They can supply water on the dock, but the depth at the end of the dock is only 4-5 feet. They open most days at 1600, Sundays at noon. They have a huge menu, with everything from salads and snacks (including good rotis) to a full shrimp, steak, or fresh fish meal. They also offer showers; free if you are eating.

Xcape [$C-D] is upstairs in a big old Caribbean building. Tony and Tom, two enterprising Vincentians, run it. You sit open to the breeze with a view over the cut and eat good local food at bargain prices. The lunch menu is inexpensive enough that you might as well eat here as onboard. Friday is party night.

Boat Club [$C-D] is an informal local hangout with music. They open daily from about 0700 till late at night and serve local food with occasional Karaoke and other

St. Vincent & the Grenadines

parties. Their pool table is often in use. Behind Boat Club on the road, Chewees is a popular local hangout, with pool and cheap barbecue food.

Paradise Beach Hotel [$B] is run by Earl and Kim Hallbich, along with their Fantasea tour operation. It is large and open, they serve good local food, and it is a very pleasant place to eat. They have a captain's barbecue on Fridays from 1900. They have rooms for a night or two ashore.

Sunset Shores is a hotel, slightly formal, with a pool just behind the beach. The cooking is a blend of European and Caribbean; local seafood and steaks are both specialties.

Across the water, with a good dinghy dock, Young Island Resort [VHF: 68, $A] is a wonderful place of tropical flowers and trees, and well worth a visit for a sundowner. They have a steel band and other entertainment on a weekly basis (call for details). If you wish to dine at Young Island Resort, make reservations in advance.

Ashore

Fort Duvernette stands behind Young Island, a monument to the ingenuity of the soldiers of a bygone age who managed to get cannons up to the top. Fort Duvernette was used in the late 18th century, when the settlers were fighting off the Black Caribs from inland. Cannons face in both directions. There is a place to tie a dinghy. The 250 steps to the top have been abandoned and you can no longer get to the top.

Water sports

Diving in St. Vincent is really wonderful. The rugged shoreline is equally dramatic below the surface. Walls and reefs that drop far deeper than any sane person can dive are common, fish are everywhere ~ feeding in schools, tucked under rocks, and hiding in sponges. The long coastline and the presence of only a few divers has kept this environment pristine.

Dive St. Vincent [VHF: 68] is run by Padi/Naui instructor Bill Tewes. Bill has been here several decades and is on nodding terms with most of the fish and sea creatures. He had the honor of appearing on a St. Vincent and the Grenadines postage stamp in full diving regalia as part of an underwater series that features his photographs. He is very good at pointing out unusual fish and sea creatures. Bill offers trips to the Falls of Baleine. Charter skippers should know that Bill can pick up a group from a yacht heading north, take them to the Falls of Baleine as the yacht powers up the coast, and deliver them back at the north end of the island.

Glenroy, from Grenadines Dive, has a Dive Center in Lagoon Marina, where he can arrange a dive as well as renting tanks and equipment to charter yachts.

Fantasea Tours has four excellent boats for tours and a water taxi service run by Earl and Kim Halbich. They do coastal and whale-watching trips and often take charter guests to and from their boats in other islands. They are based in Young Island Cut, at the Paradise Beach Hotel, where Fantasea also has a cute boutique.

Those diving on their own will find the base of Fort Duvernette easily accessible, though you do have to be mindful of the current that tries to sweep you out to sea. Anchor your dinghy to the west of the Fort Duvernette dinghy dock. Follow the base of Fort Duvernette down. Almost as soon as you begin you will be surrounded by large schools of brown chromis. At 40 feet you find yourself in a pleasant area of house-sized boulders with nooks and crannies where eels, shrimps, and angelfish hide out. Large schools of sergeant majors hug the rocks, while jacks, mackerels, and schools of margates patrol a little farther out.

Other, even better dives are best done with a local dive shop, as the anchorages are dangerous for yachts and local knowledge about the currents is essential. Bottle Reef under Fort Charlotte starts at 25 feet. You descend along the foot of an underwater rock headland. On your right is a gentle slope of coral, decorated by sponges and many smaller soft corals. On the left, the headland turns into a sheer wall, adorned by deep-water sea fans. There are small bushes of black coral in several colors. At the bottom we found several cherub fish. These little critters, the smallest of the angelfish, are only a couple of inches long. You round the bottom of the headland at 100 feet and

St. Vincent & the Grenadines

ascend through huge schools of grunts and even larger schools of brown chromis that seem to explode into a variety of patterns all around. There is always a chance of finding ancient bottles. A curious current pattern here makes it possible to have the current with you the whole way.

Kingstown South is on the south side of Kingstown Harbor. You can see by looking at the sheer cliffs above and the schooling chromis below that this will be an interesting dive. The descent is down a steep slope, and this is the place to look for the unusual red-banded lobster. This colorful little crustacean is clearly marked in bands and spots of red, white, and gold. Unlike other Caribbean lobsters, it has claws, though they are tiny. We saw one when we finished our descent and three more later, as well as a slipper lobster and the more normal spiny lobster. We circled slowly anti-clockwise up the slope looking at sponges, corals, and big rocks. You often see large pelagic fish swimming out toward the sea. Among the many reef fish you will meet are spotted drums and filefish. There

are also three wreck dives in the harbor. One is an ancient French sailing frigate of which there is not much left, but you might get lucky and find a bottle.

There is a good advanced wreck dive in Camden Park. The Romark, a 160-foot freighter, sits upright on the bottom in excellent condition. It is deep (mast at 55 feet, bottom at 135 feet).

New Guinea Reef is on the east side of Petit Byahaut. This spectacular dive takes you down a wall to 90 feet where large black corals occur in bushes of white, pink, dark green, light green, brown, and red. All three black coral species are here. Fish include black jacks, parrotfish, French angelfish, and occasional sightings of the rather rare frilled goby, frogfish, and seahorses. An overhang near the bottom makes this dive visually spectacular.

BLUE LAGOON

Blue Lagoon is a pleasant anchorage with a beach and plenty of palm trees. You can lie comfortably, protected by land and reef. Large beacons mark the main shoals between Blue Lagoon and Young Island (see sketch chart). These are in fairly shallow water, so do not cut them too fine.

Two large beacons (red and green) mark the entrance channel. Pass between them. The water is deeper a shade north of the center. After that, head straight across the reef into deep water. Depths in the channel vary with the tide, from about five feet nine inches to about seven-and-a-half feet. Call Lagoon Marina on VHF: 68 to ask about the state of the tide. Do not attempt to use the deeper south entrance as it is dangerous and has gotten many a yacht in trouble. You can use the marina or pick up a mooring.

So many moorings fill the bay that there is hardly any room to anchor. The red ones belong to TMM charter company; the ones with a stripe and/or Barefoot painted on them belong to Barefoot Charters. They all stand by on VHF: 68/16. If you take a mooring, you want to be as far over to the eastern side as you can because the southwest of the bay can be choppy.

Communications

Sunsail and TMM have wifi. Barefoot has a single computer for email and other communications.

Chandlery

Barefoot Charters and Marine Center keep a good stock of spares for their boats and will help cruisers if they have a needed part, or they will order parts on request from the catalogs. They work with Budget Marine and Lewis and will bring in anything at catalog price, plus freight. They have a complete surf and kayak shop.

KP Marine, owned by Keith Howard, is the sales and service agent for Yamaha outboards, which in St. Vincent are duty-free. I have found Howard's prices to be among the best. Between KP and Howard Marine (same owner) across the street, you can buy Yamaha and Johnson outboards and Yanmar inboards. KP Marine also stocks general chandlery, with chain, anchors, rope, antifouling paint, resins, West system epoxy, some electronics, and more. Two-stroke outboard oils are available wholesale for those

with large engines. They sell to both local fishermen and powerboat enthusiasts. They are in Calliaqua opposite Howard Marine.

General yacht services

The Lagoon Marina and Hotel [VHF: 68] is a pleasant marina with wide floating docks. It is the base of Sunsail, which operates both the hotel and the docks. Electricity (110/220-volt, 50 cycles) can be arranged at the dock. Top up on water, fuel (both diesel and gasoline), and ice. Services include showers, laundry, and communications. Tradewinds cruises are also based here. You will find a boutique, food store, bar, restaurant, beach bar, dive shop, and canvas shop.

Mary Barnard and Seth run Barefoot Charters and Marine Center [VHF: 68]. They are the only charter company here that has an ASA-accredited sailing school. Their dock is on the outside of the reef, with about 6.5 feet at the end at low tide, and they have about 6 moorings outside and 20 moorings inside. They offer diesel, laundry, water and ice, full communications, a travel agency, and air charter service. They rent reliable moorings ($15 US a night). Barefoot has 5 lovely balconied rooms with views available for nights ashore.

The St. Vincent Yacht Club is outside the reef. Reg and Reggie Adams have built a docking facility along the foreshore to the east of Barefoot. The depth off the dock is about 6 feet on the eastern end and 7 feet on the western end, but the water gets deeper rapidly and deeper-draft boats can come in stern-to on the western part. Multihulls can easily make it on the eastern end and when they finish pulling boulders out, monohulls may get in too, but check out the depths first. The docks have water and electricity and they are building a fuel dock (not quite finished). A dangerous wreck lies just west of the planned fuel dock, so take care. They have a restaurant and shop, and seven very pleasant spacious room for rent, with big balconies overlooking the bay. A haul out suitable for multihulls is planned.

TMM charter company [VHF: 68] is based here and has about 20 reliable moorings in the lagoon, many in the calmer areas, and they can usually rent you one at

YOUNG ISLAND

COASTGUARD

TMM

SVG YACHT CLUB

BAREFOOT
DRIFTWOOD

LAGOON
MARINA

BLUE LAGOON

St. Vincent & the Grenadines

Blue Lagoon

a reasonable rate. They will send a guide to bring you in either reef pass (depending on your depth and the tide), if you call them between 0800 and 1600. Manager John West is happy to give advice and a helping hand to any yachtspeople with problems, as is Miranda in the office. They also manage yachts and will hold faxes.

Technical yacht services

Barefoot Charters and Marine Center has an excellent services center. This includes a large new sail loft run by Phillip Barnard, who really knows about racing sails as well as cruising ones. They sell and service both Doyle and North Sails, and will take care of the measurement and fitting. They repair sails, as well as working with cushions and canvas, can make bimini frames, and have a machine to weld Weblon and True Tarp, so you can get a stitch-free top that does not leak. They can do small onboard weld repairs. They are agents for Harken and can help out with rigging.

Barefoot repairs and maintains all kinds of diesel engine and can do good gel coat matching and cosmetic repairs. In addition, they have an electronics workshop. They are dealers for Raymarine and Tacktic. You can buy new electronics or get your broken units repaired, whatever the make

Howard Marine [VHF: 68] fixes all makes of outboard and they are agents for Johnson. They are happy to fix all diesels, and are agents for Yanmar.

St. Vincent Marine Upholstery and Canvas will repair sails, make new cushions, and any canvas work. It is run by Shem and in Lagoon Marina. He can also help with rigging problems with Kemuel, but any wire or parts will have to be ordered.

Verrol at Nichols Marine has an efficient mechanized workshop where he repairs and reconditions alternators and starter motors in a few hours. They come back look-

ing and working like new. Call him on the telephone and he will come and sort out your problem, wherever you are in St. Vincent. (In Bequia you can leave things for him with GYE.) Verrol's workshop is in Belaire, just behind the airport, which is closer to the south coast than to town. Oscar's Machine Center is a few houses down from Verrol. Oscar is good and can do all manner of jobs on all kinds of metals and can resurface engine blocks or fix your old winches.

If you need a marine surveyor, Joe Brown works not only in St. Vincent and the Grenadines, but also anywhere in the Caribbean. He is Lloyds approved and has his own trawler for visits to other islands.

Transport

Blue Lagoon is a good place to leave your boat while you explore ashore. If you decide to do this by taxi, Robert of Robert Taxi [VHF: 68] is a real gentleman and very reliable. He works with Elvis, who is also good. You can ask about car rentals at the desk.

Provisioning/fun shopping

Blue Lagoon Marina has a small food market and next door the handy Prince and Queen's Boutique sells batiks, local handicrafts, books, and souvenirs, as well as essentials, like suntan cream.

Take a bus or taxi towards the airport for the big supermarkets there.

Restaurants

Barefoot's Driftwood Restaurant and Lounge [VHF: 68, $B-C], is very comfortable, with a touch of elegance, and a great open view south to Bequia. It is run by Leslie and Winston who open daily from 0730 till late evening. They have a big choice of excellent food, with pizzas, salads, pasta, fresh seafood, steak, and chicken. It is sometimes packed in the evening, so to be sure of a table for

eat. drink. *drift*.

restaurant & lounge

Mediterranean cuisine with Caribbean flare
pizza. pasta. grill. enjoy!

Call 456-8999 for reservations
located at Barefoot Yacht Charters, Ratho Mill, St. Vincent

eatdrinkdrift.com

Young Island cut from close to Beachcombers

dinner, make a reservation. If you blow it, you can always eat at the bar.

Black Pearl Restaurant [$B-D], upstairs in Lagoon Marina, has a view over the marina and bay. The bar is a great hangout and the restaurant is good, reasonably priced and open from breakfast to dinner. For lunch you can get anything from soup or a burger to a hearty local meal. The dinner menu has lots of fresh seafood, and a selection of vegetarian and meat dishes.

Flowt Beach Bar [$D, closed Tuesdays] in Lagoon Marina is a shack on the beach, with seats on the sand. They open at noon and keep going till the last person leaves. You can get good local grilled fish, burgers, and chicken, along with chips or vegetables.

Surfside Restaurant [VHF: 68, $B-C], hangs out over the water at the St. Vincent Yacht Club. It is run by Sue, and is open every day from 1100 till 2100. They do pizzas and snacks, along with fish and chicken.

Take a stroll into Calliaqua (just a few steps from St. Vincent Yacht Club) and check out Maryna Bar and Grill [$C-D] in the green building. It is owned by Don Martin who was doing chart check-outs when I first came here and told me what to put in the guides; he still does chart briefings for Sunsail. They open Monday to Saturday from 1000 and serve good snacks and meals, including rotis, seafood chowder, and grilled fresh fish.

Ashore

Blue Lagoon is ideally situated to visit St. Vincent's interior, especially the east coast and the volcano. I would encourage everyone to visit Montreal Gardens in the Mesopotamia Valley. The drive through this rich agricultural valley is reward enough in itself, with spectacular views in every direction. Montreal Gardens, right at the head of the valley against the steep mountains, is spectacular. Owner Tim Vaughn and his team maintain these flower gardens impeccably. There are winding paths, bridges, steps, and a river, all among brilliant tropical flowers. The only sounds are running water and birdsong. He charges a very nominal fee for entry. You could easily enjoy an hour or two here (open December to August).

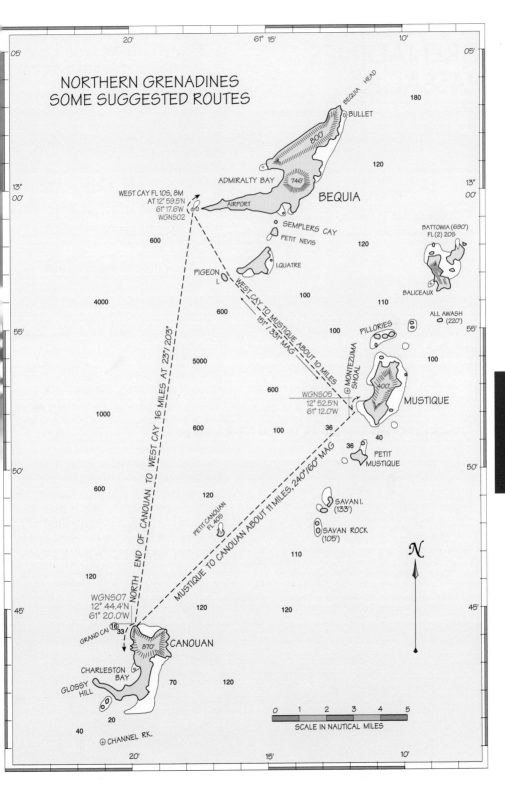

NORTHERN GRENADINES
SOME SUGGESTED ROUTES

BEQUIA HEAD

BULLET

800

180

+

746'

120

WEST CAY FL 10S, 8M
AT 12° 59.5'N
61° 17.6'W
WGNS02

ADMIRALTY BAY

AIRPORT

BEQUIA

SEMPLERS CAY

PETIT NEVIS

BATTOWIA (690')
FL (2) 20S

600

120

PIGEON
I.

I.QUATRE

120

BALICEAUX

+

WEST CAY TO MUSTIQUE ABOUT 10 MILES
151° / 331° MAG

100

110

ALL AWASH
(220')

4000

600

100

PILLORIES

100

5000

600

100

⊕ MONTEZUMA
SHOAL

400'

100

1000

600

100

WGNS05
12° 52.5'N
61° 12.0'W

36

MUSTIQUE

40

36

PETIT
MUSTIQUE

NORTH END OF CANOUAN TO WEST CAY 16 MILES AT 23° 203°

600

120

SAVAN I.
(133')

MUSTIQUE TO CANOUAN ABOUT 11 MILES, 240°/60° MAG

PETIT CANOUAN
FL 40S

SAVAN ROCK
(105')

110

N

120

120

120

WGNS07
12° 44.4'N
61° 20.0'W

120

120

GRAND CAI
33

16

CANOUAN

870'

CHARLESTON
BAY

70

120

GLOSSY
HILL

20

40

⊕ CHANNEL RK.

0   1   2   3   4   5

SCALE IN NAUTICAL MILES

St. Vincent & the Grenadines

NORTHERN GRENADINES PASSAGES

Bequia and Mustique, in the northern Grenadines, are both frequently visited by yachtspeople. Although only about eight miles apart geographically at their closest points, they are very different from each other.

Navigation

A strong current sets to the west throughout the Grenadines. Its effect is particularly noticeable in the Bequia and Canouan channels, so whether you head north or south, it is advisable to point east of your destination and check your bearings periodically to see how much you are being set. There is least set when the tidal stream runs counter to the regular current, but this is a mixed blessing since the seas become rougher, and sometimes positively uncomfortable. The roughest seas are to be found just north of Canouan and off the Bequia side of the Bequia Channel, especially up by Bequia Head. It is not unusual for the current to be going in two different directions on opposite sides of the channel.

St. Vincent to Bequia

The passage from Young Island Cut and Blue Lagoon in St. Vincent to Bequia is usually pleasant, off-the-wind sailing. It is closer to the wind if you are coming from the west coast.

Although Admiralty Bay is hidden till you get quite close, you can usually see the headland that you have to round, because it stands out against the more distant land behind. Look behind you to see which way you are being set by the current, and make adjustments so you stay on course. Big seas can lead to a little exciting surfing, and one often covers the eight or nine miles in about an hour and a half. Be prepared for the Bequia Blast after the lee of Devil's Table. Many drop their sails here, but if you fancy an exhilarating short beat, keep going. When approach-

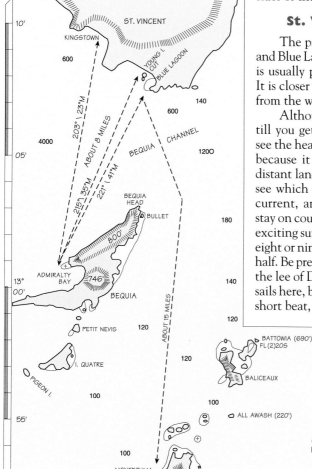

ST. VINCENT TO BEQUIA AND MUSTIQUE

ing Devil's Table, you might notice what appears to be a madman zooming around your yacht, standing up in a tiny inflatable and being badly bounced by the waves. Fear not, it is just Kenmore Henville, who makes his living taking photographs of arriving yachts. If he takes your yacht's picture, he will bring a proof for you to see. There is no obligation to buy. If you want to be sure of a picture, call him in advance.

Sailing the other way is a different matter. To make Young Island or Blue Lagoon from Admiralty Bay, you normally have to tack to windward against a foul current. It usually takes two hours and can take three or more. It is generally quicker to tack or motor sail up the Bequia coast and then shoot across from Anse Chemin, the bay just southwest of Bequia Head. This is fine in calm weather, but on rough days you can sail straight into a range of liquid mountains near Bequia Head. If the seas are rough, head straight over to St. Vincent and then work back up the coast.

Sailing to the west coast of St. Vincent is usually a fine reach.

St. Vincent to Mustique

The trip between St. Vincent and Mustique is about 15 miles, and in good going it takes two and a half to three hours. The seas around the north end of Bequia can be very rough, but one often gets an exhilarating reach. Whether you are sailing north or south, keep well off Bequia Head and the Bullet, as the current pulls you down that way. Otherwise, just strap everything down, hang on tight and ride 'em!

Bequia to Mustique

Most people approach Mustique from

Admiralty Bay. The easiest way is to round West Cay and sail out between Pigeon Island and Isle de Quatre. As you approach Mustique, Montezuma Shoal is a real danger, more so now since the big beacon washed away and has been replaced by a buoy. Keep well clear.

There are passages between Semplers Cay and Petit Nevis, and between Petit Nevis and Isle de Quatre, but they can be very rough and the current extremely rapid. Furthermore, there is a reef extending well south of Petit Nevis, so serious thought should be given to prevailing conditions before choosing either of these routes. It is an easy seven-mile reach from Friendship Bay to Mustique or back.

Bequia to Canouan

As you round West Cay (Bequia) and head south, it will be possible to see Petit Canouan. If the visibility is good, Canouan itself will be in sight. Glossy (Glass) Hill, the southwestern point of Canouan, is joined to the rest of the land by a low isthmus that stays below the horizon till you get quite close, so from a distance Glossy Hill appears as a separate island.

Mustique to Canouan

This trip can be a rolly run, with the wind right behind. I often tack downwind to make it a reach.

Canouan

Deep draft vessels (over 12 feet) should avoid Grand Cai, a small, isolated 16-foot shoal about 0.75 miles west of Jupiter Point at 12° 44.490'N, 61° 20.645'W. Seas in this area are often 6-8 feet high.

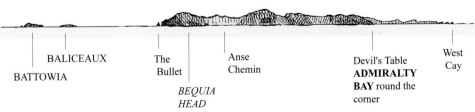

BALICEAUX		The	Anse		Devil's Table	West
BATTOWIA		Bullet	Chemin		**ADMIRALTY**	Cay
		BEQUIA			**BAY** round the	
		HEAD			corner	

Approaching Bequia from St. Vincent

St. Vincent & the Grenadines

Bequia at a glance

Regulations

Port Elizabeth is a port of entry for St. Vincent and the Grenadines. The procedure is simple. Customs is open weekdays 0830-1800 (overtime after 1600). On Saturdays, they open 0830-1200 and (overtime) 1500-1800. Sundays and holidays, they open (overtime) 0900-1200 and 1500-1800.

The entry charge is $35 EC per person per month, unless you leave within that month, in which case you pay again when you reenter. In addition, charter yachts based outside St. Vincent are charged $5 EC per foot per month plus a $125 occasional license fee. You can cruise here as long as you wish. You will normally be stamped in for a month, and then return for extensions, which are in the same office and easy to obtain. Forms may cost a few dollars.

Overtime fees are Sundays/holidays customs: $63 EC, immigration $50 EC, other days: customs: $45 EC, immigration $35 EC.

Jet skis and the like are strictly forbidden throughout the Grenadines, as is spearfishing by visitors (see also *St. Vincent*).

Garbage must be taken to the facility by the market, or you can pay Daffodil to take it. Do not give it other vendors.

Shopping Hours

Office and bank hours are as for St. Vincent. Most stores open from 0800-1200 and from 1400-1700.

Telephones

Card and coin phones may be found near the tourist office. You can buy cell phone cards in lots of stores. See also *St. Vincent*.

Holidays

See *St. Vincent*.

Transport

Inexpensive buses run to many parts of the island. (Ask in the little tourist office on the quay.) Taxis are plentiful and reasonable. Sample taxi rates for up to four people are:

	$EC
Most rides	20
Longer rides	25-40
Tours	81 per hour

(5+ $6 US per person, per hour)

Rental jeeps and motorbikes are available. You need to buy a local license, which costs $65 EC. Drive on the left.

Easter regatta, Lower Bay

Bequia

Bequia has long been a favorite of yachtspeople. Isolated enough to remain relatively unspoiled, yet lively enough to be stimulating and entertaining, it provides a blend of the old and new that many find perfect. It is well connected with St. Vincent and the other Grenadines, both by the new airport and by the cheaper and more traditional ferries. Some yachtspeople leave their boats anchored in Bequia and take a ferry over to visit St. Vincent.

Bequia is an island of sailors and boats, linked to the outside world mainly by the sea. The old traditions continue. Boats are built on the beach in the shade of palm trees. Everything from little "two bow" fishing boats

to grand schooners is built by eye, using only simple hand tools. Bequians travel all over the world on cargo vessels, and quite a few have ended up owning their own. Some are intrepid fishermen who venture all over the Grenadines in little open boats.

The island has an active whaling station in a low-key and traditional way. By IWC agreement, local whalers can take four whales a year, but in some years they do not get any. The whaling season is from February and April. At this time of year, humpback whales leave their northern feeding grounds and head south to mate and bear young. Few people are left in Bequia with the skills necessary to hunt them ~ a daring feat in

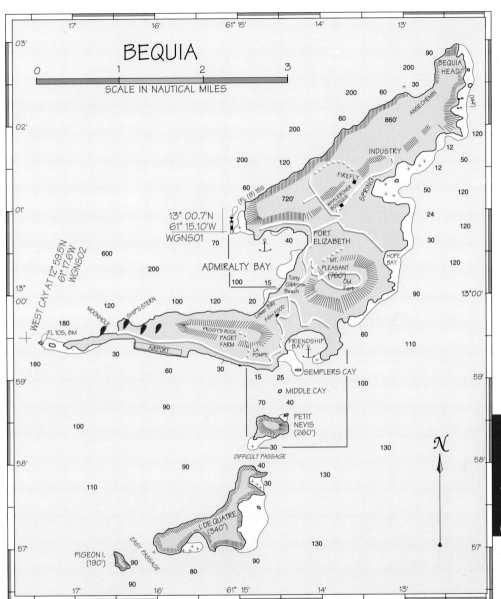

an open sailing boat, using hand-thrown harpoons. On the rare occasions that they make a kill, the hunters tow the whale to Semplers Cay for butchering.

Much of Bequia's tourist industry is based on visiting yachts, so you will find good yacht services, restaurants, shops, and handicrafts. Best of all, Bequia people understand yachting.

Bequians are a proud people, descendants of settlers who came from North America on whaling boats, from farms in Scotland, from France as freebooters, and as slaves from Africa.

Bequia's main harbor is Admiralty Bay. There is a harbor on the south coast called Friendship Bay and a daytime anchorage at Petit Nevis.

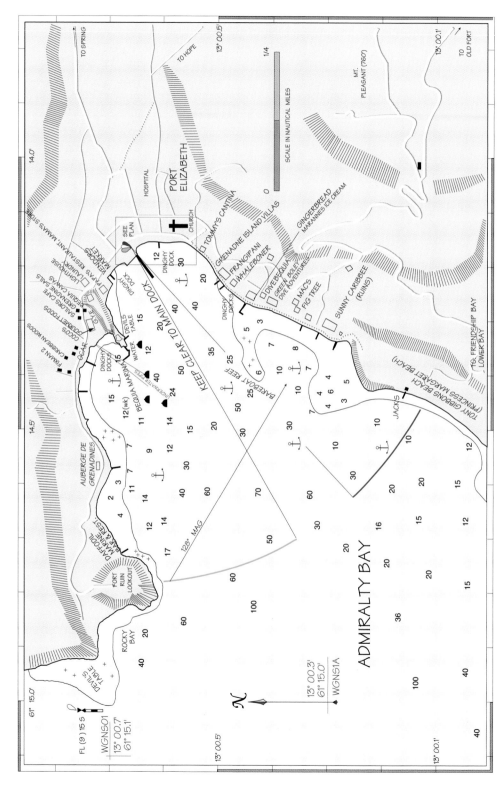

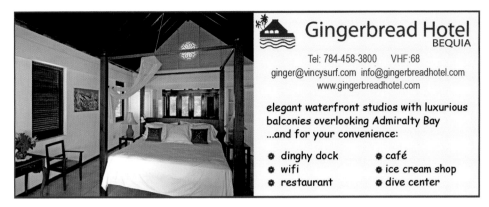

ADMIRALTY BAY

Admiralty Bay is a huge, well-protected bay with Bequia's only town, Port Elizabeth, at its head. Small hotels, bars, restaurants, and shops spread from town along both shores, strung together in the south by a path that runs along the shore. Several yacht services are grouped together in Ocar on the northern shore. Others are in Port Elizabeth. Good dinghy docks are spaced around the bay.

Navigation

The entrance to Admiralty Bay is straightforward. As you approach from the north, the bay begins to open up, and you can see two fine beaches, Lower Bay and Tony Gibbons (aka Princess Margaret) Beach, separated by a distinct headland. East of Tony Gibbons Beach, from the Sunny Caribbee into town, it becomes more built up.

When approaching, allow plenty of room for Devil's Table, which extends a good way from shore; it is marked by a yellow and black beacon. Once in the harbor, take care not to hit the shoals that lie offshore between the eastern end of Tony Gibbons Beach and the Green Boley. Yachts anchor inside some of these shoals, so it looks like tempting empty space. If entering at night, avoid the unlit, heavy metal buoys near Bequia Marina. These are used for big ship tie-ups, and two of the smaller ones have hoses running underwater to the shore.

Anchor well clear of the local ferry channel to the main dock. The ferries are large and need plenty of turning room. Keep out of their way at all times. Yachts may not tie up to the ferry dock or the dinghy dock.

There are many places to anchor. Some choose a spot up in town, off the Frangipani Hotel. The water is deep, and it takes lots of anchor line and sometimes a couple of tries to get hooked in the muddy sand.

The area by Bequia Marina is calm. Avoid anchoring on the wreck that is at 13° 00.67'N, 61° 14.47'W and another (Tail

St. Vincent & the Grenadines

Wagger) a few hundred feet farther east. They both have at least 12 feet of water over them, but have tied up many an anchor. Avoid anchoring on the underwater fuel pipes that run from below Cocos to two of the smaller buoys. Some yachts anchor off the Old Fig Tree and the Sunny Caribbee. This area is mainly 8 to 10 feet deep, shoaling toward the shore, shoaling outwards from the western headland and from the Gingerbread. Shallow draft boats can go practically anywhere here, but those with deeper draft need to use caution.

Sometimes this is a beautiful spot, calm as a lake, the water decorated with floating pink blossoms from the white cedar trees that line the shore. Yet in times of bad northerly swells, it is untenable. The banks on both sides of the harbor (8-20 feet) contain patches of hard sand and dead coral, which makes for poor holding. You need to let out ample chain and make sure you are well hooked.

Tony Gibbons Beach is one of the easiest and prettiest anchorages, yet within a reasonable dinghy ride to town. Holding is good in sand close to the beach. It occasionally becomes rolly in northerly swells, when landing a dinghy on the beach can be hazardous. The new dinghy dock at Jack's helps. Lower Bay is also easy and picturesque, though a little farther away and more subject to swells.

Moorings are available, and the usual charge is $50 EC per night. They are uncontrolled and (except Daffodil's) without legal standing. The customs office posts a warning about them. Some are better than others. Some people know Bequia well and trust a particular mooring owner. For a stranger, it is a problem. I have dived on many of them and have found most poorly designed and executed, and they break free quite often. In general, I do not trust them. On the other hand they sometimes hold better than the way some bareboats anchor. If you take one, snorkel on it to make sure it is okay. Ask for a receipt, or at least know to whom you are

paying money. The moorings on the south side, on the bank off the fig tree are occasionally untenable in bad northerly swells, which usually arrive in the middle of the night. If you anchor close to an empty illegal mooring, you cannot be made to move. Similarly, if you take a mooring and an anchored boat swings too close, you must move if they were there first. Rely on your judgment: the vendors are **only** interested in collecting the fee. Keep this in mind when they give you advice about shore services. Daffodil, Phat Shag, African, and Bequia Dive Ventures probably check their moorings more often than most.

Regulations

Port Elizabeth is a port of entry. Customs and immigration, along with the post office, are in a comfortable office right behind the ferry dock. Formalities are simple ~ just one single-sheet form, or better still, preclear on line with easeaclear.com. Customs opens weekdays at 0830-1800 (overtime after 1600). On Saturdays, they open 0830-1200 and (overtime) 1500-1800. Sundays and holidays (all overtime) they open 0900-1200, and 1500-1800. Fees are given in *Bequia at a Glance* (page 241).

There is a five-knot speed limit in the harbor. This applies to dinghies, tenders, and water taxis, as well as to yachts and ships. If you need to speed into town, do so only in the main shipping channel in the center of the harbor. Currently, small, fast boats are the most serious danger to life and limb in this harbor. We have already had one death and several bad accidents. Is five minutes worth it?

Communications

In many cases you can email from your yacht with wifi. But if you go to an internet place, most are air-conditioned, and many will help you with overseas calls, either net-to-phone or via the operator, at rates that are better than the public phones.

Bay-wide wifi comes from Sam Taxi

DEVIL'S TABLE

ADMIRALITY BAY

TONY GIBBONS BEACH

(RMS), Bequia Tech, HotHotHotSpot (ACS), and Mega network. Most signals are now good. Sam is also available in Young Island Cut. HotHotHotSpot is available in many other islands.

The Fig Tree, Maria's French Terrace, Whaleboner and Sail Relax Explore have free wifi for customers, as does Gingerbread. Frangipani has wifi, but may charge.

When you need a computer, RMS, run by Ros, is conveniently placed just opposite the market and very close to the market dinghy dock. Ros has eight computers. RMS is also a digital photo center where you can download and print digital pictures, as well as make posters and burn CDs. Ros does customs brokerage, photocopying, phone and fax, typing, laminating, and creating cards and flyers. She rents Digicel phones and sells the cards to go with them. Ros is the agent for Sam Taxi tours, a main yacht agent for St. Vincent and the Grenadines, which handles the big boats, from customs clearance (even in the Cays or Cumberland) to arranging fuel bunkering. On the taxi side, they have both regular Bequia truck taxis

and a larger, air-conditioned bus.

Bequia Land and Home also has a good internet section. You can sit at their computers or bring your own.

Campbell's Bequia Technology Center (look for the Digicel signs), next to Andy's, has a savvy owner and has a bank of computers. They also do phone, fax, software engineering, CD creation, photo work, and more.

ACS Computer Services runs the HotHotHot Spot wifi system. Owner Antoinette is a certified network engineer. ACS is next to Coco's Place, but it can be hard to find it open.

General yacht services

Bequia Marina (VHF:16 sometimes) is open to the general public for docking and water. They can take yachts up to 150 feet long and 4 meters draft (stern to). Electricity is 110-volt 30-amp, 240-volt 50-amp, 3-phase 100-amp, 50 Hz. They are open 0800-1600, Monday to Saturday.

Daffo at Daffodil's Marine Services has made a name for herself with a great alongside water, fuel, ice and laundry delivery

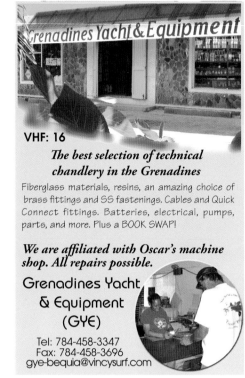
system. Nowhere in the Caribbean is this easier. Just give her a call [VHF: 67] and the service boats arrives right alongside. For laundry and ice delivery or garbage pick-up, they will send a smaller boat. Daffodil usually carries block ice as well as cubes. Her laundry is fast, efficient, and properly washed and dried.

Miranda also collects and delivers laundry. She does a good job and can be reached at Miranda's Laundry [VHF: 68].

You can also call Lighthouse Laundry [VHF: 68] for laundry pickup. They have a big laundry by the power station and have showers for a fee. Handy Andy has machines where you can do laundry yourself.

Grenadine Yacht Equipment fills cooking gas bottles, including French ones. It takes overnight. Cube ice may be found at the Gingerbread Cafe and the Frangipani.

You can go alongside a low-sterned vessel, Kingfisher [VHF: 09], which acts as a floating fuel dock selling water, ice, and Venezuelan diesel. The Venezuelan Diesel has about the same sulfur content as local, but it arrives in fishing boats whose tanks can

be dirty. Orton King, who is selling the fuel, filters it with a 20-micron filter. Some boats use this fuel regularly and have no problems (it is cheaper). It should work if your motor filters are 20 microns or more, but watch out if you use finer filters. The saving in price will not be enough to cover new filters and mechanic's fees.

When it comes to garbage in Bequia, please continue to observe the following: put your garbage in the big dumpsters near the head of the market dinghy dock (no charge). Or call Daffodil Marine any time and they will collect it from you at a charge of either $3 EC (small bag) or $5 EC (large bag). They take it to the main dump, not to town. Never accept offers from anyone else to "take your garbage!"

African (Winston Simmons) looks after boats when people go away and can organize work to be done on them. He will also help with provisioning or anything else. He does deliveries, has a charter cat, and rents moorings (593-3986, VHF:68).

Local water taxis are painted brightly and bear such names as Outernet, African,

McCarthy, and Radio. Just call any water taxi on VHF: 68. Charges for 1-4 people are: in the harbor or to Princess Margaret Beach, $20 EC; Lower Bay, $25 EC. Try to choose water taxi drivers who drive slowly and carefully. Try Didi 455-5681, African 593-3986, or McCarthy 495-3425. McCarthy provides an excellent service every morning by delivering bread around the anchorage from around 0700. He is a low-key salesman, so you will have to watch out for him and give him a shout, or call him on VHF: 68. Vendors sell lobster.

Superyachts requiring help can check with RMS in Bequia (see *Communications*), or they can contact Erika's Marine Services in Union. Verna May, Erika's Bequia representative, is very helpful and easy to deal with.

Bequia is the home of *Caribbean Compass*, the Caribbean's best, waterfront paper. Pick up your free copy practically anywhere around town.

Chandlery

Bequia has several places to buy chan-dlery and fishing gear. Happily, they all seem to use completely different suppliers, so the range is pretty good. Make the rounds and check the best buys. What you don't find in one, you will probably get in the next, and find cheaper in the third, just after you've already bought it.

Grenadine Yacht and Equipment (GYE) [VHF: 16] has a yacht chandlery that is especially good on technical things, including an excellent stock of brass pipe fittings, stainless steel fastenings, resins, electrical bits, and a huge stock of batteries, Danforth anchors, marine accessories, and parts. This is a good place to get your gas bottles filled. It is connected with Oscar's Machine Shop in St. Vincent and they will accept work for him (see *Technical yacht services*). They also have a bookswap.

Wallace & Co., right in town, is both a duty-free chandlery and a fishing store. They are the Icom agent and carry a full range, down to small, waterproof, hand-held VHF radios. They also sell rope, blocks, shackles, stainless yacht hardware, stainless chain, Delta anchors, fenders,

St. Vincent & the Grenadines

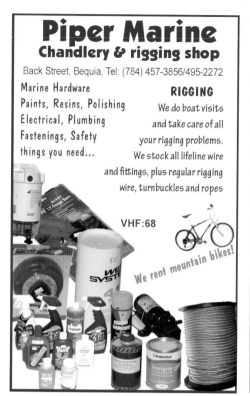
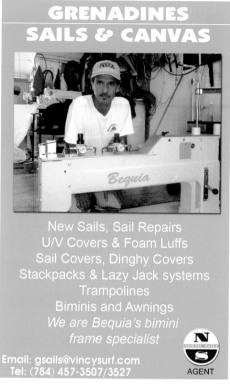
flags, West System epoxy, and first-rate safety gear. There is often new and interesting stock. This is also an excellent fishing store, with numerous lures, rods, and both Penn and Shimano reels (sales and service). Jergen and Bip both have biology backgrounds and will give you good advice on lures and rigs. In addition, they stock snorkeling gear and some diving equipment.

Piper Marine store, under Alick's sail loft, is another interesting chandlery. Piper has an excellent stock of cleaning products and consumables, plus lots of general chandlery, including cloth and West System epoxy, pumps, lights, safety gear, and much more. Piper rents mountain bikes, and he is a rigger (see *Technical yacht services*).

Lulley's Tackle Shop is upstairs in the Courts building. You should wander up here and take a look. This is the oldest fishing shop in Bequia, and it is still used by many of the island's professional fishermen. It has a wide range of fishing gear, snorkeling gear, and knives. They carry heavy commercial gear as well as sporting equipment. They have a vast variety of lures, and you can get ready-made tackle that is very easy to use, as well as rods.

Caribbean Woods sells South American hardwoods and has a good woodworking shop as well, where Cliff will cut that special bit of wood to size or make you a fancy book shelf. Upstairs is an excellent paint shop with paints, fillers, sandpaper, and resins, as well as good tools, including power sanders, bits, and cutting blades.

For general hardware, check out Bequia Venture.

Technical yacht services
Sails/Canvas/Cushions

Several places do sail and canvas work and all are good. Grenadines Sails is owned by Avell Davis, a Bequian who has spent years making sails in Bequia and Canada. His shop is close by Bequia Marina. Avell is the North Sails representative and works with Andrew Dove out of Guadeloupe to get you a fast quote for a new North Sail. Avell has the widest range of experience, from traditional, handmade sails to modern, high-tech ones. New awnings, covers, and alterations can

easily be done in the loft. Avell does excellent biminis and bimini frames.

Bequia Canvas, near GYE does just about everything but sails: interior and exterior cushions, awnings, boat covers, dinghy covers, and biminis. It is an efficient operation run by Chris Lochner from Germany and Norrell from Bequia. They keep a wide range of materials, including closed-cell foam. Wander by and you might find just the tote bag or ditty hanger you have been looking for. You can also call them on the phone and arrange for Chris to come to your yacht to discuss a job.

Alick [VHF: 68] is in Port Elizabeth, on a back street, not too far from the town dinghy dock. Alick is low key, personable, thorough, and reasonably priced. You can ask him about new sails, awnings, cushions, and covers. Alick (who trained under Lincoln Simmonds) is an excellent man to tackle that devilish splice in one of those new ropes. He will even show you how to do it. At his store he keeps a stock of fabrics, foams, and webbing, which you can buy for your own project.

Technical yacht services
Other Services

Don Lewis at the chandlery Piper Marine [VHF: 68] is the man to fix your rigging problems. He carries rigging wire, a full range of life-line wire, and press fittings. He will be happy to come to your yacht where he will get his nephew, Jason, to go up the mast to do whatever is needed. He lives on a sailboat himself. Give him a call or drop by the shop.

Just down the road from Wallace & Co., you will find Robin of Simpson Engineering, aka Fixman 2 [VHF: 68]. Robin came into mechanics from working on racing cars in England and is good with gas engines, diesels and their associated electrics. But he is also a generalist, so you see washing machines, outboard motors, shiny engine innards, and more in his workshop. He is the man in Bequia for stainless and aluminum welding and for machining. He is an excellent choice for almost any problem except refrigeration.

KMS Marine Services [VHF: 68] is run by Kerry Olliviere from Mount Pleasant.

Kerry worked for many years for various charter companies where he learned to fix everything that usually goes wrong: diesel engines, starters, alternators, outboards, refrigeration, watermakers, electrical gadgets, and, of course, heads, macerator pumps and plumbing. Kerry can weld, and is often asked to install solar panels. He works closely with GYE and can arrange high tech welding and machining through them in St. Vincent.

Alan Reynolds of Yachtfix at Daffodil Marine is another excellent generalist who can turn his hand to almost anything. His background is in electronics, and while he can help with them, he does not have spares. He will be excellent at solving your electrical problems and he is a first rate mechanic, both diesel and outboard. If that were not enough he also built Daffodil's fine deck for her restaurant. You can often find him over there.

Sam Saville of Knock Refrigeration provides excellent service for both refrigeration and air-conditioning. You will find him two doors up from GYE, or call him on his cell: 529-1682.

Tyrone Caesar at Caribbean Diesel [VHF: 68] spent nine years as an engineer on cargo carriers and several more working for large organizations such as Cummins. He is a well-trained diesel mechanic, especially with Perkins, Northern Lights, Detroit Diesels, GMs, and Yanmars. You often find him along the waterfront. Go chat with him and see if he is the man for your job.

Oscar has an excellent machine shop in St. Vincent, with full machining, milling, and turning gear, and he can fix just about anything, as well as welding stainless and aluminum. He owns GYE in Bequia. Oscar is near Verrol Nichols of Nichols Marine, the starter and alternator magician (Verrol will fix anything and send it back looking like new). You can arrange to leave work for either of these specialists at GYE, or get KMS Marine Services to come and deal with it for you.

Winfield Sargeant and his team come well recommended for varnishing, handpainting, cleaning, and polishing. Winfield comes by in his own launch. It is easiest to contact him by VHF: 68 or by phone.

Handy Andy is a good, two-part poly-

St. Vincent & the Grenadines

Porthole ▮ᵥ▮ Shoreline
Restaurant & Bar   Mini Market

Your corner store & restaurant
Fine Wines, Rotis & Wholewheat Bread

Apartments for rent - sea view

Dinner by reservation

Full Meals
soups
lobster
steak
fresh fish
Rotis
snacks

Phone: (784) 458 3458, Fax: (784) 457 3420
We open Monday to Saturday, early morning
till late at night. Need us on Sunday? Call:
(784) 458 3636

urethane spray painter. He can still occasionally be persuaded to tackle a job. Bequia also has many shipwrights and carpenters.

Provisioning

Bequia is quite a good place to stock up on provisions. Doris Fresh Foods [VHF: 68/16] is almost legendary in Bequia. It is a great, air-conditioned supermarket on the back street where you will find excellent cheeses and deli foods, good wines, local chutney, gourmet items, and good, fresh produce. You will not find a better selection of frozen meats. Baked goodies include 8-grain bread, which tastes good and keeps well, making it popular with those setting out to sea. Fresh French bread is baked daily in season, as are croissants and fancy pastries. Among my favorites here are the packets of delicious frozen conch and callaloo soup. So far, Doris has been unmatched for variety and availability of harder-to-find foods.

Noeline Taylor's Shoreline mini-market is associated with her Porthole restaurant, so you can shop from early in the morning to late at night. If you see it closed, just ask in the restaurant and Noeline will open it for you. You can pull your dinghy up on the beach just outside, making it convenient for carrying cases of beer. It is well stocked with most things, including wine, French baguettes, and whole-wheat bread baked daily. Shoreline closes on Sundays, but if you need to provision, you can always call and they will open it for you.

Eileen's Market is a super little specialty shop run by Eileen from L'Auberge, and set under the restaurant. They cut fresh fish (and some meat) into small portions and vacuum bag and freeze it for you so it is all ready to go. Their selection includes lobster, conch, snapper, king fish, yellow fin tuna, mahi mahi and more. They have some nice deli items and specialty foods.

Mama's in the restaurant Papa's, has a giant walk-in freezer and cooler and stocks good cheeses, wines, and meats. You can buy your wine here, pay corkage, and have it for dinner in Papa's.

Farther down the road, O. King, the beer wholesaler has the best buys in cases of beer.

Knight's Trading is one of the older and larger of the Bequia supermarkets. They stock almost everything except fresh produce, and their prices are often good. They will deliver to the dinghy dock. You can do one-stop shopping here, as upstairs they have a lumber/hardware/electrical store. Knight's has a smaller outlet on Front Street.

Euroshopper has a small outlet on the back street by Alick's sail loft.

Select Wines, next to the Bistro, has a well-organized and large selection of wine, soft drinks, beer, cheese, meat, French bread, and lots of specialty items like chocolate-covered hazelnuts. In addition, they have a fair selection of regular canned and dried foods. They open from about 0800 to 2200, so it is almost never too late to shop.

Bequia Foodstore offers a good selection of canned and dry goods. It is open daily from 0800-2000, making it convenient for late shopping.

In the Shoreline Plaza, Lina's is a great little bakery/delicatessen. They bake several times a day and have a whole selection of

good bread, both yeast and sourdough. They sell Danish, pain au chocolat, and more. Get a cup of excellent coffee here in the morning and sit outside under the umbrellas. Return for a lunchtime sandwich. Lina's also offers specialty foods, including the Caribbean's widest selection of pepper (the spice).

Gourmet Foods, under Coco's, sells wine, frozen meats and vegetables, deli foods, and specialty foods, wholesale and retail. It is a branch of the larger store in Calliaqua, has some tables outside, and serves good sandwiches and croissants.

You can buy fruits and vegetables in the market. The selection is good, but high-pressure Rasta salesmanship has driven many locals and regulars to Doris, or to the quieter stalls you will find dotted around the main street. (Check out the notice painted on the wall of the market.)

The Gingerbread Cafe has baked goods, coffee, and a few other items. Maranne's has yogurt and homemade ice cream.

In Lower Bay, Nature Zone is a small organic garden run by Jacqueline Meleno. You can find a few fresh items here, straight from the garden.

Fun shopping

The waterfront in Port Elizabeth is colorful, with vendors selling t-shirts, model boats, and handicrafts in the market, and along the street.

The building of model boats has been a Bequia specialty for generations. Craftsmen will build any design to order, but all-time favorites are the model whaling boats, both full and half models. They are artfully built and beautifully painted. Check out Mauvin's, near the market, or Sargeant's, closer to Bequia Marina.

More recently, Kingsley has taken the coconut boat tradition to the level of real artistry with his glossy coconut boats. You

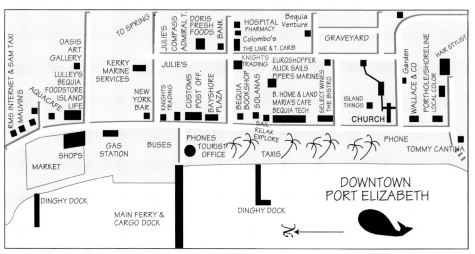

DOWNTOWN
PORT ELIZABETH

can see some at the Oasis Art Gallery which also features the wonderful art of L.D. Lucy, as well as having special exhibits of visiting artists and local craftspeople. They normally open after about 1000, but if you want to be sure, give L.D Lucy a call (497-7670).

Bequia has a wide range of small, pleasant boutiques. The new market has its own dinghy dock. Many shops here sell t-shirts, souvenirs, and gifts, and there is an ice cream shop and a bar.

Zilla's Island Life (well, the sign may still say Island Style if Zilla has not got round to changing it), is a wonderful Aladdin's cave with everything from furniture to pareos. The products they bring in are cool, and while you could fill a house here, you can also find just what you needed to decorate the boat, and a lot of it is very reasonably priced. There is jewelry, decorative boxes, fancy hats, pareos, wooden bowls, and many handy serving trays from Bali.

One part contains art by Pinky, an excellent local artist, including paintings (some hang in my boat), hand-painted calabashes, decoration, and clothing. Zilla also sells our cruising guides.

Solana's, run by Carmette and Solana, is packed with hand-painted t-shirts, shorts, and batik work, as well as handicrafts, jewelry, books, videos, flags, phone cards, and maps. Solana's is also the Federal Express agent, and they sell Digicel cards. Buy second-hand books here, and the money will go to help local children. They also have a lovely house for rent overlooking Tony Gibbons Beach.

The Bequia Bookshop is well laid out

and spacious, with an excellent range of nautical books and charts, local books, videos, and novels. They also sell postcards, and art by local artists, including the popular Caron Nichols. Scrimshaw, locally hand-crafted by Sam McDowell, is on display, as are sailors' valentines, made by Sam's wife, Donna.

Manager Cheryl J. also runs Sweety Bird, a garden cafe out back with elegant teas, coffee, fresh juices, and a great lunch at local prices. A good place to read the novel you have just bought, or wait for the

St. Vincent & the Grenadines

ferry. Cheryl has a reading club for kids every other Saturday and always needs volunteers to help the kids. If you are interested, ask her about it.

In the Bayshore Mall you can find boutiques, a barber, and a travel agent.

Sail Relax Explore has hammocks, great canvas bags, cushions, sail bags, and underwater cameras.

Island Things, by the church, has the best range of souvenirs and small crafted household items. Garden Boutique, nearby, has batik.

Upstairs in the churchyard, behind Island Things is a fascinating rattan furniture shops, all made in Guyana. They also sell hammocks and many baskets.

In a spacious upstairs location, Local Color has both a good collection of clothing and a selection of handicrafts.

Along the waterfront, the Whaleboner Boutique sells handmade clothing from screened and batik fabrics; they also sell shorts and locally made model boats. The real treat is to visit their new silk-screen factory, shop, and bar on the road to Spring (on the way to the turtle sanctuary). Here you can see the fabric being silk screened upstairs and buy fabric and clothing in the shop. Owner Angela Hinkson is often around, but otherwise Xavier will look after you.

The Green Boley Boutique has colorful appliqué pictures, locally made clothes, and souvenirs.

Restaurants

The waterfront has a wonderful mixture of bars and restaurants. The Frangipani

Hotel [$A-B, VHF: 68, closed September] is owned by Son Mitchell, ex- Prime minister of St. Vincent and the Grenadines, and has been in his family since the turn of the last century. The upper floor of the main building used to be the family home and downstairs was the storehouse for the Gloria Colita, which, at 131 feet long, was the largest schooner ever built in Bequia. In 1940, she disappeared at sea and was later found drifting empty in the Bermuda triangle. Today Son's daughter, Sabrina, ably manages the Frangipani. By day, it is a good place to meet people and enjoy a great fresh tuna sandwich for lunch. By night, they offer romantic candlelit dinners of Caribbean specialties. Everyone comes by on Thursday nights when they have a barbecue and jump up to a steel band. They also have music on Mondays in season.

Gingerbread [VHF: 68, $B-C], also managed by Sabrina, is in an impressive Caribbean-style building with highly intricate gingerbread trim and an immensely high wooden roof supported by mast-like poles. The spacious upstairs dining room has a grand harbor view. The atmosphere is enlivened by good, un-amplified groups on weekends in season. The food is delicious, with curries a specialty. Reservations are advisable in season, or stop in for a drink. The Gingerbread is also open for breakfast and lunch. The coffee shop under the trees sells coffee and baked goodies. In the same compound check out Maranne's and try her famous gourmet ice cream, frozen yogurt, or sorbet. Everything is homemade from fresh ingredients.

Ginerbread Hotel, managed by Pat Mitchell, has delightful rooms with big balconies, looking right over the harbor.

Jacques is a Frenchman who, with Eileen, has spent 22 years in the restaurant business. Auberge des Grenadines [$B-C] is on the waterfront on the north side of the harbor, with a dinghy dock, and is very popular.

During the lobster season, Jacques and Eileen keep a large, live lobster tank full in their restaurant. The lobsters go from tank to plate in a matter of a few minutes; it does not get fresher. Jacques has specialized in lobster for years, and you can expect them to be done perfectly. You can get excellent French and Creole food here as well as good rotis and light lunches. Their lunchtime salad nicoise with lightly seared fresh tuna is the best I know in the Eastern Caribbean.

Jacques has entertainment most Sunday, Monday, and Tuesday nights. His current band (Stan and Cora) plays blues music. While here, check out Eileen's Market (see *Provisioning*)

Lars and Margit from Sweden run several restaurants that rate among the best in Bequia. On the north side of the harbor, they have Devil's Table in Bequia Marina [$A-C, open at 1500 closed during the summer]. Devil's Table is built out on a dock over the water, and is mainly open to the view and the air, but it is protected from the rain by a series of little roofs. Small lights and candles produce a delightful atmosphere. They often hire promising young chefs from Sweden to run it. The food is consistently excellent and beautifully served. An unusual feature is that they have meals to suit all pockets, all perfectly prepared. If this is the Devil's Table, don't worry about sinning. They sometimes have entertainment on Friday and Saturday.

Lars and Margit also have Jack's Bar, [$B-C] on Tony Gibbons Beach. Dinghy over and tie up on their dock. Jack's is big and open, built of wood and canvas. The location is fabulous, right on the beach. They open every day from 1100 for drinks, snacks, lunch, and dinner. The lunch menu is posted on the board and changes daily, though their hamburgers are always featured, as is the sandwich du jour. They offer specials

St. Vincent & the Grenadines

259

of fresh fish (often tuna, lightly seared) and meat. The food is elegant and wonderful. On Tuesdays in season they have a big barbecue with live music, and on Sundays they have afternoon music.

The third restaurant in this group is Papa's [$C-D] up on the hill above Bequia Marina and managed by Gert. It has an informal clubby atmosphere with comfy lounging seats as well as a giant deck with a view over the harbor. This is the place to come for a big sports event like the superbowl as they can project TV right on the wall. They open every day for lunch and dinner with both a menu and daily specials. The food is straightforward and includes burgers, chicken, and sandwiches. On Wednesday nights they have Mama's Italian night, which is popular, and on Saturday nights they have live music.

There are plenty of first-rate places to get good local food. Noeline Taylor's Porthole [VHF: 68, $C-D] is a popular meeting place for breakfast, morning coffee, lunch rotis, an afternoon beer, or a relaxing dinner. Noeline always has local fresh juices and a large menu, with everything from snacks to freshly caught fish. All these are available for lunch and dinner. Check out the menu posted outside showing the daily specials. Entertainment is usually on Wednesdays and Sundays. Noeline has the biggest bookswap in Bequia, so you often see people browsing through the shelves. There is a very nominal charge that enables Noeline to keep the books in good order. Let Noeline know before you do your swap.

Cheryl's Old Fig Tree [$B-D], is along the waterfront close to Mack's Pizzeria; just

follow the coastal path. This restaurant is right on the water and open to the bay. The food is local and delicious for breakfast, lunch or dinner. Cheryl, who is always around and welcoming, also runs the cruisers VHF net in the morning at 0800, and she runs a children's reading group here every other Saturday and always welcomes volunteers from yachts to help children read. If anyone is looking for a place for a meeting, scrabble competition, or other event, it is likely here they will come. Cheryl plans a monthly poetry club. In season she has live music on Tuesdays and Fridays.

Daffodil [$B-D] has a new bar/restaurant, on a spacious deck built out into the bay. You don't get closer to the water than this and you can tie your dinghy close to your table leg. Drop by for a sundowner and see what is on the menu. Food is usually simple, good and inexpensive, but on occasion Daffodil does a more elaborate fare and gives out fliers to the yachts. If you need somewhere to stay ashore, she has nice rooms with a view.

The Hinkson family own and run the Whaleboner [$C-D]. It is conveniently situated next to the Frangipani. Much of the food comes from their farm, so you know it is fresh. True to its name, the bar, stools, and entrance have all been built of whalebone from the old whaling days. Angela and her daughter Ruth cook good snacks, pizzas, chicken, and fish. They also do full evening meals at a reasonable price, including curried and roast pork. The meat comes from their hand-raised animals. Chicken and fish are always available, as is lobster in season. Come for the daily happy hour (1700-1800)

On top of Peggy's Rock

and enjoy entertainment on Monday nights, in season, and on other special occasions.

Aqua Cafe is upstairs, opposite the market and has a great harbor view. It is worth going to check out their bar, which is built like a local trading boat. They open daily from 0830 until. Owners Gary from the UK and Trudy from Guyana will welcome you warmly. The cafe is emphasized in the mornings with good coffee, croissants and breakfast dishes. The offer a hearty local lunch at a ridiculously reasonable price, and in the evening they are a bar which serves pub food. On Friday night they have a DJ with music to appeal to all ages and on Saturday nights a live band, starting around 2115.

Coco's [VHF: 68, $C-D] is upstairs in the first building on the road behind Bequia Marina. They have an excellent view of the yachts at anchor and decoration is real Caribbean style. Coco is famous for good, local cooking, especially of seafood. In sea-

son, they do a fabulous Sunday buffet lunch, and they generally have music on Tuesdays and Fridays.

When you get tired of local food, Tommy Cantina specializes not only in your favorite Mexican dishes, such as tacos, enchiladas, and burritos, but also in seafood and lobster (in season). The location is perfect for sunset, taking in the whole sweep of Admiralty Bay. They open every day, including Sunday nights, when many others are closed.

Mac's Pizzeria's [$C-D] tasty pizzas are legendary among yachtspeople, with many choices, including lobster pizza. You can also get quiches, salads, soups, and goodies from their bakeshop, along with daily specials. The atmosphere is congenial, and it is inexpensive enough that you can gravitate here any time you do not feel like cooking. In season, it is essential to make a reservation. They also do take out.

Maria's French Terrace (formerly Ma-

ria's Cafe) is upstairs on Front Street, with a large, open balcony that overlooks life below and the harbor. This restaurant offers French cuisine. Check it out.

Next door, The Bistro [$C-D] is open to the main street. They have hearty meals, pizzas, and hamburgers, as well as local fish, shrimp, and lobster. It is also a great place to enjoy a few drinks or a cup of coffee and watch the world pass by.

For a cheap and cheerful lunch, consider Colombo's [$D]. They cook excellent pizza and pasta, and their lasagna is great. (You can buy it by the tray for a party.).

On back street, the Lime Garden has a cheap bar where you can sit and relax, and they often fire up the grill for a bargain meal.

Other local restaurants include Lyston Williams's Green Boley [$D], the best value for rotis, snacks, and local meals; Isola Mc-Intosh's Julie's Guest House [VHF: 68, $C], where advance booking is necessary; and the Pizzza Hut, which is self-explanatory, but which also sells French bread.

Tantie Pearl's [VHF: 68, $B-C] is an aerobic 5- to 7-minute walk up a steep hill behind the cemetery. The restaurant is perched on the edge of a steep slope with a bird's-eye view of the harbor. Tantie Pearl offers good, local food, but book before you go.

Behind the slipway is the Sailor's Cafe [VHF: 68, $C-D]. Owner Elfic Grant, aka The Singing Chef, is entertaining and runs a good, clean establishment. You can drop in for soup and some good Chinese fried rice or chow mein. For more elaborate fare, you need to book in advance. The bar makes a pleasant hangout; ask about happy hour.

Heading west, opposite the next dock down, a tiny street goes up the hill. On your left is Hendi's, a little rum shop with outside, under-a-tarp seating, run by Henry and Dianne. This is a cheap and cheerful local experience and lots of fun. They do good local meals, much of it barbecue. You need to give them a little notice.

On Tony Gibbons Beach, you can find Willie among the jewelry salesmen. Willie does a great beach barbecue to order, which was highly recommended to me.

These are just the restaurants in Admi-

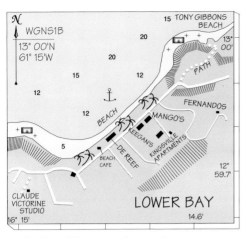

ralty Bay. There are also good restaurants in other places, and taxi fares are reasonable ($12-20 EC). (See also *Restaurants* in *Friendship Bay*, later in this chapter; it is a long walk or short drive away.)

For a change away from the boat and some special time out, consider Firefly Hotel [$A-C] over at Spring (connected with the Firefly in Mustique). This delightful and secluded hideaway looks across a field of palm trees towards the east coast, with the feel of being in the country. It is a great escape from the boat. The manager, Rodney, is very welcoming and friendly, as are the rest of the staff; they will make you feel at home. Managing director, Elizabeth, is often around. The food is very fresh; a lot of it comes from the estate, augmented by fresh local fish and meats.

They have a lunch and dinner menu which you can always choose from, but in addition they offer several specials. Friday night is barbecue night; Saturday night is Jamaican jerk night. The great curry lunch on Sundays is well worth coming for. On Wednesday lunch they do traditional Creole food, which attracts a lot of local people.

As part of your island tour, consider taking their estate tour, it is only $10EC a person and Keith will show you all around and tell you about the local plants and their uses.

Should you want a real getaway from the boat, they have rooms. Massage and beauty treatments are available on request.

Another mile down the same road, at the next big beach, called Industry, you will find Dawn's Creole. This is set in a big stone building on the beach, open to the sea. Dawn and Willie serve local food at very reasonable prices, and are open daily for breakfast and lunch. They cook excellent callaloo soup, burgers, fish and lobster sandwiches, and daily specials. You can book a dinner here but let them know before 1400 that you are coming. Every full moon they run a big evening barbecue buffet. Call them to make sure you have the day right and to let them know you are coming.

While in this area, visit the Whaleboner silk-screen factory (see *Fun shopping*).

Lower Bay has one of Bequia's best beaches, set in a low-key, rural atmosphere of fishing boats and drying nets. Great for swimming by day and romantic on a full-moon night, it is a popular place to hang out, especially on Sundays. Recently, people have begun to gravitate there for an evening of inexpensive seafood dinners. Lower Bay makes an acceptable anchorage in settled conditions and is within dinghy reach of Admiralty Bay. However, there is usually enough swell to make landing on the beach

a damp affair, so it is better to take a cab over ($15-25 EC). By day, it is interesting to dinghy to Jack's Bar, walk down Tony Gibbons Beach, and then go over the next bluff to Lower Bay.

Once you arrive, there are several local restaurants to choose from. De Reef [VHF: 68, $C-D], right on the beach, is the most famous, popular for lunch, and is a major gathering place for locals on Sundays. You can get chicken, fish, conch, or sandwiches any day of the week. Their hot conch souse

is delicious. By night they serve three-course dinners by reservation, and from time to time, they throw a wild fete.

Mango's Beach Bar and Grill [$B-C] is a run by Richard and Molly, who have breathed life into this rather lovely open-beamed restaurant. It spreads across the street to the beach with seating inside, outside, right overlooking the beach, or roadside. Find the spot that suits. They open every day from 0900 until late, creating a relaxing atmosphere with free wifi and a big TV for sports events in the bar. You can eat lunch, dinner, or snacks right on the beach and they do great grills: lobster, fresh local fish, angus steaks, baby back ribs, and more. It is very popular on weekends.

Keegan's [VHF: 68, $C-D], opposite the beach, offers inexpensive three-course dinners featuring chicken, shrimp, fish, or conch. By day, they do fish or chicken 'n chips and snacks.

Fernando's Hideaway [$C], run by Fernando, is simple, low-key, and serves very good meals of local fish and meat. Fernando is a fisherman and catches the fish himself. Advance reservations are pretty much essential. It is down a back road. Take a taxi so you can find it easily.

While you are in Lower Bay, consider seeing if you can visit the home of French artist Claude Victorine. Claude's main medium is painting on silk. She creates superb cushion covers, wall hangings, and fabrics that are guaranteed to add a touch of class to any boat or home. Paintings are also on show. Claude often accepts visitors during the day when she is there. She is delightful to talk to, and the sight of her pretty little

Lower Bay

house perched up in the hills is well worth the walk. She closes on Fridays.

Transport

Two different companies run ferries over to St. Vincent: Admiralty Transport and Bequia Express. The Admiral makes four trips on weekdays and two or three on weekends. The first ferry normally leaves Bequia at 0630, and the last returns at 1900. You can get details on the times of all ferries in the Bequia Tourist Office by the main dock.

You can rent mountain bikes at Handy Andy's or at Piper's Marine store.

Local buses can be useful for getting around the island, especially if you are going down to La Pompe or Paget Farm, both of which can seem like a never-ending walk. Just watch for one and stick out your hand.

Taxis are fairly inexpensive in Bequia and sightseeing is highly recommended. (Check out some of the attractions under *Ashore*.) If you call a taxi in advance, they can meet you outside the Gingerbread or Frangipani. Most of the taxi drivers are good.

There may be one or two who hustle a bit too much. Those I mention are pleasant, punctual, reliable, and always straightforward and informative about the island and its people. Gideon has three taxis, works well with the yachts, and is always listening to VHF: 68. His rates are reasonable and he also has four-wheel-drive rentals.

The Ollivierre family has been involved in Bequia boatbuilding from way back. Lubin Ollivierre (De Best) was one of the first taxi drivers and will be happy to tell you about what changes he has seen and what he knows of the history. He also has jeep rentals. Sandra and Curtis Ollivierre have a couple of bright yellow taxis and some four-wheel-drive cars for rent. They listen to VHF: 68.

Sightseeing cab fares for four people are only about $30 US an hour, or $6 US per person over 5. You can see a lot in an hour, and the whole island in four hours. If you just want to visit Spring, Friendship, or Lower Bay, or want to try somewhere different for

St. Vincent & the Grenadines

dinner, hop in a taxi; the island is small, so the fares are reasonable.

Ashore

If the hair on your head is beginning to resemble the stringy weed growing under your hull, then for men there is an inexpensive, traditional electric clipper barber behind the Porthole building.

Johanna Osborne, a dentist and maxillofacial surgeon now runs a clinic on Saturdays above Knights on Front Street. Call for an appointment: 529-0745.

Bequia has good walks. You can dinghy to Tony Gibbons Beach and walk to Lower Bay. If you laze on the beach and swim, keep an eye on your handbags and cameras.

Watch a sunset from Mount Pleasant, or walk to Friendship Bay, Spring, or Industry for lunch or dinner and enjoy the great variety of views along the way.

If you want to go on an adventurous hike, then Brent "Bushman" Gooding will be happy to guide you. He knows all the trails. Call him at 495-2524.

You will find Bequia is far more than the waterfront. The hills of Mount Pleasant are almost like another world. If you are not inclined to walk, take a cab one way or both. You can see all the best and most scenic spots in a leisurely 3-hour tour. Each place you visit seems so different that sometimes Bequia feels like several islands in one. Highlights include an old fort looking over the harbor, Bequia's summit, Mount Pleasant, the beautiful windward beach of Spring, and a visit to the home of the late Athneal Ollivierre, the island's head whale harpooner, where there is a small whaling museum. The taxi drivers are proud of their island and are knowledgeable guides.

The Old Hegg Turtle Sanctuary at Industry is a great destination. Brother King takes turtle eggs and rears turtles till they are old enough to have a better chance of survival. The establishment of the sanctuary has done much to raise environmental consciousness in Bequia. There is a small charge ($5 US) to visit, which goes toward the cost of feeding and housing the turtles.

On the way back, stop at the new Whaleboner Silk Screen factory, shop, and

Start of the hike to Peggy's Rock

bar, right along the road.

You can hike to Hope, a lovely, remote beach where the shallow water sets up long lines of breakers often suitable for bodysurfing (but watch the undertow).

There is an exceptionally pleasant hike (about 40 minutes each way) to Peggy's Rock, right on a mountain ridgeline with a spectacular view of Admiralty Bay. You start by the Bequia Whaling and Maritime Museum. Take a taxi or bus there; it is on the road to the airport. Hike details may be found on doyleguides.com

You can visit the other Bequia Maritime Museum in town in exchange for a contribution ($5 US suggested). Lawson Sargeant, the original model boat builder, runs it. Inside are some awesome, historically correct, giant models of whaling boats and schooners, along with photos of historic Bequia boats and the harbor from about 50 years ago. It is best to call for an appointment (495-8559/457-3685).

Tennis courts are available at Spring, Friendship Bay, and Gingerbread. If you come at Easter, you can get involved in the Bequia Regatta, a four-day extravaganza of local boat races, yacht races, and lots of partying. Christmas is also a popular time in Bequia, but "Nine Mornings," which starts some two weeks before Christmas, can make the town anchorage throb with disco music through the night.

You can also get off-island. Bequia has a very special day-charter boat, the Friendship Rose, a sailing schooner, which for years was the island's only ferry. Given the price of mooring in Mustique, some yachties figure it is worth taking a day tour on the Rose instead. They also do diving, waterfall, and other tours that are not as easy on your own boat. Their office is in town and you can check out their itinerary. Their Grenadine Island Villas rents and sells villas, so when the whole family comes to visit, you can house them ashore.

Bequia has a very active youth sailing program to get the youngsters learning. They have a fleet of small sailing boats plus one or two J 24s. The boats are kept opposite the Bistro. If you feel like getting involved by contributing some time or money, Handy

Andy is the man to talk to.

Water sports

Diving in Bequia is excellent and not to be missed by scuba fans. For the uninitiated, it is an ideal place for a resort course. There are two dive shops in Admiralty Bay.

Dive Bequia is the dive shop near the Gingerbread, owned by Bob Sachs. Sachs is one of scuba's greatest enthusiasts and Bequia's most experienced diver. His wife, Cathy, is charming and an excellent teacher, especially for kids, or for those who are nervous (a view endorsed by quite a few reader emails). Call Dive Bequia [VHF: 68/16], and Bob or one of his staff will arrange to collect you from your yacht. Return to the bar later to socialize with them and other divers. Their seaworthy dive boats make getting in and out easy and allow for occasional diving and exploring trips to the St. Vincent or the other Grenadines.

Bequia Dive Adventures [VHF: 68] is on the waterfront next to Mac's Pizzeria. It is run by Ron, an instructor, and Laury, a master scuba diver trainer, both from Bequia, and also Dave from Minnesota, who joins them for part of the season. They are an experienced team that operates with small groups and does all levels of training, from resort courses through assistant instructor training. They are happy to do boat pickups and dropoffs.

Both dive shops have retail sections with snorkeling and diving gear for sale. Both will help with equipment service or rental and tank fills.

For those diving on their own, the most accessible good dives are around Devil's Table. There is a reef extending from the black and yellow beacon to the shore. There are moorings, so you can tie up your dinghy. (The moorings belong to the dive shops, so leave plenty of line so they can tie up alongside you.) From the shallow inshore end you can dive out along one side of the rocky shoal, and back on the other. The depth at the outer end of the reef is about 65 feet. There are plenty of different corals and reef fish. Sergeant majors can often be seen guarding their eggs. An even prettier dive is along the stretch of coast from inside

St. Vincent & the Grenadines

this reef northwards to Northwest Point.
There is a sloping reef all along this shore.
The maximum depth is about 60 feet at
Northwest Point. Coral formations include
lots of pillar corals, and there are usually
large schools of blue chromis. Garden eels
undulate over the sand. On both dives you
must mind the current.

More exciting dives are far from the
anchorage, and the current makes them drift
dives. Flat Rock Drift Dive is on Bequia's
northwest coast, starting at the western
end of Anse Chemin. This is a gentle, easy
dive where you hardly have to use your fins,
and there is time to examine all the little
creatures. You swim along a captivating reef
that slopes gently into sand at 60 feet. You
will see an excellent selection of soft and
hard corals, lots of fish, arrow crabs, lobsters,
tubeworms, and anemones. A couple of spotted snake eels hang out here, and you can
often see a ray.

The Boulders is a pleasant drift dive
about two-thirds of the way between Admiralty Bay and Moonhole. A gentle descent
60 feet down a coral slope takes you into an
area where hundreds of fish, including huge
schools of blue chromis and sennets, make
ever-changing patterns as you drift with the
current. Barracudas patrol up and down;
moray eels, lobsters, crabs, and shrimps can
be found. The reef gets deeper till you come
to the boulders, which are tall rock formations, each about 20 feet high, starting from
a bottom depth of 93 feet. There are tunnels to pass through and holes and caverns
that provide hiding places for nurse sharks,
groupers, angelfish, and jacks. As you return
to the dive boat, you may see a frogfish or
seahorse.

Pigeon Island has beautiful dives. The island slopes off steeply to around 100 feet. There are walls, overhangs, rifts, and hollows decorated by deepwater lace coral. The visibility is generally excellent, and you will see huge schools of blue and brown chromis, big groupers, passing pelagic fish, and sometimes rays and turtles.

The Wall (West Cay, northern side) is an adventure dive down to 114 feet, with dramatic vistas, the odd large pelagic, and lots of great stuff to examine along the wall on your way up. Moonhole (outside the Moonhole complex) offers temporary anchorage, though I would leave a crew member on board. Make sure you are anchored in sand and do not tie to the dive moorings. The easiest dive is to start right in the bay and follow the reef around the point to the east, watching for currents. This is a gentle dive to 60 feet, with hard and soft corals and a variety of smaller fish.

Snorkeling is good around Devil's Table and along the coast to Northwest Point. The dive shops also offer snorkeling trips.

MOONHOLE TO FRIENDSHIP BAY

If you are sailing from Admiralty Bay to West Cay, you will undoubtedly catch sight of Moonhole. This rather isolated community, founded by the late American architect Tom Johnson, is not easily accessible by either land or sea, there being no road or good anchorage. Moonhole houses are certainly different; the original was built under a natural arch known as "Moonhole." It was abandoned when a huge boulder fell from the ceiling and crushed the empty bed. The other houses grow out of the rocks without straight lines or right angles. They have huge arches, fantastic views, and lovely patios. There is seldom glass in the windows and the breeze is constant. There is no electricity. Moonhole is a special kind of vacation home for the right people. The architecture is worth marveling at as you sail by.

Bequia's new airport is built along the south coast. There is a fishing dock about

Friendship Bay

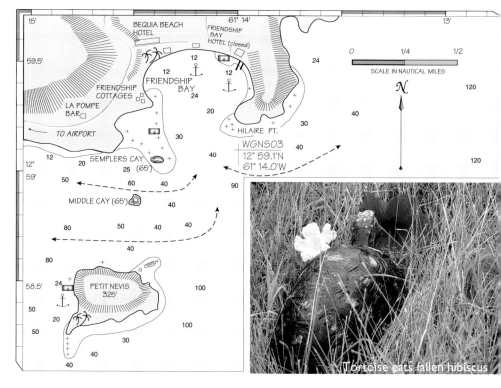

Tortoise eats fallen hibiscus

a third of a mile to its east, off Paget Farm, where in an emergency you can get ashore from a tenable, if rolly, anchorage.

FRIENDSHIP BAY AND PETIT NEVIS

Friendship Bay, on the south side of Bequia, is gorgeous, with a lovely white beach. The anchorage is secure, with good holding, and in times of northerly swells, it provides better protection than Admiralty Bay. A small swell often creeps in from the southeast, but you can cut the roll with a second anchor from the stern to keep yourself into the swells.

Navigation

A reef extends from the shore to Semplers Cay and beyond. Don't try to sail in or out that way, as some have. On the opposite side of the harbor, there is a reef extending out a fair way from Hilaire Point (locally called "Hillary"). Keep in the center of the channel. Once inside, anchor in the east of the bay or off the old Friendship Bay Resort

dock. Note that a reef extends from the west side of the Friendship Bay Resort dock down to the beach.

Communications

Bequia Beach Hotel has wifi in the bar, and you can carry your computer there. Check out also Friendship Bay Hotel if they open again.

Ashore

On the western half of the beach is an excellent, Swedish-run hotel, the Bequia Beach Hotel; one of Bequia's largest and finest. It starts on the beach and flows uphill to the road. When people want a holiday in Bequia in fair luxury, this is where they come. If your grandmother wants to visit you and would be happier ashore, this is a great option.

Their Bagatelle Restaurant [$A-B] is delightfully open, set right on the beach, with waves lapping just outside. The food is a fusion of local and European cuisine, beautifully cooked and served, making this a very popular destination, not only for people

anchored in Friendship Bay but also as a "getaway" from Admiralty Bay.

Another hotel on the eastern side of the bay has been closed for a few years. It has been bought and just may reopen during the life of this guide.

For something much more local, check out the Diamond Bar Fish Food on a bend in the road to La Pompe, where people often hangout at the bus stop. Owner Michael cooks good fish and seafood at unbeatable prices. Well worth the short steep climb to the door. They open 1000-2200, except Sunday, when they open at 1600.

To the east of the Friendship Bay Hotel progress has been made on the Bequia Heritage Foundation Historical and Cultural Museum. To date the foundations are in and some of the walls up. If funding comes in, we will see a complete building sometime soon. The building will house Bequia's traditional whaling, blackfish, and fishing boats and a canoe. A walk-around platform, always open, will ensure that you can see the exhibits. You may be able to beach your dinghy under the museum and walk. Otherwise, take the road that goes around the back of Friendship Bay Hotel and the museum will be on your right. If museums interest you and you would like to help, volunteer, or support, contact Pat Mitchel at the Gingerbread Hotel.

Water sports

The best snorkeling in Friendship Bay is between Semplers Cay and the shore. You can also try the reef along the shore to the west of the old Friendship Bay Resort dock.

PETIT NEVIS

Petit Nevis was the original whale-rendering island. It makes an interesting daytime anchorage with good exploring. The snorkeling along the shore is good, although the current can be strong out of the lee. If passing southward, note the long, southerly reef.

Mustique at a glance

Regulations

The water around Mustique is a conservation area and Mustique charges fees for staying here. Mustique is a private island, access to parts of the island are sometimes restricted. See Mustique text for details.

If you need clearance, customs and immigration are at the airport, normally 0800-1600, but the island is small they cannot be too far away out of hours.

Jet skis and the like are strictly forbidden, as are spearfishing and anchoring without supervision. Water-skiing is not permitted in the yacht anchorage area.

Vessels carrying more than 25 passengers are not allowed in Mustique.

Shopping Hours

Corea's food store: Mon-Sat, 0800-1200, 1500-1800. Boutiques: 0900-1200 and 1400-1800. Some boutiques, Ali's and Corea's, open Sunday mornings.

Holidays

See *St. Vincent*.

Telephones

Most Mustique numbers start (784) - 488 + four digits. If you are using a private phone in Mustique, you just dial the last four digits of 488 numbers. The most used such phone is in Basil's Bar.

Basil's, 8350
Coreas, 8479
Firefly, 8414
Dive shop, 8486
Mustique Moorings, 8363
Horse riding, 8316
MMS (bike, mule rental) 8555
Mustique Company, 8424, F:8409
Airport, 8336, Customs 8410
Immigration 8348, Police 8339
Doctor, 8353
Cotton House, (784)-456-4777
See also *St. Vincent*.

Transport

Bikes can be rented from Mustique Mechanical Services (MMS).

Taxi numbers are:
Boom Boom, 455-2084,
Johnny, 530 6285, Michael, 528-4205
Brego, 488-8877

ST. VINCENT

A

BALICEAUX

PILLORIES

MONTEZUMA SHOAL

BRITANNIA BAY
MUSTIQUE

Mustique

M ustique, a privately owned island, was developed by Colin Tennant as a playground for the colorful, rich and famous. The owners bought the island from him and restricted further development. House prices have soared from about a million to over ten times that much. It is now owned by the 0.1 percent, usually business people who value their privacy and don't want nautical yahoos with cameras hiding behind hedges, mistaking them for aging rock stars and models.

Mustique, although private and exclusive, has been kept as friendly and open to yachting visitors as possible. In an age where whole islands are becoming gated, they have been exemplary. However, some restrictions sometimes apply (see *Regulations*). Please help keep it open. Use common courtesy: stick to the roads, do not walk up people's driveways or onto private property. Use the beach south of the anchorage for beach time, or the Cotton House beach if you are hanging out at the beach bar there. Take scenic photos for your own use, but do not photograph residents. Press photography is only allowed by permission of the Mustique Company.

Mustique only has about 90 large houses on the whole island, plus one hotel, a guesthouse, a beach bar, a few boutiques, a small local village, and a fishing camp. About half the houses are available for rent when the owners are not in residence. As you would expect for an island of this type, prices are geared to the well-heeled.

What is wonderful about Mustique is that much of the island has been left wild and there are some great trails and not much traffic. As other islands sprout buildings like some invasive weed, much

St. Vincent & the Grenadines

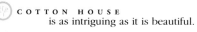

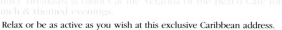
of Mustique remains beautiful and unspoiled; an island where you can hike or bike in peace on one of the best preserved Grenadine islands, with fabulous beaches and shady pathways.

Navigation

Montezuma Shoal is about half to three-quarters of a mile west of Britannia Bay. It presents a real hazard and has ground pieces off the hulls of a cruise ship, a large charter yacht, and many a bareboat. It is marked by a red and black buoy. Stay at least a quarter of a mile away. If you come from the south, do not follow the coast too closely as there is quite a reef extending seaward from the southern point of Britannia Bay.

The only permissible anchorage is in Britannia Bay. (Special day charter groups wanting a lunch stop in Endeavour Bay must contact Berris Little of Mustique Moorings in advance.) Britannia Bay has sparkling clear water and is a lovely area for swimming and snorkeling, though it is generally rather rolly.

Regulations

The Mustique Company controls all the coastal waters of Mustique. Well-maintained Moorings are provided for yachts up to a maximum of 60 feet. Yachts over 60 feet must anchor outside the moorings under the direction of Berris Little, the harbormaster (Mustique Moorings VHF: 16/68).

There is a conservation fee that entitles you to a three-consecutive-night stay. This fee in $ EC is: up to 70 feet $200; 71-85 feet $300; 76-100 feet $400; over 100 feet $500. Berris collects the fees and gives you an official receipt. His hut is at the end of the jetty.

Thirty moorings are for yachts under 60 feet and there is no extra charge for these. Each buoy is equipped with a swivel on top. Attach your own lines through the swivel. Use two lines, one to each side of your bow. Never use a single line from one side of the boat through the mooring to the other side. Yachts of 6- to 7-foot draft can use any mooring, and deeper yachts should use the outer moorings over sand. If all the moorings are taken, contact Berris Little for anchoring

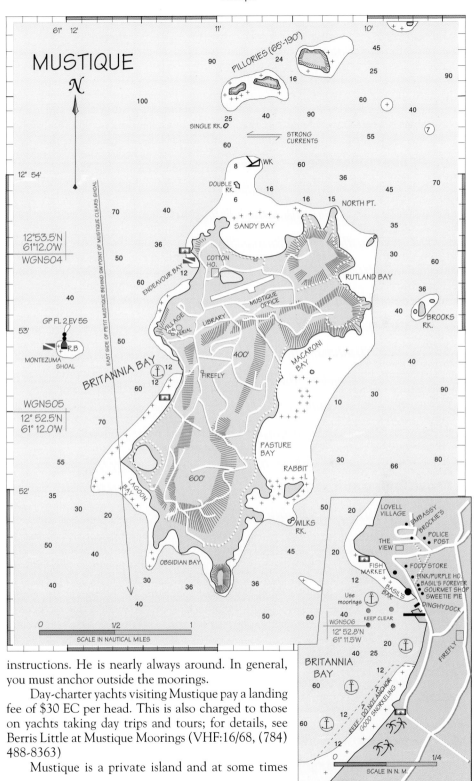

MUSTIQUE

N

PILLORIES (65'-190')

SINGLE RK.

STRONG CURRENTS

WK

DOUBLE RK.

SANDY BAY

NORTH PT.

12° 54'

12°53.5'N
61°12.0'W
WGNS04

COTTON HO.

ENDEAVOUR BAY

RUTLAND BAY

MUSTIQUE OFFICE

BROOKS RK.

GP FL 2 EV 5S

53'

VILLAGE
AERIAL

LIBRARY

400'

MACARONI BAY

R.B

MONTEZUMA
SHOAL

BRITANNIA BAY

FIREFLY

WGNS05
12° 52.5'N
61° 12.0'W

PASTURE BAY

RABBIT I.

600'

LAGOON BAY

WILKS RK.

52'

OBSIDIAN BAY

SCALE IN NAUTICAL MILES

EAST SIDE OF PETIT MUSTIQUE BEHIND SW POINT OF MUSTIQUE CLEARS SHOAL

LOVELL VILLAGE

EMBASSY

BROCKIE'S

THE VIEW

POLICE POST

FISH MARKET

FOOD STORE

PINK/PURPLE HO.
BASIL'S FOREVER
GOURMET SHOP
SWEETIE PIE

BASIL'S BAR

DINGHYDOCK

Use moorings

KEEP CLEAR

WGNS06
12° 52.8'N
61° 11.5'W

FIREFLY

BRITANNIA BAY

REEF - DO NOT ANCHOR

GOOD SNORKELING

SCALE IN N. M.

instructions. He is nearly always around. In general, you must anchor outside the moorings.

Day-charter yachts visiting Mustique pay a landing fee of $30 EC per head. This is also charged to those on yachts taking day trips and tours; for details, see Berris Little at Mustique Moorings (VHF:16/68, (784) 488-8363)

Mustique is a private island and at some times

(mainly Christmas and Easter) land access may be restricted, in which case you will be informed. Even at these times, there is a designated visitor area which goes from the local village, past the anchorage south along the western shore as far as the salt pond and you can walk the salt pond trial. You can always arrange to visit Cotton House, Firefly, and customs. Ask Berris Little for details.

Communications

Mustique has an excellent library, where you can catch up on the internet (four computers) or read the latest magazines and peruse their books. You can send faxes or make photocopies. Contributions of good books are always welcome. They open Monday to Saturday 0900-1300, 1500-1800.

There is wifi around Basil's and Sweetie Pie, and you might be able to get it at anchor.

Services

Garbage disposal is at the head of the dock. There are four taxi drivers who often wait there. If not, phone the taxi numbers in *Mustique at a Glance*.

When you realize the roll is so bad you will never be able to sleep a wink, contact Firefly House or The Cotton House to see if they have available rooms. (Basil's Bar can put you in touch.)

Provisioning and shopping

Corea's supermarket has a good selection. Augment this with fresh fruit and vegetables from Stanley's little stall, where the prices are reasonable. Then go to Basil's Gourmet store for wines, cheeses, fine coffees, and specialty foods (also for local/nature books and music cds). For fish, try the fish market in the fishing village, where you can buy fresh fish and lobster in season. You can also get fresh produce from Cecilia, from Monday afternoon to Thursday, at a stand on the road to the local village.

Come morning, many Mustique residents put on the coffeepot and head down to Sweetie Pie Bakery [VHF: 68] to stock up on fresh croissants, pain au chocolat, and Danish, along with many other pastries. French owner Ali bakes these, plus many kinds of excellent bread. Ali will be happy to discuss charter boat requirements. Ali opens 0700-1200, then 1600-1800. This is the place to come for over 150 daily and weekly newspapers in almost any language.

Ali also has Ali's Cafe between the Pink and Purple houses. This a great place with comfortable seating where you can get coffee, ice cream, lunch time sandwiches, and baked goodies at reasonable prices, open 0800-1800. If you need household hardware, get a taxi to take you to the Mustique Depot.

The Purple House is an excellent boutique run by Susie, who has a collection of swimwear, casual and not-so casual clothing, hand-crafted gifts and souvenirs, games, hats, pareos, hand-painted calabash art, costume jewelry, and more. The Pink House has a more complete range of elegant clothing, plus some casual clothing and kids' togs, and a big selection of jewelry.

Basil has two shops: Basil's Boutique is in Basil's Bar, and Across Forever, on the other side of the road, is an antique and collectibles shop. Basil travels to far eastern ports and brings back his favorite items for the shops, plus the famous Basil's t-shirts and bags.

The Cotton House has a boutique on the left, just before Endeavour Bay, in the same building as the Gym.

Restaurants

Stan and Elizabeth, from England, own a guesthouse and bar/restaurant called Firefly [$A, VHF: 10]. It has a dramatic view over the floodlit swimming pool to Britannia Bay. The atmosphere is elegant and a touch formal, yet friendly, making it popular with those who spend time on the island. Regulars gather round the bar in the evening and a piano occasionally inspires one of them to play for a while. Their food is excellent: an inventive blend of Caribbean and European cuisine using fresh ingredients. You will love the desserts. Wander up for lunch or dinner. The short walk will whet your appetite, but for those who prefer to ride, a staff member will come and collect dinner guests from the dock. Reservations are advisable.

For superb cuisine in lavish elegance, don your best evening pants or a dress (it is somewhat formal) and call the Cotton

House [VHF: 68, $A]. It is about a 15-minute walk, but if you make dinner reservations they are happy to come and get you. Cotton House, owned by the Mustique Company, and run by GLA, is a member of the Leading Small Hotels of the World, and is one of the fanciest hotels in the Caribbean. Originally an 18th century coral warehouse and sugar mill, it was artfully created by the late British designer, Oliver Messel.

They usually have top chefs and, when on form, their dinner restaurant, the Veranda, produces the best cuisine on the island. The Beach Cafe, right on the beach in Endeavour Bay, is a perfect for a morning coffee and pastry, ice cream, or lunch of fresh fish or lobster (1230-1500). The Beach Cafe sometimes opens in the evening (they have movie nights) and is available in the evening for private functions. You can enjoy cocktails and delicious tapas, including sushi and sashimi, at the Tree Garden Lounge from 1830-2230.

For a real treat, renovate your body with a visit to the Cotton House Spa, featuring ESPA treatments and a gym. Cotton House

has a museum in the sugar mill with some good pre-Columbian pottery and stone work (ask for the key).

Basil's Bar [VHF: 68, $A-B], informal, and popular is built of thatch and bamboo and perched on stilts over the water, with waves lapping underneath. This is the Caribbean's most famous beach bar and is the place to meet people, to contact other establishments on the island, to relax and look at the sunset, or just to get off your rolling boat for dinner (seafood and lobster specialties). Many come for the popular Wednesday night barbecue buffet, which is followed by a jump-up. Basil organizes a superb two-week blues festival towards the end of January to early February, which also visits Bequia.

When you tire of the fancy, visit the local village where Lisa Lewis has a restaurant with an incredible view of Britannia Bay, naturally called The View [C-D]. Turn left opposite the police station (under Brockie's), and walk till you see the sign. Or take the short cut up the hill: take the little path at the side of the boutiques, bear left at the bird

St. Vincent & the Grenadines

Britannia Bay by Stanley's market

cage, turn right on the road, and then left up the steps shortly after. At the top turn left and you are there.

Lisa opens breakfast to dinner every day. For lunch Lisa does a big trade in take-out for both locals and residents, so you can walk in for a meal. If you are coming to dinner give her a little warning. She is personable, hardworking, and will cook you a delicious meal with good fresh vegetables for a very reasonable price. Her fish is fresh and sautéed conch delightful. You can also get beef, mutton and chicken. Saturday night she does a popular barbecue. If you need a night ashore, Lisa has some rooms.

Other village restaurants include Brockie's owned by Becky, and Selwyn's Embassy Bar [both $D], which serve good lunch specials every day. Brockie's has chicken and chips in the evenings and both will cook a good dinner to order. If you want to just hang out for a drink, try Piccadilly Sports Bar or Hill Top Bar.

Ashore

A taxi tour will give you a quick overview. To really enjoy the beauty of this island, rent a mountain bike or go hiking. Basil's Gourmet store has great books on the natural history of Mustique and the species you find here.

Please note that while you are welcome to use the picnic shelters (no charge), they are by reservation only. Talk to Berris Little or call Jan O'Neil 488-8378.

If you turn right at the main dock and follow the road south, staying on the path that follows the shore, you will have a delightful walk. It joins a trail that goes around the salt pond, and also brings you to a perfect beach at Lagoon Bay.

If you get more ambitious, follow our map taking the roads that lead to Obsidian Bay. Head south from the dock, staying on the road. After about 20 minutes you will pass a couple of roads on your right and see gate posts on the road; continue up. You have to turn left at a junction where there is a concrete shed on the left corner and a grate across the road. (If you reach Obsidian House, you have just missed this turn.) Go on up the hill, and where you have a choice of concrete (left fork) and dirt track (right fork), take the dirt. This brings you to Obsidian Bay from where you can follow a rough trail right down the east coast to Pasture Bay. From here you can walk back to Britannia Bay (total hike 3.5 hours).

There is another excellent hike around North Point, from the north round to the

east, till you can see Macaroni and Pasture Bays. For this one you need to get a taxi to drop you off at the trail head right by L'Ansecou House. The trail starts down what looks like a nameless private drive, but just before the "private" sign the trail leads off to the right. It follows the coast, sometimes along open cliff, sometimes bounded by dry scrub trees. By the time you have walked back to Britannia Bay it will take about 3 hours, though you can bail out halfway at Rutland Bay. Keep your eye open on all hikes for the wild land tortoises.

Horseback riding is done in the cool of the day, at 0800, 0900, 1500 or 1600. Mountain bikes are available through Mustique Mechanical Services or Mustique Moorings.

Water sports

You can go sailboarding or diving at Mustique Water Sports [VHF: 68]. Brian Richards, the dive instructor and manager, is very good and will pick divers up from their yachts when space is available. The water is generally very clear and diving is pleasant.

Walk-in Reef is just off the dive shop dock and ideal for beginners. At South Britannia Drift Dive you let the current carry you through a delightful garden of soft corals as you watch large schools of Bermuda chubs and Creole wrasses. The occasional sight of an eagle ray makes it perfect. The wreck of the Jonas, a 90-foot dredge, lies in 40 feet of water on the east side of Montezuma Shoal. Beautiful coral formations there are home to barracudas and nurse sharks. At Southeast Pillory Drift Dive, the current sweeps you along a steep slope, which drops from 20 feet to 90 feet. The scenery is always changing as you go along, with lots of reef fish and large soft corals. Dry Rock (on the south side of Petit Mustique) is the place for the big fish: schools of barracudas, nurse sharks, and rays. You often see turtles, too.

Tortoises are plentiful

St. Vincent & the Grenadines

CHARLESTOWN BAY

Canouan (For information on holidays, customs, etc., see *St. Vincent*)

*C*anouan is an island of two parts. The Canouan Resort Development Company (CRD) owns and has developed the northern half of the island, which is managed by The Canouan Resort at the Carenage. This larger half is gated, with guards at the entry points, and locals and visitors alike need permission to enter.

The original airport has now about doubled in size and the extended runway can take private jets. The injection of new money by CRD has rapidly transformed Canouan in just a few years. The southern part has moved from a sleepy backwater of small wooden houses and fields of pigeon peas to a prosperous settlement of big cement houses. As a result, this part of the island is still finding itself, culturally and architecturally.

Canouan has spectacular beaches, great views, and lovely walks almost anywhere. It is well worth looking at the fabulous wind-ward reef-protected lagoon.

The Moorings has a small base here right next to the Tamarind Beach Hotel. This brings charterers into the heart of the Grenadines, allowing them to cruise with short, easy sails.

Navigation

Deep draft vessels should avoid Grand Cai, about 0.75 miles west of Jupiter Point. While this shoal is generally about 36 feet deep, it has on its western side a small isolated 16-foot shoal at 12° 44.490'N, 61° 20.645'W. Seas in this general area are often 6-8 feet high, further reducing the depth. It badly damaged the keel of a sailing super-yacht. It is too small to cause a noticeable difference in the sea state and is normally of no consequence to yachts with less than 10-foot draft.

Landing planes come in low to the air-

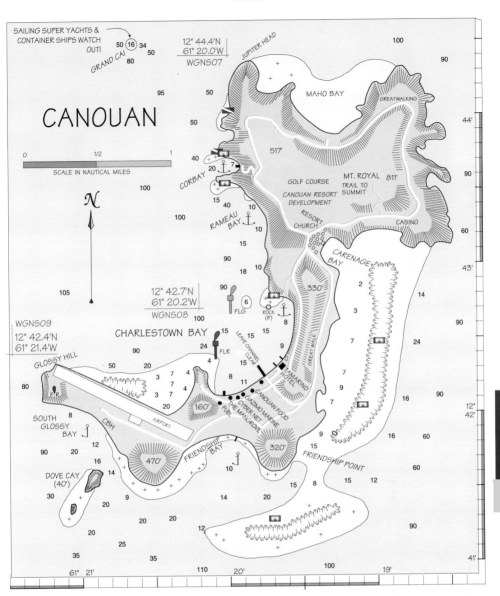

CANOUAN

SCALE IN NAUTICAL MILES

port; so give the western end of the runway good clearance.

Rameau Bay is a pleasant spot, far from the village. You may have to try a couple of times to get the anchor dug in, and the wind shifts around, so two anchors are advisable. Make sure you do not damage the coral. Corbay is a small anchorage, but one of the most protected on the island. It is sometimes used for bringing materials in, so it is occasionally noisy. At other times, it is great. If you anchor off the landing dock, you may have to move if cargo arrives. Watch out for the

reefs off both headlands: the north one has good snorkeling and diving.

Charlestown Bay is the main anchorage and the entrance is marked by a red and green beacon on either side. Pass between them. You can anchor anywhere in the bay except close to Tamarind Hotel Beach, where you must leave at least 200 yards clearance. The anchorage can be pleasant, but northeasterly winds with northerly swells will make it uncomfortable and, in extreme conditions, untenable. The holding is fairly good in sand, poor in weed. Leave a large,

St. Vincent & the ...adines

SOUTH GLOSSY BAY

FRIENDSHIP BAY

clear channel into the big dock for ferries.

On windy days, the wind gets held up in the hills and then shoots down from the north in intense gusts. Boats swing every which way.

Regulations

Customs and immigration are at the airport.

Communications

You can check out your email at Tamarind Beach Hotel internet cafe and wifi in reception or at Cyber Net. Cyber Net is way down the road on the right, well past Canouan Food. It is open every day and if the owner, Hamlet, and his assistant are absent, ask at K & W market across the road.

General yacht services

There is a large ferry dock off the beach, a Moorings dock, and a dinghy dock off the Tamarind Beach Hotel. In big swells they are all dangerous. The big ferry dock is high and difficult. The Moorings don't really have room for visiting yacht tenders. The Tamarind Beach Hotel dock is good as long as the swells are not too big.

Garbage is a problem. You will find bins ashore on the main street behind the ferry dock, but they are small, so you need to take in several small bags, rather than a big one.

Marcus [VHF: 16], helped by his cousin John, rents moorings for $50 EC a night and sells ice, water, gasoline, and, in emergency, diesel, which he will bring alongside in his tender. He also has a taxi and a water taxi, and if you are taking an island tour he will pick you up from your yacht. Many of Marcus's moorings are in front of the Tamarind Beach Hotel. (If you anchor inside these you are too close to the hotel.) He has others, so if you do not find one give him a call.

Moorings listen to VHF: 16 and will try to help with information or in an emergency. They post daily weather reports and are helpful.

Tamarind Beach Hotel [VHF: 16] sells bread and ice at the Palapa Restaurant. They have a massage and body-care center and taxis are available. Ask at reception.

Diesel and gas are sold at the gas station behind the southern end of the beach.

Technical yacht services

Gazimo Marine Services is owned and run by Earl who worked for years in a Toronto marina repair shop. He is a great guy who can deal with any problem you have, from a clogged head to a jammed winch. He is an excellent diesel mechanic and can fix outboards. He has tons of experience fixing broken charter yachts, and his ex-boss, Robert, who has a holiday house here, occasionally likes to help out.

Earl's partner Deborah helps in the shop and runs a cafe as part of the workshop. You can get good espresso coffee, sandwiches, soft drinks, beers, and more.

Provisioning and shopping

Canouan Food Limited is on the main street and opens 0800-2000, except Sunday,

0900-1200 and 1600-2000. They have a good selection for a small market, including quite a few local and imported vegetables. If you are buying cases of beer and more than you can carry, they will deliver to the dock.

Some other small markets are quite good, and market stalls on the street leading to the ferry dock have local produce. The bank has an ATM.

Shop in Tamarind Beach Hotel's new Gastronomy, a fancy delicatessen, selling freshly made food, bread, and the finest pasta, wines and liqueurs.

Restaurants

The Tamarind Beach Hotel [VHF: 16, $A-B] is part of the Canouan Resort Development, and yachts are welcome. This elegant hotel has two waterfront restaurants under picturesque thatched roofs that have been built in the traditional South American style and a beach bar.

La Palapa is the larger restaurant and is open for breakfast, lunch, and dinner. You will want to wear at least long trousers, a sports shirt, and sandals for dinner, as it is somewhat formal. Try to make reservations in advance, as space is limited.

The informal Pirate Cove Bar and Restaurant opens at 1600. You are welcome barefoot and in shorts. Comfortable seats in a garden setting overlooking the bay make this an ideal hangout. Meals are available anytime it is open, and the menu includes seafood and meat dishes, as well as pasta. They bake excellent pizzas after 1900.

The beach bar opens from 1000 to 1800, with drinks and snack meals.

Mangrove [$C-D] is an excellent local restaurant owned by Albert, who also owns Canouan Food Limited. It is quite far down the road, just where the airport road turns up the hill. The beach location is perfect, the prices and food are local, with very inexpensive lunches and moderately priced dinners, including fresh fish and lobster. They open for lunch and dinner every day.

Marcus's sister Phyllis has a cute little restaurant [$D] on the main street opposite the road that comes from the town dock and a few steps to the left. It opens for lunch and dinner. (To be sure about dinner, call 593-

Tamarind Beach hotel dinghy dock

4190 or talk to Marcus.) If you happen to be here on a Thursday, Phyllis does a big and popular barbecue cook out, starting at 1630 and going on into the evening.

Frontline [$C-D] is a cute little restaurant upstairs opposite the road that leads to the town dock. It is owned by two delightful women, Cinty and Aneka. You can get a traditional saltfish breakfast here, very inexpensive sandwiches for lunch, and for dinner they have fish or chicken and chips. They will cook you a full dinner given a little notice. They bake all their own bread.

Come out of Moorings, turn sharp right and Crystal Sands [$C-D] restaurant, bar, and apartments is on your left behind a big lawn. Anella is usually around and cooks breakfast, lunch, and dinner. She does good seafood, including a highly recommended lambi. She has rotis and other light lunches. For dinner she needs a couple of hours' notice, but it will be worth it.

Canouan Resort is in the northern part of the island, with tennis courts, villas, 180 rooms, a casino, a golf course, and a beachside restaurant and bar overlooking a fancy swimming pool. An even fancier hotel is now under construction. A variety of visiting options may be possible if it not too crowded. Call: 458-8000.

Other restaurants include: Pompoy's Bar and Restaurant, Tip Tip Bar (opens at 1900, for a meal call Chester Deroche in advance 458-8021), Honey Chrome, and Glimpses Bar.

Ashore

A taxi tour of the island only takes about an hour. Contact Marcus (VHF:16) or Phyllis (593-4190), or ask in the Tamarind Beach Hotel. The hotel can also arrange for you to hike to the island's highest peak with Randy. A walk to the east side of the island will show you the wonderful, reef-protected lagoon.

Opposite Canouan Foods is a pan yard where you can sometimes listen to steel bands practicing.

OTHER ANCHORAGES

A really rolly anchorage can be found by the Canouan Beach Hotel (CBH) in South Glossy Bay. The water here is gorgeous, and so is the beach. I would recommend it for a lunch stop.

You can dinghy to the beach, swells permitting. Currents make swimming ashore inadvisable. The CBH restaurant is usually open.

Keen snorkelers might be interested in a daytime stop at Friendship Bay on Canouan's south coast. Approach past Glossy Bay, pass inside or outside Dove Cay and associated rocks, and follow the coast, keeping a good lookout for coral heads. Friendship Bay is usually a bit rolly, but is the best anchorage in large northerly swells. You can use the fishing dock for your dinghy. In settled conditions you can dinghy up the windward side of Canouan inside the reefs, where the snorkeling is excellent. (You can get some of the way up with about 6-foot draft, but this is only for very experienced navigators in exceptionally calm conditions.)

Water sports

At least ten good dives can be found in Canouan. There are walls with giant boulders and sloping reefs, and sharks, turtles, and rays are often spotted. For those diving on their own, the easiest spot to anchor for a dive is in Corbay. Dive to seaward of the rocky headland on the northern side of the bay. You can also dinghy north up the coast and look for your own spot. Another good dive, if you are anchored in South Glossy Bay, is right around Glossy Hill. Watch out for currents. Snorkeling is good around the rocks in Rameau Bay.

Canouan Dive Center is based in the Moorings complex. Manager Vaughn Martin is very well qualified and helpful; it is are a Padi operation. They are happy to pick people up off the yachts here and further down in the Grenadines. They do the diving for Palm Island.

SOUTHERN GRENADINES PASSAGES

From Canouan to Carriacou, the Grenadines huddle together, each just a short hop from the next. The islands are generally small and quiet.

Any island with a few inhabitants will also have a rum shop where you can meet people and learn to drink Jack Iron ~ a powerful, rough, white rum, sometimes distilled far from government inspectors. A small shot is poured into a glass, and the idea is to down it all in one gulp, preferably without tasting. Then you reach for a large glass of water to put out the fire.

Navigation

The current sets to the west most of the time, so head east of your destination until you have got the feel of its strength. The southern Grenadines are strewn with keel-hungry reefs. This is the area where people make the most mistakes, and several yachts have been lost. Usually this is because they misidentify islands. If you approach this area with just a shade of apprehension and self-questioning, you should be okay.

Several navigational beacons help. Most of them are on the edges of shoals, so keep well clear.

Sailing south

When you round Glossy (Glass) Hill at Canouan, you must be sure you know which island is which. Mayreau lies in front of Union, and some people see the two as one island and then mistake the Tobago Cays for Mayreau. If you are heading for the lee of Mayreau, your compass heading should be around 225-230° magnetic. If you find yourself sailing between south and 200°, you are probably heading for the Tobago Cays ~ and trouble.

Tobago Cays. If you approach the Tobago Cays from the north, the easiest and best route is as follows: after you round Glossy Hill, head for the middle of Mayreau (about 228°magnetic). As you approach

St. Vincent & the Grenadines

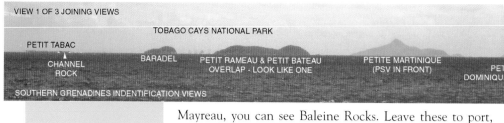

TOBAGO CAYS NATIONAL PARK

PETIT TABAC

CHANNEL
ROCK
BARADEL
PETIT RAMEAU & PETIT BATEAU
OVERLAP - LOOK LIKE ONE
PETITE MARTINIQUE
(PSV IN FRONT)
PET
DOMINIQU

SOUTHERN GRENADINES INDENTIFICATION VIEWS

Mayreau, you can see Baleine Rocks. Leave these to port, giving them reasonable clearance, and sail on until you are about halfway between them and Mayreau, before heading up into the Tobago Cays. Line up the day markers in the Cays if you can see them. (Note: Petit Rameau and Petit Bateau look like one island for much of the approach.)

An alternative and much trickier approach is to head a bit to the east of Mayreau from Glossy Hill, and then sail 100 yards to the east of Baleine Rocks, between the rocks and the northwest end of Horseshoe Reef. This entrance channel is about a quarter-of-a-mile wide, and Horseshoe Reef is often not visible, so caution is advised. The current can be strong, so make sure you are not being set down onto the rocks. Once past the rocks, hold course until the day markers line up (see Tobago Cays sketch chart), then head up into the islands.

Mayreau. When approaching Mayreau, you have to avoid Dry Shingle, which only has a stump of a marker. Pass close to Salt Whistle Bay. When sailing round the lee of Mayreau, watch out for the reef off Grand Col Point, which is sometimes marked by a red buoy, but the color and even the buoy itself are not reliable. Pass well outside this reef. When heading over to Palm or Union, you need to head well up, at least to the middle of Palm Island, until you figure out how much you are being set down, as the current can be very strong. Watching the airport on Union against Carriacou gives an idea of current set. Union's deadly windward reef (Newlands Reef) extends halfway to Palm Island, so you have to sail almost to Palm before heading west into Clifton Harbour. Note that there are three red beacons on Newlands Reef. You leave these to starboard as you head into Clifton.

VIEW 2

SALT WHISTLE BAY

CARRIACOU   MAYREAU

PALM ISLAND

PETIT DOMINIQUE

BALEINE ROCKS

VIEWS TAKEN WHILE ROUNDING GLOSSY HILL

Swing in a curve well outside them.

Grand de Coi, between Union and Palm, is a dangerous reef. It is not quite as bad as it was, as the center part of it is now usually above water and so visible. There is a yellow and black beacon on its western side. You must always pass to the west (Union Island side) of this beacon, keeping well clear. Numerous yachts have run aground here, and several have been destroyed, usually coming from PSV to Palm or Union. The following pointers may also be helpful in gauging your position.

All directions: When there is a gap between PSV and Petite Martinique, you are too far south to hit Grand de Coi. When this gap is closed, keep clear of Grand de Coi by watching the western side of Mayreau against the Union Island airport. If you keep the west side of Mayreau behind the airport you will be west of Grand de Coi. A gap between the two stands you in danger.

For all directions south: Sail down to the entrance of Clifton Harbor, then pass west of the Grand de Coi beacon.

To Carriacou: Head toward the northwest coast. When you approach Hillsborough, it is safest to pass to the west of Jack a Dan before rounding up into town.

To PSV: When you have passed Grand de Coi, steer for the east side of Carriacou until PSV bears due east, then head on in, passing well to the south of Mopion, Pinese, and all their surrounding reefs. Keep an eye on current set and compensate if necessary.

A much trickier and more dangerous way is to pass between the two little sand cays, Mopion and Pinese. The course from the lee side of Grand de Coi is around 165-170° magnetic, though with current you may have to head considerably more to the east. A bearing of 160° magnetic on

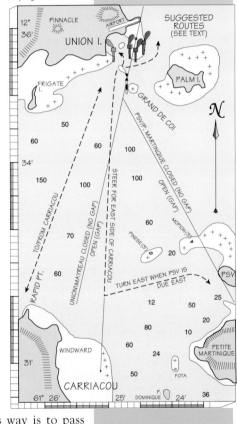

SALT WHISTLE BAY

THE PINNACLE

VIEW 3

MAYREAU

UNION ISLAND

CATHOLIC ISLAND

CATHOLIC ROCKS

St. Vincent & the Grenadines

Carriacou   Mayreau   Union Island   Glossy Hill   Catholi Island

North Canouan affords an ideal spot from which to identify some of the islands to the south

the highest peak of Petite Martinique takes you close enough to eyeball your way in. Mopion usually has a small thatch shelter on it. Always sail through the center of the passage, and do not round up too soon, as the reef extends about a quarter of a mile southwest of Mopion. Recently, this has been easier because another small sandbar formed closer to the edge of the reef (see our PSV and Petite Martinique chart). Treat this passage with caution.

Sailing north

From Carriacou to Clifton and Palm: The safest route is to pass to the west of Jack a Dan, and then follow the coast up to Rapid Point. From Rapid Point, aim for the east side of Union, checking on the current set by watching Frigate Island against Union. As you near Union, you should be able to see the reefs between Frigate and Clifton. Do not get too close to these, as the current and wind are setting you down on them. On the other hand, keep a good eye out for the Grand de Coi reef to the east. Stay to the west of the beacon that marks this reef (see also Grand de Coi notes, above, under Mayreau).

From PSV to Union: Sail due west till you are on a line between the east coasts of Carriacou and Union, before changing course to Clifton. Before the gap closes between PSV and Petite Martinique, edge westward till the finger of land on the western side of Mayreau disappears behind the new Union Island airport. Pass to the west of the Grand de Coi beacon. Experienced sailors could head out between Mopion and

Pinese and then head for the Pinnacle until the finger of land on the western side of Mayreau disappears behind the new Union Island airport, or until the Grand de Coi beacon is identified. Always pass well to the west of the Grand de Coi beacon.

From Palm northwards: Always sail round the lee of Mayreau. Pass to the west of Grand Col Point, staying well clear of the reef. Then, as you get to the north of Mayreau, stay well east of Dry Shingle (marked by a black and yellow beacon), which extends eastward from Catholic Island.

Approaching the Tobago Cays from the south: Sail round the lee of Mayreau, then head straight up toward the middle of the Cays. If you are tacking under sail, favor the Mayreau side of the channel when passing Baleine Rocks to avoid the one-fathom shoal to their south. There is a southern entrance to the Cays, but it is tricky and should not be attempted without local knowledge. Many charter yachts have run aground here. However, if you are in the Cays on a quiet day with good reef visibility, you could try leaving by this route.

When leaving the Cays to go north: The safest route is to sail from the anchorage to the north end of Mayreau, then head north after you have passed Baleine Rocks. There is also a channel to the east of Baleine Rocks about a quarter of a mile wide. From the Cays, you have to head just south of the rocks until you reach the channel and then turn north, or you are in danger of hitting the western edge of Horseshoe Reef.

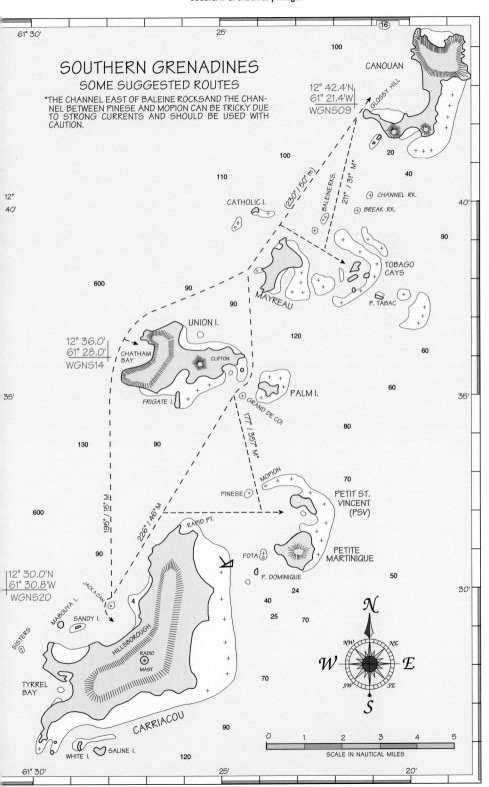

SOUTHERN GRENADINES
SOME SUGGESTED ROUTES

*THE CHANNEL EAST OF BALEINE ROCKSAND THE CHAN-
NEL BETWEEN PINESE AND MOPION CAN BE TRICKY DUE
TO STRONG CURRENTS AND SHOULD BE USED WITH
CAUTION.

CANOUAN

12° 42.4'N
61° 21.4'W
WGNS09

GLOSSY HILL

100

100

110

CATHOLIC I.

BALEINE RKS.

211° / 31° M*

CHANNEL RK.

BREAK RK.

20

40

90

(230° / 50° m)

600

90

90

MAYREAU

TOBAGO
CAYS

P. TABAC

120

60

UNION I.

12° 36.0'
61° 28.0'
WGNS14

CHATHAM
BAY

CLIFTON

60

PALM I.

FRIGATE I.

GRAND DE COI

80

130

90

177° / 357° M*

70

MOPION

PINESE

PETIT ST.
VINCENT
(PSV)

600

195° / 15 M

226° / 46 M

RAPID PT.

PETITE
MARTINIQUE

12° 30.0'N
61° 30.8'W
WGNS20

JACKADAN

FOTA

P. DOMINIQUE

50

90

4

40

24

MABOUYA I.

SANDY I.

25

70

SISTERS

HILLSBOROUGH

RADIO
MAST

70

N

NW   NE

TYRREL
BAY

W   E

SW   SE

S

CARRIACOU

90

0   1   2   3   4   5

WHITE I.   SALINE I.

120

SCALE IN NAUTICAL MILES

St. Vincent & the Grenadines

DIVING IN THE SOUTHERN GRENADINES

The normally clear water makes diving in the southern Grenadines wonderful, though currents can be strong, and many dives have to be done as drift dives.

Since the creation of the Tobago Cays National Park, diving within the park must be with a local dive shop. This covers the area from well to the west of Mayreau through to the outside of World's End Reef.

One call and a dive boat will come by and pick you up from your yacht in the Tobago Cays, Mayreau, or Union.

Grenadines Dive [VHF: 16/68] is a pleasant, relaxed, dive operation in Union Island run by Glenroy Adams from Bequia. Glenroy has incredible experience in this area, and has done much for environmental education in Union, and for the conservation of the Tobago Cays. Glenroy will collect you from your yacht in Union, Mayreau, PSV, or the Tobago Cays. If you are short of ice or have run out of bread, he will happily bring some along on his way out.

See also Canouan Dive Center under Canouan.

You can still dive on your own in Canouan, Union, and PSV. In Union, you can dive on the outer edge of Newlands Reef which is very easy from your yacht. In Chatham, you can dive on the northern headland and the coast farther north, and in PSV you can dive on the north side of the reef around Mopion.

Dives within the park include the wreck of the World War I gunboat, Purina. It is marked on our chart. While you can certainly get some elegant views of large schools of fish, framed by pieces of wreckage, this dive does not compare in scenic beauty with the reef dives. As it is only 140 feet long, neither is it a dive where you keep moving along, looking at the view. The beauty of this dive is that you don't move ~ you are already there. This is a dive where you stop rushing around and instead get on more intimate terms with the fish and sea creatures, of which there are a great abundance. Since the fish are very tame, it is ideal for underwater photography.

Surface currents over the wreck can be strong, but down on the wreck it is not usually a problem. I like to start with a slow exploration to see the layout and also get a feel for the kinds of fish that are around. Then I examine each part of the wreck, concentrating on the invertebrates and letting the fish come to me as they will.

Diving outside Horseshoe Reef on either side of the small boat passage is pretty, but watch for current, though in this area it is mostly on the surface. Farther north, the current can be very strong, and it is more suitable as a drift dive. Diving is also good on the reef outside Petit Tabac.

Diving in some of the cuts among the reefs between Mayreau and the Cays is spectacular. Discovered by Glenroy, this area is called Mayreau Gardens. If you manage to dive one of these in clear visibility, it could turn out to be the dive of your holiday. There is usually a lot of current, so we are talking drift dives, sometimes so rapid that you come to the surface over a mile from where you went down. You hardly need to fin. The current does all the work while you get wafted through a delightful garden of hard and soft corals, sponges, and fish. My favorite part is on the southern side of the gardens, coming out along the southern edge of the reefs. A sloping reef drops to a sand bottom in 40-60 feet. The reef has a wonderful texture made up of all kinds of corals. Boulder, pillar, and plate corals rise in a variety of intricate shapes. Some areas of huge sea fans are so large you can play hide-and-seek behind them. The special luminous quality of the light, typical in the Grenadines, seems to extend below the waves. Massive schools of brown and blue chromis engulf you from time to time, swimming inches from your mask. A few yards away, schools of snapper and jack swim by purposefully, creating a flurry of nervousness in the chromis. Angelfish, trumpetfish, large boxfish, and brightly colored parrotfish are all there as well.

BARADEL
PETIT BATEAU
PETIT TABAC
PETIT RAMEAU
JAMESBY
TOBAGO CAYS

SALT WHISTLE BAY, MAYREAU

Mayreau

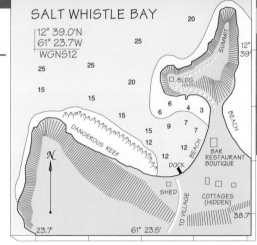

SALT WHISTLE BAY

12° 39.0'N
61° 23.7'W
WGNS12

20
25
12° 39'
25
25
25
20
15
15
SUMMIT
BLDG.
6
6
4 3
BEACH
9
7
15
7
15
12
12
BAR
RESTAURANT
BOUTIQUE
12
BEACH
12
DOCK
N
DANGEROUS REEF
SHED
TO VILLAGE
COTTAGES (HIDDEN)
38.7'
23.7'
61° 23.5'

ayreau is rimmed with pristine beaches and there are spectacular views from up on the hill. Most islanders are happy to see you and it is well worth exploring on foot. Visit both the village and the windward beaches. A road now runs from Saline Bay to Salt Whistle Bay, with many side roads. All the waters around Mayreau are part of the Tobago Cays Marine Park. Park visitation fees are not being collected, but there is no diving on your own.

SALT WHISTLE BAY

This spectacular bay has a sweeping half-moon beach and Salt Whistle Bay Club is tucked away behind it. The resort is so well hidden in the trees that people who sail in the bay often question whether it is really there.

Enter right in the middle of the bay, as there are reefs to the north and south. The northern reef

St. Vincent & the Grenadines

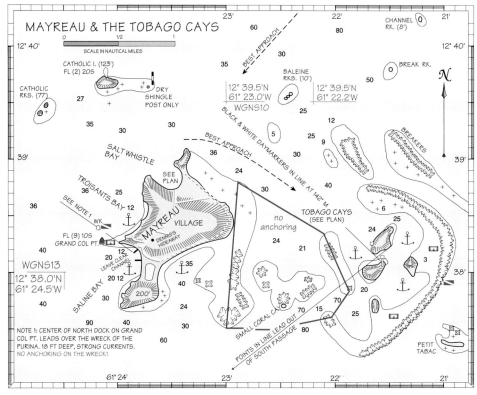

is about 6 feet deep and not usually much of a problem. The southern reef is dangerous because both wind and swells will help drive the inattentive navigator hard onto the coral. Boats often come to grief here, so take care. The holding in the bay is good in sand, if you avoid the weed patches. It can roll in northeasterly swells and winds.

There is a dock you can use for your dinghy, but no other yacht services.

Locals offer moorings for rent. One boat was badly damaged when the mooring dragged. I would not trust them. You can anchor among the moorings; they have no legal standing or rights.

Restaurants/Ashore

Salt Whistle Bay Club [VHF: 16/68, $B] was built by Tom and Undine Potter, and is now run by their daughter Natasha. They did an excellent job of being unobtrusive; it blends in so well with the surroundings, that you might not even realize it is there.

It has a whimsical, woodland atmo-sphere: the dining area is set in the open among the trees, and each table is built of stone, with its own thatched roof. You might almost expect the Mad Hatter to wander by. It is a perfect place ot hang out at the bar or dine. The menu changes daily, the food is usually delicious, fresh seafood is always available.

Just to the east, behind the beach, Salt Whistle Bay Club has another beach on the windward side, where shells and drift-wood wash ashore. Snorkeling on the reefs and rocks in the bay is fair, but sometimes murky. A new road leads up to the village from near the hotel dock, and Curtis runs a taxi service up.

On the south side of the dock, beach shacks offer seafood meals [$B]. Black Boy and Debbie is lively and in the middle. Richard's Last Bar before the Jungle has the best name, and towards the dock Yellow's is owned by Yellow Man who also delivers fresh bread, croissants, and banana bread in the morning if you ask the night before.

Salt Whistle Bay

TROISANT BAY

Troisant Bay lies between Salt Whistle and Saline Bays. It is not as protected as those bays, but still reasonably calm in most conditions. Tribu Resorts are developing this bay as private residences and plan a long dock, beach bar and restaurant at the southern end of the bay. The seabed is mainly an excellent grass bed, so wait till they put in moorings, as anchors will tear up the grass.

SALINE BAY

Saline Bay has a lovely, long beach. A large electric-generating plant is on the slope overlooking the bay. It has bright lights that shine over the bay at night but, thankfully, you do not hear it from the anchorage.

As you approach Saline Bay from the north, keep to seaward of the red buoy that marks the long reef off Grand Col Point. It is placed right on the edge of the reef, so do not cut it too fine. If the buoy is not in place, give this reef a very wide berth, as it extends much farther than most people can imagine. The outer part of the reef is 12°38.25'N, 61°24.14'W.

Saline Bay has plenty of room to anchor, the holding in sand is good, but avoid the weedy areas. Leave a clear channel for the ferries, with room for them to turn. Try to anchor on patches of sand where the holding is good.

When cruise ships anchor, Saline Bay does a quick imitation of Coney Island. Luckily, the crowds are always gone before nightfall.

Communications/services

Dennis's Hideaway and Combination Cafe both offer internet. Dennis has a desal plant by the main dock and sells water. You can tie your dinghy to one of the two docks.

Ashore

Basic supplies and sometimes fish, are available in several small groceries. Both

St. Vincent & the Grenadines

293

Salt Whistle Bay

Combination Cafe and J and C's have mini markets. A few handicrafts are available in small shops tucked in people's houses. Occasionally, a vendor sets up by the roadside.

Yachting visitors support several Mayreau-owned restaurants and a few handicraft and t-shirt outlets ~ all good for the local economy.

Dennis's Hideaway [VHF: 68, $B] is owned by Dennis from Mayreau, who used to be a charter skipper. This was the first restaurant here and has the nicest atmosphere, with an open bar and dining area beside a pool and a two story sunset view tower.

Late afternoon is the best time to meet other yachting folk. Dennis has a great flair with guests and when he is around, you will get excellent local cooking. Dennis's Hideaway also has a modern guesthouse. Dennis is building a beach bar down by his desal plant near the dock.

Almost opposite Dennis is Annie and Alexander's The Combination Cafe, and First Stop Supermarket which has a delightful rooftop bar. Stop here and enjoy a drink or cup of coffee, and pick up some of their freshly baked bread. They also open for meals from breakfast through dinner. (One reader highly recommends the fish sandwich.) Alexander was a chef in Salt Whistle Bay for many years.

Friendship Rose [$B-C], run by Rose, is next. It is a bar where Rose will happily cook you lunch or dinner to order.

Continue uphill for J & C Bar and Restaurant [VHF: 68/16, $B] on your left. It has the best view of the harbor. It is owned by Jean and Claude and is large enough to take a huge group. Jean and Claude are friendly, make a big effort, and their large portions of fish and lambi are excellent value. They have a water taxi and divide their time between here and Salt Whistle Bay.

Robert Lewis "Righteous" is a well-known Rastafarian, and you can groove to Bob Marley and other good sounds and have some good talks with Robert at Righteous & de Youths [VHF: 68, $B]. This is the cool hangout for both locals and visitors. The restaurant is an ongoing art form of construction and decoration and is the character spot on the island. Robert is welcoming and friendly, and he has a small boutique as well as a restaurant.

BEQUIA

CANOUAN

DRY SHINGLE

SALTWHISTLE BAY

GRAND COL POINT

SALINE BAY, MAYREAU

James Alexander has the Island Paradise Restaurant [VHF: 68, $B]. It is well up the hill, with a birds-eye view. This is not a place to come if you are in a hurry, as everything is cooked from scratch, but their Creole fish and curried conch are well worth the wait. They have the biggest sound system on the island, and for those who want to groove to some sounds, they can turn it up after dinner.

A little higher on the right hand side of the road, Jenella's Honey Cone serves good food at a reasonable price.

A walk east from Saline Bay along the salt pond will bring you to some long, pristine beach on the windward side. It is possible to walk north along this beach, almost to the end then look for the trail which goes in and out of the bushes. It is unmarked, but easy enough to follow all the way back along the coast to Salt Whistle Bay.

Water sports

Snorkeling on the reef coming out from Grand Col Point is fair.

WINDWARD ANCHORAGE

There is a pretty good anchorage on the eastern side of Mayreau. It is open to the south and can roll, but is excellent in unusual conditions, when northerly or westerly swells make the western anchorages untenable. Approach from the south in good light and identify the reef that extends east off the southeastern part of Mayreau. Follow this reef in. Be careful of the reefs to the east of the anchorage as some are hard to see.

The Windward anchorage is within the Tobago Cays National Park protection zone so no fishing is allowed.

Tobago Cays

The Tobago Cays

The Tobago Cays are a group of small, uninhabited islands, protected from the sea by Horseshoe Reef. The water and reef colors are a kaleidoscope of gold, brown, blue, turquoise, and green. Small sand beaches blend into luminous clear water. On cloudless nights, the stars are cast across the sky like wedding confetti thrown in an excessive gesture of bonhomie. Even squalls can be dramatically beautiful as they approach from afar. The anchorage is, however, open to the full force of the ocean winds, which are sometimes strong.

The best approach is between Mayreau and Baleine Rocks, staying south of One Fathom Bank. Black-and-white day-markers help you get the approach right. Petit Rameau and Petit Bateau look like one island for most of the approach. Don't cut corners, lest you land on a coral head.

You can anchor just west of Petit Rameau, in the cut between Petit Rameau and Petit Bateau, to the north or south of Baradel, or between Baradel and the other islands. Shallow draft yachts can anchor to the east of Baradel. Moorings are available in the Cays for $45 EC a night, but are neither compulsory nor particularly reliable. They mainly surround the turtle watching area. Do not anchor between the moorings and the turtle watching area.

There are strong currents in the cut anchorage, so bow and stern anchoring may be necessary.

When heading south out of the Cays, it is safest to pass round the lee of Mayreau, though the Cays do have a southern channel (South Exit) that is okay as an exit for the experienced when the light is good. Avoid using this southern route as an entrance, as it is hard to find, and many charter yachts have gone aground in the attempt.

Regulations

Tobago Cays is a national park. Park fees are currently $10 EC per day per person, which rangers come to collect. Superyachts should call in advance for advice on where to anchor. While Mayreau is included in the park, no fees are collected in Mayreau anchorages, but diving regulations apply. Yachts are asked to use holding tanks, this

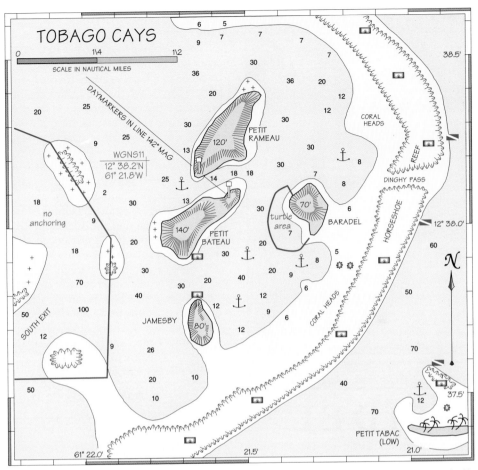

will keep the water clean for swimmers in what can be a crowded area.

This magnificent park offers the most spectacular anchoring in the Eastern Caribbean. Enjoy, and help others to do so, by obeying regulations and being considerate.

A 6-knot speed limit is in effect in the Tobago Cays. This applies to all vessels, dinghies, water taxis, and sailing boats. Please obey it and keep a good look out for swimmers. People swim throughout the anchored yachts, to the reef, and to the islands. The speed limit precludes water skiing and many water sports. However, sail and kite boarders may exceed the speed limit, but only in the area north of Petit Rameau.

Enjoy snorkeling and looking at the fish and turtles. They are there because this is a conservation area and no fishing is allowed. You may not collect or harm any kind of sea-creature, including the corals. Do not take souvenirs of any kind, including shells and rocks.

A turtle-watching area has been established around the beach in Baradel. It is marked by a series of linked buoys. If you wish to snorkel here, either anchor your dinghy outside or take it directly (and very slowly) into the beach and pull it up on the sand. No anchoring or drifting with your dinghy is allowed, and you should not run your dinghy through this area except to go to and from the beach. Approach turtles slowly, and no closer than 6 feet. (If you are still and they come closer, that is fine.) Though they look calm and peaceful, they are easily frightened if you chase or try to touch them.

No fires may be made on the beaches, and the vegetation ashore is part of the park and should be left alone.

Do not discharge any oil, chemicals or other waste into the water, or pump your

St. Vincent & the Grenadines

bilges in the park. Avoid using bleach and strong cleaners that get flushed overboard.

Those wishing to scuba dive in the park may only do so with a local dive shop.

Some people get so excited at the beauty of the Tobago Cays, that they think the way to complete the experience is to play their favorite music at top volume for the whole anchorage to hear. Cathartic as this might be for them, it may not be what others want. Keep any noise you make on your boat from music, generators, and windmills low enough that your neighbor cannot hear it.

Anchoring is permitted behind Horseshoe Reef and around the islands in sand only. Adventurous and experienced skippers could sail outside Horseshoe Reef (the approach is easiest from the south exit) and find temporary anchorage in Petit Tabac on sand bottom only. This is strictly eyeball navigation and for calm weather. Even so, it is small and rolly. Yachts should not anchor among any of the reefs between Petit Rameau and Mayreau, except in the anchorage we show directly east of Mayreau.

Ashore

Local boat vendors ply the Cays during the season, selling everything from ice, bread, and lobsters to jewelry. They are a friendly bunch and very obliging if you need them to bring you ice or bread the next day. If you want to be left alone, they will do that, too. They offer great beach barbecues and water taxis to places like Baradel.

Rasta Richard Phillip on Jah Live and Larston Browne of Lordag Velocity 2 are among the good barbecuers and they are helpful and have been highly recommended.

Rondel Weeks on Mr. Quality and Wilma Stowe at Petit Bateau are the only authorized vendors selling the Carriacou Fidel Productions art t-shirts. Each one is a painting by a local artist reproduced on a shirt. Felix-Turtle design by Carriacou artist Felix is the most popular, so popular that one vendor has copied the shirts and pretends to be the artist.

Engine in Free Spirit and Willie in Free Willie are among the good and helpful vendors.

BALEINE ROCKS

SMALL BOAT PASSAGE

P. RAMEAU

BARADEL

P. BATEAU

JAMESBY

MAYREAU

TOBAGO CAYS MARINE PARK

PETIT TABAC

St. Vincent & the Grenadines

Water sports

The snorkeling on Horseshoe Reef is good, though recent hurricanes have damaged some hard corals. The reef near the small boat passage is in the best condition. Fish are plentiful and there are lots of turtles. It can be choppy out there, and anywhere near the small boat passage you will meet current. If you have beginner snorkelers on board, the east beach on Petit Bateau (facing Baradel) has some snorkeling that starts in calm, shallow water. The dinghy approach through the reefs is tricky. For turtles, check out protected turtle area just west of Baradel.

The Tobago Cays are excellent for sailboarding. The designated area for this, when you want to go more than 6 knots, is north of Baradel. Experts can sail out through the small dinghy passage into the ocean.

To go scuba diving, contact Grenadines Dive, who will come and collect you from your yacht. Currents can be very strong and most dives are done as drift dives.

Palm Island

Palm Island

Palm Island [VHF:16] was for many years an uninhabited island called Prune Island. John and Mary Caldwell fell in love with it, built a small hotel, and planted palm trees. John was a real character, and his early sailing experiences are outlined in his famous book, *Desperate Voyage*. John had a long and interesting life. After he died, Palm Island was bought by a big hotel group and upgraded to a first-class resort.

The anchorage is off the docks, and holding is fair in 15 to 20 feet, with a sand bottom. The anchorage can be rolly, so try it for lunch, and if you feel comfortable, stay overnight.

You can use the dock for your dinghy, but use a stern anchor to keep it from riding underneath where it will be damaged. Leave plenty of room for local boats to come onto the outer end and south side of the dock.

Ashore

Palm Island's Casuarina Beach is one of the most beautiful beaches in the Windwards: a gorgeous expanse of golden sand, lapped by translucent turquoise water ~ the ultimate picture-perfect Grenadine beach. When you step ashore, turn right and you will find a boutique that sells essentials, casual wear, and souvenirs. The Coco Palm [VHF: 16, $A] beach bar and restaurant is a few steps farther on. It is open to the sea and serves elegant light lunches and heartier dinners. It is pleasant, but geared to the well-heeled in secluded surroundings.

Patrick Chavailler has an art gallery on Palm Island. He is the Palm Island doctor and helps yachting people in an emergency (458-8829). He does great underwater and boating scenes and undertakes yacht commissions. He also prints his work on tiles (fabulous) and offers limited edition prints. Ask reception for directions, or visit him in the Anchorage Hotel in Union.

Yachts are welcome to enjoy the beach area around the Coco Palm and the shoreline to the south. You can walk along Casuarina Beach if you stay fairly close to the water's edge. (One chain above high water is public.) Please respect the privacy of the hotel rooms and facilities. If you think you might want to stay here someday and want to look around, talk with a security guard; he may be able to arrange a tour.

Union I.

Union is a great island to visit. It stands out from afar with its dramatically mountainous outline. Clifton, the main harbor, is protected by a reef that shows off its brilliant kaleidoscopic colors and patterns as you sail in. If you anchor out on the reef, the water to your east is an expanse of brilliant green-turquoise; you can jump in the clear, clean water and snorkel on the reef. Ashore, the main town, Clifton, is charming and colorful, with a picture perfect market around a green. Union Islanders are welcoming and friendly and there is an excellent choice of restaurants and bars where you can sit outside and watch life in the town. Provisioning is good. The roads and trails offer the best hiking and biking in the Grenadines.

CLIFTON

Clifton is a bustling small port with a cosmopolitan atmosphere; the center of yachting in the southern Grenadines. It has a thriving day-charter industry, with tourists flying into the small airport daily to tour the Grenadines.

When approaching Clifton from the north, it is necessary to sail halfway over to Palm Island to avoid Newlands Reef (keep well outside the three red beacons on its outer edge). When approaching from the south, give Grand de Coi a wide berth.

Clifton Harbour is protected by Newlands Reef, and it has a small reef in the center. The main entrance is just south of this center reef and marked by red and green beacons. It is possible to sail to the east of the center reef and up behind Newlands

Clifton

Mayreau

Grand de Coi

Palm I.

Palm to Clifton showing routes

St. Vincent & the Grenadines

CLIFTON HARBOUR

Note the reefs and entrance

Reef toward Green Island. This area off the outer reef offers a visually great anchorage, but if you prefer to be nearer to the action, anchor anywhere off the town. Leave a wide channel with turning room for the ferries.

A coastguard dock and station are in the southern part of the harbor.

Do not anchor close to any of the innocent-looking, empty mooring buoys. Come 1700, the large day-charter boats will return and pick them up regardless.

Locals offer moorings for rent but many have gone adrift with serious consequence, and taking one is risky. Some venders put you on private moorings figuring once you have paid them it is then going to be your problem when the owner comes back and you have to move, often just as night falls. I hear lots of bad mooring stories in Union, and boats have been damaged when moorings break; it is safer to anchor.

Regulations

Clifton is St. Vincent's southern port of entry for customs clearance. Check with customs in the fishing complex weekdays from 0830-1630; at other times, including Sundays and holidays, you will find them at the airport. (Overtime is charged after 1600 and on weekends.) Immigration is in the new tourist building opposite the market and also at the airport. As long as the airport is open, clearance is available there. Clear customs as soon as you go ashore.

Communications

You can surf the net and do phone calls and faxes at Erika's Marine Services [VHF: 68] or the Internet Cafe above Buffalo Trading. Both have good equipment and are helpful, and both have bay-wide wifi. Erika's is agent for UPS; the Internet Cafe is agent for Digicel. Aquarium and Captain Gourmet offer free wifi. Both Lime and Digicel have offices on the main street.

General yacht services

You can leave garbage in the dumpster on the fishing docks, or give it to Lambi's boat for a small fee. Dinghy docks are at the Anchorage, Bougainvilla, and West Indies; also Clifton Beach Hotel and Lambi. The

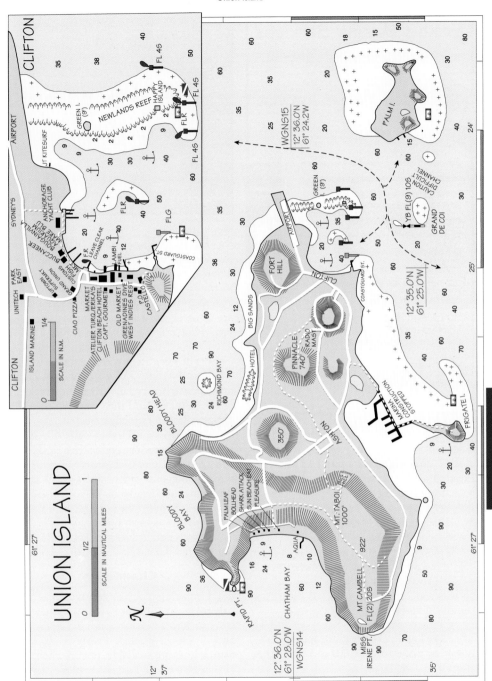

Anchorage is one of the best and while they sometimes charge a $5 EC user fee, this is fully refundable against drinks, meals, bread, ice, or anything you might want to buy there,

Ice is available at Anchorage Yacht Club, Bougainvilla, Grand Union, Lambi, and many rum shops. Unitech fills cooking gas bottles.

Jean-Marc's Bougainvilla [VHF: 16] is a marine mall with stern-to berthing for

about 20 boats. They sell water (they have a desal plant), and ice. It is also the home of the L'Aquarium restaurant and Mare Blu Boutique. Wind and Sea charters have a base here, and they do many day tours in the Grenadines. Air and sea charters are available, and this is the Grenadines base for Switch Charters.

The Anchorage Yacht Club [VHF: 68/16] has a 12-berth marina where you can tie stern-to a floating dock, and they can supply water, electricity, ice (block & cube), fax, laundry, and showers.

Clifton's gas station has a small dock adjoining Lambi's on its south side, and this is a great place to get outboard fuel. They also sell diesel, but it is only 4-5 feet deep alongside. You could drop anchor and come downwind bow-to in 7-8 feet of water. They can truck to big boats on the main wharf on demand.

From time to time, people import Venezuelan fuel which is cheaper but can have a high cost in terms of breakdowns and clogged fuel filters.

Erika's Marine Services [VHF: 68] is on the waterfront; speak to Heather or Chillie. Their services include laundry (boat collection and delivery), yacht clearance, full provisioning, and an internet station. They are a travel agent and can book tickets for you. They are the UPS agent, rent DVDs, have a good bookswap, and a water-taxi. They will even help you out for cash on a credit card if the ATM is broken. They offer full superyacht service, with agents throughout St. Vincent and the Grenadines, and a private plane for emergencies.

Clifton Beach Hotel [VHF: 68, $B-C] has about 9 feet at the end of their dock. You can come in here alongside or stern-to to buy ice and get your laundry done. Water is sometimes also available. You can also come stern-to at Lambi for water, and ice. Docking is free to dinner customers.

If you need to fly out, check Joy James at James Travel, Eagle's Travel, or Erika's.

Chandlery

Unitech has a chandlery with mechanical and yacht hardware items, and they now carry such things as second-hand equipment and dinghies. Elodie's lovely ready-made fishing lines are available, not only here, but also in L'Ateleier Turquoise, Mare Blu, and several other stores. Unitech rent kayaks by the day or week.

Technical yacht services

If you need something fixed, talk to Laurent at Unitech, just at the beginning of the road to Fort Hill. They repair all kinds of gas-

oline and diesel motors, including outboards. They weld iron and stainless, and they do fiberglass and electrical repairs. They get new parts from Martinique. Unitech sells cooking gas and can fill most boat cylinders.

Almost opposite Unitch, Island Marine Special [VHF: 16] is run by Earl Allen, a good diesel mechanic.

Slic has a sewing machine and can do emergency sail repairs and other canvas work. Ask for him near Park East

Provisioning

Provisioning in Union is good. The local market opposite Erika's is colorful and photogenic. Vendors have an excellent selection of fresh fruits and vegetables in colorful stalls around a green.

Bertram and Signa's at Island Grown, grow much of what they sell in their farm up in the hills.

Some vendors, like Jenny, have fridges, where they keep greens such as spinach and callaloo so, if you don't see what you need, ask.

Another local market is farther down the road towards Grenadines Dive.

Nicolas and Linda's Captain Gourmet [VHF: 08] is on the main street opposite the Clifton Beach Hotel. This great little store has good buys on French wines. They sell fresh French bread and yogurt, frozen shrimps, steak, smoked salmon, and many other meats, along with cheeses and whipping cream for the charter cook. You will also find coffee and many French dry goods. Outside seats make this a pleasant place for a coffee break. They offer a full provisioning service for yachts and will deliver to your dinghy. Nicolas and his father Robert are pilots, with a small plane that helps them bring in new stock. Nicolas is also involved with JT Kitesurfing School (see watersports) and he started the youth sailing program here with Optimists.

More small supermarkets will cater to your other shopping needs. Uptown Supermarket is a new, clean, and pleasant mini supermarket. Owner Stephanie stocks cream and cheeses, along with the regular items and a good selection of drinks. In the same building you will find the Vet Store and Sophie's Therapeutic Massage and Nail Care. Round the back is the office of the environmental group Sustainable Grenadines

Grand Union often has lots of basics and fresh local chicken. Lambi has wine, packaged food, fresh food, pork and beef from Lambi's farm, and general hardware and household goods.

Buy your local bread from Cash 'n Carry, just by the turn to the market. It is freshly baked, inexpensive, and good. For fancier French bread, croissants, and Danish, check out the Anchorage Hotel, the bakery on the

Bougainvilla Hotel, Union Island, T: 784 494-8880
The most beautiful boutique in Union Island

dock at Bougainvilla, and Captain Gourmet.

Need pet food? A vet has now opened a little store in the small mall on main street. Susie, who works with the vet store, Heather from Erika's, and Gary from Union have started an Animal Kindness charity. They get the fur back on strays, food in their bellies, cut down on random pet procreation, and provide animal education in the local schools. Susie is on first name terms with every dog in the island. They have had a big impact. You can ask about it in the vet store or at Erika's.

Fun shopping

Union is becoming quite the place for boutiques. Robert and Annie-France's L'Atelier Turquoise (Beads and Art gallery) displays original paintings and local handicrafts and souvenirs. These include great locally painted calabash art, figures from Haiti and lots to attract the eye. But the main attraction of the boutique is Annie-France's lovely jewelry made from semi-precious stones, including the lovely larimar stone, and beads. Each delightful item is hand crafted, special, and sold at affordable prices.

I have known Charlotte since I first started writing guides, when she ran the Ponton du Bakoua in Martinique. She moved to Union and ran the Anchorage Hotel during its best years. Now she has come out of retirement and opened Mare Blu in Bougainvilla. Charlotte has created a beautiful boutique, using artistic design and lighting, so as you come in you have the feeling of entering Aladdin's treasure trove. It is fun to visit and you will find a little of everything: elegant casual wear, hats, art, carvings, ornaments, fancy bags, jewelry, and books, as well as practical stuff like sunblock and flip flops. This is the place to buy postcards and stamps. You can write them over a coffee in L'Aquarium and bring them back and Mare Blu will mail them for you.

Juliet's Romeo Boutique is in the market and opens most days. Juliet stocks casual wear, t-shirts, souvenirs, and decorative items, as well as locally made jewelry

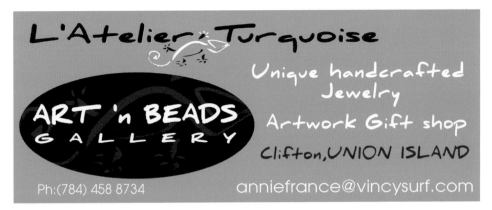
and metal sculptures. Kazia from Martinique has Kazia's Madinina Showroom with lots of t-shirts, overpainted tie-dye items, Felix's sculptures, some applique, and souvenirs. Other shops to check out along the street inlcude Roots, and Music Shop Art & Craft. The Clifton Beach Hotel has the Sunseekers Shade boutique, with a wide range of casual clothing, souvenirs, and books.

The Grenadines Gift Shop is at the airport. They have batik wall hangings, t-shirts, souvenirs, carvings, film, and hard-to-find camera batteries. You can send your Fedex packages from here.

Castello Paradise is unique: a garden bazaar with a distinct feel of the East, a combination of alcohol and art. It includes a grotto, sculptures, quaint architecture, and more. There are several little boutiques that include the work of Jutta Hartmann, and at least three bars. The best is the Pelican Bar, up Rocky Birdland hill at the end of the garden, which has a view of the harbor. You pay a $5 EC entrance fee to this hill, redeemable at the bar. Add in cages full of parakeets and you have a place that will fascinate kids. The pig farm next door adds a rural element.

There are several other small stalls and shops for local handicrafts, and many ladies hang out t-shirts for sale in the fish market buildings.

Lulley has a branch of his fishing tackle store here, a great place to get all kinds of fishing equipment, from rods to hooks.

Up beyond Castello, Kandy Cream is the place for ice cream and cake.

St. Vincent & the Grenadines

Clifton

Restaurants

Both Anchorage and Bougainvilla have shark pools; sharks and other sea creatures are sometimes in residence.

Union has become the jump-up center of the Grenadines, and you will find plenty of entertainment and some fun restaurants.

Marie is originally French, but made Union her home so long ago it was just about when I started writing guides. She has been involved in several good business, but Ciao Pizza [$C-D] is the best. She cooks excellent fresh fish, and seafood specials, pastas, great gazpacho, and, of course, pizza. This is the place to come for a really good lunchtime smoked fish salad. She is right in town, opposite the main dock; you can sit outside and watch the world go by.

The West Indies [$B-C] is on the waterfront by Grenadines Dive, with its own dinghy dock. Joëlle, the owner, and her assistant, Jean-Jacques, look after their customers very well. The ambiance is casually elegant French, the cooking is French/Creole, and the prices are reasonable. Their local conch dishes and beef tenderloin are excellent. Save enough room for dessert, if possible; chocolate mousse and chocolat liegeois are among the choices. Their soups, salads, and panini sandwiches are wonderful for lunch. The bar is a popular hangout for many locals. This restaurant has remained a favorite for many repeat visitors.

L'Aquarium [$B-C] has a perfect location in the Bougainvilla complex, open to the harbor and the breeze, with a spectacular saltwater aquarium for decor. It is owned by Sonia from Paris. It is open all day and she has plenty of space, so there are comfy seats for relaxing as well as dining tables, making it a good meeting place where you can have an espresso while using their wifi. They have a lobster tank, so the lobster is fresh, and they cook other excellent seafoods, as well as Argentinian beef. A second specialty is perfect Italian pizza and pasta. Save room for crème brulée. Ask about their occasional entertainment.

Sonia also has the tiny waterfront bar La Cabane, just outside with a few seats. Here they cook crepes, baguettes, pain au chocolat, and croissants and they make

Clifton's reef anchorage

sandwiches.

Buccaneer [$C-D] is a new two-story restaurant next to the Bougainvilla complex. Manager Asha is helpful and usually around. They serve a good plate of food here at a reasonable price. They have a Friday lunch barbecue, a Saturday creole lunch, plus Thursday night Karaoke. A new flat screen TV was just about to arrive, making this the place to watch that important game.

Bert and Camille's Twilight, next to Marie's, is another good hangout bar, as Bert plays guitar, and Camille knows how to keep everyone happy. They cook good fish burgers.

The Anchorage Yacht Club [VHF: 68, $A-B] is pretty with a delightful view of the harbor. It is owned by the Palm Island group and managed by Patrick Chavailler, the doctor and artist from Palm Island, who brought it back from ruin. They have a dinghy dock and a pleasant bar for relaxing. Their restaurant is open all day every day. They have a big tapas menu as well as a comprehensive menu. Patrick's painting are on show (and for sale) which also helps with decoration.

If you need a night ashore, Anchorage offers special rates for those on yachts.

Lambert is smiling these days, and why not? His Lambi emporium [VHF: 68, $B-C], consisting of a supermarket, a big waterfront restaurant, and some rental rooms is going well. Each time I come, his building seems to have crept farther out to sea. The conch shell walls give a rough-and-ready atmosphere. The food is reasonably priced and local, as is the entertainment, with lively steel bands every night in season. Lambert also sells very inexpensive takeaway snacks on the road side.

The Clifton Beach Hotel [VHF: 68, $B-C], run by Marie Adams-Hazell, has a perfect, open waterfront location and its own dinghy dock. The bar is a popular meeting place. After you have finished shopping, try one of their sandwiches. You can also visit for dinner, or the occasional jump-up.

Limelite, open to the main street, is the place to take a break and watch the world go by and it is the last bar to close at night. Its presence here began the improved look of the main street.

St. Vincent & the Grenadines

The cheapest and fastest food is Teroy William's Big Citi, upstairs, opposite the market. He opens all day from about 0700 to 2200 with a great view and cafeteria style food.

For other good and inexpensive local food, visit T&N [$B-D], which is another pleasant place to watch life go by. Alternatively, walk down the road and check out Evergreen, by Castello's, or Jennifer's Restaurant and Bar [$C-D], a little farther up the road. Both serve West Indian food at a reasonable price. Or check out Paula's, opposite the old market. You might want to visit Cruiser's Bar above Erika's.

If you are anchored near the reef, you will notice Janti's Happy Island [$B-D], built on the edge of the reef. Janti is the only man in the Caribbean I know who created his own island by hand. He formerly had a bar in Ashton, but could not find enough customers. He also worked for tourism, trying to clean up the town. One headache was a huge pile of conch shells left by fishermen on the beach. Janti solved both problems by taking the shells from the beach and using them to build Happy Island. It is perfectly placed for snorkeling by day and for taking a sundowner at night. You can tie your dinghy right outside. This is Union's most informal bar, it is fun, and has a lovely view as sunset turns to night. You can come here for a simple desert-island barbecue dinner or a lobster-and-champagne special. Janti is often helped by Andrea.

Transport

Water taxis will be happy to take you ashore: $10-20 EC one-way for your group, depending on where you are anchored. Eat with Lambi and he will arrange it for free.

Sam Young usually parks his taxi by the fishing port close to Bougainvilla, look for him or call (433-6002); or try Rosmund Adams (526-4500 not on Saturday).

Ashore

While in Clifton, visit the SMMA interpretation center on the main square. There is not much in here, and the staff don't seem that interested in visitors, but it may improve. They are supposed to have educational movies about the park and marine matters, and a big aquarium.

Union offers great hiking and biking, with views of the island's beautiful turquoise waters, from Clifton right over to Ashton and Frigate Island. The road system enables you to bike all over the island. Two obvious close viewpoints for walkers are Fort Hill and the road that leads from opposite the hospital back past the Pinnacle and into Ashton. Farther afield, the roads that rise from Richmond Bay to circle round Bloody Bay and Chatham are beautiful, and the road from Ashton to Mt. Campell has great views to the south. Off-the-road hiking includes the ridge along the western mountain range and, for excellent views, take the well-marked trail to Big Hill, from where the adventurous can rough it up to Mt. Taboi. The Pinnacle

View from the hill on Frigate Island

FRIGATE ISLAND ANCHORAGE, UNION

is one of the hardest climbs, with a dramatic, 360-degree, precipitous view. Looked at from afar, an iguana-like rock lies on the top. The approach is right under the iguana, on the Clifton side of the hill. Hardy adventurers could try this with a cutlass, but it would be smart to find a guide. Doyleguides.com has more detailed directions.

Water sports

You will find information on the dive shops and some dive sites under the Southern Grenadine diving section. Clifton is the base of Grenadines Dive [VHF: 16/68].

Jeremie and Linn, together with Nicolas, run JT Pro Kitesurf Center, which is based in the Anchorage Hotel. These are top professionals and teach at all levels. Many of their customers are sailors who want to learn to kitesurf or become better. They also do great full moon parties in the season. You will find them close to the airport. Check them out or visit their web Kitesurfgrenadines.com

Day-charter boats leave every day to visit the other Grenadines. The main operators of the cats are Land and Sea and Palm Island (Captain Yannis). Then there is Martin's Scaramouche, the lovely Carriacou-built schooner, whose presence enhances the view, and is a great addition to any photo of the Tobago Cays.

FRIGATE ISLAND

Frigate Island, although just over a mile from Clifton, is generally quiet and well protected in normal conditions, and exceptionally so in strong northeasterlies. You can anchor in the lee of the island, but enter carefully, as the bottom shelves quickly. Construction started on a large development, including a 300-berth marina. The company went bankrupt, and the project stopped.

You are within dinghy reach of Ashton, the other town on Union. Ashton is local and delightful, with lower prices than Clifton. It has a good dock for leaving your dinghy. You will find small restaurants, friendly rum shops, and several small supermarkets.

Walking ashore is pleasant. Those with a head for heights and a firm grip can scramble high up the hill on Frigate Island for a view. For more ambitious hikes, there are Big Hill and Mt. Taboi. You can find good snorkeling on the reef on the windward side of Frigate. Be careful of the current.

St. Vincent & the Grenadines

Chatham Bay

CHATHAM BAY

Chatham Bay, on the lee side of Union, is a large and magnificent anchorage, with a long sandy beach to the east and a steep headland to the north. Anchor anywhere in the north part of the bay. (You may have to move if the fishermen are seine netting.) The wind tends to come over the hills in shrieking gusts. There is a long beach to explore and good snorkeling around the rocks off Rapid Point. The fish life here is particularly rich and attracts all kinds of birds, including pelicans. A rough road leads to the northern headland, and a path leads to the center ridge, and from these, roads go to Ashton or Clifton. The hiking all around is lovely.

Sunday is often popular with locals who come over for lunch.

Services/Ashore

If you want to avoid Clifton and have not yet cleared, one of the boat men will run you to town and back to clear customs for about $150 EC, or Seckie will take you by cab for about $120 EC. The Palm Leaf boat sells fresh bread and ice in the mornings.

At the north end of the beach, five master barbecuers compete to give you an entertaining lunch or dinner on the beach. They charge about $65-100 EC depending on whether you want fish, chicken, ribs or lobster. These bars are rough, ready, and lots of fun. Some try a hard sell from their boats. If you have the time, walk ashore, check out the people and places, then choose. They will need to know a couple of hours in advance that you are coming.

Sun, Beach and Eat is run by Seckie and Vanessa and is one of the larger buildings, where they will look after you well; ask about their beach games. They serve fish, chicken, ribs, lobster, and land crabs, and a bonfire is often lit after dark. They can arrange for a big drum dance and other entertainment for groups and will organize special events like birthday parties. They always do a big full moon party with live music. They are occasionally there all day, more often in the evening. They can arrange to bring you over from Clifton if you don't make it to Chatham.

Palm Leaf is at the north end, and is run by Jerry, who is very pleasant, laid back, and not at all pushy. He is often there during the day when the others don't show.

Bollhead is next door. His family owns a building in Clifton and he had a bar there. He now does barbecues in Chatham. He will keep you well entertained and fed. Someone torched his place a few years ago, but he got back up running and often draws a crowd. It is a happening bar. He has a very quiet generator and plays music so you can dance on beach in the moonlight. Bollhead's boatkick, Andel, catches fish and lobster early in the morning and sells to yachts.

Shark Attack was the first to offer beach barbecues here. It was hard work, because everything had to come by boat, but he became popular. Eventually, the government put in a rough road. This made life so easy that others saw what he was doing and set up in competition. Shark Attack keeps up his tradition of great barbecues of fish and lobster.

Pleasure, who has hung out at Chatham even longer than Shark Attack, originally sang for him, and now has Pleasure's Bar, under a big tamarind tree. It is close by the road and the path that leads to the rest of the island. He and his wife Rosita are very pleasant and will cook you fresh fish or lobster, and he is a little less expensive than the others. Pleasure plays guitar and will provide a little music for your entertainment.

Way down at the south end, Antonio

SUN BEACH & EAT
TEL: (784) 531-6965 (784) 530-5913
VHF: 16

Chatham Bay, Union I.
Happy Hour
   3pm-6pm
Breakfast
Lunch
Dinner
Full moon
   party
Taxi

Your hosts
Seckie & Vanessa

has opened Aqua in two wonderful, open, thatched buildings; a bar and a restaurant that are joined by a swimming pool. This is a completely different experience from the others: a lovely boutique resort, comfortable and elegant, perfect for when you are beach-barbecued out and want somewhere quiet to relax. Manager Lesia is helpful and they are open for a light lunch [$D]: rotis, sandwiches, and grilled fish. Their shrimp and lobster rotis are excellent. They are also open for a gourmet style dinner [$A]

Antonio had just put in an inventive and artistic dinghy dock, using giant rocks placed by nature. He is the southern agent for JT Yachting. You can ask about water.

St. Vincent & the Grenadines

View from Aqua dock

PSV & Petite Martinique

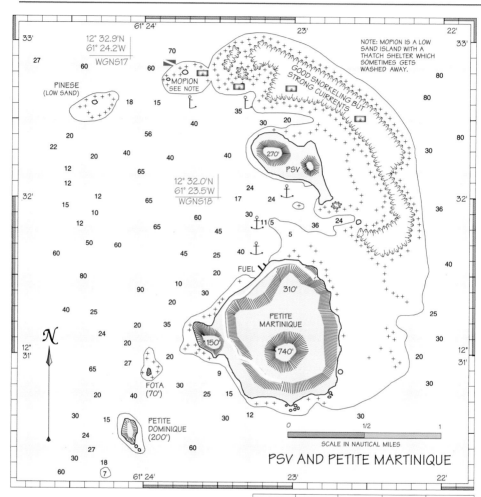

PINESE
(LOW SAND)

12° 32.9'N
61° 24.2'W
WGNS17

MOPION
SEE NOTE

NOTE: MOPION IS A LOW
SAND ISLAND WITH A
THATCH SHELTER WHICH
SOMETIMES GETS
WASHED AWAY.

GOOD SNORKELING BUT
STRONG CURRENTS

12° 32.0'N
61° 23.5'W
WGNS18

PSV

FUEL

PETITE
MARTINIQUE

310'

150'

740'

FOTA
(70')

PETITE
DOMINIQUE
(200')

SCALE IN NAUTICAL MILES

PSV AND PETITE MARTINIQUE

SPA

DINING
ROOM
& BAR

BEACH
BAR

DINGHY
DOCK

DOCK

REEF

PSV
ANCHORAGE

12° 32'N
61° 23'W

SV (Petit St. Vincent) and Petite Martinique lie just a short sail southeast of Union. PSV is part of St. Vincent, and Petite Martinique is part of Grenada.

PSV

PSV (VHF: 16,) was probably the first Caribbean boutique hotel. It is a quiet and exclusive resort, where the guests get pampered in secluded stone cottages. Each cottage has a flagpole that is used to summon the butler room service, which soon appears in a mini-moke. The hotel does well at top Caribbean rates: probably the Caribbean's most successful boutique hotel.

It was built by the late Haze Richardson,

who operated it since its inception until 2007. It is now managed by husband & wife team Matt & Anie Semark along with an excellent local crew. The island and resort were purchased, in late 2010, by Phil Stephenson and Robin Patterson. During the first year the new owners have heavily invested in renovating the entire island and all her cottages. New additions are the Yacht friendly Beach Restaurant 'Goaty's' Bar, and a new spa complex.

The main anchorage is shown on the chart. There is current in the anchorage and, if the wind drops, yachts will swing about. The reef off the dinghy dock extends farther than some think.

Mopion is a very popular daytime anchorage (see *Water sports*)

Ashore

When you go ashore keep in mind that this is a very exclusive and luxurious resort, so please be respectful. If we are to continue to be welcome this is essential. You should only come ashore by the Dingy Dock on the leeward side. You are welcome to walk along the shore and shore road from the dinghy dock to the new beach bar and boutique. All other areas are private for in-house residents only, which include the guest cottages and the western end of the beach, past the beach bar. Private areas are clearly sign posted.

You are welcome to visit the main bar and restaurant upstairs, though for this smart casual attire is expected (no bathing costumes by day, or shorts and t-shirts for dinner). Reservations are essential for dinner.

The hotel bar, with a great view of the bay, is open all day long and it is a great place to take a drink - especially those frozen daiquiris and fruit specials they are so good at.

Goatie's Beach Bar is more causal and built with visitors in mind, so shorts, t-shirts and even bathing togs are fine, up until sunset when slacks and a sports shirt or similar are appropriate. It is open from 1030-2000,

St. Vincent & the Grenadines

with the restaurant side of it is open from 1000-1800. They will keep the restaurant open for dinner for parties of six or more if you let them know a few hours before. They have tapas, great salads, sandwiches and burgers, pizza, pasta and grilled seafood, and meat.

On Saturdays they often have a beach barbecue with a steel band. Come for the barbecue or just to listen and visit the bar. On many Tuesdays they have a classic movie night, with a big screen set up in beach bar.

The Spa is also open to people visiting on yachts with all kinds of massage and beauty or health treatments. Chaperoned island and cottage tours are available on request after 10.30am. Book by radio, phone, or ask in the bar or office.

If you are dying for a long walk, Petite Martinique is within dinghy range.

Water sports

The snorkeling on the surrounding reefs is good. Mopion makes an exciting destination for a picnic by dinghy. You can anchor close by as a lunch stop. You can feel your way into anchorages in the reef north of PSV for excellent snorkeling. Pinese makes a fair dive.

PSV

PETITE MARTINIQUE

Getting tired of all the tourists? Petite Martinique (PM), the last outpost of Grenada, is small and enchantingly authentic. I love to overnight here, take a long walk, and have a meal ashore. It is also a good place to take on water and fuel and look for bargains on beer, liquor, and wine. The inhabitants live by boatbuilding, seafaring, and fishing (and, in days of old, smuggling). There are usually several cargo vessels at anchor, and the docks are far busier than the roads. The many fancy new houses are recent, but some of the older wooden, pitched-roof houses are photogenic, especially at the eastern end of the island. PM is a lot larger than it looks. If you turn right from the dock, the road winds round to the south side of the island. It is possible to walk all the way round, but the eastern part is a thorny scramble with no real trail. You will find the people here friendly and welcoming, and the island has a bank, several shops, and a restaurant. For the adventurous explorer and snorkeler, Fota and Petite Dominique are within range of a seaworthy dinghy.

If you are coming north from Carriacou, you can clear out and visit PM on your way to Union. Most yachts come over directly from PSV or the Grenadines, and, indeed, it is these yachts that keep the fuel dock and restaurant alive. Although PM is part of Grenada, it is generally accepted that no one is going to sail from PSV to Carriacou to clear in, then sail back to visit PM, so to date the authorities have not worried about yachts overnighting as part of their Grenadines cruise, and many do. Anchor anywhere off the fuel dock among the other boats. PM can also be visited by seaworthy dinghy from PSV. You can leave your dinghy on the inside part of the fuel dock.

The holding in PM is in soft mud and not always easy. Use plenty of scope, and if it is blowing hard, use your engine to keep the boat in place to allow the anchor time to sink in the mud before you put strain on it.

The best thing to do is eat at the Palm Beach Restaurant. Then you can pick up one of the two bright red moorings (marked with their name) that they keep for customers.

If you do have a problem, a big, shallow (8 to 12-foot deep) patch of easy anchoring sand is clearly visible about half a mile north and a little east of the docks. It is a fair dinghy ride in, but okay.

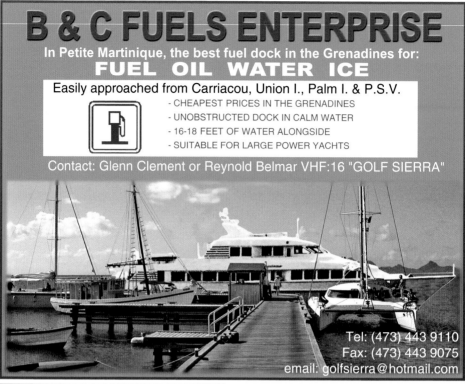
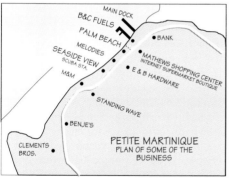

PETITE MARTINIQUE
PLAN OF SOME OF THE
BUSINESS

General yacht services

Glenn Clement and Reynold Belmar own B & C Fuels [VHF: 16 Golf Sierra], the best and most convenient fuel dock in the Grenadines. Easy approach and fair prices have made this the main refueling station for large power yachts and bareboats. You can approach the dock into the wind, and it has about 16-18 feet of water alongside. They sell high quality diesel, gasoline, water, cube ice, and cases of beer or water.

Chandlery & technical yacht services

E&B hardware is on the left as you walk down the main road heading west. It is upstairs, over E&B supermarket, in the same building. Owner Emrol Logan keeps a good supply of resins, cloths, and a little yacht hardware, plus fishing gear, along with general hardware and a lot of plumbing bits. Emrol repairs outboards, so you can bring your broken one here to get it fixed.

The Clement brothers can fix anything. They build boats, weld stainless and alumi-

Communications

Odinga's Millennium Connection, a pleasant boutique in Matthew's Shopping Center, has high-speed internet access at reasonable rates. Other computer services include printing. They are normally open until about 1800, but in an emergency you can probably find someone in the adjoining house.

Palm Beach Restaurant has free wifi for their customers.

num, repair diesel engines, and often help out charter companies with a breakdown in the area.

Shops, restaurants, ashore

Matthew's Shopping Center is a great addition to PM. It is worth coming to PM just to replenish your wine, beer, and liquor lockers at Matthew's unbeatable prices. This is also the largest of the local shops, and you can top up on all your groceries. This complex also has Odinga's (Matthew's daughter) Millennium Connection, which has stacks of clothes, shoes, jewelry, and more. Adjoining is a gift shop with handicrafts. They also have a pleasant rental house, if you fancy a longer stay.

Petite Martinique has a very pleasant restaurant, The Palm Beach [VHF: 16, $B-C]. It is owned by Peterson, Augustina, and Emmanuel Clement. Emmanuel is the manager. The setting is perfect: a pretty garden shaded by palms, right on the beach. They serve fresh seafood from the local fishing fleet, with chicken for those who don't like fish, lambi, or lobster. The food is first-rate; try the lobster bisque, if it is on the menu. If you are anchored in PSV, they have a free ferry service to and from your yacht. This works for lunch or dinner and if you want time to hike or shop or wander around you can talk to Emmanuel about this. It is a great way to add PM to your PSV visit, and if you do not want to eat at Palm Beach, Emmanuel can bring you over as a water taxi. Palm Beach have two customer moorings you can use and free wifi. Palm Beach also have rooms to rent.

Almost next door, Melodies [VHF: 16,

"Tasha P Radio"] is a fancy new guesthouse, built right on the beach. It is managed by Reuben Patrice, local headmaster and a racing sailboat enthusiast. They have a bar/restaurant, but cook meals to advance order only.

If you keep going down the beach, you will come to Francis and Emma's Seaside View. This beachside supermarket makes loading the dinghy easy. They keep a good stock of basics, and for those looking for a room, they have some sweet, little self-contained cottages just behind. You can rent scuba gear here (see *Water sports*).

There are several other small supermarkets (minimarkets would be a better description), rum shops, and snack shops dotted around the island, along the west-running road. Standing Wave [$D] is a local supermarket, rum shop, and restaurant. Farther down, M&M is a supermarket. A mobile vendor is often around selling fresh fruits and vegetables.

Water sports

The Seaside View Supermarket has a very professional-looking setup for filling tanks and renting scuba gear. It is mainly for local fishermen, but they are happy to rent to yachts, and, if your dinghy is small, ask owner Francis Logan if he can arrange for a local boat to take your group to the dive sites. This is much less expensive than going with a dive shop. This is not a sports establishment and has none of the safeguards that go with a dive shop, so satisfy yourself that the gear is in good condition and within its scheduled test period.

St. Vincent & the Grenadines

Grenada &
Carriacou

Hiking the Seven Falls trail

Carriacou at a glance

Regulations

Carriacou is part of Grenada and, if you are coming from another country, you must anchor in Hillsborough and clear customs at the foot of the jetty before visiting any other port. If you arrive on a holiday, ask a taxi driver to take you to the nearest customs officer. The new one-page form makes life easier, but you still need to first check with immigration, customs, then port authority, making it a long-winded affair. Those clearing outside normal office hours (0800-1600 on week-days) will pay a reasonable overtime fee.

Monthly customs cruising permits are $50 EC for up to 40 feet; $75 EC 40-60 feet; $100 EC 60-80 feet, and $150 over 80 feet. In addition, port charges are $8.10 EC per person, except the skipper. Once you have entered, you do not pay the monthly fee for months spent on the hard.

If you plan to leave within 72 hours of clearing in, you can get outward clearance at the same time.

Visitors may not spearfish in Grenada waters and anyone caught doing so will be heavily fined and may be banned from returning to Grenada waters. The waters surrounding Sandy Island, the Sisters and the northern side of Tyrrel Bay is a ma-rine park, The Sandy Island / Oyster Bay Marine Protected Area (SIOBMPA). In these areas, anchoring is not allowed, but moorings are provided in Sandy Island. The charge for being in the marine park is $10US or $25 EC per day. Diving in the marine park must be with a local dive shop. Do not fish in the marine park.

Holidays

See *Grenada*. Also, the Carriacou Regatta usually takes place at the end of July. For details check their website: carriacouregatta.com

Shopping hours

Shops and offices normally open from 0800-1200 and 1300-1600. Saturday is half day and most places are closed by noon. Banks open weekdays 0800-1200, and 1300-1500, and on Fridays 0800-1200, and 1500-1700.

Telephones

If you do not have cell phone you can look for a card and coin phone. You buy cards for the phones in post offices and selected shops. For the USA, dial 1 plus the number. For other countries, dial 011 + country code + number. (If the local area code starts with a 0, leave it off.) For collect and credit card calls, dial 0 + country code + number. When dialing from overseas, the area code is 473, followed by a 7-digit number.

Transport

There are inexpensive ($1.50-$6 EC) buses running to most villages. Taxis are plentiful. Linky Taxi (VHF: 16) is a good driver, used to working with yachts. Sample taxi rates are:

	$EC
Hillsborough to Tyrrel Bay...	35
Tyrrel Bay to Airport............	40
Island tour (2.5 hours)..........	200
Mini tour (1.25 hours)..........	100

Rental cars are available (check our directory). You will need to buy a local license, which costs $30 EC. Drive on the left.

Airport tax for international flights is $50EC, for flights between Grenada and Grenada, $10 EC.

Windward

Carriacou

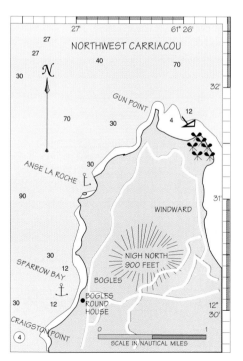

NORTHWEST CARRIACOU

27'   61° 26'
27
27
40   70
30   N
32'
GUN POINT
70   12
30   4
ANSE LA ROCHE   30
90
31'
WINDWARD
30
SPARROW BAY 12
NIGH NORTH
900 FEET
BOGLES
30 12
12°
BOGLES
ROUND 30'
HOUSE
CRAIGSTON POINT
4
0   1
SCALE IN NAUTICAL MILES

"*his is an island with over a hundred rum shops and only one gasoline station.*" Frances Kay, Carriacou.

Carriacou is enchanting. The inhabitants live by farming, fishing, and seafaring, and must number among the friendliest in the Caribbean. Just about everywhere in Carriacou is of interest, but Windward should definitely be part of your tour, as should the road running from Windward to the north end of the island. Windward is the traditional center of boatbuilding and it is here that you can see the fishing fleet arrive under sail. If you cannot afford a taxi, take a bus over to Windward and hike. A destination with a great view is the hospital, which sits high on the mountain overlooking the harbor.

Carriacou has lovely anchorages, pleasant hiking, a yacht haul-out facility, several yacht services, dive shops, entertaining bars, restaurants, and cafes.

322

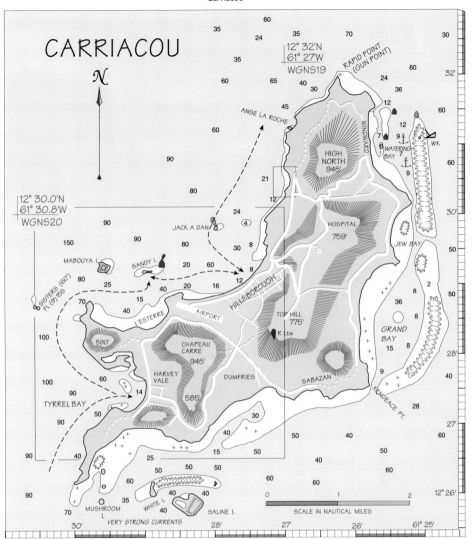

Navigation

Carriacou is a Carib word meaning "island surrounded by reefs," but do not worry: the approach down the west coast is simple enough. When sailing from the north, it is safest to pass to the west of Jack a Dan before heading up into Hillsborough. If you take the trickier route east of Jack a Dan, watch out for the large reef, which is about 4 feet deep, about one-third of the way between Craigston Point and Jack a Dan. Favor the Jack a Dan side of the channel (but not too close). You can anchor almost anywhere off the town. Hillsborough is a good anchorage, except in bad northerly swells, when you will be better off in Tyrrel Bay.

There is a flashing green light on Jack a Dan and a flashing red light on the buoy east of Sandy Island.

Two anchorages north of Hillsborough are worth a thought. Anse La Roche has a perfect beach, with a big rock on the south side. It is good for temporary anchorage for a swim and beach visit, but northerly swells make it untenable. Sparrow Bay (home to Bogles Round House) is a good anchorage, except during bad northerly swells, but even in moderate swells it will be hard to beach the dinghy. When coming from Hillsborough, pass outside Jack a Dan.

The adventurous might want to poke into Windward and Watering Bay on the

north east coast. The entrance is easier now that Jerry (the rescue tug man) has buoyed it. Leave the first green buoy on your left (red right returning) and you will find yourself in a vast, fairly protected lagoon. You can explore a long way up into this lagoon with a draft of 6 feet, but go carefully as it is all eyeball navigation.

HILLSBOROUGH

Hillsborough has a special charm of its own: a pleasant town built right on a perfect beach. As you walk down the main street, you catch glimpses of the sea through gaps between the buildings. A new tourist office faces the main dock. Pop in for maps and information, including cultural events.

Regulations

Hillsborough is Carriacou's only port of clearance. For details see page 321. When you clear in, you must first visit immigration in the big block behind the tourist office, then customs and port authority on the dock.

Communications

Three good internet stations in Hillsborough are reasonably priced. Digi-Soft, a computer store, is upstairs in the M&M building. Turn right off the dock and keep walking. They have a good set of computers for the internet and also sell disks, CDs, hardware, and games, and they rent DVDs.

Services Unlimited, upstairs at Bullens, has internet, computer, DHL, copying, and desktop publishing. They open weekdays 0800 till 1600, Saturdays, 0800 till noon.

Ade's Dream is close to the main dock and has an internet computer room in their office at the back. For phone and fax, try Lime (Cable and Wireless) or Ade's Dream.

Transport

Matthew Raymond, aka Linky Taxi [VHF: 16], is a good and reliable cab driver, used to dealing with yachtspeople, and he always carries his phone with him. If you need something done, he can help. He has two cabs: a big new luxurious one, and a smaller one run by his sister. Linky also has a select fleet of very nice jeeps available for rent.

Provisioning

Supermarkets are on the small side, but have most essentials, though you will have to visit the market or local streetside vendors for fresh produce.

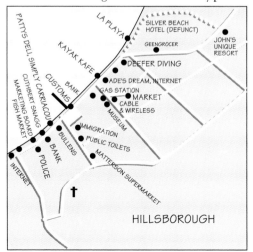

HILLSBOROUGH

Liquor prices are good. Check Ade's Dream and Bullen's. Both of them also stock hardware and cosmetics. Unity Supermarket is on Church Street.

One place not to miss is Patty's Deli. Christine, a Carriacou woman who was brought up in England, is charming and helpful and sells all the things the other supermarkets do not in her pleasantly cool air-conditioned shop. Freshly baked French bread, croissants, and other baked goodies come out of her oven around 0900, and you will find cold cuts, yogurts, cheeses, fine frozen meats and fish, good wines, heavy long-lasting bread, wheat wraps, regular milk, lots of sauces, and coffee. Christine provisions bareboats and yachts with a little notice and you can purchase your stores VAT-free if you have cleared out.

Fun Shopping

Simply Carriacou is a charming little boutique in the same building as Wendy's Deli, and is owned by her sister in law, Karen. It has artistic crafts, including beautifully painted calabashes, art t-shirts, local paintings, good locally made jewelry, locally made health care products, clothing, and more. Karen rents villas and cars, and she books tours and anything else you might want in Carriacou.

You can find banks, travel agents, and many quaint, small variety stores, each crammed with its owner's ideas of what sells in Carriacou. If you go round to enough of them, you will find a wider selection of products for sale than on many a larger island. Bullen's has a pharmacy; turn right from the dock onto the main street (left-hand side).

If you have broken shoes, even high heels, help is at hand; turn left off the dock, and look for Jam Rock Family, the shoemaker.

Restaurants

La Playa [$C-D], open 1000-2200, except closed all Thursdays and at 1800 on Sundays, is an entertaining beach bar presided over by Kathyanne and owned by the Green Roof people. You can get food anytime they are open and they offer generous hamburgers, fishburgers, soup and

Grenada and Carriacou

environmental efforts in Carriacou and owns a couple of powerboats to take you on snorkeling trips and expeditions to the offshore islands. He also builds model racing boats. A good place to meet him is at Snagg's Place [$C], his bar, which is a great hangout on the beach. On occasion, if the group is right, he will organize a lobster bash or fish cookout.

The Green Roof [$B-C] lies about half a mile north of town on the coast. This Swedish establishment is owned and run by Asa and Jonas. It has a nice view and a bar that is open all day. It serves fresh fruit juice and good coffee, along with regular drinks. They open for dinner (reservations essential).

In the other direction you can walk 10 minutes towards the airport for a good roti at Annie's Roti Shop, just across the road from the beach

Bogles Round House [$A-B] is special. It is too far for most to walk, but you can anchor off Bogles and dinghy ashore or, if you have a group of six or more, they will provide free transportation from Hillsborough or Tyrrel Bay, or you can take a taxi. The Round House comes right out of a children's book, with its circular structure and white roof supported by a tree in the center of the room. Round windows have been made out of old farm implements and wheels. You expect gnomes and wizards to be in attendance.

Roxanne, the chef, spent many years in the merchant navy and ended up in the galley on the Onassis yacht. She loves food, and her cooking is a fusion of Caribbean and Mediterranean flavors. They make their own bread.

This small place is excellent and popular, so make reservations. They close Wednesdays, and only serve lunch on Sundays.

Ashore

You can use the low part of the main dock, but you may need to use a stern anchor to stop your dinghy from mashing up in swells. The taxi square is in front of customs. There is a gas station in town and many youths are willing to fetch ice.

The museum is worth the short walk and is open Monday through Friday 0900-1545. It has an eclectic collection, from

sandwiches. It is a perfect placed for that sunset drink or as daytime hangout; try their homemade ice cream. You can anchor right off La Playa and dinghy ashore as long as there are no big swells. If you have to come into Hillsborough to clear customs, this makes a perfect place for lunch.

Kayak Kafe [$C-D], run by Sally, opens for breakfast and lunch and will open for dinner by special request. The drinks are done separately in a little bar that specializes in fresh juices, but also sells beer. The food menu changes but includes good sandwiches, salads, local fish dishes, soups and desserts.

Deefer Dining is part of the dive shop, but they serve lunch and it is a good place to meet divers.

Laurena II is cheap, cheerful and serves generous portions of local food. They open around noon.

New Wave Restaurant [$C-D] is part of Ade's Dream. The dining room hangs out over the beach, with the gentle sound of waves brushing the shore. It serves reasonably priced local food and does takeout.

Cuthbert Snagg [VHF: 16] is active in

Arawak pottery to the island's first telephone exchange.

For a taste of local life, hang out in the rum shops all around.

Should you happen to arrive towards the end of July or early August, you may witness the famous Carriacou Regatta. It is no secret that the best trading and sailing sloops in the islands are built right here in Carriacou. Once a year they get together to race on this festive weekend. The boats they build today are unbelievably fast and sweet, and if you are lucky enough to see one sailing into harbor, it is a joy to behold.

Carriacou also has an interesting Maroon Festival towards the end of April: carriacoumaroon.com/

Carriacou is one of the last unspoiled islands. One reason for this is that much of the land does not have clear title. However, if you are interested, there are lots available at Craigston Estates, overlooking the sea. Contact Renwick and Thompson or Down Island Realty.

Water sports

Diving is very good, with excellent visibility. With the creation of the new marine park, you must now dive in the park with a dive shop, though you are welcome to snorkel on your own. The Sandy Island / Oyster Bay Marine Protected Area (SIOBMPA) has 15 dive sites that are less than 10-minutes boat ride from either Hillsborough or Tyrrel Bay. New dive sites to the north of Hillsborough are being explored.

Sandy Island has a sheltered shallow site that is a favorite with both divers and snorkelers. Other popular sites include Sharky's (home to several nurse sharks) and Whirlpool (so called for its champagne-like bubbles which are caused by volcanic activity), both of which are at Mabouya. Sisters Rocks, features two sites outstanding for their black coral and masses of aquatic life. Aquatic life frequently seen within the SIOMPA include, several species of moray eels (green, spotted, chain-link, and chestnut), sea horses, spotted eagle rays, southern stingrays, nurse sharks, angelfish, frogfish, and a multitude of blennies.

Deefer Diving is owned by Gary Ward from London and Alexandra Holler from Austria who have taken over the Silver Diving dive shop. They are very welcoming, well qualified instructors who run a good dive shop with enthusiasm and care. Both are experienced Padi staff instructors and offer a variety of courses, from beginner to pro, as well as fun dives for certified divers. Courses include Recreational Sidemount diving, a new technique affording longer dives and greater control in the water. The dive center retains a Padi 5-star centre status and remains one of the most qualified dive centers in the Windwards. Like all dive shops in Carriacou, they only go out with small groups.

The dive center is open from 0800 to 1800 and walk-in business is welcome; Oceanic scuba and snorkeling gear is on sale. A pick-up service from your yacht in Tyrell Bay or Sandy Island can be arranged.

They also run the friendly Deefer Diner as part of the shop, a place to take snack between dives or a post-dive drink.

Grenada and Carriacou

PSV   PM

JACK A DAN

SANDY ISLAND

PARADISE BEA

SANDY ISLAND AND L'ESTERRE BAY

This area is now comes under SIOBM-PA. Moorings are provided at Sandy Island and it costs $25 EC or $10 US per day per yacht to be in the park. Yachts should use holding tanks.

Sandy Island is nothing but a flawless strip of sand, surrounded by perfect snorkeling and diving reefs. Pelicans and seagulls will be your neighbors in this wonderful anchorage.

Sandy Island has changed rapidly in recent times. The beach suffered such degradation that all the trees died, but then a hurricane threw up a coral capping, leaving great tide pools and providing the island some protection. Locals have planted trees. Be respectful of all beach plants and vegetation: they may be the only things holding the island together.

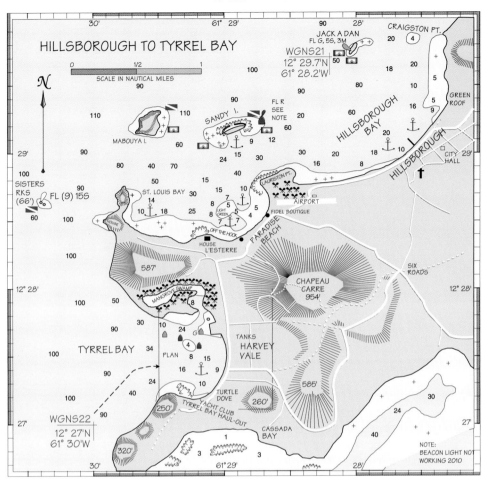

You can carry 7 feet quite close to the middle of the island, but watch out for the reefs north and south, and the odd shallower spot. There is not much room to drag in Sandy Island, so check your mooring.

L'Esterre Bay, with the long and beautiful Paradise Beach, is right opposite Sandy Island and is within dinghy reach.

Moorings are planned near Off the Hook. Keel boats can head from Sandy towards the white house with terracotta roof on the headland west of Paradise Beach. Skirt the really bright green water, then turn east once past it, and you are in the right spot if the moorings ever get put in.

Ashore

You can dinghy to L'Esterre, the home of Sandra's Fidel productions. This little container-boutique is unquestionably the best in Carriacou. Everything is locally and artistically made: original calabash art, handmade soaps, jewelry, Zaka masks, Putumayo CDs, Art Box, Rasta hats, bamboo and coconut craft, Art Fabric batik, and original paintings and prints.

Fidel produces art on t-shirts: good-quality reproductions from local artists sold through their website, fidelproductions.com, or in shops up and down the islands. Treasure in Mustique, Art 'n Beads in Union, and Imagine in Grenada sell them. Mr. Quality, and Mr. Bob sell them in the Tobago Cays. Fidel also produce mojos, each an original, using exotic beads from many materials, often accented with gold and silver, sold in Fidel and other shops.

There are several good little bars here, including Joan's [$D] next to the boutique. Joan does a good and inexpensive lunch and will also cook dinner on order.

Off the Hook [$B-D] is much farther down the beach. You can dinghy over from Sandy, pick up a mooring if they become available, take the longish walk from Tyrrel Bay, or catch a bus. Curtis Malcolm opens his restaurant every day from 0900-2300. It is in an open beach area with fishing boats, giving

it a pleasant local feel. It makes a great beach hangout. Curtis cooks local fish, lobster, and lambi, serves good pizza, and claims to have the best fries in Carriacou. Some nights they show movies, and men can always get a haircut as Curtis is a professional barber. Dinner reservations are appreciated.

Sandy Island

TYRREL BAY

Tyrrel Bay is huge, well-protected, and very popular with cruisers. A few vendors may come out offering wine, beer, and produce. The taking of mangrove oysters is no longer allowed, so do not buy any.

Businesses line the waterfront. A road separates them from the sea. The shore used to be thickly wooded with manchineel and seagrapes. Most of these were cut down to increase the visibility between the boats and the businesses. When Hurricane Lenny threw record-breaking swells into the bay, it devastated the unprotected shoreline and destroyed much of the road, turning several properties into beachfront real estate. The government then built the big seawall that now lines the waterfront.

Navigation

Tyrrel Bay is deep and wide and easy to enter. Despite this, a surprising number of

people manage to run aground. The buoys are rather confusing. Whatever the original color, they end up Pelican-guano white on top and rusty underneath. Buoys may be added or removed at any time without notice. There is a reef in the northern part of the bay, towards the center. The deepest channel is to the north of this reef and is marked by three buoys. However, the reef that is most often hit is along the southern shore. There is a small cul-de-sac in this reef called Bareboat Alley, and people manage to go right up in here and run hard aground. Two large unlit mooring buoys lie in the middle of the southern channel. It is easiest to enter the bay just south of center. You are not in danger of hitting the northern reef until you are over halfway across the bay. You can pass closely on either side of the big mooring buoys safely, though keep in mind that buoys should not be relied upon.

MABOUYA

MAIN SHIP CHANNEL

BAREBOAT ALLEY

CARRIACOU MARINE

Holding is good if you can find clear sand, but rather poor in the weedy areas.

Communications

Carriacou Children's Educational Fund (CCEF) has free bay-wide wifi, funded by local businesses, and based in the Slipway Restaurant. Go in to find out how to link up, and you will be given an opportunity to make a contribution to CCEF. If you have items for the annual yacht auction take them to the shop at After Hours. The Matterson's very kindly store them, and the auction is held there. Lambi Queen, Yacht Club and several other bars have wifi.

General yacht services

Leave your dinghy at Carriacou Marine, Slipway Restaurant, Lazy Turtle, the main dock, or pull it up on the beach. Garbage bins are dotted around; try not to overwhelm them.

Carriacou Marine [VHF: 16, ex Tyrrel Bay Yacht Haul Out] is a charming small boatyard and marina. As we went to press it had been bought by Pierro and Trevor who

Grenada and Carriacou

Map labels:
12°28'
MANGROVE SWAMP
5 5 5
TYRREL N BAY
8 8
6 (WK) 2
20 10
16 40
35 4 40
REEF
40 MAIN DOCK
RECALIMED LAND FOR MARINA, HAULOUT & CONDOS
SWAMPY JO'S
IN STITCHES
ALEXIS
LIZ'S PLACE
SCRAPER
P. CONCH SHELL
12°27.5'
34 16 8 (WK) 16
12
8
6
AFTER OURS'
ARAWAKDIVERS
9
TWILIGHT
OLD RUM SHOP
MOORING BUOYS 14 12
24 12 12
9
3 1 11 6
1
12 LAMBI QUEEN
BAREBOAT ALLEY
8
+ ROCK 8
SLIPWAY LAZY TURTLE
HAUL OUT & CARRIACOU MARINA MARINE RESTAURANT LUMBADIVE
TOOL MEISTER
61° 29.5' 61° 29.0'

beam and 8-foot draft. It is one of the more environmentally friendly yards, with a wash-down catchment so that no toxic paint goes into the sea, and they have vacuum systems to suck up the dust. They can take about 17 boats.

Normal opening hours are 0800-1600 Monday to Friday and 0800-1200 on Saturdays.

This yard is excellent for general work and do-it-yourself jobs. It is absolutely first-rate for mechanical services, welding, and fabricating, thanks to Dominique and Uwe (see below). For environmental reasons, they are not currently spraying boats, sandblasting, or encouraging major fiberglass repairs, as they lack an enclosed area to contain the fumes and dust.

A good little chandlery is planned and in the meantime anything can be shipped up from Budget Marine or Island Water World, occasionally as quickly as four hours.

Carriacou Marine includes a fair-sized building with a laundry, showers and toilets,

were working on an exciting new upgrade. One of the first things they were putting in was a secure storage unit, so you can store gear off your boat.

You can come to the dock or the outside of the eastern travel lift dock to take on water. They have convenient docking with space for about seven yachts, both on the finger dock and outside of the marine hoist dock.

Yachts are hauled on a 50-ton marine travel-lift. They can take up to 18-foot

a small shop, ice and rooms for rent for those that prefer to stay ashore. They are building a pleasant cafe where you will be able to drink and eat, and the whole area has wifi.

Gerry owns various tugs and can provide a 24-hour marine emergency service for yachts that go aground or start to sink. He is the right person to contact if you need a hand, as his prices are fair. Call 407-0927 or contact him through Slipway Restaurant.

My Beautiful Launderette, owned by Daniella, is next to the Alexis Supermarket. They will do your wash for you, but if you are obsessive enough to want to do it yourself, you can (the price is the same). They have seats where you can lime while your laundry is washing and a book exchange so you will not be bored if you wait. They open 0700-1800 daily.

Next to Lambi Queen, Jack's Shorebase Services is a laundry combined with a small supermarket. The laundry opens 0830-1630 weekdays; the supermarket stays open longer.

You can arrange diesel fuel (duty-free if you have cleared out) by the big storage tanks at the head of the main dock. It is piped down the dock. Enquire at Bullen's supermarket in Hillsborough. This is excellent fuel, not the bargain-basement rough Venezuelan fishing boat fuel available farther up the Grenadines. You can take the same fuel at B&C in PM, which is an easier dock.

The McQuilkins, a Carriacou family, are building a large marina/haulout/shopping and condominium complex on the far side of the main dock. This, the largest development in Tyrrel Bay, is progressing at a leisurely rate.

Technical yacht services

In Stitches is an excellent canvas and sail repair shop run by Andy, who is helped by Petra and the team. Andy lives on his yacht Yellow Bird, and drives an old BMW bike with a sidecar. You can call him on VHF: 16. The shop is ashore. They are very helpful with all kinds of canvas work, upholstery, sail work (they offer new sails with the Quantum label), and bimini tops, and they make very decorative custom flags.

Dominique [VHF: 16], of Carriacou Aluminum Boats, does wonders in aluminum, from building a new dinghy to fixing a broken mast. He also welds and polishes stainless steel. Biminis are one of his specialties. His wife Genevieve sews sails and offers therapeutic massage for bad backs and sore necks. You will find him on his trimaraft workshop, not far from the boatyard.

Uwe, at Tool Meister, runs an excellent machine and mechanics shop. People come here from all over the Grenadines to get their problems solved, and much of his work is with cargo ships. He can completely rebuild your old engine or help you buy a new one and install it properly. He can fix just about anything that is broken and machine new parts if they are unavailable. Uwe is so busy that he has a closed sign permanently posted on his door just above the Lazy Turtle, but if you go and find him, he may try to help.

Transport

Linky Taxi [VHF: 16] is helpful and friendly, and has a good-sized minibus for island tours and shopping trips, backed up by a smaller minibus run by his sister. He is

SLIPWAY RESTAURANT

(473) 443-6500

Open
lunch & dinner
Tuesday to Saturday
Open Sunday for lunch
Reservations appreciated

**Tyrell Bay
Carriacou**

Old boatyard atmosphere amid boats bits & tools

info@slipwayrestaurant.com
www.slipwayrestaurant.com

always ready to come. He can rent you one of his modern Jeeps.

Bubbles [VHF: 16] has a fancy, air conditioned bus with spacious seats.

Cycling is a great way to see Carriacou ~ especially off the main roads where cars won't go. You can rent bikes from Lambi Queen.

Provisioning

There are several little supermarkets that stock a supply of liquor and beer, along with bread, canned and packaged food, eggs, and chicken. Some also have electronic goods and household supplies. If you don't see what you want, it is worth asking. The Carriacou Marine store is good for liquor and basics and will probably upgrade. Twilight Supermarket [VHF: 16] is run by La Qua and Diana Augustin. They sometimes have block ice on hand and, if not, you can get them to order you a block for the next morning. Alexis Supermarket is run by the Alexis family, who own a fleet of boats, including some of the ferries that run to Grenada. The newest supermarket is After Ours', which sometimes has goodies not found in the others.

Fresh food is sold by Denise in a stall opposite In Stitches. Her sister, Donelyn, has another stall, called Empress Elisha Palace, which sells clothing and produce next door.

Restaurants

The Lazy Turtle [VHF: 16, $B-C] is on the waterfront with a dinghy dock. Jean Baptiste from Brittany runs it and sometimes his partner, Auro Ghosh, who has American and East Indian roots, is around. They have big decks, so you sit looking over the water, Dinghy in and tie to their dock.

This is a friendly place where they cook excellent Italian pizzas, pastas, and salads, as well as a few specials like tiger shrimp flambéd in Ricard (delicious), so come for their lobster pizza or shrimp pasta. They open every day about 0900 which is popular with the internet crowd who gather here for an early beer and free wifi. They take orders till 2200, so if you arrive late, you can still get a meal. They occasionally have live entertainment.

Daniella (My Beautiful Launderette) and Kate have opened an excellent new restaurant next the Yacht Club. It called Slipway [$B-C, VHF:16] and uses the old Slipway building, complete with a boat in the roof, planers, routers, and other tools, all left standing but artfully converted to form bars, and tables. The menu changes daily and is posted on a blackboard. Daniella greets guest warmly and keeps everyone happy out front, while back in the kitchen Kate cooks like an angel. The food is simple, but very good, and very reasonably priced. They are closed on Mondays and for Sunday dinner. Otherwise they are open 1130-1400 for lunch and 1800-2100 for dinner. Sunday's brunch, is popular and runs from 1130-1530. Tie up your dinghy on their dock right outside. Phone: 443-6500 or VHF:16.

Trevor and Piero are going to open a new cafe at Carriacou Marine, somewhere in the old yacht club block. This is worth checking out as a cafe, bar, and restaurant.

Lambi Queen [VHF: 16, $C-D] is a cute restaurant with a patio railing made from old barrel planks with curved surfaces. The Sylvester family owns it. Edwin goes out fishing, and his son, Sherwin, cooks up the catch in good Carriacou home-style. Nightly happy hour is from 1730-1830. They often have a party on Fridays. They have a small dinghy dock.

The Twilight Restaurant and Bar [VHF: 16] has a pleasant, intimate atmosphere; the walls are brightly decorated with paintings, many from local artist, Canute Caliste. Owner and chef, Diana Augustin cooks spicy West Indian Creole dishes with fresh fish, lobster, lambi, chicken, and pork. Happy hour is 1800-1900. They have one perfect table across the road hanging over the beach.

Natasha's Bayside Restaurant and Bar [$C-D] sits open to the breeze next door to In Stitches, with one waterfront table across the road. Natasha opens weekdays from 0830 till the last customer leaves. This is the place to come for good local food. Walk in for breakfast or a lunch of soup or roti. Dinner is possible on weekdays, but you must book.

The Old Rum Shop [$B-C], run by Casana and Timothy, is a great hangout where you can meet people and play dominoes. They sometimes do meals featuring fresh fish, conch, and lobster, but they need about a half-hour notice to get in gear.

The Conch Shell [$C-D] is just down the street that leads back from Scraper's. You will need to give advance notice.

After Ours' has built a handsome new building that is a restaurant, nightclub, conference center, and stage. They open from time to time for occasional music, discos, live bands, and other entertainment.

Joann's Swampy Jo's, down in the swamp, is cheerfully painted and Joann will welcome you. Her bar opens at 0800 and runs until late.

The Mighty Runaway, a jovial calypsonian and ex-policeman, has opened a local bar just above Tool Meister called Runaway's Hideaway. If you go talk with him, he will cook you a good barbecue.

There are several other inexpensive hangouts, including Liz's Place [$D] which

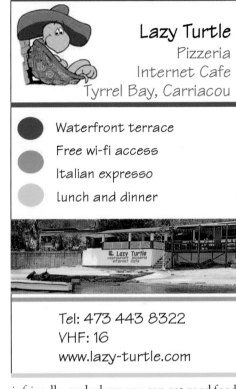

Lazy Turtle
Pizzeria
Internet Cafe
Tyrrel Bay, Carriacou

- Waterfront terrace
- Free wi-fi access
- Italian expresso
- Lunch and dinner

Tel: 473 443 8322
VHF: 16
www.lazy-turtle.com

is friendly, and where you can get good food at bargain basement prices.

Ashore

The mangrove swamp in Tyrrel Bay is part of the new marine park and is protected. Switch off the donghy motor and listen to the peace. (Take insect repellent.) You often see herons and sometimes iguanas. Yachts are not allowed in except during a hurricane warning. Taking oysters without a license is forbidden.

There are plenty of hiking possibilities, including a pleasant trek up Chapeau Carre, the second highest peak on the island, which offers panoramic views all around. (Hiking instructions are on doyleguides.com)

Water sports

There is plenty of good diving. All the marine park dive sites are within a 10-minute ride and right off the Sisters is an excellent dive where you find a sloping reef of soft and hard corals, decorated with many sponges. Lots of fish gather here. You are bound to see

angelfish and stingrays and turtles are likely. There are also superb dives off Round Island and Kick 'em Jenny, and you can do these on your own, but it is better to go with a dive shop. Here the fish life is outstanding, with sharks, rays, and big pelagic fish. There are 200-foot walls, caves, and many reefs. Since it is a long trip, dive shops do it as a two-tank dive in fair weather only.

Georg Schmitt and Connie Hagen own Arawak Divers [VHF: 16], they have been in Carriacou longer than the other dive operators. Georg has lived in Carriacou since 1994 and no one knows the local waters better. Georg does both commercial and pleasure diving. Connie, like Georg, is a Padi instructor. Both Connie and Georg came from Germany. Their shop is based in the After Ours' building and they are happy to pick customers up off their yachts in Tyrrel Bay or Sandy Island. Just call them on VHF 16. Their groups are always small and they do private dives. They are good, low-key and welcoming. They are very much into photography, and their photos are superb. This gives them a keen eye for unusual small critters like flatworms, frogfish, seahorses and nudibranchs. They know all kinds of small sites where they can find particular creatures.

They have two dive boats: the largest is a 32-footer for the distant sites. They are the Carriacou Trans Ocean base and rent kayaks (a good way to visit the mangrove swamp).

Lumbadive [VHF: 16] is next to Turtle Dove. It is run by two French Canadians, Diane and Richard, who speak English and French and teach Padi courses in both languages. They also own a dive shop in Montreal.

PASSAGES BETWEEN CARRIACOU & GRENADA

Unfortunately, none of the islands between Carriacou and Grenada affords good shelter. Isle de Ronde can be used in a pinch. The anchorage is in the bay on the

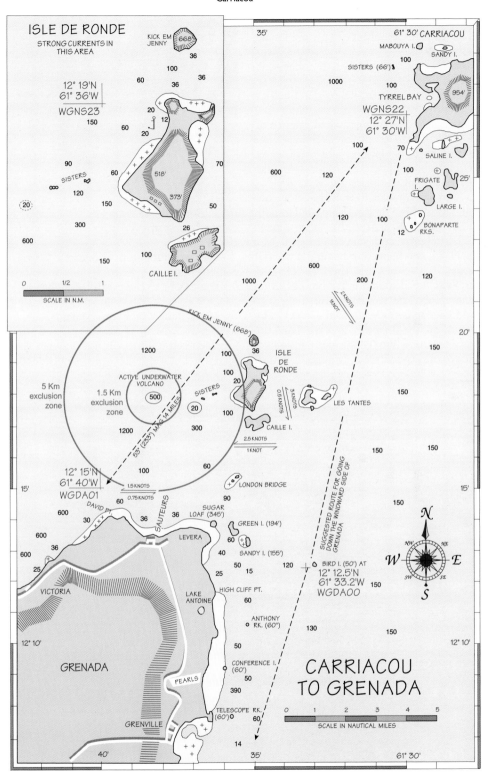

ISLE DE RONDE

STRONG CURRENTS IN THIS AREA

KICK EM JENNY 668

12° 19'N
61° 36'W
WGNS23

SISTERS

518'
373'

CAILLE I.
26

0   1/2   1
SCALE IN N.M.

61° 30' CARRIACOU

MABOUYA I.
SANDY I.
SISTERS (66')
TYRREL BAY
954'
WGNS22
12° 27'N
61° 30'W
SALINE I.
FRIGATE I.
25'
LARGE I.
BONAPARTE RKS.

2 KNOTS
1 KNOT

KICK EM JENNY (668')

ACTIVE UNDERWATER VOLCANO
500

5 Km exclusion zone

1.5 Km exclusion zone

ISLE DE RONDE

LES TANTES

SISTERS
20

CAILLE I.

3 KNOTS
0.5 KNOTS

2.5 KNOTS
1 KNOT

12° 15'N
61° 40'W
WGDA01

1.5 KNOTS
0.75 KNOTS

53° (233°) MAG. 14 MILES

LONDON BRIDGE

DAVID PT.
SAUTEURS
LEVERA

SUGAR LOAF (345')

GREEN I. (194')
SANDY I. (155')

HIGH CLIFF PT.

VICTORIA

LAKE ANTOINE

GRENADA

PEARLS

GRENVILLE

40'

ANTHONY RK. (60")

CONFERENCE I. (60')
390

TELESCOPE RK. (60')

14

35'

SUGGESTED ROUTE FOR GOING DOWN THE WINDWARD SIDE OF

BIRD I. (50') AT
12° 12.5'N
61° 33.2'W
WGDA00

CARRIACOU TO GRENADA

0   1   2   3   4   5
SCALE IN NAUTICAL MILES

N
NW NE
W   E
SW SE
S

15'

12° 10'

61° 30'

northern side of the west coast, but it is likely to be rolly, even for lunch. This is a shame, as the snorkeling is excellent and the island has some good walks. About 20 inhabitants live on the south coast.

It is impossible to anchor at either Kick 'em Jenny or the Sisters, but both are interesting and may be approached reasonably closely, weather permitting. Both have large nesting bird populations, and you can see boobies and pelicans, particularly on the Sisters. Beware of the strong currents.

An active volcano that lies about two miles west of Isle de Ronde erupted in both 1988 and 1989. It, too, has been named Kick 'em Jenny, and you certainly will get a big kick if you happen to be on top when it erupts. To prevent this, the Grenada government has declared a 1.5-km exclusion zone around the volcano at all times (not enforced; it is for your own safety). The exclusion zone increases to 5 km when the volcano is rumbling (For the current status of the volcano, check: www.uwiseismic.com, or follow the links on www.doyleguides.com.)

Kick 'em Jenny (the big rock) has the reputation of kicking up a nasty sea as you go north, and this is particularly true if the tide is running east.

When sailing from Grenada to Carriacou, the fastest way to go is to hug Grenada's lee coast right to the north before heading to Carriacou. Unless the wind is well in the south, take a tack into Sauteurs, as the west-going current is weakest close to the Grenada coast. This will not only get you up faster, but it should keep you outside the 1.5 km volcano exclusion zone.

Regulations

Grenada, Carriacou, and Petite Martinique make up one country, with ports of clearance in Hillsborough, St. George's, Prickly Bay, Phare Bleu, and St. David's Harbour. Customs cruising permits per month are $50 EC up to 50 feet; $75 EC, 50-60 feet; $100 EC, 60-79 feet; and $150 over 80 feet. You do not pay for months spent in a yard.

You may clear in and out at the same time for stays up to 3 days (72 hours).

There are also port charges of $8.10 EC per person, excluding the skipper. Entry is on a single page form. You can download it from the website: grenadagrenadines.com/boat_customs.html.

Normal office hours for customs are 0800-1145 and 1300-1545 on weekdays. At other times you will be charged overtime fees that always seem to be higher in Grenada than in Carriacou. If you have any questions about yachting, including security, contact MAYAG: (473) 416-7135, mayagadmin@gmail.com.

Visitors may not spearfish in Grenada waters or scuba dive on your own within marine parks. Collecting or damaging coral and buying lobster out of season are strictly forbidden. (Lobstering season is October 31 to April 30.)

Those wanting to take dogs ashore will need a valid rabies certificate.

Holidays

January 1, New Year's Day
February 7, Independence Day
Easter Friday through Monday, March 29-April 1, 2013, and April 18-21, 2014
Feb 22, Independence Day
May 1, Labor Day
Whit Monday, May 20, 2013 and June 9, 2014
Corpus Christi, May 30, 2013 and June 19, 2014
Emancipation Day, first Monday in August
Carnival, Second Monday and Tuesday in August
October 25, Thanksgiving
December 25, Christmas
December 26, Boxing Day

Shopping hours

Shops and offices normally open 0800-1200 and 1300-1600. Saturday is a half day and most places are closed by noon. Banks normally open weekdays till 1500, and on Fridays to 1700.

Telephones

Cell phones (Lime or Digicel) are the way to go, though some card and coin phones still remain. For overseas calls dial 1 for the USA and NANP countries; 011 plus the country code for other countries (see page 19). For collect and credit card calls, dial 0, then the whole number. When dialing from overseas, the area code is 473, followed by a 7-digit number.

Transport

Inexpensive ($1.50-$6 EC) buses run to most towns and villages in Grenada. If you are going a long way, check on the time of the last returning bus. Taxis are plentiful. Sample taxi rates (for four, normal hours) are:

	$EC
Prickly Bay to St. George's	50
Airport to St. George's	50
Airport to Prickly Bay	40
Prickly Bay to Grand Anse	30
By the hour	52
Short ride	20

Rental cars are available (see our directory). You will need to buy a local license, which costs $30 EC. Drive on the left.

Airport departure tax is $50 EC though it is usually included in the ticket.

Hiking with Henry Safari

Grenada

*G*renada, a spectacularly beautiful island, has lush green mountains, crystal waterfalls, golden beaches, and the fragrant spice trees that give the island its epithet "Isle of Spice." Come from late January to early March to get the added bonus of seeing the hills ablaze with hundreds of bright orange, flowering immortelle trees: pure magic.

Grenada's history has been lively, with early wars and revolutions. More recently, things got exciting with the transition to full independence in 1974. Most Grenadians felt this was premature, and instead of jubilant celebrations, the island was on strike and in protest. Nonetheless, independence was thrust upon her, and Grenada came of age under the rule of Sir Eric Gairy, a flamboyant and controversial figure who had a very divisive effect on the population. This resulted in the 1979 left-wing coup by

Maurice Bishop, who greatly admired Fidel Castro. Bishop attempted to turn Grenada into a socialist state. He improved medical care and education, but he did so at the cost of freedom: anyone who opposed him was thrown in jail, and all independent newspapers were banned.

However, this didn't insulate him from opposition within his own ranks. Second-in-command, Bernard Coard, his wife Phyllis Coard, and members of the army took Bishop prisoner in 1983. After a massive crowd freed him, an army group executed him along with half his cabinet. At this point, the US, along with Grenada's eastern Caribbean neighbors (the Organization of Eastern Caribbean States), launched a "rescue mission" and were welcomed with open arms. Now, 30 years later, this is old history, and looking back over these last years, Grenada as an independent county has experienced the

340

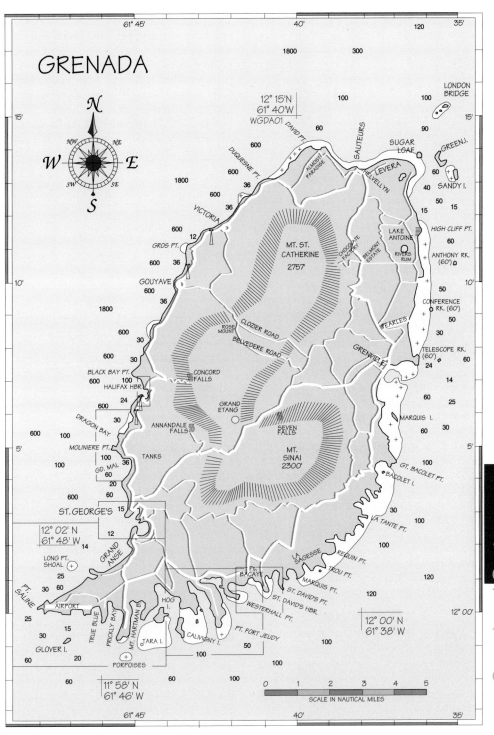

GRENADA

best, most democratic, and most productive years since it was colonized. Grenadians are a warm and hospitable people, exceptionally so once you get off the main tourist route.

From a yachting point of view, Grenada is developing rapidly. Haul out facilities are found in St. David's and Prickly Bay. Marina facilities can be found in St. George's, Clarkes Court Bay, Prickly Bay, Phare Bleu Bay, and Mt. Hartman Bay. St. George's has a big state-of-the-art Camper and Nicholson marina, as well as a yacht club. Two big chandleries now supply yachting gear and legislation has been passed that encourages yachting by allowing for low-duty supplies, parts, and chandlery for yachts.

The yachting act also allows you to clear out at the same time as you clear in, as long as you are not staying more than 3 days.

Grenada is host to a few important yachting events, as well as smaller club races. The Grenada Sailing Festival, a week of racing and social events organized by an independent company, is held in January. All entrants are welcome, from serious racing boats to live-aboards. The festival is lively and entertaining, with colorful local boats racing off Grand Anse Beach.

The South Grenada Regatta, a series of three races out of La Phare Bleu, always has competitors singing its praises and is held during the last weekend in February.

When the organizers get it together (not every year), the Round Grenada Race takes place in March. Multihulls are always welcome in this event, and all classes start together.

The Grenada Yacht Club organizes other races and Grenada has a strong marine trades association called the Marine & Yachting Association of Grenada (MAYAG) (www.mayag.org).

The interior

Few islands are as photogenic as Grenada, with houses surrounded by flowers, mountains, rivers, and rainforest. Sometimes when you are hiking along a river amid nutmeg trees, it has an uncanny resemblance to early pictures of the Garden of Eden. A swim in one of the waterfalls will leave you feeling wonderfully refreshed, your hair and skin feeling extra soft. Concord Falls are in beautiful countryside, and anyone with a spark of adventure should hike the extra half hour to the upper falls. Seven Falls are the best: a lovely one-hour hike. You need a guide if you want to make it to Honeymoon Falls, another half-hour from Seven Falls. Concord and Seven Falls are on private land, and the owners levy a small charge.

In 2004, Hurricane Ivan did huge damage throughout the island, especially in the rainforest. The island has mostly recovered, and the rainforest is coming back well. While it is growing the hiking is, in some ways, better than ever: the views are better, and the paths drier.

The most beautiful road in Grenada runs from Gouyave to St. Andrew. It has two forks, the Clozier is the prettier, Belvedere the easier. You snake across the heart of Grenada through verdant agricultural land, with lovely mountain views.

Grand Etang is a crater lake, and the Forest Center is close by. You often see monkeys where the buses stop. Trails are laid out so you can wander into the forest. There are wonderful hikes, including one halfway across the island (four hours). The road from St. George's to Grand Etang goes through some lovely forest, and you can include a detour to the Annandale Falls.

Grenada has its own organic chocolate factory, the brain child and passion of Mott, who loves sailing so much that he delivers chocolate to Carriacou in a tiny beach cat. They make high-octane bars that are 71 and 82 percent cocoa. Let them melt in your mouth for a creamy, chocolate flavor, unlike any other commercial brand. It makes the perfect gift. Better still, come and see where the chocolate comes from at Belmont Estate, a typical and very picturesque country farm, where the cocoa beans grow. Take the tour ($5 US) and watch how cocoa is extracted from the big fruits using the sun and a people-powered dance shuffle. They will show how the Grenada Chocolate Factory takes these beans and processes them, using solar-powered, handmade, and vintage machinery. The beans are roasted and ground. Some are squeezed into cocoa butter and some blended into a smooth,

Grenada and Carriacou

Antoine Rum Factory does not run every day and it is more fun to go when everything is up and running. You can call in advance to find out (442-7109 or 442-4537). The location fits in well with visiting Belmont Estate. Both places serve lunch.

There are two very special places for a great country meal. Petite Anse [$B-D] has a delightful location, hanging over its own beach, a five-minute drive west of Sauteurs. Phillip and Annie built this mini hotel after crossing the Atlantic on the Arc and chartering for four years. You can swim in the pool and walk in the beautiful gardens, past cottages tucked amid flowers and trees to the beach.

They serve fruits and vegetables from their own estate, fish and lobster from local fishermen, and much of their meat is from local farmers. Their restaurant, with its wide ranging menu, is popular with both locals and visitors. They offer yachts their local rate for a weekend escape.

Helvellyn [$B-C, closed Sunday] has a gorgeous location at the northern tip of the island, to the east of Sauteurs, perched on a cliff overlooking the Grenadines to the north. Hang out and enjoy the picturesque garden, or follow the tortuous path down to a secluded beach below. You relax for lunch in the shady gardens of a lovely local family home. In the distance you sometimes hear the buzz of kid's kites. Helvellyn is run by Karen from Grenada and Badre from Morocco. They serve an excellent authentic West Indian lunch, and have a wonderful pottery on the property, including Moroccan work, and will always open it for visitors. You need to book with a minimum of two people, and they are only open for the winter season (442-9252).

The Rosemont Estate cooks good local meals and sells flowers in a wonderful setting on the road between Gouyave and St. Andrew. They do not open on Saturdays, and booking the day before is advisable.

Fish Friday in Gouyave is a great event, fun, and inexpensive, with lots of vendors selling different seafoods. Drive, take a taxi, or join a tour. McIntyre Bros. do a particularly good tour that you can usually join. They arrive about 1800 and leave about 2100, which gives you plenty of time there.

rich cocoa paste. These are combined with sugar to become your perfect chocolate bar. Their Belmont Estate shop sells all kinds of delicious chocolates laced with local fruits that are only available there. New lines of chocolate bars include Salt-i-licous (salt on the bottom) and nib-a-licous (with little bits of cocoa inside - a wonderful texture).

Many years ago I used to keep an eye on a coconut plantation for a friend. To get there I passed the River Antoine Rum factory, where they made strong white rum called Rivers. I fell in love with this place, which still runs much as it has since the mid-1800s: a giant water wheel crushes the cane, the dry stalks are burned to heat up the juice, and large wooden scoops manually move the hot juice from one big cast-iron bowl to the next as it gets hotter (they call these bowls "coppers," as the original ones were made of copper). They now open this estate to visitors and give tours for $5 EC, which gets you a full explanation and a taste of the rum. (Ask for the strongest rum, drop a bit of ice in the glass, and watch it sink.) River

Grenada and Carriacou

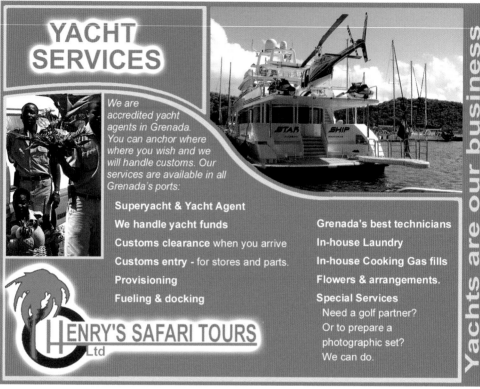

For hiking, Henry of Henry's Safari Tours [VHF: 68] is the best man to contact. (Note call sign: Henry Safari Tours.) Henry specializes in hikes and knows the trails well, including Seven Falls. He also does turtle-watching tours from May to August. Most other taxi drivers are reluctant to get their feet muddy, but there are a few exceptions, including Selwyn Taxi, who will hike and keep you happy. (See our section on *Prickly Bay*.)

Adventure Grenada, owned by Randal Robinson, specializes in adventure tours: all-terrain jeeps, tubing rivers, and mountain biking. They can pick up small groups; larger groups could contact Henry's Safari Tours to get them to the action.

If you prefer the adventure and economy of a great hiking guide who gets everywhere by local bus (this makes for easy one-way hikes across mountains), contact Telfour Bedeau (442-6200). He knows hikes all over Grenada. This works best when you are anchored near a bus route.

Keep in mind that all Grenada's anchorages are within an easy taxi ride, so wherever

you anchor, read about all the anchorages.

Navigation

There is a major light on Point Saline, visible for 18 miles both to the north and south, flashing (2+1) every 20 seconds. There is a lower-elevation (6+1) flashing light on Glover Island, and another at the western end of the airport runway. The lights have not always proven to be reliable.

Grenada uses the IALA B (red right returning) rule. Unless you draw more than 10 feet, you will not have to pay attention to the two big-ship channel buoys outside St. George's or use the leading marks.

The west coast of Grenada is steep-to: a quarter of a mile offshore clears all dangers except Long Point Shoal.

Some people like to sail down Grenada's east coast. It can be rough, but trolling for fish is usually rewarded. It is only advisable in settled weather. Stay well off Grenada's east coast. Pass close inside Bird Island, but outside all other islands. Keep well away from the Porpoises as you come along the south coast. They can be difficult to see,

especially in the afternoon, with the sun in your eyes. Some of the coast lacks landmarks, but you can clearly see Grenada Marine in St. David's Harbour, and look out for the development at Westerhall. Prickly Point has a distinctive saddle shape, and a conspicuous house that looks like a lighthouse.

Grenada's west coast is a marine park and has several lovely anchorages perfect as a last stop for northbound yachts, especially charter yachts that take off after lunch. In the case of northerly swells Grand Mal and Halifax are the most protected. Snorkel on park moorings to make sure they are in good shape.

HALIFAX HARBOUR

Protected Halifax Harbour, once lovely, has been turned into a dump. A huge garbage pit borders its southern side, and the port authority dumps old wrecks here. The southern beach is still pretty if you can get past the flies and the smell of

Grenada and Carriacou

HALIFAX HARBOUR
BEAUSEJOUR BAY
HAPPY HILL
DRAGON BAY
MOLINIERE POINT
GRAN

HALIFAX HARBOUR

12°07.0'

60
20
20
60
60
12
12° 06.7'N
61° 45.0'W
WGDA02
50
150
100
80 50 30
60
30
27
HIGH
TENSION
CABLE
60FEET
26
25
BRIZAN
16 20 12
12
6
3

TO
CONCORD
FALLS

WHITE
HOUSE

RIVER

RIVER
06.5'

GARBAGE
DUMP

CLIFFS

N

TO ST.
GEORGES

0   1/4
SCALE IN N.M.

45.0'   61°44.7'

Regulations

A marine park area follows the coast from Beausejour to Grand Mal. You should find moorings in Happy Hill, Dragon Bay, and the northwest of Grand Mal Bay. The white moorings south of Moliniere Point are for yachts. The rest are for day charter boats who have complete priority. These go back by late afternoon, after which using one will not do any harm. The charge for taking a boat in the park, around $10 US, is sometimes collected; make sure you get a receipt. Snorkel the mooring to make sure it is in good shape and if you prefer to anchor you can anchor off Sunset View in Grand Mal, and in Beausejour Bay. Personal watercraft are not allowed.

HAPPY HILL

burning garbage.

If you brave it, tuck well in, as the water in the middle is very deep. High-tension cables have been strung across both parts of the bay. The lowest wire is about 60 feet above sea level. On the north side, avoid anchoring too close to the low end of the cables. A big landslide marks the southern headland, the result of a major road building dynamite blunder.

Happy Hill (Flamingo Bay), just north of Dragon Bay, can be very peaceful, and is good in everything but bad northerly swells. The narrow beach is backed by a hill, and on the hill is a large, old, silk cotton tree. There is good snorkeling and diving on both sides of the bay around the rocks. Use a mooring. You can anchor in sand in Beausejour Bay, the next bay to the north, but it is a little more susceptible to swells.

DRAGON BAY

Dragon Bay is delightful, with a palm-lined beach and good snorkeling on both sides around the points. Use the moorings.

You can pick up a dinghy mooring just round the corner in Moliniere Point where you can visit Grenada's underwater scupture park created by Jason Decaires Taylor and made world-famous by photos in National Geographic. Snorkel off your boat and look for the statues.

Ashore

Dragon's Hideaway Bar and Grill [$D] is a great little beach bar in Dragon Bay owned and run by Garvin Gibbs. It is easily accessible from the moorings in the bay or from those south of Moliniere Point. Garvin spent many years in the US and UK, and he loves yachting customers, has wifi in his bar, sells ice, and will fill jerry jugs with water. His bar is open every day from about 0800. He grills fresh fish, chicken and pork and serves them with local vegetables. Getting him on the phone can be difficult, but turn up with an open mind and relaxed time schedule and you will find it great fun and excellent value. This makes a perfect last night in Grenada before you head north.

GRAND MAL

Grand Mal is a well-protected anchorage most of the time. The water is usually clean and the long beach attractive. There are gas storage tanks in Grand Mal and two buoys offshore that are used for unloading tankers. Pipes run out from the small dock to the buoys, so avoid anchoring in this area. Anchor south of them, just outside the fishing fleet, and off the Sunset View. You can also pick up a mooring on the north side of the bay, south of Moliniere Point. The snorkeling is good here and it is the most protected area in northerly swells.

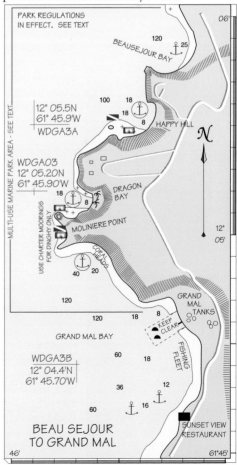

Grenada and Carriacou

Dragon Bay, part of the new marine park area

Ashore

The Sunset View [$C-D] was created by Horatio Brizan, who also owns the Tropicana in town. It hangs out over the water, and you can dine in the fresh air, open to the sea and the anchorage. The cooking good, there is sometimes live entertainment on Fridays and Saturdays. Tie to their dinghy dock, using an anchor to keep your dinghy clear. They can supply water from this dock; you have to edge your boat as close as its draft will allow and tie with your bow towards the dock, and then hope the hose is long enough. If using the restaurant, anchor close by where you can keep an eye on your boat. (See also *Dragon Bay*.)

ST. GEORGE'S

St. George's is built on a ridge, with the sea on one side and the protected Carenage on the other. The houses mingle with shrubs and trees, giving splashes of bright color against a background of dark green. From afar, it is as neat and pretty as a picture-book illustration. The old brick buildings are capped with old "fish scale" tile roofs. The buildings are a reminder of long ago when the profitable journeys were outward bound, laden with rum, spices, and fruit, and returning sailing ships would arrive "in ballast" of bricks.

As you enter the harbor, you see Fort George and the hospital on your left. A little farther in, the channel divides in two: to the left is the protected Carenage, surrounded by the city of St. George's. To the right is the lagoon and the big new Port Louis Marina, with some of the larger and fancier yachts facing out toward the town. The lagoon is a yachting center, complete with a yacht club, the marina, supermarkets, restaurants, and a chandlery. The eastern side, near the chandlery,

350

has been made into a pleasant park along the water, and you will find convenient dinghy docks to help you explore ashore.

Navigation

The town of Gouyave, about 8 nautical miles north of St. George's, now has a very fancy dock. You can find good temporary anchorage off the dock. This could be useful for picking up or dropping off people once you have cleared in.

A large cruise-ship dock has been built and considerable land reclaimed off the Esplanade.

The lagoon has two marinas, otherwise, the anchorage is outside the harbor, south of the channel. You can anchor anywhere along the coast as far as the last headland before Grand Anse. This is usually calm, but occasionally rolly. The holding is not great and Jr. Cuffie rents legal moorings for $10 night; he will collect. This is a good service, but snorkel and check the mooring as some of the ropes were chaffing in 2012, and I saw no sign of maintenance.

Leave the red buoys to starboard and head on into the lagoon. Most of the lagoon has been dredged to over 15 feet deep, with a few corners that are about 10 feet deep.

If you wish to tie up in the Carenage, call the Grenada Port Authority on VHF: 16. Yachts over 200 tons need a pilot to come here or to Port Louis. Seven entries qualifies you to enter on your own.

St. George's, showing the cruise ship dock

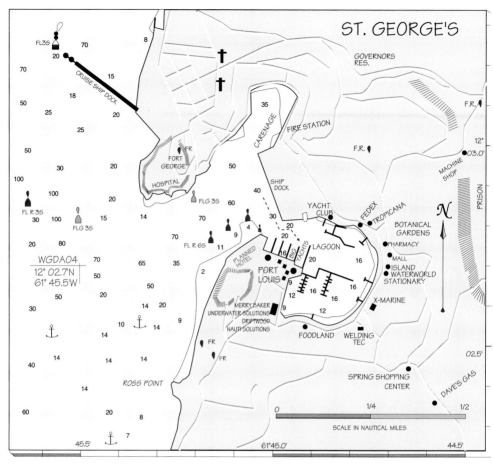

No town in the Windwards is completely free of theft. Always lock up the boat and dinghy. The marinas have security.

Regulations

The customs office is in Port Louis. They open weekdays 0800-1600; weekends and holidays 0900-1400. They can come in outside these hours by request. If you have any kind of time pressure, consider using the registered agents: Henry's Safari's Tours or Spronk's Mega Yacht Services. They are on excellent terms with the officers, can often arrange pre-clearance, and they can clear you from anywhere in the island. For visits of up to three days, they can arrange your inward and outward clearance at the same time. You can hand your passports and papers over and feel free immediately. It is not very expensive.

Communications

Weather and local information are available on a cruiser's net that operates at 0730 on VHF: 68 (except Sunday).

Island Water World has wifi access that covers the lagoon. It is free (charity contributions accepted). Other wifi is also available. The marinas have phones and fax. Port Louis has plug-in internet.

The Fedex office is near Tropicana, and DHL is in Renwick and Thompson

General yacht services

Camper and Nicholson's Port Louis Marina [VHF: 14/16] is a fancy and lovely new marina: very spacious, and beautifully gardened and laid out. Customers can lounge in the swimming pool overlooking St. George's, and climb the tower to photograph their yacht below.

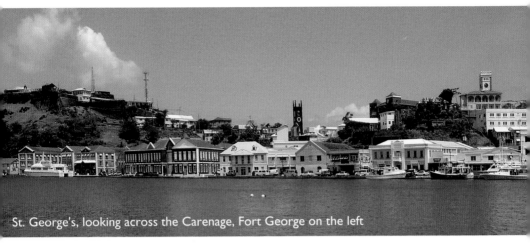

St. George's, looking across the Carenage, Fort George on the left

The marina includes 10 berths for yachts up to 300 feet long, 16 berths for yachts up to 120 feet long, and over 140 berths for smaller yachts. To reach the dinghy dock you have to go right round all the docks, though at low tide you might be able to short-cut under the dock in front of the office.

The berths have electricity, cable TV, plug-in internet, and water. The big boat berths have all kinds of voltages at 50 cycles (60 cycle is planned). High speed fuel (duty free) is planned.

Port Louis has an excellent team. Danny Donelan is in charge of marketing and sales, along with customer welcome and service. The professional office staff will make sure you have all the help and resources you need. Docks are for sale. Danny Donelan will be delighted to tell you how this works.

Port Louis is home to the Moorings charter company and Sea Sun Adventures day tours. The 1782 Bar is the place to chill out (see *Restaurants*).

The Grenada Yacht Club [VHF: 6/16 "GYC"], includes a modern marina with berthing for about 43 boats and a fuel dock that has both diesel and gas. The docks have electricity (110/220-volt, 50-cycle) and water, and the rates are reasonable. The Yacht Club is informal. You can send a fax or get your mail during office hours: 0800-1700 (address mail to Grenada Yacht Club, P.O. Box 117, St. George's, Grenada). Showers, laundry, and garbage disposal are available. Henry Safari picks up empty gas bottles, and drops off filled ones on Mondays and Wednesdays.

Taxis and other services can be arranged. The Yacht Club bar opens at 0900 and stays open till 2200. The restaurant is open every day and is good (see *Restaurants*). The Yacht Club also runs a sailing school program.

The super-yacht agents work well together. Spronk's Mega Yacht Services is run by Roger and Claire Spronk, who own Bananas (see *True Blue*). They have a desk in the Sea Sun Adventure office. They are registered yacht agents and clear yachts in and out, arrange visas, fueling, docking, flowers, travel arrangements, taxis, car hire, laundry, crew placement, repairs, flights, and anything else a large yacht could need. Spronk's are also building a private marina in Petit Calivigny Bay (see *Clarkes Court Bay*). This will be have easy berthing for the largest of yachts, and make a convenient Grenada base. They are excellent at full superyacht provisioning, which means large yachts can be fully provisioned from scratch in Grenada. Their Gourmet Store in True Blue stocks all the best quality frozen fish and cuts of meat, and they own an 8-acre farm for fresh produce. Where possible, they source locally, but for exotic and special items they work with all the big international yacht provisioners.

Henry, of Henry's Safari Tours [VHF: 68], is a superyacht agent who also works well with cruisers. He understands that they have different needs and budgets, which has given him an excellent reputation with everyone. He owns the laundry at Port Louis (plus two others), fills everyone's cooking gas cylin-

Grenada and Carriacou

353

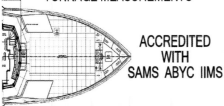

ders, and has a fleet of taxis, plus Grenada's most colorful service vehicle. He collects and delivers to all Grenada anchorages.

Henry does customs clearance for yachts and their stores and for superyachts, he helps with immigration for arriving crew. Other services include dinner reservations at no charge, garbage collection, dock space, fuel, technicians, and he makes travel or shoreside arrangements. Henry can also arrange full provisioning. He loves his job, and it shows. Having worked with yachts for some 30 years, he knows just about anything a yachtsperson may want. He learns a few extra tricks each year as new things come along, whether it involves banking, finding a golf partner, or arranging an unusual permit.

Brian Sylvester at Blue Water Yachts has a store in Port Louis Marina (see *Provisioning*). Brian does full yacht provisioning and offers the full gamut of superyacht services from arranging docking and clearing customs to arranging for technical help and day tours. Brian has a hotline to Ricardo Moultire, the authorized battery service technician for ACR Electronics who can replace the batteries in your EPIRBs and PLBs. Through Ricardo, Brian can also arrange high-tech filtration for fuel, oil, gas and aviation fluid. Other services in the marina are given under *Technical yacht services*.

Bob Goodchild owns Flying Fish Ventures. Bob trained as a boatbuilder in the UK and is now a marine surveyor and a member of the International Institute of Marine Surveyors (IIMS) and the Society of Accredited Marine Surveyors (SAMS). He can do tonnage measurements and MCA compliance inspections up to category 2 through his membership in the Yacht Designers and Surveyors Association (YSDA). Bob has been in Grenada for years, is very professional and good, and is also a great guy to deal with. He has now been joined by Neil Batcheler who has a marine and mechanical background, and some of you may know him from Island Water World in Grenada.

Bob also has some pleasant apartments to rent behind Whisper Cove Marina.

Grenada and Carriacou

355

Chandlery

Island Water World has a big branch of their huge and very successful Caribbean marine store on the lagoon road opposite the marina. They have an excellent range of stock at duty-free prices, including batteries, yacht hardware, winches, electronics, outboards, fishing gear, ground tackle, stoves, charts, and cruising guides. If there is anything you need that they do not have, look at their large catalog, and they can bring catalog items in quickly. On the first Wednesday of the month they run a book/DVD swap coffee morning for charity.

Ace Hardware is on the Maurice Bishop Highway (behind *True Blue*). This is Grenada's best general hardware/car parts/household/gardening store. You can get everything here from a dinghy pump to a new tea kettle.

Bryden and Minors stationary store is next door to Island Water World, and they may well have ink for your printer. They sell computers and printers.

Marine World, on Melville Street, caters to Grenada's fishing fleet, they are opposite the fish market. They stock fishing and snorkeling gear and charts, as well as safety gear and some hardware.

Technical yacht services

Two business specializing in looking after and fixing boats have offices in Port Louis. Horizon Yacht Management is owned by James and Jacqui and works well with their charter company, Horizon Yachts, in True Blue. They have a good team of technicians under manager John Pirovano who specialize in maintaining and outfitting yachts while the owners are away. They can repair or install any systems, and can arrange for your haul out and paint job, oversee any work you may be doing through other contractors. Horizon are agents for new Bavaria Yachts, Fontaine Pajot Cats, and Sea Ray and Meridian power boats. They have a full yacht brokerage.

Mark and Anita's Island Dreams, a long established business with a fine reputation, has a base here. Mark and Anita are good people to look after your yacht while you go away, fixing anything that needs doing at the

same time. Some jobs they do themselves. For the rest they bring in the right people, and they do everything from a simple repair to a complete refit. Yard work in either of the boatyards can be arranged through them and they will supervise, ensuring the work is done properly and on time. (They do much guardianage for Spice Island Marine). They have a professional web site for customers where you can see the last time they checked your boat, how the voltage was, what work was done and more. If you want, they will have your yacht hauled, painted, fueled, launched, and ready to leave when you arrive. If you need overnight accommodation on the way, they will arrange that. They can store your yacht in Port Louis, Phare Bleu or other places by arrangement. Yard work needs to be discussed with them at the beginning of the project. They offer gear storage facilities, a big help if the interior is being pulled apart. They represent Little Ships brokers.

Brett Fairhead's Underwater Solutions has boats in several harbors, a base in Port Louis and they work all over the island. They are good enough to get asked to do jobs throughout the Caribbean. Brett is one of the Caribbean's most experienced commercial diver and he has done everything from working under ice to underwater welding in the tropics. He trains and works with a team of Grenadian divers, who clean yacht hulls and props, remove shafts and rudders in the water, carry out underwater damage survey and repair, including underwater welding, as well as untangling anchors.

They can undertake salvage work and have a small tug to assist in this. They also do bathymetric depth contour surveys and install pipelines, moorings, and channel markers. They do anything underwater, large or small.

Turbulence Sails has a station in Port Louis. They handle all sail repairs as well as canvas and cushion work. They are Grenada's main riggers and will come sort out your rig and hydraulic problems. They are also a first-rate electronics shop and can fix all your instruments (see *Prickly Bay*).

Grenada Marine (see *St. David's Harbour*) can repair all boat systems and they sell electronics, engines, watermakers and more. They have an office in Port Louis and can do

Grenada and Carriacou

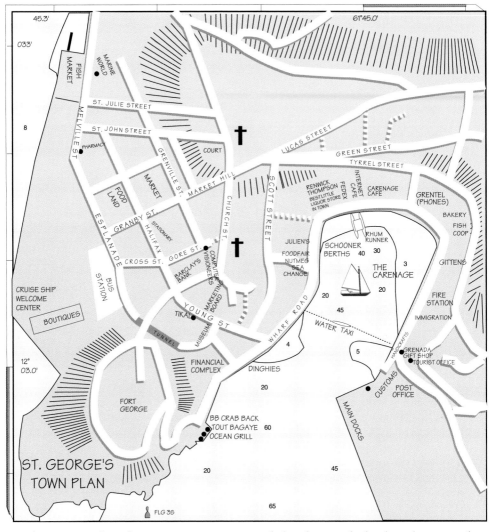

ST. GEORGE'S TOWN PLAN

in-the-water work at the marina.

Driftwood offers fine yacht woodwork, from fancy joinery to replacing a plank or teak deck. It is owned by Steffen who worked for many years with Chippy in Antigua. Here he is helped by Pierre, who worked for some years with Woodstock in Antigua. They are a good and reliable team who work on all sizes of boat. If a woodworking job involves glass or composite work, they can do that as well, which considerably simplifies some jobs.

X-Marine, run by Nicolas and Mark, is the best place to go for any kind of major structural repair in glass, composite, or carbon fiber. Their shop is on the lagoon,

and they have a dock where boats can be brought alongside for work. They can work on boats hauled in the yards. They fabricate anything in glass or carbon fiber, they spray Awl-Grip, and they can oversee any boat project, however major. If you want a new boat, these are the people to build it for you. They plan a welding shop for aluminum, stainless, and titanium, and a full mechanical shop for engine repair.

Michael Cadore of Protech Engineering Services teaches electrical engineering and refrigeration at the local technical school. He makes boat visits, is good, and fixes all fridges, and air conditioning systems, as well as appliances like washers and driers, and

any DC or AC electrical system. He also fixes both gas and electric cooking stoves. He carries tools in his van, listens to his cell phone and will come to any Grenada port.

Basil St. John at Lagoon Marine Refrigeration Services is also good, but hard to find. You can also try Dexter Hayes (Mr. Cool) at Subzero Air Control.

Albert Lucas runs an excellent machine shop and is usually there every day. He will often do small jobs while you wait. Finding him is more of a problem, as he has no sign. Turn right at the Tropicana roundabout,

then left on the main road. Head uphill at the next roundabout. Albert is on the right-hand side of the road on the corner, just before Blue Danube. You climb a few steps to reach his workshop, which is on the left.

Francis Hagley runs a first-rate metal working shop on the lagoon called Welding Tec, which does all stainless and aluminum welding and fabrication. He will make good stanchions, swim ladders, bimini frames, hard tops, or radar arches, or just fix up whatever it is you have broken.

Clarkes Upholstery is run by Vernol

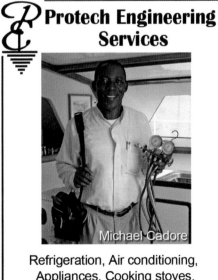
Grenada and Carriacou

Port Louis, looking towards the Carenage

Clarke, a Grenadian who does upholstery and is equally good at canvas work for biminis, covers, and awnings, all at competitive prices. Yachts are about half his business and he will come to measure and fit, not only in St. George's, but any of Grenada's anchorages.

Jeff Fisher is the local Neil Pryde Sails representative. He can measure up and quote for a new sail, and advise on re-using any expensive sail hardware you have. He will also fit the sail when it arrives.

Nauti Solutions offers mechanics and carpet cleaning: perfect when you have a classic fail while fixing your engine on the carpet. It is run by Danny, an Australian mechanic, good at fixing all engines, inboard or outboard. His office is Port Louis, his boat in Prickly Bay, and he works all around. He will also fix windlasses and watermakers. His wife, Lesley, is excellent at carpet cleaning, and general yacht cleaning.

Panabread, at AJS Enterprises, is the man for signs and carvings of all types.

Tan Tan Sam is excellent for hand varnishing, painting, cleaning, and polishing. Call him on his cell: 403-9904. He often works with Sean Thomas (406-4258/419-7454), who also does good work. Ashley, (456-9003), is another good professional as is Thadius (410-6224) who often works with Island Dreams. These men will work in any marina.

Randy, who works with Sea Sun Adventures, fixes outboards (416-4715).

Al Bernadine in Gouyave (444-8016) is good with alternators, starters, and power tools. He has a small machine shop. If you call him he can arrange for you to drop off what you want fixed in St. George's.

Alan Hooper is a marine surveyor. His cell is 409-9451.

Check also all the marine services in the south coast harbors. Most will come to St. George's.

Provisioning

The Merry Baker, owned by Nigel and Merry Fairhead (parents of Brett from Underwater Solutions), is just inside the lower road to the marina. It is a dreamy homemade bakery where they cook all kinds of wonderful breads (they vary day to day) and baked goodies, as well as producing their own ice cream, selling frozen meals and juices for takeout, and offering such delectable homemade products as whisky marmalade. They sell wines, beer and soft drinks (the only things not homemade). Come and take a coffee in the morning to check it all out. Return for one of their excellent sandwiches at lunch (especially on a Friday when they have "build a burger" lunch). But bring a big shopping bag, for the delicious breads and other items you will want to take back afterwards; their olive bread is the best I know in the Caribbean. Merry Baker opens weekdays 0730-1700, Saturdays, 0800-1300.

Blue Water Liquors, part of Blue Water Yacht Services, has an office with a convenience store and wine shop in Port Louis. This company is owned by Brian Sylvester and he does full yacht provisioning as well as acting a general yacht agent organizing anything the big yachts need (See General yacht services). Blue Water Liquors opens at 0830 and stays open till the last customer leaves around 1900 or later. Look in the freezer for frozen meats and fish, they also do frozen meals to order. As workers have found, this is the cheapest place to buy a cold drink.

St. George's is a first-rate place to provision, with comfortable, air-conditioned supermarkets. The newest is Foodland, in the lagoon. It has its own dinghy dock and is often open quite late at night. Foodland has an excellent selection of regular items and a pleasing delicatessen section. It offers a five percent discount to charter yachts.

You can take your dinghy from the lagoon over to town. If you take this guide with you, our town map will help.

St. George's is a busy place, with plenty of traffic, including buses laden with people and goods, playing loud music, cars, and trucks weighed down with building materials. Sometimes it seems like they are all honking at once. People will shout "taxi!" at you, and vendors may offer fruits from baskets.

Most shops open from 0800 to 1200 and from 1300 to 1600 on weekdays. Banks are open only till 1500, except Friday, when they open to 1700. The post office is open over lunch but closed all day Saturday. Most shops close Saturday afternoon and Sunday (though you can still shop, see *Grand Anse*). The lovely old financial complex, which used to house the post office, has been restored, creating some of the fanciest government offices in the Windwards.

Those wishing to buy wine or liquor should visit Renwick and Thompson's Best Little Liquor Store in Town [VHF: 16 "Rhum Runner Base"]. You can tie your dinghy close to the shop. Their selection includes over 125 different wines. Duty-free prices are available for case lots, but allow at least 48 hours for processing. Duty-free has to be delivered after you clear out. On large orders, delivery to Prickly Bay is possible. At Renwick and Thompson you can send your DHL packets and organize money through Western Union. They offer land and water tours and have an agricultural section where you can find useful hoses and hose fittings. If you are interested in land in Grenada or Carriacou, they have some of the best for sale.

Food Fair is conveniently close to the

water, and you can tie up nearby. Food Fair is an excellent supermarket, open weekdays till 1730, except Friday, when they are open till 2045. On Saturdays, they close at 2000. They, too, offer a five percent discount to charter yachts.

Visit the local market, preferably on a Saturday morning. It is a riot of color, where determined ladies under big umbrellas sit amid huge heaps of vegetables. It is one of the most interesting markets in the islands, and you can get fresh produce, spices, and handicrafts. If you need a new watch battery or repair, there is stall in the market that specializes in this and they can often fix your watch on the spot. The Marketing Board, on Young Street (opposite Tikal), has some of the best prices on fresh produce, although the range is limited.

You can usually get a good selection of fresh fish in the fish market.

Henry B, one of the Port Louis Taxi drivers, has a herb farm and can supply fresh herbs as well as prepared dried herbs for cooking. These include his own soup herbs,

Grenada and Carriacou

Young Street, St. George's, Tel:473-440-2310, freddy@tikalgrenada.com, www.tikalgrenada.com

which add flavor to any soup.

Fun shopping

Port Louis has a few boutiques and more will follow. Fidel Productions sells great art t-shirts, commissioned from Caribbean artists who receive royalties. They stock hand-painted calabash art, Moho jewelry, decorative items, and souvenirs; all are attractive and of good quality.

Young Street, in St. George's, has several attractions. Tikal was the first Grenadian gift shop when Jeanne Fisher opened it in 1959. It is stacked with quality arts and crafts and beautiful fabrics. You will find paintings, maps, hammocks, ornaments, casual shirts, nautical charts, books, and more.

Across the road and a few steps up the hill is Art Fabric. The shop is a riot of colorful batik fabrics, clothing, and household items. Batik demonstrations are available on request.

Upstairs opposite Tikal is Jim Rudin's Art Gallery. Jim is a lovely man who has worked with the arts in Grenada most of his life. He always has a big range of paintings and prints on display, many by local artists.

The museum, in a lovely old building, is well worth a visit for the small entrance fee. They have excellent cultural events at 1730 most Friday nights. Stop by and ask for a program. It includes jazz, good pan, storytelling, and local dance. They also have the museum bistro upstairs (closed Sunday), run by Oliver Vargas. It opens at noon and serves tappas, using fresh produce, and stays open into the evening some nights.

St. George's is best explored when you have plenty of time and no errands. There are wonderful views wherever you go. The more panoramic are around the fort and by the cemetery (go up Church Street and keep going). There are plenty of steps and narrow alleys to explore. With the advent of the cruise ship dock, the focus of tourist shopping has moved into the cruise ship area, with a mall of bright and cheerful shops selling everything from fresh juice to jewelry, with tons of souvenirs.

Restaurants

The 1782 Bar and Grill [$A-D] is a big, informal restaurant, open to the breeze in Port Louis. It is the sister restaurant to the excellent Aquarium, and owned by Uli. Since it is the only marina restaurant it has a wide-ranging menu to suit everyone, from the admiral to the cabin boy, and the food is very good. You can dine finely here on fresh fish and shrimp or the best steak. Or you can get pizza, pasta, salads, burgers, and sandwiches. They open every day.

The Marine View Restaurant [$C-D] in the Yacht Club has a friendly, clubby atmosphere, is run by the staff, and is both good and very reasonable. They do a bargain daily special which is served at lunch and at dinner if there is any left. You can get rotis and sandwiches as well as delicious dinners with the emphasis on seafood, including shrimp and fish. The bar opens at 0900, the kitchen an hour later and stays open into the evening. The kitchen closes on Sundays.

Horatio Brizan's Tropicana [$C-D], on

the lagoon, is an inexpensive restaurant: cheap enough for any time cooking seems too much of a chore. The food is Chinese plus they serve good rotis, fish, and lambi dishes. It is excellent value for lunch or dinner, with a separate and speedy takeout section. If you need a night ashore, they have inexpensive rooms upstairs.

In town, the Nutmeg, overlooking the Carenage is one of the city's older establishments. You have not really spent time in St. George's till you have had lunch at the Nutmeg, they also serve dinner.

If you follow the Carenage right round town to the end, you come to a restaurant corner. You can tie your dinghy right outside, and these restaurants all have an open view of the harbor.

Brian and Anna Benjamin are the warm and welcoming owners of BB's Crab Back [$B-C, closed Sunday]. Brian grew up with his grandmother, Acil, in Grenada, till he was eleven and left for England. She bestowed on him a love of cooking and fresh food. In England, he trained as a chef and had a famous West Indian restaurant in Ealing. He has now returned to his roots. He cooks Caribbean food with a European flair. If he can get a group together, Brian does cooking sessions, where he takes people to the market to buy the food, comes back, and they all learn how to prepare and cook it. You can tie your dinghy to the railing, but may want a stern anchor.

Ocean Grill [$A-B] has a wonderful, wide deck, open to the view and the breeze. You can tie your dinghy pretty much onto your table leg. They have very inexpensive lunches geared to locals and more upmarket food in the evenings, using good quality meats and fresh seafood.

In the lagoon, The Roof Top is perched at the top of the Mall near Island Water World. It is a good spot to hang out and owner Gloria Cyrus offers a big range of tapas.

Patrick's continues in a tradition started by Mama of a giant local feast, featuring a vast array of local dishes, so you can taste everything one-time; a real experience.

Transport

Taxis that most often deal with yachts are all members of the Marina Taxi Association. They can be found in all Grenada's marinas, including Port Louis, and set a high standard for reliability and good customer service. In Port Louis, Keith, from K&J Taxi, is a good choice. He is courteous, knowledgeable, interested in the history of the island and the use of herbs. He volunteers his taxi to take yachties up to Mount Airy for the weekly reading group (listen to VHF 68 at 0730).

Grenada and Carriacou

Grand Anse

GRAND ANSE

Grand Anse is what most people have in mind when they think about the Caribbean: a generous, two-mile sweep of white-gold sand, backed by shady palms and almond trees. Planning restrictions have prevented buildings from being overly intrusive.

Anchoring is forbidden right off the beach, but the St. George's anchorage comes almost to the beginning of Grand Anse. It is within easy dinghy range of St. George's. The dinghy dock is at the eastern end of the beach, and from here you can walk. Grand Anse contains a wealth of shops and restaurants and is easily visited by bus or taxi from St. George's or Prickly Bay.

Communications

Onsite Software Support, by the banks, has everything for cybernuts: disks, print heads, and ribbons. They offer free stand-up email access for visitors. They repair notebooks, desktops, and their software.

Provisioning

When you get behind the beach and onto the main road, Grand Anse is a big shopping strip lined with malls, from Food Fair Mall to Excel Mall. Cars and buses hurtle down the road with little thought for pedestrians. Stay on sidewalk and take care when crossing the road. Grand Anse is good for Sunday shopping; both Real Value and Value Garden are open mid morning.

The two main supermarkets are Food Fair, in the Shopping Center, and Real Value, in the Spiceland Mall. Food Fair is an excellent supermarket with a big range of products, including fruits and vegetables that are mainly local and refreshed frequently. Charter yachts are offered a five percent discount.

Real Value is like a US supermarket, with the biggest variety, including specialty foods. When a container arrives (usually on Thursdays), you get the widest choice of overseas produce and an excellent deli section. The aisles are wide, and everything is attractively displayed in a spacious setting. You can shop here on Sunday mornings.

Spiceland Mall includes The Wine

Shoppe, a good place for retail wines. They open 1000-1900, Monday to Saturday.

Just down the road, many banks have ATMs for Visa or MasterCard. Gittens Drugmart is a full pharmacy, with everything from newspapers to prescriptions. A travel agent is in the same block, farther down.

The Marketing Board runs Value Garden in the Excel Mall. This offers a good selection of local products and produce at the best prices. They are open Sunday mornings.

La Boulangerie (Marquis Mall) is a great bakery, with croissants, baguettes, Italian county bread, quiches, cheese cake and more. Stock up for your next charter, or just drop by for lunch (see *Restaurants*).

While shopping and eating, keep an eye out for Sugar and Spice Ice Cream. It is made in a tiny factory in Prickly Bay using fresh local ingredients, from the coconut they grate themselves to the chocolate from the Grenada Chocolate factory. Their coffee break is especially delicious, as is their soursop.

Fun shopping

Grand Anse is an easy bus ride from Spice Island Marine Services or St. George's. This is a wonderful shopping area, with three malls, street-side shops, and hotel boutiques.

If you come by dinghy, it is worth checking out the local craft market just behind the beach.

The Big Bamboo in the Marquis Mall is Grenada's best surf shop, with surfing essentials from sunblock to boards, along with snorkeling gear in case you fall off, beachwear, and a load of accessories. They also have a wide range of casual clothing, sandals, good sailing shorts, beach bags, and t-shirts, which make great souvenirs when you want to make one of your relatives envious. Patrina, the owner, is very friendly and happy to offer sailors a five percent discount for cash (mention that you read it here).

Food Fair is part of a pleasant shopping center where you will also find Imagine, a terrific handicraft store with batiks, woodcraft, hand-painted t-shirts, Spice Island cosmetics, and books. Other shops include Hubbard's Home Center, Mitchell's Pharmacy [open till 2100], Sandra's hairdressing salon, and Magic Photo Studio. Rick's Cafe, [$D] in the mall, offers local dishes, fast foods, coffee, and a full range of ice creams. Eat them in the pleasant seating area in the mall square.

Spiceland Mall has a host of small shops where you can buy everything from stationery and shoes to clothing and music, as well as electronics, kitchenware, and hardware. I have found nice boat throw-rugs in Linens and Things. You will find music, a big hardware store, and a fresh fast-food corner, good for fresh-squeezed juice and lunch.

Marcelle and Peter Toussaints lived for many years in the UK. Their gift shop, Presents, in Excel Mall, includes a wide range of classy local and international gifts, games and toys, and books. This mall also has three mini-cinemas.

Upstairs in the Foodfair Mall, is Dr. Mike Radix, a GP who has been treating yachtspeople for years, and opposite Spiceland Mall is Ocean House, with surgeon Robbie Yearwood.

Toothache? Grenada not only has good, highly-recommended dentists, they are easily visited in Grand Anse. Many cruisers have been helped by Dr. Roxanne Nedd at the Sunshine Dental Clinic. Her clinic is next door to Excel Mall. She has been very busy of late so it is welcome news to announce two excellent new Grenadian dentists, with all the most modern equipment at Island Dental Clinic, above Gittens Drug Mart, opposite the roundabout. Dr. Tara Baksh trained in the UK and Dr. Victor Samaan trained in the USA. They can do everything from extractions and root canals to complex crowns. If you need implants, visit Dr. Yaw in Prickly Bay opposite North South Wines. He is a first rate dental surgeon.

Restaurants

A great little Italian quarter has sprung up in Le Marquis Mall. Pepeo's La Boulangerie is both a great Italian bakery and a restaurant. They open every day for a breakfast of baked goodies, serve the best coffee and have pizza, pasta dishes, quiches, and salads for lunch or dinner. They also have delicious desserts like tiramisu, cheese

Carib
SUSHI
439-5640
At Le Marquis Mal
Open weekdays: 11.30 am - 2 pm, 6 pm - 9 pm
Saturday: 12 noon to 2 pm, 6 pm - 9 pm
Sundays: 6.30 pm - 9 pm
At Sushi Shop, True Blue, (473) 439-8991
open:11 am - 6.30 pm

cake, and many pastries.

Next door, another Italian, Michele, has Carib Sushi, a great little Japanese restaurant. On the sushi side, good Oriental chefs use fresh local fish (tuna, dorado, and wahoo), lobster, and lambi, as well as imported salmon, for the best sushi and sashimi. On the cooked side, they offer shrimp, vegetable and fish tempura, beef, tuna tataki (lightly seared), and other Japanese dishes. They open for both lunch and dinner but are closed in between. Maybe because the food is so healthy, you see some good-looking, healthy people here. They do takeout, which could be handy for charter yachts.

Next door is Tortuga, an Italian wine bar, owned by Marco. They serve a big range of wines by the glass or bottle and appropriate food when you want to make meal of it.

On Grand Anse Beach, Umbrella's [$D] is a perfect beach hangout open every day except Monday. Pull your dinghy up on the beach, sit under the umbrellas outside, or up on the roof, or you can sit inside. They have an extensive drinks menu, from cocktails to

local juice and food to go with it, the emphasis is on salads, sandwiches, burgers, fish and ribs. Save room for some fancy American-style desserts. They are often rated among the best places in Grenada on Trip Advisor.

Coconut Beach, a French restaurant [$A-B] managed by Scratch, has a superb location on the water's edge on Grand Anse beach. French cuisine has been adapted to local foods.

Lawrence Lambert is a Grenadian who spent some years in Canada and then returned to buy the Flamboyant Hotel and villas, and the Beachside Restaurant [$B-D]. It is at the western end of Grand Anse beach, with a sweeping view to St. George's. I know many yachtsmen who have used the rooms from time to time, and the restaurant has good West Indian and continental food, with a steel band on Wednesday nights in season.

Their Owl Sports Bar has two big TVs to keep you on top of the latest games.

The beautiful, but shallow Morne Rouge Bay is a short ride or healthy walk from Grand Anse. There is a complex here called the Gem Holiday Beach Resort. They run the Fantazia 2001 disco, which is open on Wednesdays for Oldie Goldie night, and on Fridays and Saturdays with live music.

Water sports

Grenada has many dive shops, all keenly competitive and happy to take yachtspeople. If you call one, they will collect you from the marinas or docks. All dive shops are Padi or Naui establishments with all kinds of courses, including introductory resort courses. We mention just a couple of the Grand Anse dive shops: Aquanauts [VHF: 16], who have their main base in True Blue, also have a base in Spice Island Inn. Dive Grenada, run by Phil Saye, is based at the Flamboyant Hotel. They offer a friendly and flexible service to divers and are a Padi Golden Palm 5-star shop.

Grenada has a variety of good and interesting dives. For sheer drama, you cannot beat the Bianca C, a 600-foot cruise ship that sank in 100-165 feet. The wreck is vast, and mainly broken, but there are splendid views up at the bow, and the swimming pool is still intact on the deck. Large schools of small

Racing off Grand Anse

snappers, some midnight parrotfish, and a few barracudas get framed by the wreckage. This is an advanced dive, and most dive shops will insist you do one other dive first.

Flamingo Reef starts just outside of the north end of Happy Hill Bay and continues along the coast toward Dragon Bay. This colorful and lively reef offers a changing seascape as you swim along. There is a good balance of healthy hard and soft corals, with a dense, tall forest of waving sea whips, sea rods, and sea fans at the top, on the seaward end. This is the place to look for the flamingo tongue that gives the dive its name. Many grunts, squirrelfish, wrasses, parrotfish, and trumpetfish swim along the sloping reef. Large schools of brown chromis pass by. Deeper on the reef, you have a chance of seeing large groupers. In the sand are mixed schools of spotted and yellow goatfish, probing the bottom with their barbels.

Dragon Bay and Moliniere Point join together and are the easiest dives to get to with your dinghy. Use one of the park moorings. You can start on the south side of Dragon Bay or go out from the little bay in Moliniere Point. These dives have a mixture of large sand and coral patches, going from shallow water down to about 60 feet. Much of the reef in this shallow area is densely covered with a variety of corals and sponges.

When you get to about 30 to 40 feet, you meet a drop-off that goes down another 25-30 feet. Sometimes it is a steep slope, at other times a sheer wall. A few rock outcroppings make for dramatic valleys, and deep, sand-filled gullies are cut into the drop-off.

Boss Reef starts outside St. George's Harbour and continues to Point Saline, a distance of at least two and a half miles. It varies in width from 200 to 500 yards. It is possible to do many dives on this reef. Currents are strong here, and it is best done as a drift dive with a dive shop. A popular dive is the middle section, swimming wherever the current takes you. The depth here varies from about 30 to 60 feet. The reef rises from the sand to a somewhat level top that is broken by deep gullies and holes that drop down to sand. This is an exceptionally good dive for coral variety. The top is completely covered in an array of corals, all packed close to each other. There are lots of brightly colored fish, with large schools of blue and yellow Creole wrasses, accompanied by blue and brown chromis. Grazing parrotfish and big schools of doctorfish will pass you by on the reef, and you will see schools of smaller grunts and perhaps a large Spanish grunt. Look under corals and in holes for spotted drums.

Grenada and Carriacou

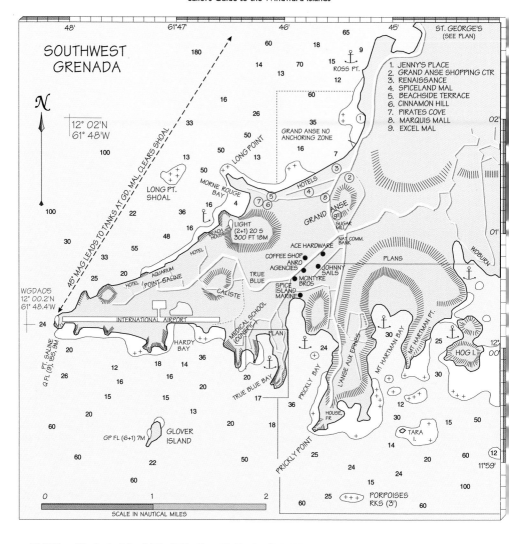

PT. SALINE TO PRICKLY BAY

When sailing between St. George's and Point Saline, keep well clear of Long Point Shoal. Head west from St. George's and continue till you are on the line between Point Saline and the tanks at Grand Mal, before heading for Point Saline. Reverse this procedure when you return.

Alternatively, coast hoppers may prefer to explore this shore, which has several pretty beaches. You must, however, be very careful of Long Point Shoal, and only approach when there is good light and you can see the reefs. It is possible to eyeball your way

inside Long Point Shoal, but don't cut too close to Long Point, as shoals come out about 150 feet from shore. As you round Long Point heading west, you will see the beautiful Morne Rouge Bay, which, unfortunately, is only about 4 feet deep (perfect for multi-hulls). You can sometimes find lunchtime anchorage just outside Morne Rouge Bay.

As you sail round Point Saline and head toward Glover Island, Prickly Point is the farthest headland that you see. When closer, Prickly Bay is easily identified by all the yachts inside and the handsome houses

on the hill. There is plenty of water for most yachts to sail inside Glover Island. There is one good anchorage, just before Prickly Bay, called True Blue. St. George's University and Medical School is conspicuous; it looks like a town, and is on the west side of True Blue.

Ashore

Two restaurants lie along the north shore leading to Point Saline. Because of their prime beach locations and excellent reputations, many people make the effort to visit them, usually by cab.

Approach Uli and Rebecca's Aquarium Beach Club [$B-D] by taxi or rental car. The setting is spectacular, under some giant rocks that form a headland at the end of an idyllic deserted beach. The architecture has made the most of these features, and the dining room is open to the view. They have created interesting corners and also an open beach bar. The fresh barbecued seafood is excellent, and this is a great place to come for a quiet, romantic, seafood lunch or dinner, or to bring a group and make it what you will. The Aquarium Beach Club is popular on Sundays, when people come to swim and snorkel. Rebecca is an artist and some of her work decorates the walls. You get to the Aquarium by driving past the airport terminal, and looking for the sign on your right. They now offer some of the most gorgeous rooms in Grenada, above the restaurant in their Maca Bana villas.

On a calm day, you can anchor off The Beach House [$A-B], in the bay west of Morne Rouge Bay, and get your dinghy ashore to enjoy this elegant beachside restaurant, which is managed by Stanley Minors. Alternatively, take a cab. Come for lunch and enjoy the beach, or make it an evening treat (especially good when the moon is up). The food is first-rate.

Grenada and Carriacou

True Blue

TRUE BLUE

True Blue is the bay just west of Prickly Bay. It is a beautiful little bay, colorful and clean, and it makes a lovely anchorage. Russ and Magdalena, owners of True Blue Resort, have spent much time both cruising and working for charter companies, and they love boating customers. A small marina is part of the hotel, and a delightful wooden walkway over the water connects the two.

A distinctive small island is at the entrance. Enter in the middle of the bay between this island and True Blue Point. Go straight up into the bay and anchor inside, take one of the moorings, or tie up at the marina. The water is about 25 feet deep at the entrance to the bay and 13 feet deep up to the outside of the marina. A small surge enters from time to time, when the wind goes south of east. The waves are smaller than in Prickly Bay, but shorter and steeper. This works better for many monohulls, which roll less, but some cats wobble more. If there is a problem, put out a stern anchor to hold you facing out of the bay and into the seas. That will fix it.

Everything in True Blue is easily reached by dinghy to Spice Island Marine Services, then a short walk.

Communications

True Blue has wifi, you can use the high-speed email station, and the office will send and receive faxes. Bananas has free wifi.

Services

Jacqui and James manage the True Blue Marina and use it as a base to run Horizon Yacht Charters. It takes about 25 boats and, in addition, they have 15 reliable moorings for rent. The mooring fee is $40 EC per night, with less expensive monthly rates. Mooring is optional, as there is tons of room to anchor. The marina has diesel, water, electricity (110-220 volt, 50 cycles), wifi, showers, and toilets. You can get propane tanks filled and they will get Henry's Safari to come get your laundry. Their office sells ice, cruising guides, and Horizon t-shirts. Jacqui and James will look after you well and help you get any kind of repairs you may need. They look after boats when the owners go away and will undertake major

370

project management. They have an office for this in Port Louis.

You can rent a car at the hotel.

Spronk's Mega Yacht Services is down the road at Bananas. It is run by Roger and Clare. They provision boats and are super-yacht agents. They do customs clearance, arrange docking, find or import parts, organize airline tickets or transportation, and source flowers or anything else (see *St. George's*).

Provisioning/fun shopping

A few steps from True Blue, in the direction of Spice Island Marine Services, is the Bananas complex, run by Roger and Claire Spronk. Downstairs is a pharmacy and minimarket. But go upstairs to the office for the gourmet store. They stock top quality frozen food, especially fish and other seafood (everything from oysters to black tiger shrimp), and quality meat cuts, as well as burger and sausage. They own an 8-acre farm for produce. This is the place to get your pickled ginger and wasabi powder. They supply many of the local hotels, as well as

private homes and all kinds of yachts. Walk in and check them out. They also deliver sizeable orders.

Magdalena, at True Blue Resort, runs Truebluetique, which is small, but packed with a tasteful collection of handicrafts, ob-

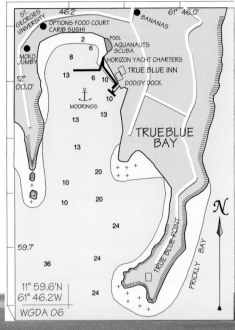

jet d'art, jewelry, souvenirs, and useful items.

Restaurants

The Dodgy Dock [$B-C], True Blue Hotel's restaurant, is perched over the bay on stilts, with a dinghy dock. The food is very good and blends Mexican, Caribbean, and European flavors, all made from local ingredients. They have snacks, a full menu, children's menus, and daily specials.

Steel band music is played on Tuesdays. Friday is Latin night with Latin music and Mexican food. Saturday is music night in season. On Sundays, they serve a full roast beef brunch with Yorkshire pudding. Advance reservations are a good idea, especially for a waterside seat. Russ (from the UK) and Magdalena (from Mexico) rank among the most friendly of patrons and are especially welcoming to those on yachts. Their nightly happy hour is 1700-1800.

Other facilities include a conference room, a small open playground, and a swimming pool. Rooms are available to yachtspeople at special rates.

Esther and Omega run an interactive and entertaining cooking demonstration, that includes tasting on Thursdays at 1500 ($10EC). On Monday at 1650 they have a local rum tasting session. Check the special events on their website, including a kid's Easter treasure hunt and Christmas events.

Imaginative in concept, Bananas [$B-C] was designed by two yachtsmen: Roger, who owns it, and Don, who helped build it. It is a cool restaurant, hangout, and nightspot, with lots of interesting corners and pretty waterways. Bananas has a sports bar with a big TV, and free wifi. Outside, Carib Cave [$D] is Grenada's first wood-fired pizza oven, for excellent pizzas with cold beer. This is also the place for burgers and snacks.

Their restaurant [$C-D] is above, on a canvas covered deck pleasantly open to the breeze. It opens every day for dinner, and sometimes in season for lunch. The food is good and very reasonably priced, with emphasis on fresh seafood and meats.

Bananas is Grenada's hot entertainment spot with something always going on within

 Full-Service Marina

 Accomodation

 Dodgy Dock Restaurant

 Le Conch Spa

 Aquanaunts Dive Center

 Sanvic's Car Rental

 TrueBluetique

True Blue: Truly Perfect

Walking distance to Spice Isle Marine, Special Sailors Hotel Rates, Daily Happy Hours.

www.truebluebay.com
windward@truebluebay.com
Phone: (473)-443-8783

TRUE BLUE BAY
BOUTIQUE RESORT
GRENADA

Grenada and Carriacou

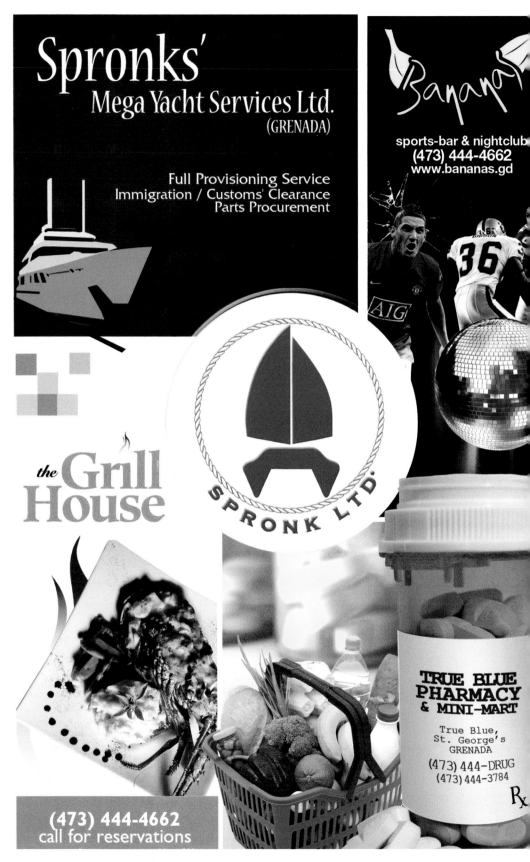

Prickly Bay

PRICKLY BAY

(Also known as L'Anse aux Epines, pronounced "Lans O Peen.")

Prickly Bay is pleasant, a well-to-do area of fancy houses, many of which have well-tended flower gardens. At the eastern head of the double-headed bay is a palm-fringed beach. The buildings are overcoming the green areas as people build larger and larger mansions, but you still live with the sound of birds by day and tree frogs by night. St. George's is only 15 minutes away by car, and the airport and Grand Anse are even closer. Spice Island Marine Services is at the western head of the bay, on the True Blue side, and Prickly Bay Marina is in L'Anse aux Epines on the east side of the bay. This makes everywhere from True Blue Bay to Mount Hartman within easy dinghy/walking distance. Buses are plentiful from the True Blue roundabout, at the beginning of the dual carriageway, (Maurice Bishop Highway), a short walk from Spice Island Marine Services.

A prominent house at the end of Prickly Point looks just like a lighthouse. This makes it easy to recognize.

Prickly Bay is easy to enter, but don't get careless. There is a reef in the middle, opposite Prickly Bay Marina, that is just deep enough (6-feet) to be hard to see. A second, deeper (9-feet) reef lies a few hundred feet to its west.

Reefs also extend nearly all the way up the eastern shore, and one should give the

the complex. They have hosted everything from concerts and magic shows to boxing matches, and their sound-proofed disco, and big sports TV screens are a fixture. The easiest way to check out the action is to check out www.bananas.gd.

If you are walking at night from either True Blue or Spice Island Marine Services, take a flashlight, and be cautious on big party nights.

Walk towards the university for more attractions. Options Food Court is a series of small shacks, each selling something different, including the Sushi Shop, pizza and ice cream, and Rumours Vegetarian. Tables have free wifi and power.

Water sports

True Blue is home to Gerlinde and Peter Seupel's Aquanauts Grenada. They are a Padi 5-star Golden Palm Resort and take people diving, do all kinds of courses, fill tanks, and rent diving equipment to those going on charter. They offer nitrox and rebreathing dives and training.

Dinghy up to their dock, or they will collect divers from docks in Prickly Bay. Aquanauts has three very large and well-equipped dive boats. Calmer summer weather offers the exciting prospect of exploring special sites off Grenada's south coast, or going up to Isle de Ronde.

Grenada and Carriacou

True Blue headland reasonable clearance. Prickly Bay Marina has put in a marked channel in the middle of the bay. This keeps an entrance channel clear of anchored boats, which can help the big yachts.

Occasional southerly swells can make the bay uncomfortable, though a stern anchor will do much to restore a sense of calm.

Regulations

Prickly Bay is a port of entry, with the customs at Prickly Bay Marina. They normally open every day of the week. Customs officers often have duties on the way in, so they sometimes arrive more like 1000 than 0800. Anchoring is forbidden within 600 feet of the beach, as this area is reserved for swimmers. Small buoys mark the area.

SPICE ISLAND MARINE

LEAVE CLEAR CHANNEL

PRICKLY BAY MARINA

TRUE BLUE

LEAVE MARKED CHANNEL CLEAR

PRICKLY BAY

Communications

A cruisers' net operates on VHF: 68 at 0730 weekdays. It includes weather and local information, including coming events.

Prickly Bay Marina has a good little internet station with high-speed wifi access and some computers. Their wifi covers the docks and the marina. If you are farther out in the bay, HotHotHot Spot and Cruisers wifi provide coverage. Hothothot spot has another base in Clarkes Court Bay and many others up island. Cruisers wifi covers several Grenada anchorages, including St. George's and the Clarkes Court Bay, and they have a station in Trinidad.

Spice Island Marine Services has wifi and computers for the use of those on the slip. Restaurants with wifi include De Big Fish, Bananas, and Dodgy Dock.

General yacht services

Dinghy docks and garbage disposal are available both at Prickly Bay Marina and Spice Island Marine Services (by De Big Fish). Prickly Bay Marina has fuel and water. You can bring the boat in, or use jerry jugs. Essentials sells ice.

Henry's Safari Tours [VHF: 68] has a sub-base in the marina, with on-the-spot laundry, and cooking gas collection station. For emergency service, call him on the radio [VHF: 68]. Spice Island Marine Services has coin-operated laundry machines.

Prickly Bay Marina [VHF: 16] is a charming, small marina where fresh green lawns are dotted with palms and almond trees. It has an informal atmosphere and docks for about 25 yachts. They have stern-to docking, showers, electricity (110/220 volt, 50 cycle), diesel, gasoline, water, and

Grenada and Carriacou

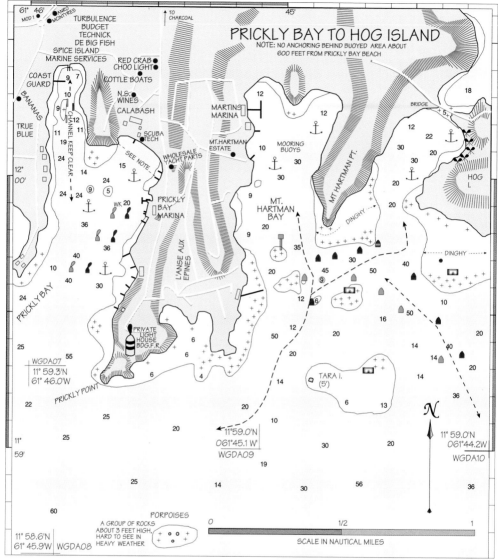

PRICKLY BAY TO HOG ISLAND
NOTE: NO ANCHORING BEHIND BUOYED AREA ABOUT
600 FEET FROM PRICKLY BAY BEACH

ice. The marina is managed by Davide who will make you feel right at home. Darren, also on the management, has been upgrading the yachting facilities at a steady pace. They have put in an excellent dinghy dock, upgraded the shop, and are improving all the buildings.

This marina houses Henry's Safari Laundry, Enza Marine, Essentials Mini-mart, and the Marina Tiki Bar and Restaurant (see *Restaurants*). The new owners of this marina have built some very fancy condominiums and plan a bigger marina. Those interested in the condos can ask in the marina or look

for Champy Evans.

Davide at the marina offers absentee yacht and project management and he can get technicians (many their own maintenance staff) to fix any boat problem you may have.

Spice Island Marine Services [VHF: 16] is a pleasant boatyard, with room for 200 boats. It is in the northwestern corner of Prickly Bay, on the True Blue side. It is easy to walk from here to all the places we mention in True Blue Bay. It is a family business and Junior Evans is in charge. Their travel lift can take boats up to 70 tons and 25-foot

Grenada and Carriacou

beam. At present, yachts of up to 10-foot draft can come in at high tide and they have one 12-foot draft boat they manage to drag in. They have a mast crane and hydraulic stacker with mast racks for those storing their masts off the yacht. They have tie-downs for all boats in the hurricane season, and secure cradle berthing is available. The yard keeps cats separate from monohulls. Their staff includes a team that washes and chocks, does AwlGrip spray painting, osmosis treatment, hull polishing, woodworking, and antifouling. Sailmaking and rigging are done by Turbulence; welding and fabrication by TechNick. The yard is secure and kept in excellent order.

Yacht crew can do their own work or arrange approved outside contractors through the yard. The yard has electricity (110/220 volt, 50 cycle), wifi, and good water pressure. Spice Island Marine Services can look after your yacht while you are away, as well as arrange all the work. While you work, life is made easier with showers, toilets, a coin operated launderette, email (yard customers only), and De Big Fish waterfront bar (see *Restaurants*). Budget Marine Chandlery is also based at Spice Island Marine Services.

Superyachts can get any help they need in this area from either Henry's Safari Tours or Bananas (see *St. George's*).

Chandlery

Budget Marine has a big, duty-free (to foreign yachts) chandlery at Spice Island Marine Services. You will find a good collection of general and technical chandlery, including everything you need for your haul-out. This is a good place to find anything from an inflatable dinghy or Tohatsu outboard to a new galley stove. This branch is part of Budget Marine's Caribbean chain, and anything that is in the Budget catalog that they do not have in stock can be brought in by Fedex or, if you have time, by their regular shipping schedule. They currently open weekdays 0800-1700, Saturdays 0900-1200. Bring in your boat papers for the first visit to get the duty-free prices.

Technical yacht services

Turbulence Grenada, based in Spice Island Marine Services, has impressive workshops that handle sails, rigging, and electronics. It is owned and run by Richard and Joelle, who are French, but who have lived in English islands almost forever. They are helped by about 10 employees. Richard is a very experienced rigger and sailmaker (and racing helmsman). He used to prepare maxi boats for major races and is well qualified to advise and handle complete new deck layouts. The store is divided into three sections. The rigging shop is long and well equipped to deal with swaging and all rigging problems up to 16-mm wire or up to 10-mm rod rigging. They keep materials to make spinnaker poles on hand and can order whole new rigs through Sparcraft. They stock all the necessary ropes for running rigging and sheets, as well as the blocks and winches (including electric) to help you get them in tight. They repair big boat hydraulics and are agents for Navtec. They stock and install Profurl roller furlers.

The Turbulence sail loft is large, and you see them working on everything from sailboard sails to massive mainsails from maxi-yachts. They produce sails themselves under the Turbulence logo, and if they get too big for that (or if you prefer), they are agent for Doyle Sails and North Sails.

They make biminis from scratch and can tackle all other canvas work. Sheldon heads the Turbulence electronics department. They will repair your electronics, whatever the brand, and are agents for NKE, Brookes and Gatehouse, and Ray Marine, and they supply and install these brands of instruments and autopilots. All branches of Turbulence are also available in Port Louis in St. George's and Grenada Marine in St. David's Harbour, where Louis, from Switzerland, is manager.

In the same yard, TechNick Yacht Services is run by Nick and Karen. Originally from England, Nick has spent years in the Caribbean and is a citizen of Dominica, where he helped put up the aerial tramway. He may be the only qualified mechanic who also has a degree in biology. He was the Moorings southern area technical manager for a while. Nick is good, he welds and does metal fabrication in all metals, and he plans to open a machine shop soon. One of his big specialties is the building of arches and supports for dinghies, biminis, and solar panels. Nick is very knowledgeable about all boat systems, and can often give good advice.

Cottle Boat Works is a full marine joinery and carpentry shop. Owner Jim Cottle sailed to Grenada on his yacht, J. Jeffrey, and has over 37 years of experience in the business. Jim has a large, new, modern shop near the Red Crab, full of excellent, top-grade machinery. You get to it by taking the

Grenada and Carriacou

381

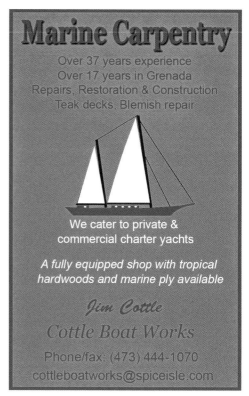
left side road just beyond the Red Crab, and looking on your left. Jim basically does all his own work, so you can be sure of a good job. Teak decks are one of his specialties, along with wood repairs and fine joinery work. Jim can also fix dings, burns, and other blemishes in varnish. He keeps a good supply of teak and other hardwoods on hand. Many of his customers come from the large charter yachts. Jim is very happy to work on yachts staying either in Prickly Bay, Mount Hartman Bay, or St. George's. He can get booked up, so if you have a big job, discuss it with him as long in advance as possible.

Anro Agencies, run by Robert Miller, is a classy operation. They are agents for BMW and Subaru, as well as Mariner and Mercury outboards, Mercruiser engines and outdrives, Yanmar and Perkins diesels, and several brands of generators. They sell and install new units, do warranty work, repair broken engines, and will make boat visits. All new engines can be bought duty-free from their bonded warehouse, and parts may be imported duty-free. They will normally come to any of the Grenada ports to pick up broken outboards to fix. Their shop is a few hundred feet down the road from Spice Island Marine Services, on the Maurice Bishop Highway, the dual carriageway between the roundabouts. They are within easy walking distance of Spice Island Marine Services on the east side of the road. They stock quite a few engine related accessories in the Quicksilver range and their prices can be quite competitive. They import sports boats by Trinidad's Formula 111.

McIntyre Bros., also on the Maurice Bishop Highway, is within easy walking distance of Spice Island Marine Services, next to the roundabout on the east side of the road. They have qualified diesel mechanics and can fix most engines. They are the sales and service agents for Yamaha outboards and can arrange sales to yachts at duty-free prices. They will come and pick up your Yamaha for repair from most of the marinas.

McIntyre rents cars and will deliver to the boatyard or marina. In addition, they do excellent hiking and sightseeing tours, and arrange weddings.

Enza Marine [VHF: 72], in Prickly

Bay Marina, is owned and run by Greta, a pleasant ex-air force major. Enza does repair work on yachts, using mechanical, electrical, and electronics engineers, as well as refrigeration, air-conditioning, and watermaker specialists. They do outboard repairs, especially 4-stroke. They do some machining and metal fabrication and are agents for Perkins, Northern Lights, Kiss windmills, and Iridium phones. They can source any parts you might need at short notice and have them brought in. You can discuss new installations with them. There is pretty much nothing electrical or mechanical that they cannot do. They are reliable and have a good reputation and charge accordingly.

Johnny Sails and Canvas [VHF: 16/66] is a sail loft just down the Dusty Highway that leads north from Spice Island Marine Services. Johnny and his team can do excellent work, from sails to canvas and cushions, though scheduling can take time.

Many day workers are available for on-board painting, varnishing, and other work. These include Charlie, Winston, and Julian, normally known as Sam or Tan Tan, who has been around yachts for years and who spent quite some sea time as a private yacht skipper. You can also check out Slim and Curtis.

For computer repairs and IT you can try Christian and Anand's ModOne by the True Blue roundabout, or Onsite Software Support in the Marquis Mall (see *Grand Anse*).

Transport

There are some excellent taxi drivers around. They have now organized themselves in the Marina Taxi Association which covers all the ports in Grenada. It is easy to call Marina Taxi [VHF: 16]. The Prickly Bay branch has a small office in Prickly Bay Marina. All their drivers are good and one is nearly always available.

If you are renting your own car, McIntyre's are close by, will quickly deliver a car, can provide a local license, and have staff who are used to dealing with yachts.

Provisioning

The Prickly Bay Marina shop, Essentials [VHF: 16] is a convenient mini-market. They are open Weekdays from 0800-1800, Saturdays, 0800-1600, and Sundays 0800-noon. They have most things you need, including a little fresh produce and frozen fish and meats, and it is convenient for buying cases of beer and other drinks. They also sell ice.

For more than that, bus or cab to the malls in Grand Anse (buses go from the True Blue roundabout). A little closer is the small local open market by the L'Anse aux Epines roundabout.

People needing to stock up on their wines will be delighted by North South Wines, a short walk from the boatyard, close by the Calabash. They stock wines from all over the world, including Europe, Australia,

Grenada and Carriacou

South America, and South Africa. You can sit down in a comfortable atmosphere, discuss your needs, and they can recommend wines for different menus. They have a large enough range to satisfy the superyacht owner, as well as those with more modest needs. This is a wholesale outfit, so wines are sold by the case, but they are often willing to mix cases for yachts, and they will deliver to your yacht. If you buy a case of wine and don't want it all at once, they are happy to store it for you in their temperature-controlled rooms. Opening hours are weekdays 0800-1600. They have a retail outlet called the Wine Shoppe in Spiceland Mall (see *Grand Anse*).

Restaurants

The Marina Tiki Bar and Restaurant [$B-D], right in Prickly Bay Marina, is a favorite yachty haunt. You can get great thin-crust Italian pizzas, good meals, and other daily specials that are usually reasonably priced. They have the most popular happy hour in L'Anse aux Epines, when free pizza snacks sometimes make the rounds, a clever move as you really want more after a taste. Happy hour is 1700-1900 nightly except Saturday when it runs from 1700-2200. Friday is the most popular night, with steel band from 1800, followed by more music. Sunday night is movie night, and they have competitive bingo on Wednesdays. The cruisers net gives information about their quiz nights and other attractions.

On the True Blue side, De Big Fish [$B-D] is the bar/restaurant at Spice Island Marine Services. The location is pleasantly open to the water, with a large dinghy dock.

They open for lunch and dinner every day, except Sundays, when they occasionally open for breakfast.

Owners Kim (from Trinidad) and Rikky (from the UK) have managed to create a friendly atmosphere with good service and are very much geared to cruisers, who use it as a meeting place. It is very casual and kid friendly, and also popular with residents. They have a happy hour on Tuesdays, Fridays and Saturdays, with live music early on Tuesdays and Saturdays. The daily lunch specials are a bargain, and their menu is wide ranging with everything from burgers to fresh fish.

The gourmet will favor the Red Crab [$A-B], run by George Mueller and his son, Scott. They blend West Indian and continental flavors with skill and imagination and do excellent seafood from fresh seared tuna to lobster, as well as prime steaks. It is the first choice of local residents when they want to eat really well in a quiet atmosphere. Most choose to eat out on the pleasant patio, but there is also seating inside. It is a just short walk from Prickly Bay Marina.

The Choo Light [$C-D] is run by the Choo family from Hong Kong. The prices are so reasonable that you can eat here any time you don't feel like cooking. The atmosphere is informal and the staff welcoming. They have a full range of dishes: seafood, vegetarian, and meat that all come with plain rice. Their ginger shrimp and fish are good and they sell takeout.

The Calabash Hotel [$A] has a very fine, up-market restaurant in a pleasant atmosphere and with excellent food. They prefer you to be dressed fairly smartly, but this

is a great choice when you want somewhere really special; reservations are essential.

Mount Hartman Estate Cave House [$A] is another exclusive restaurant within walking distance of Prickly Bay or Secret Harbour. It is a lovely sculpted building with high ceilings and an open view down over Secret Harbour. The food is good, you can eat a la carte, or they offer a two-course meal, which is quite reasonable for such a top-class establishment. It is good for a special night out, but reservations are essential.

Charcoals is about half a mile down the main road on the right. It is worth the walk for the first-rate grilled foods, fresh local juices, the best Angus beef burger, and daily specials at reasonable prices. They open for dinner on Monday and Tuesday and for lunch and dinner Wednesday to Saturday.

Ashore

You will find tennis courts at the hotels and a golf club in Golflands. Ask for directions.

Everything in True Blue is now easily accessible from Prickly Bay; dinghy to Spice Island Marine Services and take the short walk down the road.

There is a very easy walk between Prickly Bay and Secret Harbour Marina in Mount Hartman Bay. From Prickly, just turn right out of the boatyard road and take the first left. When you come to the T-junction, turn right, then left.

Water sports

Scuba Tech is the waterfront dive shop on the Calabash beach, a Padi/Cmas shop. This pleasant dive shop is owned and run by Sabine, Jochen, and Carsten. They do all the usual courses as well as nitrox and rebreathing. The can do annual visual tank inspections and fills, and help repair equipment. They dive with small groups, using a 32-foot pirogue. They visit all the sites, on both the south and west coasts, including the Bianca C.

If you are after big fish, ask about their wreck sites south of Prickly Bay. San Juan, a small wreck that sank in 27 meters, is 1.5 miles south of Grenada. Herma 1 was sunk in 2005, is 170 feet long, and is four miles south,

Grenada and Carriacou

and 30 meters deep. King Mitch is 200 feet long, 6 miles south, and 37 meters deep.

These wrecks are in open, rough water, so are weather dependent, challenging, but very exciting. They attract lots of nurse sharks, rays, and spadefish, and turtles often drop by. On one of their better dives on San Juan here they saw 17 nurse sharks and four eagle rays.

They usually meet at 0845 to gather equipment for a two-tank dive at 0900. If you have gear, they could pick you up from Prickly Bay on their way out.

They can help out with small underwater problems and mooring work. For dedicated professional dive work, see Underwater Solutions in St. George's.

THE SOUTH COAST BEYOND PRICKLY BAY

(See sketch charts pages 378 and 393)

The south coast of Grenada has beautiful and protected anchorages, as well as some great restaurants, several marinas, a boatyard, and other facilities. A mass of reefs provides interesting, if somewhat murky, snorkeling. The area should be treated with caution: eyeball navigation is essential. On our charts, we have marked as "too shallow" several areas of relatively shoal water (12-15 feet) that extend well offshore. In normal conditions you can sail over these, but when the going gets rough, seas start breaking on them, and they are best avoided. The Porpoises, about half a mile off Prickly Point, awash and hard to spot, are as nasty a group of rocks as you could find to get wrecked on.

Buses run between the south coast and St. George's.

The buoyage system, such as it is, is privately maintained, with a lot of markers placed by individuals for their own purposes. Very few buoys stay in the same place over two years. My sketch charts include the markers that were there when I looked in 2011. Markers have proved extremely unreliable,

and, when out of place, dangerously misleading. Visit this coast for the first time in good light and rely on your own navigation skills, not on the buoys. When you know the area and know which buoys are in place, they may be helpful on later visits.

The exceptions to this are the buoyed channels into Phare Blue Marina and into Grenada Marine in St. David's Harbour. These channel buoys are well-maintained.

Entering Mt. Hartman Bay and Hog Island is tricky, as new shoals have arisen in the channel. The main reefs are easy to see in good light. The new shoals, 6- and 9-feet deep, are not as easy to spot. From Prickly Bay, pass about midway between Prickly Point and the Porpoises. Look out for Tara Island, a tiny coral island about a foot high. Leave Tara to starboard, passing halfway between it and Prickly Point. Head for Mt. Hartman Point, eyeballing your way through the reefs. For Hog Island, follow the inner reef up to Hog Island, leaving the red buoys to port. For Mt. Hartman, pass between the red buoy and the green beacon.

An alternative is a deeper channel south of Hog Island. For this, approach the western tip of Hog Island on a bearing of magnetic north, and eyeball your way around the reefs as you approach Hog. To leave, pass close by the reef just south of Hog Island, and head out on a bearing of 170° magnetic. In both directions, make sure the current is not setting you to the west. A 14-foot bank lies on the west side of the channel, so deep-draft yachts need to be particularly careful. Last time I passed, two green buoys marked the inside part of this channel.

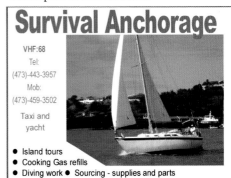

Photo labels: SECRET HBR MARINA · MT HARTMAN BAY · MT HARTMAN PT · HOG I. ANCHORAGE · TARA I.

MOUNT HARTMAN BAY

Mt. Hartman Bay is deep and well protected (see chart *Prickly Bay to Hog Island*, page 378), with a modern marina. This is a great area for dinghy sailing or sailboarding, as there is protected water all the way to Phare Bleu Bay. By land, it is a 10-minute walk to Prickly Bay. (From the marina entrance, turn right, walk up the hill, and round the corner; keep going till you come to a crossroads, turn right again, and then take the next small road on the left. When you come to the next main road, turn right again, and the marina is on your left.)

General services

Secret Harbour Marina [VHF: 16], with 53 berths, has a lovely location in a peaceful bay. Fuel, water, ice, showers, telephone, wifi, fax, laundry, dinghy dock, 24-hour security, and electricity (110/220/380V, 50 cycle) are among the marina services. Duty-free fuel is available. They can take any size of yacht from the smallest cruiser up to huge superyachts. The maximum draft on the deepest dock is 20 feet, and a yacht of this depth will have to be careful entering the bay. If you have any questions, call the office who will be helpful in assisting you in docking at the marina, or in finding any services you might need. The marina also has lovely self contained cottages along the waterfront to rent. Each is beautifully appointed and has a delightful balcony over the water.

There is no customs station here, so if you want to come straight here, call Secret Harbour Marina and they can arrange for one of the yacht agents to clear you.

Technical yacht services

George, a taxi driver whose call sign is "Survival Anchorage," refills propane bottles, looks after yachts when owners are away, helps source parts or other things, and can do underwater work, including hull and prop cleaning. He is willing to do overnight passages for those needing an extra hand. He delivers boats in the Windwards, or helps deliver them farther, and he can act as pilot

Grenada and Carriacou

SECRET HARBOUR MARINA

DOCKAGES

Situated in the south coast of Grenada, is one of the Caribbean's finest marinas. Located outside the hurricane belt in the well-protected and sheltered waters of Mount Hartman Bay, is considered one of the safest marinas in the Caribbean. All this, is located 10 minutes from the entertainment and shopping centers, and 15 minutes from the point Salines International Airport.

COTTAGES

Are you looking for a place to leave your boat and relax at the same time, experience «Secret Harbour» here you can find twenty (20) fully furnished cottages located in the beautiful gardens with spectacular view of the marina and the bay.

Our tropical gardens and lush vegetation surround you with luxury and charm from your arrival to your departure.

SECRET HARBOUR MARINA OFFERS

- 53 slips marina accommodating boats up to 200 ft, 42 stern-to-slips and 11 alongside slips, 20 ft draft is the deepest dock.
- High capacity electricity 110/220/380V (50Hz) and water at each slip.
- Fuel, gas, oil, garbage and ice. Duty-free fuel available.
- Long and short-term slip rental, full security.
- Telephone, fax, internet and laundry facilities.
- Beach Volley and Restaurant-Bar. Friday Night Barbecue, also Taxi and Island Tour services.
- Shopping Bus service two days per week.

EACH COTTAGE HAS

- Air conditioned bedrooms.
- Beautiful view of the sea and the marina
- Elegantly decorated.
- Kitchenette with fridge.
- Microware and coffee machine.
- Bathroom with shower.
- Daily maid and laundry services available.
- Car rental and Island Tours.
- Free wifi internet connection.

Tel: (473) 444-4449 / Fax: (473) 444 2090 · Email: secretharbour@spiceisle.com · VHF : 16/71
Website: www.secretharbourgrenada.com
Facebook Secret Harbour Marina

around the reef-strewn south coast. He has his own yacht for day sails or island passages.

Ashore

Secret Harbour Bar, Restaurant and Pizzeria is open every day from 0900 until the last order. The location is pleasant and the spacious dining room is open with a view of the bay. They often run a barbecue and sometimes have special party nights.

Winston Brizan is a good, reliable taxi driver and is usually on hand to take you from this marina.

George (Survival Anchorage), the taxi driver mentioned in *Services* above, takes people on "Village Life" tours. He will take you to some of the small villages and introduce you to some of his friends to give you an understanding of village life in Grenada.

HOG ISLAND

North of Hog Island is a huge, protected bay. When you anchor, there will be just a finger of horizon to remind you the sea is still

there. This is one of Grenada's most popular cruising hangouts. Yachties enjoy the peace and Roger's ramshackle shack bar that takes up a good chunk of the tiny beach. Access to shore is available at Mt. Hartman Bay and Woburn. On Sundays the cruisers get together for a popular barbecue at Roger's Bar.

See pages 378 and 393 (charts) and pages 386 for navigation into Hog Island. When you get in, anchor anywhere between Hog Island and the mainland.

A construction company now owns Hog Island and Mt. Hartman Estates and plans a massive development, currently stalled. So far they have built a bridge to link Hog Island to the shore (no more sailing yachts through the narrow channel, but you can dinghy through).

In the land behind Hog, I noticed a lot of grazing horses. I tracked down the owner, Wendell Wilson, who owns Amistad Stables and can take you riding (440-4175/533-8221).

On the image: WOBURN, CCB MARINA, HOG ISLAND, CLARKES COURT BAY, WHISPER COVE, PETITE CALIVIGNY, CALIVIGNY ISLAND, HOG ISLAND TO CALIVIGNY ISLAND

CLARKES COURT BAY

This huge and sheltered bay, with Woburn at its head, has lots of anchoring possibilities: you can explore and find your own spot. It is linked to protected bays to the east and west, offering miles of safe dinghy navigation. You will find marinas and dinghy docks.

In the old days, big sailing ships would anchor here to take on rum that was brought down the river to the head of the bay by small boat. Calivigny Island lies at the entrance to Clarkes Court Bay. It was privately purchased in 2001 and is being developed. As part of this development, the deepest part of the entrance channel has been buoyed. These buoys are privately maintained, and have proved unreliable. Check for yourself that they are in position. You need to enter fairly close to Calivigny Island to avoid all the reefs and shoals that extend south of Hog Island. Once inside, you can anchor almost anywhere that takes your fancy.

One popular anchorage is off Calivigny Island just north of the island, off the beach. The bottom shelves steeply, so make sure you are well hooked. Calivigny Island is privately owned and guarded. The beaches, like all Grenada beaches, are public. You should not use the dock, go behind the beach, or use any of the owner's beach huts. But you can pull your dinghy on the beach, have your picnic ashore, and swim. Keep it clean. Guards may check you out, but they know the law. One time we visited, two big labradors came running out and tried to knock us over with their wagging tails, and then lick us to death. We loved it.

You can find good anchorages between Hog Island and the mainland, on the windward side of Hog Island. Another delightful little anchorage is in Petite Calivigny Bay, with good snorkeling around Petite Calivigny Point.

Both Calivigny and Hog are dotted with hardy little frangipani trees. Their leaves fall in the dry season, leaving only sweet-smelling, delicate white flowers.

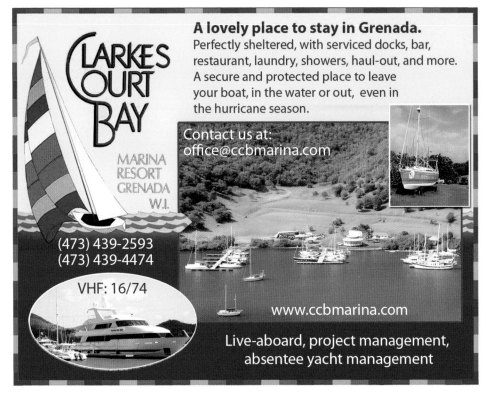
Communications

Clarkes Court Bay Marina has wifi or plug-in, as does Whisper Cove Marina. Bring your own computer. You can probably pull in Cruisers wifi or Hothothot spot onboard.

General yacht services

Clarkes Court Bay Marina [VHF: 16/74] is the brainchild of Bob Blanc. The atmosphere is peacefully rural, with a cooling breeze. This is a small, friendly and personal marina, and a secure place to leave your boat if you want to travel. Bob spent years in Canada building top-quality floating docks, and used this technology when he returned to Grenada. He has 56 slips. Each with water and electricity, both 110 and 220 volt, 50-cycle. The minimum depth at the inside dock is about 7 feet, deepening to at least 15 feet at the outer berths.

This marina is approved by some insurance companies for the hurricane season, if the yachts are left in double spaces and tied off to the docks on each side. To lighten the load in a warning, Bob has some hur-ricane moorings. You can rent these during the winter.

Bob can store yacht ashore, at the moment fairly light boats, lifted by crane. He plans a 30-ton Sealift system soon for yachts up to 10 foot draft and beam no problem. Prices are reasonable; do your own work.

The marina has toilets, showers, a laundromat and the Oasis Bar (see *Restaurants*). You are asked to use the shore toilets or a holding tank to help keep the place clean. Bob is personally at the marina much of the time. He looks after yachts when customers travel abroad, and he undertakes project management if you have any work that needs to be done.

Whisper Cove Marina is a small, pleasant, and friendly docking facility between Petit Calivigny and Woburn run by Gilles and Mary. It is well protected by a groin. They have 12 berths for boats up to 60 feet and 10-foot draft, with electricity (220 volt, or 110 with a transformer); water comes by a long hose. They have hurricane moorings in case of a storm, and these are available for

rent outside the hurricane season (or free if you want to tie up to one for a meal). They have a laundry machine, wifi, dinghy dock, the Meat and Meet shop (see *Shopping*), and a bar and restaurant (see *Restaurants*). They look after their customers well and have a bus for airport runs.

Cruisers love their do-it-yourself workshop with its vice, drill press, and other tools. If you need a hand with very simple welding, Gilles may help. You can drop off propane tanks and laundry for Henry's Safari Tours.

Petit Calivigny Marina is under construction and already has a couple of boats pulled out and it should be fully operational during the life of this guide. It is owned by Claire and Roger of Spronk's Yacht Services. The water is deep here so they will be able to take any size of yacht up to big superyachts, who may find it handy as a local base. Initially, it will be stern-to tie up to the shore, docks will be added later. Water and electricity will be available and they plan to sell fuel. They already provide full support services (See *St. George's* for details).

Chandlery

Sherri is an efficient and enthusiastic Trinidadian who used to run Marine Warehouse and now owns Wholesale Yacht Parts, a short walk from the dock in Woburn. She can source anything you need from the US, usually at a discounted price, and have it shipped down at a 60% discount of the usual Fedex rates. If you want to ship something of your own from the US, she can help. If you are in another island, she can ship direct to you there. She is in the big 4-story building right across the bay from Clarkes Court Bay Marina. Drop by or or contact her by phone or by email.

Shopping

Whisper Cove's Meat and Meet shop is known for the best selection of meat and sausages you will find in Grenada. Gilles is a butcher who buys local animals, which he hangs and processes professionally in his modern facility. The result is that you can buy the best cuts of much finer meat than the imports found in the supermarket. He

also makes excellent sausages. They can prepare meat to order, so you can get just what you want by cut or portion, and they can freeze it. Some charter yachts do their meat provisioning here.

They bake French bread every day except Sunday, which is available from 1030, and sell wines and other supplies.

You can anchor off Woburn or any of the other bays and tie your dinghy to the village dock. Wander up to the road and turn left, and you will find a little corner store called Nimrod and Sons Rum Shop, run by Pat and Sep. You can buy ice here, along with bread, fresh chicken, lettuce, a few canned goods, beer, and rum.

Restaurants

Whisper Cove Marina Restaurant [$B-D], is a fun, French bar and restaurant, family-run by Gilles and Mary. They open for lunch Monday to Saturday for hearty fish sandwiches, excellent burgers, and fresh salads. Thursday night is chicken and fries night, and dinner on Friday and Saturday features excellent meat, which they butcher themselves, melt-in-the-mouth steak, and pork, as well as lobster and fresh fish, though they can cater to a vegetarian. They are often open for special occasions, including the occasional Sunday brunch (check the morning cruisers net).

The Oasis Bar [$D] at Clarkes Court Bay Marina is a great hangout, with a big screen TV for sports events. They open pretty early in the morning and continue till everyone leaves. You can get sandwiches till 2000. They have something going most nights, from pool to wee bowling; listen to the morning net for details. Tuesday night is movie night: bring snacks. They have live music and burgers on Wednesday nights, potluck on Saturday night, and pizza during the day on Sunday. You will find a big book swap, and a regular bus leaves for town from Tuesday to Saturday.

Woburn is home to Little Dipper [$D], the cutest small restaurant in Grenada. Joan, who owns it with her husband, Rock, the taxi driver, has cooked in several fancy restaurants and is now doing her own thing both well and very inexpensively, making this both a special experience and the best value in Grenada. Enjoy the sweeping view out over Hog Island as you taste fresh local seafood with a good variety of local vegetables. You won't find a better deal on lobster, fish, or lambi. They open Monday to Saturday from 1000-2200. They have a small dinghy dock, with a reef in front, so approach carefully along the coast from the north. The dock has a flashing amber light to help you in. It is an adventurous stroll up through mangroves, bananas, and fruit trees to reach the restaurant at the top of their land. Rock can bring you over from Prickly Bay or Secret Harbour at a special inexpensive rate.

Island Breeze [$B-D] is another good restaurant, right by the dock. The upstairs balcony is open to the breeze and has a view of the bay to Calivigny and Hog Islands. They specialize in seafood, including lobster, lambi, shrimp, and fish, which they serve in the restaurant or as takeaway. Sometimes you can watch as the catch arrives on the dock outside. If you walk down the pretty little boardwalk by the dock, you come to

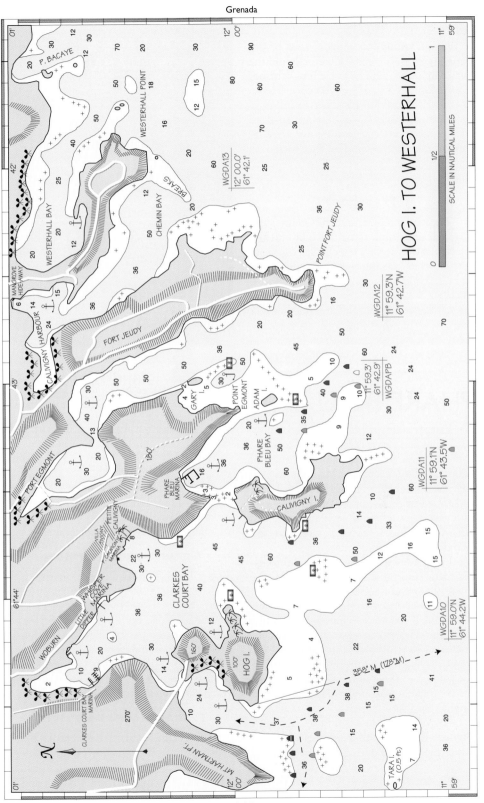

HOG I. TO WESTERHALL

SCALE IN NAUTICAL MILES

0   1/2   1

P. BACAYE

WESTERHALL POINT

WESTERHALL BAY

CHEMIN BAY

BREAKS

POINT FORT JEUDY

WGDA13
12° 00.0'
61° 42.1'

MANGROVE HIDE-AWAY

CALIVIGNY HARBOUR

FORT JEUDY

WGDA12
11° 59.3'N
61° 42.7W

PORT EGMONT

GARY I.

POINT EGMONT

ADAM I.

PHARE BLEU BAY

WGDAPB
11° 59.3'
61° 42.9'

PHARE BLEU MARINA

CALIVIGNY I.

WGDA11
11° 59.1N
61° 43.5W

PETITE CALIVIGNY

WHISPER COVE MARINA

CLARKES COURT BAY

WOBURN

LITTLE DIPPER

CLARKES COURT BAY MARINA

HOG I.

MT HARTMAN PT.

358° M (178° M)

WGDA10
11° 59.0N
61° 44.2W

11
37
38

TARA I.
(0.5 ft)

Grenada and Carriacou

Sea Quest, a local bar.

If your family is coming to stay, or you want to get off the boat, Bob Goodchild the Surveyor (see *St. George's*), has Whisper Cove Mango Cottage and Bamboo House in their own private garden two minutes' walk from Whisper Cove Marina. Situated on the regular bus service into town, they are comfortable and convenient for the marina and anchorages of Clarkes Court Bay and Hog Island.

Transport

The road running through Woburn looks so rough and rural, with the odd chicken wandering over it, that it seems impossible to imagine a bus hurtling by full of smiling faces and big shopping baskets, but it happens all the time. Whichever way it comes, you can catch it to town if you wait around Nimrod's Rum Shop. On the return run, ask for a bus going to "Lower Woburn." Take it easy on the white rum while you wait, or be prepared to miss the bus.

PHARE BLEU BAY

East of Calivigny Island, between Calivigny Island and Point Egmont, is a protected harbor, home to Phare Bleu Marina and Boutique Hotel. Dieter and Jana, the owners, have built a delightful marina/cottage hotel, with a warm and welcoming atmosphere, which has some excellent supporting services. You will be helped by Lynne at reception, and Wendy in the marina.

Entry is down a buoyed channel through the reefs. You have to enter between the shoals that extend south from Adam Island and the shoals that extend east from Calivigny Island. If you hit the channel right, there is at least 35 feet of water on your way in. It is quite straightforward if you follow the buoys, leaving red right returning. If you are not going into the marina, the best anchorage is probably in Calivigny Island, a short dinghy ride away.

Phare Bleu Marina is host to the South Grenada Regatta, with a series of races and match racing held during the last weekend in February. Docking is free and the villas are discounted for regatta participants. They

host the major parties. It is a friendly and fun event.

Regulations

La Phare Bleu is a port of clearance. Customs are open from 0800-1600, but they sometimes have to leave early. On weekends, they start later and end earlier.

General yacht services

La Phare Bleu is 50-berth marina (for yachts up to 100 feet), using mainly heavy floating docks. There is water and electricity (110/220-volt, 50-cycle), gasoline, and diesel available on the docks. Henry Safari has a laundry ashore and fills gas bottles (open 0900-1600). Wifi is free to customers (ask for the password). Phare Bleu has a good tug which can help out for rescue and recovery.

Technical yacht services

Island Dreams also have a branch here, with another office in Port Louis. Owners Mark and Anita look after your yacht while you go away, fixing anything that needs do-

Phare Bleu Pool Bar Restaurant

ing at the same time. They do everything from a simple repair to a complete refit. For a more complete description, see *St. George's*.

Dave and Jane Royce at The Canvas Shop will take care of all your upholstery and canvas work. They come from the east coast of England, where Dave, a sailmaker since the age of 18, had a company making spray hoods and canvas bits for the prestigious Oyster Yacht Company. Now in the Caribbean, they have a spacious new workshop. They make very elegant biminis, dodgers, awnings, and covers, and they specialize in leather work, covering steering wheels, and grab rails. They keep closed-cell foam in stock, make cockpit cushions, and sew elegant interior upholstery.

Mike runs Palm Tree Marine, helped by several Grenadians, including Kevon. This is an excellent place to fix all your mechanical and electrical problems. They work on all brands of inboards, outboards, and generators. They are agents for Caterpillar, Yanmar, and Westerbeke and are equipped for tank cleaning. They are agents for Spectra watermakers and service all makes. They have an efficient mini-machine shop and do steel and stainless welding.

Palm Tree Marine have a van for visiting other locations. However, it is more efficient to come to Phare Bleu where their shop is, because, if they get really busy, they don't have much time outside the marina.

Restaurants

Phare Bleu's Pool Bar Restaurant ($B-C), is in a big high-roofed building open to the breeze. You sit almost on the beach. The pool and lounging area make it a great hangout, and they offer a wide ranging menu. Happy hour is 1700-1830 nightly, a favorite being the six pack of Carib on ice for $22.50.

Tuesday night is two-for-one pizza night, and so busy it is best to book. On Wednesday night they have the friendship table at 1900 ~ everyone sits at a great long table, with lots of food and you serve yourself as much as you like. Thursday night is spicy curry night, on Saturday night they have live music.

Le Phare Bleu Restaurant ($A, open for dinner) is in a lovely, old Swedish lightship, alongside the dock. It is also the marina office and cruisers' lounge. If you have time, ask to see the historic old engine room and the museum-like lounge. The restaurant offers fine dining: you eat on the upper deck in an intimate nautical atmosphere, and this is perfect for a special night out. The food in both restaurants is very good.

For those looking for an investment ashore, houses and land are for sale.

The snorkeling off Adam Island and on all the surrounding reefs is fair.

Ashore

Ashore you will find a good little mini-market that sells fresh bread daily, baked by the restaurant, as well as fresh produce, some good frozen meat, and staples.

Next door is a car rental agency, and Gary Adams; a chiropractor, sailor, and good blues musician (Doc Adams).

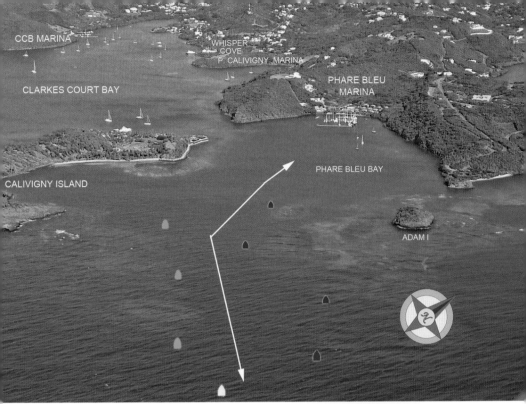

CCB MARINA

WHISPER
COVE
P. CALIVIGNY MARINA

PHARE BLEU
MARINA

CLARKES COURT BAY

PHARE BLEU BAY

CALIVIGNY ISLAND

ADAM I

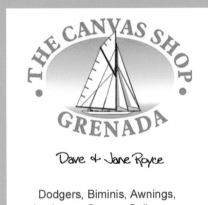

Grenada and Carriacou

PORT EGMONT

Port Egmont is a completely enclosed lagoon, surrounded for the most part by mangroves. It is quite pretty and makes a first-class hurricane hole. Enter the outer inlet fairly close to Fort Jeudy, keeping an eye out for the reefs that lie near the shore. Fort Jeudy is developed, and there are several prosperous-looking houses on the hill. Anchor anywhere in the inner harbor. Or you can also anchor outside, off the little beach at the inner end of Fort Jeudy, but keep an eye out for the shoal off the northern end of the inlet.

The southwest shore of Port Egmont, from the inner harbor all the way out to Point Egmont, is currently being developed. The inner harbor is Grenada's best hurricane hole. The main people behind this development, Andrew Bierzynski and Geoffrey Thompson, are both local, and, as developers go, have concern for the environment. They have done a magnificent job to this point, with a new bridge over the mangroves and well-laid-out roads that afford lovely views of the bay. If you sail in and fall in love with the place and want to build, contact Renwick and Thompson.

A marina is planned at the head of Port Egmont, just before the entrance to the inner harbor.

CALIVIGNY HARBOUR

Calivigny Harbour, sometimes called Old Harbour (not to be confused with Calivigny Island), is another enclosed harbor with a fine, palm-shaded beach. It makes an acceptable hurricane hole, though heavy rains can create currents that cause boats to lie sideways to the wind from time to time. The entrance to the outer harbor is between Fort Jeudy and Westerhall Point. You must have good enough visibility to see the reefs off Fort Jeudy. The shoals coming out from Westerhall Point are deeper and harder to see, though they often cause breaking seas. Stay with the devil you can see. Find the reef off Fort Jeudy and follow it into the outer harbor. This entrance can be hairy in heavy winds and large swells, and I would only recommend it to sailors with a lot of experience in reef navigation. When passing into the inner harbor, favor the Fort Jeudy side, as a shoal extends out from the sand spit. Anchor anywhere in the inner harbor.

In the deepest recesses of the bay, Mangrove Hide-Away [$C-D], run by Rhoda Benoit, is a largish informal restaurant and bar with wifi, TV, pool, and table tennis. Use their dock for your dinghy, but take care; it is due for a rebuild. They keep some macaws, and wild tortoises, iguanas, and other birds roam freely. They open every day from 0800, serve a choice of good daily specials; also pizza. Thursday nights is coconut bakes and saltfish souce, Saturday is soup day, with a choice of good local soups. Try the mannish water if you dare, but don't ask about the ingredients till you have finished.

Aubrey's is a bar/restaurant/shop/restaurant right at the entrance to Westerhall Estate, where you can also catch a bus to

WESTERHALL BAY

P. BACAYE

LITTLE BACOLET WEST

WESTERHALL BAY TO LITTLE BACOLET POINT

LITTLE BACOLET PT.

town. If you turn right at the main road and walk a while, you come to the Coop supermarket. See also Petit Bacaye, which is a fair walk away.

WESTERHALL POINT

Westerhall Point is an attractive housing development, with well-tended grounds, easily seen by walking up from Calivigny Harbour. Westerhall Bay is a protected anchorage if you tuck up in the southeast corner of the bay, behind the mangroves. In rough conditions the entrance is tricky and the exit heads straight into wind and sea. I would suggest anchoring in Calivigny Harbour and walking over to take a look before you attempt this.

Theresa has some nice, very reasonably-priced apartments overlooking Westerhall Bay, good for those in Phare Bleu or anywhere on the south coast. Call 443-5779.

PETIT BACAYE

Petit Bacaye and Little Bacolet West are two great little anchorages, so small that four boats in either would be a crowd. Space in both is limited enough that I recommend dropping the main before you enter. Petit Bacaye is an idyllic little bay, full of flowers and palm trees, with a little island you can swim out to. It has a micro-hotel of the same name [$B-D, closed Monday], with a few thatch-roofed rooms, a small bar and restaurant, and a tree top platform in the lovely gardens. It opens 1100-1800 for lunch and snacks. Take a book, swim, and laze away a day. Entering is strictly eyeball navigation. A visible rock on the western reef helps.

The entrance to Little Bacolet West is narrow: follow Little Bacolet Point and stay just outside the fringing reef. Development has just begun here. This is generally a calm hideaway.

Grenada and Carriacou

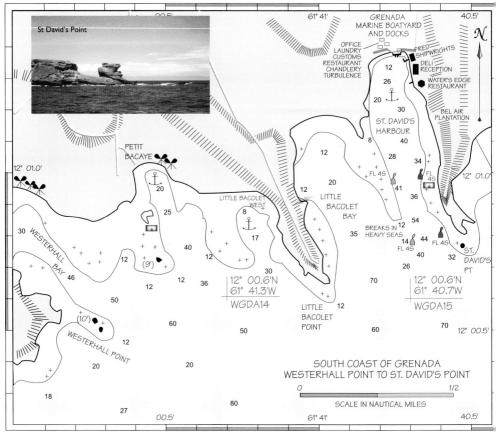

ST. DAVID'S HARBOUR

St. David's Harbour lies 1.2 miles east of Westerhall Point. Many years ago, sailing ships would sail in here to load up on spices and produce bound for Europe. Although never the site of a town, it was an important harbor. It is deeply indented enough to be well protected, and the reefs at the entrance reduce the swells when the trades turn south of east. It can rock a little, in which case a stern anchor to face you out of the bay is a good fix. Wind and current can switch around, so you need to leave far more room between anchored boats than you would expect. St. David's Harbour is a lovely bay with a narrow sandy beach, palm trees, and jungly vegetation crowding down to the waterfront. A pleasant breeze keeps things cool.

Grenada Marine, is a haul-out operation for those who want the pleasingly rural atmosphere of Grenada, and one where you will be considerably drier than in Trinidad during the rainy season. It is the kind of yard where you can swim right off the beach after work. They must do something right, as about 60 percent of their customers are repeats. Owners Jason and Laura Fletcher have 10-acres at the head of the bay and can take up to 250 boats.

The entrance is easy if you approach in good light, provided you have correctly identified the bay. The reef dividing St. David's from Little Bacolet is much harder to see than the one off St. David's Point, so favor the St. David's Point side of the channel, staying in the deep water. Part of the channel is buoyed with red and green markers. They flash about every four seconds. St. David's is well situated if you come down the east coast of Grenada, and it is an easy downwind sail from here to the other south-coast anchorages.

Regulations

St. David's Harbour is a port of entry, with customs and immigration. Customs is there every Monday to Thursday from 0800 to 1600. Immigration will come anytime.

Communications

Grenada Marine and Belair Plantation have free wifi. If you don't have a computer, ask in Grenada Marine's office.

General yacht services

Grenada Marine [VHF: 16] is a work and storage yard with room for 250 boats. They use a specially designed, 70-ton Travelift, which is 32 feet wide and is designed to haul catamarans as well as monohulls. Yachts of up to 12-foot draft can be hauled. After hauling, a hydraulic stacking trailer can put yachts close together. Early booking is advisable as the yard fills up in the summer. Jason manages the yard, and his wife Laura, the restaurant.

The yard is equipped with hurricane tie-downs for every boat and cradles are available for those who want them. Masts are often lifted for hurricane security and they have a state-of-the-art mast storage rack outside the rigging shop. Diesel and water are available on the outside of the hauling pier.

They have two huge paint sheds, so your boat can be sprayed in ideal conditions.

They have reliable moorings in the bay, and plan 300 feet of stern-to docking to accommodate any size of yacht.

The office staff are very helpful and will make your hauling arrangements, put you at ease, find you a rental car, or help with sending a fax or making a phone call.

You can do your own laundry in the machines or send it out to be done with Henry's Safari Tours. He will also fill your cooking gas bottles.

Chandlery

Island Water World has a branch of their chandlery here. This comprehensive and first-rate store carries everything you need and tempts you into buying things you just want. If you don't find it here, ask, as it may be in stock in their larger branch in St.

Grenada and Carriacou

401

GRENADA MARINE

LITTLE BACALOT POINT

BEL AIR PLANTATION

ST. DAVID'S HARBOUR
GRENADA

ST. DAVID'S POINT

George's. They have a catalog, and anything can be brought in at short notice.

Technical yacht services

The yard has about 90 employees including a good team of technicians who work in glass, spray AwlGrip, and re-gelcoat finishes. They do proper osmosis treatment. The atmosphere is drier here than in Trinidad, which is an advantage for this. In addition, they use a heat and vacuum system to dry-out the hull completely for osmosis treatment. They can airless-spray antifouling. Neils Lundt organizes most technical work. The head of the metal department, Dietmar Zuber, is one of the best in the islands. They have an office in Port Louis and can do in-the-water work down there.

Their rigging and sailmaking are run jointly with Turbulence and managed by Louis (rigging) and Martin (sails). Masts are stored in custom-made racks, so you can remove yours for extra hurricane security. They can check out your rig while you go away and do any kind of rigging repair, including a whole new rig. (They share a rod-rigging machine with their larger shop in True Blue). The sail department does all kinds of sail construction, repair, and all canvas work.

Grenada Marine's mechanical shop can handle all mechanical repairs, and they are agents for Yanmar, Perkins, Volvo, Northern Lights, and ZF drives, and some watermakers. You can buy these systems though them.

They have a full electronics shop (agents for Raymarine), as well as a complete woodwork shop.

Owners and their crew are also welcome to do simple jobs like antifouling, brush painting, and removing shafts and underwater systems.

Ashore

The Galley Bar at Grenada Marine [$D] is a restaurant and hangout for technicians, crew, and owners. It is cheap, cheerful, and right on the waterfront. They do tasty and hearty food, serve lunch and dinner daily, and are open from 0800-2100. They sometimes have live music, usually Saturdays.

Adjoining Grenada Marine is Bel Air Plantation, a really magnificent and upmarket resort, the creation of Susan Fisher, with Caribbean-style cottages set amid wonderful flowering gardens that cover the hillside right down to the sea. You can walk from the boatyard or go by dinghy. They have

a good dinghy dock outside their Water's Edge Restaurant.

For those wanting a night ashore in real comfort, this is the place to come. They offer beautifully fitted-out houses, with original art and every luxury, or simpler but elegant suites. The hotel was up for sale recently. Check to see what is still open, especially the pleasant Water's Edge Restaurant [$A-B].

Just a bay to the east is La Sagesse Nature Center, a 12-room hotel owned by Mike and Nancy. It is set in a gorgeous bay, with one of the longest and broadest palm-backed beaches in Grenada. Here you will feel you are well away from all the work. The room prices are reasonable, especially in the off-season, and, if things are quiet, they offer yachtspeople excellent discounts. Their beachfront restaurant is open all day from 0815 till 2200, with informal lunches, and romantic fine dining at night. They use all fresh ingredients and offer some of Grenada's best seafood. This is a great escape from the boatyard and work. Walk over the hill for lunch, but it would be best to book for dinner. Either way, give them a call; they offer free transport to and from Grenada Marine for meal and hotel guests.

For those farther afield, they offer a $55 US per person day package, which includes transportation, lunch, an optional nature walk, and use of the beach chairs and kayaks.

When you get tired of work and want a little trip to the country, consider visiting the Laura Herb and Spice Garden, which is a few miles down the road. It is part of an herb and spice marketing cooperative that sells Grenadian herbs and spices worldwide. They have about eight acres under cultivation in the garden, with well-laid-out trails and signposted plants. The atmosphere is peaceful, with birds singing in the trees and plenty of shady areas. You pay a $5 EC entry fee and if you ask (you should), they will give you a tour of the garden and explain the plants to you.

Grenada and Carriacou

La Sagesse

Island Foods

Ste. Anne Market

Island Food

ne of the best ways to experience local foods is to eat out. This way you don't have to slave over the stove and, best of all, no dishes to wash up. In this section we introduce you to some wonderful local fruits and vegetables, as well as some ideas about seafood. Those who cook for themselves will find recipes. For those who prefer to eat out, we will make some suggestions. But you cannot start without a drink in your hand, so why not make:

Skipper's Rum Punch: *Mix the juice from 3 limes with ¼ cup of Grenadine syrup, 1 cup of brown rum, and one liter of juice (orange, pineapple, or local passion fruit). Serve with a lot of ice and liberally grate fresh nutmeg on top.*

While on the subject of drinks, coconut water is the Caribbean's own natural soft drink. If you are driving around the countryside, you may well see a homemade barrow by the side of the road stocked high with

green coconuts. These are "water-nuts" ~ young coconuts that have not yet developed a hard inner brown husk or firm white flesh, but are full of a delicious liquid. The vendor will slice off the top of the nut for you. It is now ready to drink, straight from the shell. These days you can buy bottled coconut juice in many islands. This is a great alternative to manufactured soft drinks, but before you buy

in bulk, take care, as it does not keep more than a few days unless frozen.

If you have a blender, try making "smoothies." These are made by taking the flesh of any suitable local fruit (mango, banana, guava, pawpaw, pineapple, or soursop), adding a good slosh of rum, a good measure of ice, and then blending it. You can add lime or orange juice for flavor and you can try combinations.

Eating out

Eating out anywhere will give you a taste of local food, because even the most international of restaurants use local vegetables, seafood, and fruits. Local restaurants usually cook excellent curries and Creole-style specialties. In general, local soups are wonderful, but desserts are less interesting.

Those who go to the Windwards and eat hamburgers deserve what they get. Better to eat a local roti, the ideal lunchtime snack. A roti is curried meat or vegetables wrapped in a wheat flour tortilla-like shell. It usually comes in one of three flavors: beef, chicken, or conch. I usually go for conch (lambi). This is firm, white flesh from a large seashell and is absolutely delicious. The chicken roti is often made from back and neck and full of bones. Locals love to chew on them, but if you have not yet acquired that taste, ask for "boneless."

Nearly every menu lists lobster in season. Lobster is delicious, delicate, and easy to ruin, especially if it is frozen and then broiled. For the best lobster, eat at a restaurant where you can select your own, alive and fresh from a pool.

Island foods

Grenada is the world's second largest nutmeg producer. You will find fresh nutmegs in local markets and many boutiques. If possible buy them as a "kit" with a little grater. The outer hard dark brown husk must be removed before grating. Nutmeg is not only essential for rum punch, but excellent for spicing up desserts, soups, pancakes, French toast, and mashed pumpkin.

Coffee grows in the islands and many local coffees will get you up and going. Grenada grows excellent cocoa. Much of Grenada's cocoa is sold abroad, but some is turned into wonderful gourmet chocolate (82% cocoa) by the Grenada Chocolate Factory. Some cocoa makes it to the local markets as cocoa sticks. These contain the full fat content of the cocoa beans and make a rich drink quite unlike commercial cocoa, which is a by-product of making cocoa butter and is the compressed cocoa bean with no fat.

Canned tropical fruit juices are now becoming available in supermarkets. Flavors include soursop, papaya, and guava.

In the market you can buy turmeric, locally called saffron. It is a root that can be bought fresh or grated. It is good in curries and for coloring rice. True saffron (made from crocus flowers) is only found in the fanciest supermarkets. Hot sauces are a local specialty. Many different brands are for sale and they make good gifts.

Most islands have producers that pack wonderful peanuts and cashews in recycled beer bottles. Fish is smoked locally in some islands and is usually excellent.

Tropical leaves, fruits & roots

This is an introduction to some foods you may not be used to ~ not a complete list of what is available.

Breadfruit, plentiful and inexpensive year round, is a savior to the traveler on a budget. Originally from the Pacific, breadfruit was imported to the Caribbean by Captain Bligh for the planters as a cheap food for slaves (they awarded him 5,000 pounds for his effort). It arrived late because of the

Breadfruit

mutiny. Watch it carefully or it will cause you grief, too. It remains nice and firm for a day or two, but when it decides to go soft and rotten, it can do so almost as quickly as Bligh could order a keel hauling. (I refer here to the legendary Captain Bligh, not the real Bligh, who was a lieutenant at the time of the mutiny and moderate with punishments.) Best to cook your breadfruit first and store it after. Boil it (40 minutes in an ordinary pot or pressure cook for 10) or bake it in the oven (about 40 minutes). It will now store for some days in an icebox or fridge. Treat it like potato: mash it, cut slices off and fry it, use it in salad or stews. Mash it together with an egg and some cooked fish, season, then fry to make wonderful fish cakes. Buy one for a barbecue and cook it on the embers of a dying fire till you can slide a thin sliver of wood from opposite the stem up into the center. Cut it open and serve with salt, pepper, and lashings of butter. Try making it like mashed potato, but mash with coconut milk instead of ordinary milk. Cover with grated cheese, and brown.

Coconuts are nutritious and cheap. Many years ago I heard stories of wrecked sailors starving on desert islands because, having seen brown-husked coconuts in the supermarket, they could not recognize the real item, with its green outer shell, on the tree. Coconut milk (not to be confused with coconut water) is often used in Caribbean cooking much as one would use cream where cows are more plentiful than palm trees. These days you can buy dried and canned coconut milk ~ or you can make it yourself:

Buy an older "flesh nut" ~ one of the brown ones you buy in the market. Grate the flesh, add any water from the nut, and add ordinary water till it is covered. Leave it for a few minutes, then

Coconuts at this stage they are called water nuts

Callaloo

Dessert figs - eat very ripe

squeeze the juices from the flesh into the water. Sieve, throw out the dry flesh. The creamy liquid is coconut milk.

Callaloo, an elephant-ear-shaped green leaf (the leaf of the dasheen), grows on wet ground such as the banks of small streams. It is plentiful year round and inexpensive, and is available as bundles of leaves or, in bags, chopped and prepared for cooking. If you get the leaves with their stems, it is necessary to remove the skin from the stem and from the center vein. Always boil callaloo for 30 minutes. Eating it raw or undercooked has much the same effect on your mouth and throat as one imagines chewing on raw fiberglass would have. The discomfort is temporary. Callaloo makes a wonderful soup and if you do not cook it for yourself, eat it in a restaurant at the first available opportunity. To use callaloo as a vegetable, just boil it with a little salt for at least 30 minutes. Like spinach, it boils down to very little.

Callaloo Soup: *½ lb chopped bacon, 1 pint water, ¼ lb peeled shrimp, 2 bunches prepared callaloo (about 1 lb), 5 sliced okras, 1 sliced onion, ½ oz butter, salt, pepper, garlic, thyme, and hot sauce to taste.*

Fry the bacon and onion in butter, drain off excess fat. Add callaloo, okras, water, and seasoning. Boil for 40 minutes, then add peeled shrimp. Cook a little longer and serve. For a thicker soup, blend, then serve.

To the uninitiated, Plantains, bananas bluggoes, and figs all look just like bananas. But try putting a plantain in a banana daiquiri and you will soon know the difference. Eating (or dessert) bananas, the kind you most often meet at home, are a major Caribbean crop, but they taste much better when

eaten here as they are naturally ripened. You will also find other cultivars such as the dessert fig, which can have an almost strawberry flavor.

Regular dessert bananas also make a starchy vegetable. Use them when full in size, but still green. Peel them, chop them, and drop them into boiling water (or add to stews). Bluggoes are used the same way, but they have less sugar and cannot be eaten raw.

Plantains are cooked when they are yellow and ripe. Split them down the middle and fry them for a few minutes on each side. They are sweet and delicious and a perfect complement to any kind of fish. You can also chop them up and add them to stews or bake

Dessert bananas

Plantains

them. Whatever you do, they taste wonderful ~ unless you try eating them raw.

Ask the market ladies to make sure you are getting the kind of banana that you want. If you buy a whole branch of bananas you will find that they all ripen at once. When you get tired of just eating them raw, try the following:

Skipper's Banana Flambe (for 4): *4 bananas, ½ cup dark rum, ½ cup fresh orange juice, 2 tbsp. brown sugar, a slosh of white rum or vodka, seasoning of nutmeg, cinnamon, and allspice.*

Split the bananas lengthwise in two and put in a frying pan, add the brown rum and orange juice, sprinkle on the sugar and spices,

Island Foods

and simmer for about 5 minutes. Pour on the white rum and ignite. (If vodka, you will have to warm it gently in a pan first.)

Bananas Celeste: *from Leyritz Plantation. (for 4): 6 oz cream cheese, ¼ cup brown sugar, ½ tsp cinnamon, 4 tbsp. unsalted butter, ¼ cup heavy cream (tinned is OK), ¼ tsp cinnamon, 4 large bananas, peeled and split in half.*

Mix the first 3 ingredients. Saute bananas in butter. Lay 4 halves in a buttered baking dish, spread with half of mix and repeat on top. Pour cream over and bake at 350° for 15 minutes. Sprinkle with remaining cinnamon and serve hot.

Pumpkin

The local **pumpkin** is nothing like the North American halloween monster. It is green and yellow, with a delicious orange red pulp that is akin to butternut squash. It keeps a long time unopened and is both versatile and tasty. Remove the seeds before cooking. Boil or bake till soft and serve with butter, or boil and mash with seasoning (include a little nutmeg) and a little orange juice. If you want to make a meal out of a pumpkin, slice it longways down the middle and bake it. While it is cooking, fry onion, christophene,

tomato, and any leftovers you might have, melt in a quarter pound of cream cheese, and stuff the cooked pumpkin with this mixture. Pumpkin makes a delicious soup. Try it in a restaurant or make it yourself.

West Indian Pumpkin Soup: *1 small pumpkin, 1 chopped onion, 1 tbsp. butter, 1 chicken stock cube, ½ pint fresh cream (or two cans of cream), ¼ glass white wine, salt, pepper, grated nutmeg. Skin and seed the pumpkin and chop into small cubes. Lightly saute the onions in butter till cooked. Add pumpkin, stock cube and a minimum of water. Boil, using a lid. When soft, blend or sieve. Add the cream and wine, flavor with salt, pepper, and nutmeg to taste. If too thick, thin with milk or water.*

Local **avocados** are absolutely delicious, and reason enough to come down in the summer (available much of the year, but peak season is around August and September). Locals say you should never store them with citrus. They can be eaten as they are, flavored with a little salt and lime juice, or stuffed with mayonnaise and shrimp. If they get a little overripe, mash them with lime, finely chopped onion, garlic and seasoning. This makes an ideal dip to enjoy with your sunset drink.

Okra is a spear-shaped green pod with slimy green seeds. Avoid the large ones, which tend to be tough. They are somewhat slimy if boiled, but much less so if sliced and fried. They are good in soups.

Root vegetables: sweet potato and yam are sweet and tasty local root crops that take about 30 minutes to cook; try mashing with a little orange juice.

Root vegetables: eddo, tania and dasheen are closely related, brown, hairy roots. They can be boiled to produce a sort of white object that tastes much like wallpaper paste. But if you do things such as mashing with oodles of butter and milk, or mashing with seasoning and refrying, they can be pretty darn good, and all the local root vegetables store much better than potatoes.

Christophene has shallow ridges, is pear shaped, comes in either green or white, and grows on a vine. Somewhat delicate in flavor, it makes an excellent vegetable dish or may be added to curries or stews. Peel it and remove the seed. This is best done under water

Sweet potato

Yellow Yam

Dasheen

Papaya or Pawpaw

Christophene

Papaya cut open. Remove seeds, add lime or passion fruit, eat!

or with wet hands, as otherwise it leaves a mess on your hands that gives the impression your skin is peeling off. It is excellent just boiled with salt, pepper, and butter and is even better put in a white cheese sauce. It may also be used raw as a salad ingredient. The seed tastes good raw.

Mangos are delicious and available spring, summer, and fall, but less often in the winter. They are harder to come by and more expensive in Martinique than in the

Preparing a mango – or just peel, eat and take a bath

other Windwards. There are many different varieties. Grafted ones are bigger, better, and have fewer strings.

Pawpaw (Papaya) is a lush tropical fruit that contains digestive enzymes, making it an ideal dessert. Green when underripe, it is ready to eat when it turns yellow and becomes slightly soft. Pawpaws are available year round, but are delicate and hard to store. It must be eaten the same day it becomes ready. Slice like a melon and remove the seeds; add a squeeze of lime or, even better, add the insides of a passion fruit to flavor.

Citrus (oranges, grapefruit, tangerines, etc.) are available mainly in the winter. The quality varies from absolutely superb to dry and unusable. When you are shopping, buy

one from the market lady to try. She will open it with a knife for you to taste. This is the only way to tell how good they are. Local oranges are usually green. Despite the outside color, the inside is orange and ready to eat. Limes are generally available year round and are essential for making rum punch.

Pineapples are available most of the year and very inexpensive in Martinique, but harder to come by and more costly elsewhere. Local pineapples can be absolutely delicious. Test for ripeness by pulling on a central leaf. If it pulls out easily, it is ready. *For an easy dessert, cut out the flesh, chop into cubes, leave soaking in rum a few hours, replace in husk, serve.*

One way to serve pineapple

Soursop is available year round. It is a knobby green fruit which is ripe when it begins to go soft. It is really delicious, but messy to eat because of all the seeds. It can be blended with a little milk and ice to make an excellent drink.

Passion fruits are available May to

409

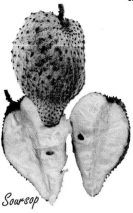

Soursop

Passion fruit, best eaten when the skin gets crinkly

Star fruit

French cashew

Wax apple

Sapodilla

November. A small yellow or pink fruit with a slightly crinkly skin and very strong flavor. Makes an excellent drink and locally-made passion fruit concentrate is usually available in the supermarkets.

Star fruits are available year round and have a light flavor that makes them good in salad or as a garnish. Locals make an excellent drink with them. Peel and eat the flesh.

Guavas, available July to December, are green-yellow fruits a little bigger than golf balls. They are excellent eaten raw, or stewed with sugar. Locals make a sweet called "guava cheese" out of them.

French cashew (plumrose) is a pink fruit with white flesh available much of the year. Wax apple is another cultivar, but has a waxier skin and paler color. Both have white flesh. Do not peel, but remove the stone. They have a light refreshing flavor and could be good as garnish. Real cashew trees (the nut) have a similar-looking fruit that is not so good to eat.

Sapodilla is a small brown fruit, available in the winter. You need a very sweet tooth to enjoy these as they are, but they make an excellent addition to fruit salad.

Sorrel is a flower in the hibiscus family, available fresh around Christmas and dried the rest of the year. Pour boiling water on a couple of blossoms to make an excellent herb tea with a flavor not unlike "Red Zinger." Or boil a bunch of the flowers with water, adding a lot of sugar and spices. Serve as a delicious iced drink.

Seafood

Although seafood in the Windwards is excellent, it is not always available in the local supermarket. The main towns of most islands have fish markets, and the one in St. George's, Grenada, is good, as is the fisherman's coop by Pointe Seraphine in St. Lucia. To get fish, you often need to first catch your fisherman. In the Grenadines, you can try asking fishermen in camps or those returning from fishing trips. Try asking any of the local people where, and at what time, the fishermen usually bring in their catch. On arrival they signal by blowing a conch horn. The fish is sold straight out of the boats when they arrive. Calliaqua, in St. Vincent, has a good little fish market where the fish generally arrive at about 1600 hours. If you see fishermen untangling a bunch of large fish from a gill net, be cautious. Sometimes these nets have been left out for some days, and by the time the fish reach shore, they are only good for salting. Among other fish you often find:

Barracuda ~ a delicious white-fleshed fish. It is probably best to find ones less than two feet long, as ciguatera poisoning is possible, though very rare.

Dolphin ~ sometimes called "Dorado" or "Mahi Mahi." This pretty fish has white firm flesh, is excellent eating, and is absolutely no relative of "Flipper."

Snapper ~ an excellent white-fleshed fish. The red snapper is most common.

Tuna ~ several varieties, dark fleshed, excellent flavor, wonderful raw as sushi.

Wahoo ~ a great eating fish with firm white flesh, as good as tuna eaten raw.

An easy way to cook most fish is to cut them into steaks or filets, season with salt, pepper, and herbs and saute them in butter or barbecue them. In my opinion, fish is best when barely cooked ~ overcooking fish turns a wonderful treat into a dry chewy disaster fit only for the ship's cat.

If you like sushi you can make some fair sushi ginger by skinning the local root (available in markets or supermarkets), slicing it very thinly then putting it in a jar with an equal mixture of vinegar and cane syrup. Leave a couple of days before using.

local ginger

I have a small freezer and hate to waste fish, so when I catch one, I filet and skin it and freeze the flesh. The head, bones, and scraps become:

Sailor's Fish Soup:

You will also need some of the flesh, plus a couple of onions and potatoes, two limes and a christophene. Optional improvements are a plantain, some carrots, green banana and local roots.

Put the head, bones, and scraps into a pressure cooker, cover generously with water, and pressure cook for about 10 minutes. Pressure cooking enables you to sit the cooker on the floor and forget it till you anchor. If you don't have a pressure cooker, a regular pot is fine. Just boil for a little longer. It may smell a bit fish-oily at this stage; not to worry. Once at anchor, save the liquid. Throw out the solids. Put the liquid into a saucepan.

Peel and cut up a couple of onions, a couple of potatoes, and a christophene. If you have them include a green banana, a few carrots, and local roots. Throw these into the liquid and add the juice of a couple of limes. Boil till cooked, and add salt and pepper to taste.

Add to this some of the fish flesh that has been chopped into bite sized pieces and cook for just a few more minutes. At this stage also add a plantain if you have one, cut up into small segments. Add hot sauce to taste. For a really rich, creamy flavor, add some coconut milk or cream at the end.

Seviche: *1 lb fresh fish, 1 finely chopped onion, 1 chopped tomato, ¼ tsp local hot sauce, lime juice, olive oil, salt, and pepper.*

Filet the fish and cut into small pieces. Put in a nonmetallic container with the onion and tomato. Season with salt and pepper. Cover with a mixture of lime juice, about one third as much olive oil and a little hot sauce. Let stand in the fridge or ice box overnight; drain before serving.

Caribbean faux gravlax: *One 3 to 4 lb tuna, ¼ cup sugar, ¼ cup salt, tbsp of peppercorns, ¼ cup dill, if available.*

Mix sugar and salt, add grated peppercorns and dill. Filet the fish. Lay half of the fish in a shallow dish and spread the other ingredients on top. Put the other filet on top to make a sandwich. Gently place in a ziplock bag. Return to the dish, place a flat board on top (must be smaller than the dish) with a 5 lb weight on it. Keep in fridge and turn every twelve hours. It is ready after 24-36 hours. Slice very thinly. If parasites could be a danger, freeze after slicing. Freezing does not impair the flavor.

Conch is a mollusk that lives in a huge spiral shell lined with a beautiful pink. The whole animal is called a conch, and "lambi"

Conch shell

refers to the meat. If you are buying from a fisherman, get him to remove the shell. Then hold the conch up by the claw, remove all the thin skin and slime that hangs from the bottom, remove the eyes and mouth, cut open the gut, and clean and remove the tough brown skin. Lastly, remove the claw. You should be left with a slab of white to slightly pink meat. Chop this up and tenderize by hammering. If you want to be sure your conch is tender, cut it up and pressure-cook it for 45 minutes. One of the best ways to cook conch is in a curry.

Curries are very popular in the Windwards due to the East Indian influence. Although simple, a curry can be made into a feast if you serve it with small bowls of garnishes to be sprinkled on top or eaten beside the curry. Some side dish possibilities are: grated coconut, crushed peanuts, chutney, chopped onion, yoghurt, chopped mango, chopped tomato, raisins soaked in rum (drain before serving), and chopped cucumber soaked in vinegar mixed with pieces of fresh ginger (remove ginger and drain before serving). Curry should be served with a bowl of steaming hot rice.

Kristina's Curried Conch: *1 cleaned and chopped conch per person, 1 chopped onion, 2 crushed cloves of garlic, 1 tsp fresh grated ginger, 1 cup coconut milk or coconut water, 1 can drained tomatoes or 2 peeled fresh tomatoes, 1 plantain, 1 tsp thyme, 1 tsp turmeric, and curry powder. Start with 1 Tbs. curry powder and work up from there, as strength can vary enormously.*

Saute the onions and garlic till tender and translucent. Add the herbs and spices and curry powder. Blend them in. Add the rest of the ingredients and let them simmer for about 20 minutes.

This same recipe will work for meat, chicken, fish, or shrimp. In the latter two cases, cook the other ingredients first and only add the fish or shrimp at the last minute. If you wish to fill out the curry somewhat, peel, chop, and add two christophenes. They will take about 10 minutes to cook.

The local **lobster** is a spiny variety without claws. It is illegal to buy lobsters with eggs (they sit in orange clusters under the tail) or during the summer when they are out of season, or those less than 9 inches long. Fines of $5000 are not unknown for first offenders.

Lobsters are best boiled alive. Submerge them rapidly in boiling water and they will quickly die. Tie up the legs and tail with string so you don't get splashed with boiling water. Boiling time is 10 to 20 minutes depending on size. You can buy smaller ones (about 2 lbs) and put them with a pint of cold water in the pressure cooker. Close the lid, bring them up to pressure and cook for about 2 minutes.

Put the cooked lobster face up on a cutting board and, with a very sharp, tough knife, split it in two from head to tail. Serve with hot garlic-lime butter. Keep the shells and any odd bits; with these you can make a delicious bisque (you can also use shrimp heads and/or skins). This way you get twice the value for money out of your lobster (or shrimp).

Seafood Bisque *(Serves 4 as a first course or lunch): Shells from 3 lbs of lobster (or the heads from 2 lbs shrimp), 9 Tbs. butter, 1 liter water, ½ cup white wine, 2 Tbsp. tomato puree, 1 chopped onion, 2 cloves garlic, 1 bay leaf, 2 Tbs. flour, 1 egg yolk, ½ cup cream.*

Saute the onions, garlic, and lobster shells in 6 Tbs. butter for about 15 minutes. Add water, wine, tomato puree, and bay leaf. Bring to the boil and simmer for 20 minutes. Strain. Mix the rest of the butter with 3 Tbs. flour, add to the stock and simmer for another 5 minutes, stirring constantly. Adjust seasoning (salt, pepper). Mix egg yolk with cream in a small bowl. Pour a small amount of soup in it and stir. Then pour it back into the soup very slowly, beating constantly. Taste again and serve immediately. Garnish with left-over bits of lobster or shrimp (if any). Reheat very gently, as boiling will ruin it. Serve with grated cheese if you wish.

Meat

Meat is pretty international. Locals use a lot of chicken, much of which comes from the USA. French supermarkets have little baking chickens which are inexpensive and taste good. If you want to be adventurous, try eating goat in a local restaurant. Local pork tenderloin is often excellent and reasonably priced.

A WORLD OF ISLANDS AWAITS...

The Caribbean Islands are a magical world that awaits your exploration. Three books, *Virgin Anchorages, Windward Anchorages* and *Leeward Anchorages*, graphically, and through spectacular aerial photography, depict dozens of favorite anchorages in their respective areas.

Each anchorage is featured in a two-page full color spread. One page provides an aerial photograph of the anchorage. The adjoining page offers advice on approaching the anchorage with navigational instructions.

Virgin Anchorages can be used in conjunction with the *Cruising Guide to the Virgin Islands. Leeward Anchorages* is a companion to the *Cruising Guide to the Leeward Islands. Windward Anchorages* is a companion to the *Sailors Guide to the Windward Islands*. All should also be used with official navigational charts.

These guides are indispensable for the cruising yachtsman or charterer visiting these legendary Caribbean islands and they make a stunning memento for the coffee table.

CRUISING GUIDE PUBLICATIONS

To Order:

Phone: (727) 733-5322 • (800) 330-9542
Fax: (727) 734-8179
www.cruisingguides.com

Virgin Anchorages $29.95
Leeward Anchorages $29.95
Windward Anchorages $29.95

If calling a Martinique regular phone from a foreign country dial + 596 596 + 6 digits
If calling a Martinique mobile phone from a foreign country dial + 596 696 + 6 digits

MARTINIQUE EMERGENCY

Ambulance, (0596) 75 15 75

Clinic (medical), (0596) 71 82 85

Cosma (Lifeboat) (0596) 70 92 92 VHF: 16

Customs, Marin, (0596) 74 91 64

Dr Delores, Marin (0596) 74 98 24

Hospital, (0596) 50 15 15

Medical emergency (emergency doctors), (0596) 63 33 33/60 60 44

Physiotherapist, Dominique Lanque, (0596) 62 44 71/(0696) 26 72 00 .

Police Emergency, 17

Police headquarters, (0596) 63 00 00

Pompiers (fire department) **18**

MARTINIQUE AIRLINES

Air France, (0596) 55 33 00/33, (0596) 55 33 08

Air Guadeloupe, (0596) 59 82 05

Air Martinique, (0596) 51 08 09

American Airlines, (0596) 42 19 19

LIAT, (0596) 42 21 11

MARTINIQUE CHANDLERY FISHING GEAR

Akwaba, (0596) 66 67 88, akwaba972@ orange.fr, fishing gear

Caraibes Marine, (0596) 74 80 33, F: (0596) 74 66 98, cell: (0696) 27 66 05 contact@caraibes-greement.fr

Carene Shop, (0596) 74 74 80, F: (0596) 74 79 16, carene.shop @ wanadoo.fr

Clippers Ship, (0596) 71 41 61, clippers-ship@ wanadoo.fr

Coopemar, (0596) 73 37 54, Fax: (0596)63 76 63, coopemar @sasi.fr

Intersport, (0596) 63 39 89

Le Ship, (0596) 74 87 55, F: (0596) 74 85 39, le-ship-martinique@ wanadoo.fr

Littoral, (0596) 70 28 70, F: (0596) 60 56 18

Mer & Sport, (0596) 50 2 75/50 67 59, F: (0596) 50 14 41

Plus Nautique, Marin, (0596) 74 62 12, plus-nautique@ mer-et-sport.com

Polymar, (0596) 70 62 88, F: (0596) 60 10 97, polymar@ wanadoo.fr, Baie de Tourelles,

Sea Services, (0596) 70 26 69, F: (0596) 71 60 53, seaser-vices972@orange.fr

W.I.N.D, (0596) 68 21 28, F: (0596) 68 21 28, wind@wind-flag.com

MARTINIQUE COMMUNICATIONS

Cyber Deli, (0596) 78 71 43

Cyber Marin, (0596) 74 77 95, F: (0596) 74 17 41, Psc@business.ool.fr

Laverie Prolaunet, Anse Mitan (0596) 66 07 79, internet & laundry.

Marin Yacht Hasr-bour, Blvd Allegre, Le Marin, 97290, Martinique, (0596) 74 83 83, F: 74 92 20, VHF: 09

Kay Zaza, Grand Anse D'Arlet, T&F: (0596) 68 74 22, kayzaza972@ yahoo.fr

Le P'ti Bateau, Grand Anse D'Arlet, (0596) 65 50 19

MARTINIQUE GENERAL YACHT SERVICES

A&C Yacht brokers, (0596) 74 94 02, Cell: 0696 73 70 27, acyb-michel @wanadoo.fr

Bichik Fuel dock, Marin, (0596) 74 70 94, F: (0596) 74 78 08, fuel, laundry, car rent

Caraibe Yachts (0596) 74 16 70/ (0696) 23 43 38, jean.collin@ caraibeyachts.com, brokers

CarenAntilles, Fort de France, (0596) 63 76 74, VHF: 16, F: (0596) 71 66 83, carenfdf @sasi.fr, haul-out

CarenAntilles, Marin, (0596) 74 77 70, F: (0596) 74 78 22, VHF: 73, carenantilles.marin @wanadoo.fr, haul out

DCML, Quai de Tourelles, (0596) 71 74 64, (0696) 91 60 48, Fax: (0596) 71 27 17, dcml.sarl@ wanadoo.fr, fuel

Dock Cleaner Ecologique, (0696)-22 04 40, dry dock

Dockwise Yacht Transit, (0596)-74-15-07, cell:0696 22 88 13 nadine@ dockwise-yt.com

Douglas Yacht Services, (0696) 45 89 75, (0596) 52 14 28, VHF: 09, doug-las@yachtservices.fr, super-yacht agent

Marin Yacht Harbour, (SAEPP), (0596) 74 83 83, F: (0596) 74 92 20, VHF: 09, port. marin@wanadoo.fr

Martinique Dry Dock, (0596) 72 69 40/72 67 48, F: (0596) 63 17 69

Pressing du Port, (0596) 74 62 66, Fax: (0596)-74-04-72 ly-sev@netcourier.com

Surveyor, (Jacques Scharwatt, (0596) 74 02 14, emcscharwatt @wandoo.fr

Somatras Marina, (0596) 66 07 74, F: (0596) 66 00 50, VHF: 09, marina3ilets@wa-nadoo.fr, Anse Mitan, marina

MARTINIQUE MISCELLANEOUS

Eau de Tiare, (0696) 37 47 50, (0596) 74 33 57

Fedex, (0596) 42 41 00

Pre Colombian Mu-seum, (0596) 71 57 05

Tourist Department, (0596)-60-27-73

MARTINIQUE SAILMAKERS CANVAS CUSHIONS

Alize Voiles, (0696) 24 66 81

Manu Voiles, (0596) 63 10 61, F: (0596) 63 65 23, cell: (0696) 90 76 33, manuvoiles@wanadoo.fr

Sud Voilerie, (0596) 58 24 69, sudvoilerie972@orange.com

Voilerie Assistance, (0596) 74 88 32, didier-et-maria @wanadoo.fr

Incidences, Marin, (0596) 74 77 47, F:74 05 38, VHF: 16, incidences.caraibes @wanadoo.fr

Voilerie du Marin, (0696) 25 94 01, dan.karner@wanadoo.fr

MARTINIQUE TECHNICAL YACHT SERVICES

Alize Composites, glass, gelcoat, paint specialist, (0696)-00-12-34/07 30 75, clippers-ship@wanadoo.fr

Altec Marine, Cell: (0696) 28 44 78 F: (0596) 74-85-65, machine shop

Antilles Greement, (0696) 50 97 07/29 16 64, antilles-greement@ hotmail.fr

Antilles Marine Services, (0596) 74 70 78, F: (0596) 74 63 71, anitllesmarine@wanadoo.fr, Marin, mechanics

Atelier Sylvestre, (0596) 50 58 91/45 45 56, F: (0596) 50 23 63, hydraulics

Aquatech, (0696) 80 94 89, polyester work

Cadet-Petit, Cell: (0696) 23 67 75, electrics

Caraibes Greement, (0596) 74 80 33, F: (0596) 74 66 98, cgmar@wanadoo.fr, rigging, electircs

Caraibes Menuiserie (0596) 74 80 33, contact@caraibes-menuiserie.fr

Chalmessin, (0596) 60 03 75/60 03 79, F: (0596) 63 49 67, welding & fabrication cooking stoves

Continental Marine, (0696) 29-51-11, Yamaha agent

Debrouilla Marine, (0696) 45 92 20, marine electrics

Diginav, (0596) 74 76 62, F: (0596) 74 76 63, diginav@wanadoo.fr, electronics

EM Composites., (0596) 62 91 95, Cell: (0696) 23 24 57, glass work and painting

Fred Chaumelle, (0696) 07 71 25, frederic.chaumelle@leposte.net

Fraicher service, (0696) 82 24 04, (0596) 74 41 10, refrigeration, air-conditioning

Hybride Diffusion, (0696) 86 67 03, polyester and epoxy fabrications and repair.

Inboard Diesel, (0596) 78 71 96, F: (0596) 78 80 75, Cell: (0696) 45 95 93, frank@inboardiesel.com, mechanics

Infologeek, (0596) 67 30 53, 0696 71 79 77, contact@infologeek.com

Jean-Michel Rolland, (0596) 71 49 28, metal fabrication

JLN, (0596) 74 16 45/(0696) 22 48 70, boat signs

La Survy, (0596) 74 63 63, F: (0596) 74 63 00, Cell: (0696) 43 07 53, la.survy@wanadoo.fr, inflatables

Martinique Diesel, (0596) 51 16 13/51 34 33, IZ, injector pumps & injectors

Maxi Marine, (0596) 63 75 49, F: (0596) 63 84 62, info@maximarinefwi.com, Mercury, Cummins

Mecanique Plaisance, (0596) 74 68 74, F: (0596) 74 09 39 Workshop, (0596) 74 72 72, pc.mecaplai @wanadoo.fr, mechanics

Moderne Marine, (0696) 82 40 72, Mercruiser engines

Meca'bats, Marin, (0696) 03 74 41, vanille-st@hotmail.com, inboard/outboard repair.

Nautic Froid, (0696) 22 71 13, nauticfroid97290@hotmail.com

Nautic Services, (0696) 45 61 60, nautic.services@hotmail.fr Marin, sandblasting & antifouling

Patrick Roget, (0696) 36 59 88, electrical work

Pochon, (0596) 38 33 45, pochon.martinique @orange.fr

Proto Meca, (0596) 78 34 49, (0696) 26 09 26, F: (0596) 78 34 50, protomeca@ hotmail.fr, metal fabrication

Renovboats, (0596) 25 01 92, Case Pilote, fiberglass and painting

Sud Marine Electronic, (0596) 74 65 56, Cell: (0696) 45 68 04, sudme@wanadoo.fr, electrical, electronics

Sea Services, (0596) 70 26 69, F: (0596) 70 26 69, rigging

Techni Marine, (0696) 40 93 72, technimarine@free.fr

Techni Marine Services, (0696) 25 84 79, F: (0596) 68 74 22, tmsmartinique@hotmail.com, refits, hull repair

Tilikum, (0696) 22 79 89/ (0596) 74 67 03 F: (0596) 74 66 63, VHF: 16 tilikum@wanadoo.fr, refrigeration

Tony Crater, (0596) 74 66 60, F: (0596) 25 65 49, welding and fabrication

Turquoise Servicing, (0596) 68 19 10, F: (0596) 68 11 07, Suzuki outboards

Yes, (0596) 65 05 24, cell: (0696) 45 29 87, F: (0596) 65 05 53, yescaraibes@ hotmail.com, electrical

MARTINIQUE TRANSPORT

Afc Aviation, 51 07 17/56 32 78, airport, aerial charter

GD location, (0596) 58 27 89, (0696) 30 09 90, gd location@orange.fr

Europcar, Central, (0596) 42 42 44, Fort de France, (0596)

Madin-Loc,(0596) 74 05 54, madin-loc @wanadoo.fr

Nad in Car, (0596) 61 14 00, (0596) 61 25 88

Jumbo Car, (0596)-74-71 77, (0696) 90 10 67

MARTINIQUE PROVISIONING

Appro Zagaya, (0596) 74 39 75, (0696) 07 16 29, F: (0596) 68 82 35, cathy@appro-zagaya.fr

Caribizz.com, (0596) 74 16 82, F: (0596) 74 16 83, VHF: 72, info@caribizz.fr

Champion at Centre Annette, (0596) 74 85 85, F: (0596) 74 90 96,

Ed Marin (0596) 59 17 13, F: (0596) 59 17 10,

Les Halles Fraicheurs (0596) 74 61 39, hallesfraicheurs@ orange.fr

Vatier, (0596) 70 11 39, F: (0596) 60 00 00, impex.vatier@ wanadoo.fr

MARTINIQUE FUN SHOPPING

Levalois Racing, (0596) 73 11 96, CS-gas, personal protection

Mymy Boutique, (0596) 74 08 37

Sea Services, (0596) 70 26 69, F: (0596) 71 60 53, fine casual clothing including *Saint James*

MARTINIQUE BANKING

Change Caraibes, (0596) 60 28 40/73 06 16

Martinique Change, (0596) 66 04 44

MARTINIQUE RESTAURANTS

Aux Poisson D'Or, (0596) 66 01 80,$C

Beach Grill, (0596) 78 34 02 $B-C

La Baie, (0596) 42 20 38 $B-C

La Foyal, (0596) 63 00 38 $A-C

Le Littoral, (0596) 71 58 98, $B-C

Le Mayday, (0596) 78 75 24, (0696) 34 50 95, $B-D

La Grande Voile, (0596) 51 41 75, $D

Le Petibonum, (0596) 78 04 34 $B

Bidjoul, (0596) 68 65 28, $D

Copacabana, (0596) 66 08 92, $B-C

Fleur de Sel, (0596) 68 42 11, (0696) 01 05 58, $A-B

La Manureva, (0596) 66 16 45, $A-B,

L'Escapade Marine, (0596)-69 64 26, $D

La Cave a Vin, (0596) 70 33 02, F: (0596) 70 33 02, $A

La Dunnette (0596) 76 73 90, $C

Le Paradisio (0596) 76 92 87, leparadisio@ wanadoo.fr, $B-C

Le Coco Neg (0596) 76 94 82, coco-neg@ wanadoo.fr $C

Le Mahot (0596) 65 24 38 evelyne.murat@ orange.fr $C

Le Tamaya, (0596) 78 29 09, $C

Lina's, (0596) 71 91 92, $D

Mango Bay, (0596) 74 60 89, F: (0596) 42 18 56, $D, mangobay@ wanadoo.fr

O Ble Noir (0596) 48 12 01, $D

Sextant (0596) 63 41 24, $D

Ti Payot, (0596) 68 71 78. $C

Ti Toques, (0596) 74 72 32, $B-D

The Crew, (0596) 73 04 14, $B-C

MARTINIQUE CHARTER

Autremer Concept, (0596) 74 79 11/ (0696) 43 55 33 info@ autremerconcept.com cats, cruisers, racers

Corail Caraibes, (0596) 74 10 76, corail.mart@ wanadoo. fr, cat FP

Croisieres Caraibes, (0596)-74 64 58, (0696) 77 45 87, Croisieres-caraibes@wanadoo.fr, trips by the cabin

Dream Yacht Caribbean, (0596) 74 81 68, F: (0596) 74 86 95, martinique@ dreamyachtcharter. com, cats and monos

France-Escales, (0696) 61 17 37, contact@escales-grenadines.com (charter by the cabin)

Kiriacoulis Antilles, (0596) 74 86 51, F: (0596) 74 73 41, kiriacoulis-antilles@ wanadoo.fr, all charter

Liberty Sea, (0596) 74 91 18, location@ libertysea.com

Petit Breton Antilles, (0596) 74 74 37, F: (0596) 74 74 43, pba@wanadoo.fr.com, all kinds of charter, boat sales

Punch Croisieres, (0596) 74 89 18, F: (0596) 74 88 85, contact@punch-croisieres. com, all charter

Regis Guillemot Charter, (0596) 74 78 59, (0696) 81 31 45, regisguillemot@ wanadoo.fr, catamaran charter

Sparkling Charter, (0596) 74 66 39, F: (0596) 74 71 89, caraibes@ sparkling-charter.com, all kinds of charter

Star Voyage, (0596) 74 70 92, F: (0596) 74 70 93, star.voyage. marin@ wanadoo.fr, all kinds of charter

Sunsail, Port de Plaisance, Marin, 97290, Martinique, (0596) 74 77 61, F: (0596) 74 88 12, sunsail.martinique@ wanadoo.fr, all kinds of charter

VPM, Port de Plaisance, Marin, 97290, Martinique, (0596) 74 70 10, F: (0596) 74 70 20, martinique@ vpm-bestsail.com, all kinds of charter

MARTINIQUE SCUBA DIVING

Alpha plongee, (0596) 48 30 34

Anthinea, (0596) 66 05 26

Case Pilote Diving Club, (0596) 78 73 75/61 60 01

Corail Club Caraibes, (0596) 68 36 36, corail@fr.st

Attitude Plongee, (0596) 66 28 73, (0696) 72 59 28

Immersion Caraibes, (0596) 53 15 43/(0696) 33 40 95, chrisreynier @gmail.com

Kalinargo, (0596) 76 92 98, kalinargo @ wanadoo.fr,

Lychee Plongee, (0596) 66 05 26,

Localize, (0596) 68 64 78, (0596) 68 68 88

Mada Plongee, (0696), 51 60 70, madaplongee@ hotmail.fr

Marin Plongee, (0596), 74 05 31, (0696), 83 13 51, marinplongee@ wanadoo.fr

Nautica Antilles, (0596) 57 15 15, F: (0596) 51 85 56

Planete Bleue, (0596) 66 08 79, planbleu@ais.mq

Papa D'Lo, (0596) 78 12 06

ST. LUCIA

ST. LUCIA EMERGENCY OFFICIAL

Customs, Castries, (758) 458-4846, 24-hour; (758) 468-4859

Customs, Marigot, (758) 458-3318

Customs, Rodney Bay, (758) 452-0235

Customs, Soufriere, (758) 459-5656

Customs, Vieux Fort, (758) 468-4933/4

Rodney Bay Medical Center, (758) 452-8621 docb@candw.lc, (multi services)

Tapion Hospital, (758) 459-2000 (multi services)

Kent Glace, (758) 458-0167, F: 458-0893, kent_glace@hotmail.com, dental surgeon

Police Marine, (758) 452-2595, VHF: 16

Marine Emergency, HELP (4357) VHF:16

ST. LUCIA AIRLINES

Air Caraibes, (758) 453-0357

Air Jamaica, (758) 453-6111, 800-538-2942

American Airlines, (758) 454-6777/6779, F: (758) 454-5935

American Eagle, (758) 452-1820/453-6019, F: (758) 451-7941

BWIA, (758) 452-3778

LIAT, (758) 452-3051-3

Travel World, (758) 451-7443/453-7521, F: (758) 451-7445, travelworldslu@hotmail.com, travel agent, car rental, tours

Virgin Atlantic (758) 434-7236

ST. LUCIA CHANDLERY FISHING GEAR

Johnsons Marine Hardware, (758) 452-0299, F: (758) 452-0311, chandlery, fishing gear

Island Water World, (758) 452-1222 F: (758) 452-433, IW-WSLIAN@candw.lc, major chanderly

NAPA, (758) 542-5034, chandlery, auto parts

ST. LUCIA COMMUNICATIONS

Lime, (758) 453-9055/6/7

Marina at Marigot (758) 451-4275, F: (758) 451-4276, marina@ marigotbay.com

Rent A Ride, (758) 452-9404/0932, F: (758) 452-0401, VHF: 16, reservations@vcrentals.com

Rodney Bay Marina, (758) 452-0324, Fax: (758) 458-0040

ST. LUCIA GENERAL YACHT SERVICES

Ben's Yacht Services, (758) 459-5457/7160, VHF: 16, F: (758) 459-5719, Cell: (758) 484-0708/721-8500, saltibusb @slucia.com, yacht agent

Fletcher's Vieux Fort Laundry. 758 454 5936; fletcherdrycleaning@live.com

Harmony Yacht Services, (758) 267-4261/518-0081/ 519-7416 VHF: 16, info@ harmonyyachtservices.com, yacht agent

Ian Desouzay (Reliant Brokerage), (758) 484-3782

Marina at Marigot Bay, (758) 451-4275, F: (758) 451-4276, manager@marigotbay-marina.com

Kessel Marine, (758) 450-0651, Cell: 758 484-3547, F; 758 450 0241,kessellc @candw.lc, surveys

Kessel Lisa, (758) 484-0555, Customs brokerage

Rodney Bay Marina, (758) 452-0324, F: (758) 458-0040, VHF: 16, rbm@igymarinas.com

Sud's Laundry (758) 285-4388

St. Lucia Yacht Services (758) 452-5057, VHF: 16, fuel

Chateau Mygo has Marigot docks see *Restaurants.*

ST. LUCIA MISCELLANEOUS

Forestry Department, (758) 458-2231/2375/2078, forest hikes

Home Services, (758) 452-0450, F: (758) 452-0071, homeservices@candw.lc, real estate

Le Spa, Marigot, (758) 458-3039

Latitude 13 Real Estate, (785) 458-3947, VHF: 16,

L'Essence Massage, (758) 715-4661

National Trust, (758) 452-5005, E: natrust@candw.lc, hikes

Marine Industries Association of St. Lucia (758) 452-2300, (758) 484-3646, comtonk@candw.lc

Morne Courbaril, (758) 459- 7340/712-5808

Soufriere Marine Management Assn., (758) 459- 5500, F: (758) 459-7799, Head Ranger cell: 718-1196, VHF: 16, smma@candw.lc,

Soothing Touch Massage, (758) 284-4606

St. Lucia Golf and Country Club, (758) 450-8522/3, F: 450-8317, golf@candw.lc

St. Lucia Marine Terminals, (758) 454-8739/42, F: (758) 454-8745, port authority

St. Lucia Tourist Board, (758) 452-4094, slutour @candw.lc

ST. LUCIA SAILMAKERS CANVAS CUSHIONS

Lubeco, (758) 454-6025, F: (758) 454-9463, allain@candw.lc, fitted sheets and matresses

Rodney Bay Sails, (758) 452-8648, (758) 584-0291, rodneybay-sails@hotmail.com Full sail loft

ST. LUCIA TECHNICAL YACHT SERVICES

BBC Yachting, (758) 716-7610/ 458-4643, bbcyachting @live.com, absentee yacht management and repair, asll systems

Chinaman, (758) 518-1234, metalwork

Calidad Communications, (758) 484-5652/384-8318, info@calidadwireless.com, IT and computer systems

Cox Enterprises, (758) 384-2269, glass & paint

TECHNICAL YACHT SERVICES (cont)

Complete Marine Services, (758) 458-3188/485-1141, info@cms-sl.com, yacht/project mangement

Destination St. Lucia Box 2091, Gros Islet, St. lucia, W.I. (758) 452-8531, Fax: (758) 452-0183, Call us on VHF: 72 "DSL" destsll @candw.lc, absentee yacht management and repair, all systems

Island Marine Supplies, (758) 452-9404/484-3706, outboard repair, Mercury agent.

Kennedy Joseph, (758) 716-0383/ 452-9013, alfalewis@hotmail.com, Paint, varnish polish, help

KL Marine (758) 450-5565, Yamaha

Liferaft & Inflatable Center, (758) 452-8306/715-9671, F: (785) 458-0679, francis@ liferaft&inflatble.com

Mac's Marine, (758) 485-1530, Mariner outboards

MarinTek, (758) 484-6031/450-0552, marintek@gmail.com electrical, refrigeration, Volvo dealer

Mermaid Marine (Elvis**),** (758) 488-5291, glass/paint

Pride, (758) 284-7948, woodwork

Prudent Repairs, (758) 459-4334, cell: (758) 384-0825, refrigeration

Quick and Reliable, (758) 520-5544/584-6544, +F: 452 9560, alwynaugustinengineer @gmail.com diesel mechanic

Quick Fix Refrigeration, (758) 484-9016

Remy, (758) 450-2000 woodworking, fixing TVs, cds, etc

Regis Electronics, (758) 452-0205, F: (758) 452-0206, VHF: 09, stlucia@regiselectronics.com

Ryte Weld Enterprises, (758) 450-8019, metal work

Scribble, (758) 452-0224, info @ scribbledesign.com, boat names, brochures

Tyson, (758) 452-5794/487-5641, cecilgirard@ candw.lc woodwork

Tony's Engineering, (758) 715-8719 /452-8575, mechanics

ST. LUCIA TRANSPORT

All Round Adventures, (758) 712-5731/458-4266, bike rentals

Ben's Taxi Service, (758) 459-5457/7160, VHF: 16, F: (758) 459-5719, Cell: (758) 484-0708/ 715-8642, saltibusb@slucia.com

C.J. Taxi Service, Rodney Bay, St. Lucia, (758) 450-5981/458-4283, Cell: (785) 584-3530, F: (758) 452-0185, VHF: 16,

Cool Breeze Jeep/ Car Rental, Soufriere., St. Lucia, (758) 459-7729, F: (785) 459-5309,

Intellect Taxi, Linus Placide, Rodney Bay Taxi driver, (758) 458-0265, 384-3016, VHF: 16

Kierean water/land taxi (758)584-2038

Mystic Man Tours, (758) 459-7783/455-9634, aimblec@candw.lc

Soufriere Water Taxi Assn., (758) 459-7239/5500, F: (758) 458-7999, VHF: 16, E: richie@candw.lc

Taxi Service Marigot, (758) 451-4406, VHF: 16

TJ's Car Rental, (758) 452-0116/268-0466

ST. LUCIA BANKING

CITS, (758) 452-1529, American Express agent

Royal Bank of Canada, (758) 452-9921, F: (758) 452-9923

ST. LUCIA PROVISIONING

Admac Ltd., (758) 451-6890, Fax: (758) 451-8995

Glace Supermarket, 758 452-8814/0514/8179, Cell: 484-1415, F: 758 452-9669, glaceg@candw.lc

BBs (The), (758) 452-0647, taylorn@candw.lc

Chateau des Fleurs, (758) 451-7422, F: (758) 452-6022

Eroline Foods, (758) 459-7125/5299, F: (758) 459-7882

Flower Shack, (758) 452-0555 Fax: (758) 452-0556, mail@flowershack.net

MariGourmet, (758) 451-4031 Fax: (758) 451-4032, marigourmet@ candw.lc

Super J Supermarkets, (758) 452-0414, F: (758) 452-9049, Rodney Bay Mall, (758) 457-2000

Starfish provisioning, (758) 452-0100/716-2109, starfishfoods@gmail.com

ST. LUCIA FUN SHOPPING

Artsibit Gallery, (758) 452-7865

Bagshaw's, (758) 452-6039

Caribbean Perfumes, (758) 453-7249, caribperfumes@candw.lc

Handicraft Center, (758) 459-3226

Jemann (758) 454-593/ 716-6797, bibiana.morgan @gmail.com

La Place Carenage (758) 452-7318, slaspa@candw.lc

Livity Art Studio (758) 488-2554

Sea Island Cotton Shop, (758) 452-3674

Sunshine Bookstore, (758) 452-2322, F: (758) 453-1879, sunbooks@candw.lc

The Art Boutique, (758) 452-8071, caribbeanart@ candw.lc

Zaka (758) 457-1504/ 384-2925, zaka-art@yahoo.com

ST. LUCIA RESTAURANTS & ACCOMMODATION

Anse Chastanet, (758) 459-7000, $A-C

BB's (The), (758) 452-0647,, $C-D

Big Chef Steak House (758) 450-0210, markjoinville@candw.lc $A-B

Captain Mike's , (758) 572-6435, $C-D,

Buzz, (758) 458-0450/ 718-0392, $A-B

Cafe Ole, Boardwalk Bar , (758) 452-8726, $D

Charthouse, (758) 452-8115, (758) 45-STEAK, ashworth@candw.lc, $B-C

Chateau Mygo, (785) 451-4772, VHF: 16, info@ chateaumygo.com, $B-D

Chef Xavier, (785) 458-2433/ 484-2433, chefxavier@gmail.com $A

Coal Pot, (758) 452-5566, F: (758) 453-6776, xavier@cand.lc, $B

Delirius, (758) 451-3345, info@deliriusstlucia.com

Discovery at Marigot, (758) 458-4767, info @ marigotbay.com, Resort, Boudreau Restaurant and several bars, $A-B

Doolittles, (758) 451-4974, $B-C

Edge (the) (758) 450-3343, bobo.b@telia.com, $A-B

Elena's (758)-458-0576, $C-D

Fire Grill (758) 451-4745, firegrillstlucia @ gmail.com

Gee's Bon Manje (758) 457-1008/488 1247/ 721-8651, $A-D

H2O, (758) 452-0351 $B-C

Harmony Beach Restaurant, (758) 459-5050/287-4261, F: (758) 458-5033, harmonyiii@ hotmail.com, $C D

Hummingbird Resort, (758) 459-7232, VHF 16, Fax: (758) 459-7033, hbr@candw.lc, $A-B

Jacques (758) 453-7249, $B cathy@ jacquesrestaurant.com,

Jalousie Plantation, (758) 456-8000, F: (758) 459-7667, info@thejalousieplantation.com

Jambe de Bois, (758) 452-0321, VHF:16, $C-D, btipson@candw.lc

JJ's Restaurant & Bar, (785) 451-4076, F: (758) 451-4146, VHF: 16, $B-C

Kimatrai , (758) 454-6328, $C-D, info@kimatraihotel.com

Key Largo, (758) 452-0282, F: (758) 452-9933, pizza @ candw.lc, $D

La Haut , (758) 459-7008, F: (758) 459-5975, Lahaut@candw.lc, $C-D

Ladera Resort (Dasheen), (758) 459-7323, F: (758) 459-5156, ladera @candw.lc, $A-B

Landings Beach Club, (758) 458-7375, $B-C

Le Chaudiere, (758) 519-7922/723-0874/457-1418, lechaudiere@hotmail.com $C-D

Mango Bay, (758) 4485-1621/458-3188, judith@marigotbay.com, accommodation

Matha's Table, (758) 459-5174, $C-D

Ocean Club, (758) 452-0351, info@ocst-lucia.com, $B-C

Old Plantation Yard, (758) 454-6040, oldplant@hotmail.com, $D

Pat's Bar, $C_D, (758) 454-5002

Pink Plantation House, (758) 452-5422, $B-C

Pizza Pizza, (758) 452-8282

Rainforest Hideaway, (758) 286-0511/ 451-4485, rainforesthideaway@yahoo.co.uk, $A

Razmataz, (758) 452-9800, F: (758) 452-9800, $C, razmataz@candw.lc,

Red Snapper, (758) 456-8377, $B-D

Sandy Beach, (758) 454-6392/721-3659, ricattigeorges @ hotmail.fr, $C-D

Spice of India, (758) 458-4234/716-0820, info@spiceofindiastlucia.com

St. Lucia Yacht Club, (758) 452-8350, VHF: 16, $D

Starfish, (758) 452-0100/716-2109, starfishfoods@gmail.com

Still Estate (The), (758) 459-5179, (758) 459-7301, dubou-layd@ candw.lc, $B-D,

Stonefield Estate, (758) 453-3483, 453-0394, $B-C

Tapas on the bay, (758) 451-2433, $C-D

Ti Kaye, (758) 456-8101/03, Ti Manje, (758) 456-8118, info@ tikaye.com

Villa des Pitons, (758) 459-7797, $C-D

Winsdjammer Landing, (758) 452-0913, in USA:800-743-9609

Zoe's, (758) 455-9411, $C-D

ST. LUCIA CHARTER

Bateau Mygo, (758)-458-3947, VHF: 16, kiteboarding cruises, bareboat, day, skippered

BBC Yachting, (758) 716-7610/ 458-4643, bbcyachting@ live.com, bareboat, skippered, day charters

Destination St. Lucia Box 2091, Gros Islet, St. lucia, W.I. Call us on VHF: 72 "DSL" Telephone: (758) 452-8531, Fax: (758) 452-0183, destsll@ candw.lc, all charter

Caribbean Yachting, (758) 458-4430 Fax: (758) 452-0742, Ben@candw.lc

Cats, 450-8651, day-charters

The Moorings, P.O. Box 101, Castries, St. Lucia, West Indies, T: 758-451-4357, F: 758-451-4230, mooring@candw.lc, all kinds of charter

Unicorn Day charters, (758) 452-8644

ST. LUCIA SCUBA DIVING/WATERS-PORTS

Action Adventure Divers (AA) (758) 459-5599, 485-1317

Buddies Scuba, (758) 450-8406

Island Divers, (758) 456-8110, cell: (758) 285-3483, diving @ tikaye.com

Scuba St. lucia, (758) 459-7000, VHF: 16

Windward Island Gases, (758) 452-1514/1339

ST. VINCENT

ST. VINCENT EMERGENCY

Botanic Clinic, (784) 457-9781, private hospital

Customs Kingstown, (784) 456-1083

Customs Chateaube-lair, (784) 485-7907

Emergency, 999 - fire, police, medical

Maryfield Hospital, (784) 457-8991/1300, F: (784) 457-8992, private hospital

Police, (784) 456-1185

Police Chateaubelair, (784) 458-2229

During Marine Emergencies call **St. Vincent Signal Station** on VHF: 16 for an appropirate relay.

ST. VINCENT AIRLINES

American Eagle, (784) 456-5000,

Air Martinique, (784) 458-4528/456-4711, F: (784) 458-4187

LIAT, (784) 457-1821, F: (784) 457-2000

SVG Air, (784) 457 5124, F: (784) 457-5077, svgair@ vincysurf.com, air charters

ST. VINCENT CHANDLERY FISHING GEAR

KP Marine, (784) 457-1806, F: (784) 456-1364, kpmarine @ vincysurf.com

ST. VINCENT COMMUNICATIONS

Anancy Communications, (784) 456-2080, agnes @caribits.com

Office Essentials, (784)-457-2235, oel@ vincysurf.com

see also Barefoot and Lagoon marina under General yacht Services

ST. VINCENT GENERAL YACHT SERVICES

Aquatic Club, (784) 458-4205, water

Bay Central, (784) 527-3298, 431-1899, water, washing machines

Barefoot Yacht Charters, (784) 456-9526, F: (784) 456-9238, VHF: 68, moorings

Charlie Tango, (784) 458-4720/493-2186/593-1882, info@ charlietangotaxi.com, moorings

Joe Brown, (784) 456-9438, F: (784) 456-9886, marine@ vincysurf.com, surveyor

Ottley Hall, VHF: 68, haul out

Sam Taxi Tours, (784) 456-4338/ 528-3340, F: (784) 456-4233, VHF: 68/16, sam-taxi-tours @vincysurf.com, Bequia, 458-3686 Union, 494-4339, shipping, customs clearance

St. Vincent Yacht Club, (784) 457-2827, stvincentyachtclub.com

Sunsail Marine Center, (784) 458-4308, F: (784) 456-8928, VHF: 68, sunsailsvg @vincysurf.com, marina

TMM, Blue Lagoon, T: (784) 456-9608, F: (784) 456-9917, VHF: 68, moorings

Wallilabou Anchorage, (784) 458-7270, F: (784) 458-7270, VHF: 68, $C-D, water

MISCELLANEOUS

Dept of Tourism, (784) 457-1502/1957, F: (784) 456-2601

Cumberland tour guides, Suzanne, (784) 454-9236, Marsden, (784) 497-3516, Abbey, (784) 531-0237,

ST. VINCENT TECHNICAL YACHT SERVICES

Barefoot Marine Center, (784) 456-9334/9526, F: (784) 456-9238, VHF: 68, barebum@ vincysurfsurf.com, sail loft, diesel repair. Electronics dept, electronics@ barefootyachts.com

Howard's Marine, (784) 457-4328, F: (784) 457-4268, VHF: 68, mechanics, inboard and outboard, haul-out

Nichol's Marine, (784) 456-4118, F: (784) 456-5884, VHF: 68, starter motors and alternators

Oscar's Machine Shop, (784) 456-4390

St. Vincent Marine Upholstery and Canvas, (784) 533-3860

TRANSPORT

Fantasea Tours, (784) 457-4477/ 5555, fantasea @ vincysurf.com

HazEco Tours, (784) 457-8634, hazeco@ vincysurf.com

Robert Taxi, (784) 593-6474/593-6009 VHF: 68, Elvis and Robert

Sam Taxi & Tours, (784) 456-4338, F: (784) 456-4233, VHF: 68/16, sam-taxi-tours@ vincysurf.com,

ST. VINCENT BANKING

Caribbean Banking Corp., (784) 456-1501, F: (784) 456-2141

CITS, (784) 457-1841, F: (784) 456-2331 Amex agent

ST. VINCENT PROVISIONING

Aunt Jobe's Market, (784) 456-1511/494-8989, F: (784) 456-2462, auntjobesales @vincysurf.com

Gonsalves Liquor, (784) 45-1881, F: (784) 456-2645, gonliq@vincysurf.com

Gourmet Food, 456-2987/2983/528-3188, charm_dev@ yahoo.com

Greaves C. K., Kingstown (784) 457 1074, Fax: (784) 456-2679, Arnos Vale, (784) 458-4602, ckgreaves@ vincysurf.com

ST. VINCENT RESTAURANTS & ACCOMMODATION

Beachcombers, (784) 458-4283, F: (784) 458-4385, beachcombers @ vincysurf.com, $B-C

Beach Front Restaurant, (784) 458-2853, F: (784) 456-9238, VHF: 68/16, $B-C

Beni, (784) 427-0405, VHF: 16, benett@ vincysurf. com, $C

Black Baron, (784) 485-7904, VHF: 16, $B

Black Pearl, (784) 456-9868, $B-D

Bounty (The), (784) 456-1776, $D

Driftwood, (784) 456-8999, $B-C

Flow Wine Bar (784) 457-0809, & **Flowt Beach Bar** (784) 593-6471, $C-D

French Verandah (784) 453-1111, frenchverandah@ vincysurf.com, $A-B

Grand View Grill, (784) 457-5487, $C-D

High Tide, (784) 456-6777, hightide@ vincysurf.com, $B-D

Little Hideaway Bay, (784) 456-0421, $B

Mareyna Bar and Grill, (784) 457-5233, $C-D

Marsy Beach Bar, (784) 458-2879/ 430-8437, VHF:16, $C-D

Mojito, (784) 433-7526/ 452-8007, $C

Paradise Beach Hotel, (784) 457-4795,info @ paradisesvg.com

Rock Side Cafe, (784) 456-0815/430-2208, $C, rosimorgan@ vincysurf.com

Surfside Restaurant, (784) 457-5362, $B-C

Wallilabou Anchorage, (784) 458-7270, F: (784) 458-7270, wallanch@ vincysurf.com, VHF: 68, $B-C

Wilkie's Restaurant, (784) 458-4811, F: (784) 457-4174, $A-B, grandview @vincysurf.com

Xcape, (784) 457-4597, Xcaprerestaurant@ hotmail.com$C-D

Young Island Resort, (784) 458-4826, VHF: 68, $A

ST. VINCENT CHARTER

Barefoot Yacht Charters, (784) 456-9334/9526, F: (784) 456-9238, VHF: 68, Email:barebum @ vincysurfsurf.com, all kinds of charter boats.

Festiva Sailing, (784) 457-5350, (866) 575-3951

Sunsail, (784) 458-4308, F: (784) 458-4308, VHF: 68, sunsailsvg@ vincysurf.com, all kinds of charter

TMM, Box 39, Blue Lagoon, St Vincent, W.I. T: (784) 456-9608, F: (784) 456-9917, sailtmm@ vincysurf. com, tmmsvg @ sailtmm.com, all kinds of charter

ST. VINCENT SCUBA DIVING

Dive St. Vincent, (784) 457-4928/4714, F: (784) 457-4948, VHF: 68, Bill2s@ divestvincent.com

Dive Center, (784) 457-4948

BEQUIA EMERGENCY

Police, (784) 458-3211,

Customs, (784) 457-3044, VHF: 16

Imperial Pharmacy, (784) 458-3373,

Bequia Hospital, (784) 458-3294, VHF: 74

BEQUIA CHANDLERY FISHING GEAR

Grenadine Yacht Equipment,(784) 458-3347,F: (784) 458-3696, VHF: 16 gye-bequia@ vincysurf.com,

Lulley's Tackle Shop, (784) 458-3420, lulley@ vincysurf.com

Piper Marine, (784) 457-3856/495-2272. VHF: 68

Wallace & Co., (784) 458-3360, wallco@ vincysurf.com

BEQUIA COMMUNICATIONS

Bequia Land & Home, (784) 458-3772

Bequia Technology Center, (784) 458-3045, F: (784) 388-8094, info@ bequiatech.com

Fedex, Solana's, (784) 458-3554,

RMS, (784) 458-3556, F: (784) 458-3571, VHF: 16/68/10, rms@ vincysurf.com

BEQUIA MISCELLANEOUS

A Caribbean Wedding, (784) 457-3209/528-7444

Bequia Land & Home, (784) 458-3116/533-0677, bequialandandhome @vincysurf.com

Caribbean Compass, (784) 457-3409,

Grenadines Island Villas, (784) 529-8046/455-0696, island-villas@ mac.com

Kenmore Henville, (784) 457-3212, Cell: (784) 529-5005, VHF: 77, marine photographer

Old Hegg Turtle Sanctuary, (784) 458-3245/3596, oldhegg@ vincysurf.com

BEQUIA GENERAL YACHT SERVICES

African, (784) 593- 3986,VHF: 68, yacht management, deliveries, moorings, provisioning

Bequia Marina, (784) 530- 9092/431-8418, VHF: 68, docking, water

Daffodil Marine, (784) 458-3942, VHF: 67,daffodil@ vincy-surf.com, water, fuel, laundry

Lighthouse Laundry, (784) 458-3084,VHF: 68, laundry

Miranda's Laundry, (784) 530-6865,VHF: 68, laundry

Papa Mitch, (784) 458-7222, VHF: 68, laundry

BEQUIA SAILMAKERS CANVAS CUSHIONS

Allick Sails, (784) 457-3040/458-3992, VHF: 68

Bequia Canvas, (784) 457-3291, F: (784) 457-3291 , VHF: 68, beqcan@vincysurf. com

Grenadine Sails, (784) 457-3507/3527, VHF: 16/68, gsails@ vincysurf.com

BEQUIA TECHNICAL YACHT SERVICES

Caribbean Diesel, (784) 457-3114/ 593-6333/ 458-3191, VHF: 68, mechanics

KMS Marine Services, (784) 530-8123/570-7612

Piper Marine, (784) 457-3856/495-2272. VHF: 68, rigging

Simpson Engineering, (784) 457-3692/526-6729, dee. williams @hotmail. com, VHF: 68, mechanics

Winfield Sargeant, (784) 458-3058/562-0882, VF: 68, friendshipside2@ yahoo. com, varnishing etc.

Yachtfix, (784) 458-3942

BEQUIA TRANSPORT

Admiralty Transport, (784) 458-3348, F: (784) 457-3577, admiraltrans@ vincysurf. com

Challenger Taxi Service, (784) 458-3811, VHF: 68, challenger-taxi@ yahoo.com

De Best, (784) 458-3349/530-4747, F: (784) 457-3408, VHF: 68, friendshipgapt @ vincysurf.com

BEQUIA TRANSPORT (cont)

Gideon Taxi, (784) 458-3760/527-2092, F:(784) 458-3760, VHF: 68, gideontaxi@ vincysurf.com, taxi, rentals

Handy Andy, (784) 458-3722, F: (784) 457-3402, VHF: 68, rentals

BEQUIA FUN SHOPPING

Bequia Bookshop, (784) 458-3905, F: (784) 457-3875, bequiabookshop@ hotmail.com

Claude Victorine, (784) 458-3150, claudevictorine @ vincysurf.com

Island Life, (784) 458-3012

Island Things, (784) 457-1600, kelcom@ vincysurf.com

Local Color, (784) 458-3202, F: (784) 457-3071, chappell@ vincysurf.com

Oasis Gallery, (784) 497-7670, bequiaboat-house @vincysurf.com

Solana's, (784) 458-3554, solanas@ vincysurf.com

Whaleboner, (784) 458-3233,VHF: 68

BEQUIA PROVISIONING

Bequia Foodstore (784) 457-3928

Doris Fresh Foods, (784) 458-3625, F: (784) 457-3134, VHF: 68

Eileen's Market (784) 457-3500, eileensmar-ket@yahoo.com

Knights Trading (784) 458-3218, F: (784) 457-3327, knightstrad @ yahoo.com

Linas, (784) 457-3388

Nature Zone, (784) 458-3793/433-5088,

Mama's, (784) 457-3443

Maranne's Ice Cream, (784) 458-3041

Select Wines, (784) 457-3482

BEQUIA RESTAURANTS & ACCOMODATION

Aqua Cafe Bar, (784) 458-3133, $D

Bequia Beach Hotel, (784) 458-1600, info@ bequiabeach.com

Coco's Place, (784) 458-3463, F: (784) 458-4797, VHF: 68, $B-D

Colombo's, (784) 457-3881, $B-D

Daffodil, (784) 458-3942, F: (784) 458-3369, VHF: 67, $B-D

De Reef, (784) 458-3412/3484, F:457-3101, $D

Devil's Table, (784) 458-3900/3222 VHF: 68, $A-D

Fig Tree, (784) 457-3008, figtree@ vincysurf.com, $B-D

Firefly Hotel Bequia, (784) 488-8414/458-3414, VHF:10, liz@ fireflybequia.com, $A

Frangipani, (784) 458-3255, F: (784) 458-3824, VHF: 68, $B, info@ frangipan-ibequia .com

Gingerbread, (784) 458-3800, F: (784) 458-3907, VHF: 68, $B-C, gm@ginger-breadhotel.com

Hendi's, (784) 593-0510, $D

Jack's Restaurant, (784) 458-3809, VHF: 68 $B

Kingsville Apart-ments, (784) 458-3404/3932, kingsville @ vincysurf.com

L'Auberge des Grenadines, (784) 457-3555, VHF: 68, $A, auberge@ cari-brestaurant.com

Mac's Pizzeria, (784) 458-3474, VHF: 68, $C-D, beqvilla @ vincysurf.com

Mango's, (784) 458-3361, $B-D

Maria's Cafe, (784) 458-3422, mitchell1@ vincysurf.com, $D

Papa's, (784) 457-3443

Porthole, (784) 458-3458, F: (784) 457-3420 $C-D

Tantie Pearle's, (784) 457-3160, $B-C

Tommy Cantina, (784) 457-3779. $C

Whaleboner Inn, (784) 458-3233, VHF: 68, whalebonerbequia @ hotmail.com $C-D

BEQUIA CHARTER

Island Time Holidays, grenadines@ vincy-surf.com

Sail Relax Explore, (784) 457-3888/495-0886/9

The Friendship Rose, (784) 457-3888/495-0886/9, friend-shiprose@ mac.com

Tradewinds Cruise Club, (784) 457-3407, info@ tradewind-scruiseclub. com

BEQUIA SCUBA DIVING

Bequia Dive Adven-ture, (784) 458 3826, VHF: 68, adventures@ vincysurf.com, dive shop

Dive Bequia, (784) 458-3504/ 495-9929, VHF: 68,16, cathy@ divebequia.com, dive shop

MUSTIQUE MISCELLANEOUS

Mustique Moorings, (784) 488-8363,VHF: 16/68

Horse riding, (784) 488-8316

MMS (bike, mule rental) (784) 488-8555

Mustique Company, (784) 488-8000, F: (784) 488-9000

Airport, (784) 488-8336

Doctor,(784) 488-8353

MUSTIQUE SHOPPING

Coreas, (784) 488-8479

The Purple House, (784)- 528-8788 boutique, elegant wear

MUSTIQUE RESTAURANTS & ACCOMMODATION

Basil's Bar,(784) 488-8350,VHF: 68, $A-B

Cotton House, (784) 456-4777, F: (784) 488-8215/6, VHF: 68, cottonhouse@ vincy-surf.com $A

Firefly Mustique, (784) 488-8414, (784) 488-8514, VHF: 10, stan@ fireflymustique. com, $A-B

The View, (784) 488-8807/532-2421, $C-D

MUSTIQUE SCUBA DIVING

Mustique Waters-ports, (784) 488-8486, VHF: 16/68

CANOUAN AIRLINES

AA, (784) 456-5555

CANOUAN COMMUNICATIONS

Cyber Net, (784) 430-4045

Tamarind Bay Hotel, (784) 458-8044

CANOUAN GENERAL YACHT SRVICES

Marcus VHF: 16, cell: 784) 492-3230 (784) 458-8375, moorings, water, fuel, taxi

CANOUAN TECHNICAL YACHT SERVICES

Gazimo Marine Service (784) 491-1177, gazimomarineservice@ yahoo.com

CANOUAN TRANSPORT

Phyllis Taxi, (784) 593-4190

CANOUAN HOTELS/ RESTAURANTS

Crystal Apts Restaurant (784)-458-8356, $C

Frontline Restaurant (784)-497-5561/492-3182, $C-D

Phyllis, (784) 593-4190, $C-D

Canouan Resort, (784) 458-8000, $A

Tamarind Bay Hotel, (784) 458-8044,VHF: 16, info@tamarind.us, $A-D

The Mangrove, (784) 482-0761/593-3364, VHF:16/68, $C-D

CANOUAN CHARTER

The Moorings, (784) 482-0655

CANOUAN SCUBA DIVING

Canouan Dive Center, VHF: 16, (784) 528-8030, info@canouandivecenter.com

MAYREAU RESTAURANTS & ACCOMODATION

Dennis's Hideaway, (784) 458-8594, F: (784) 458-8594, VHF: 16/68, $B-C

J & C Restaurant, (784) 458-8558, VHF: 16/68, $C

Island Paradise, (784) 458-8941/8068, VHF: 68, $C

Salt Whistle Bay Club, (784) 497-5145, tasha@saltwhistlebay.com, $B

Righteous & de Youths, (784) 458-8203, VHF: 68, $D

PALM ISLAND

Palm Island VHF: 16, Tel: (784) 458-8824, Fax: (784) 458-8804

Patrick Chavailler, Palm island doctor and artist, (784) 458-8829, palmdoc@vicysurf.com

UNION ISLAND EMERGENCY

Customs, (784) 458-8360

Health Center, (784) 458-8339

UNION AIRLINES

Eagle Travel, (784) 458-8179, eagtrav@ vincysurf.com, VHF: 68

UNION COMMUNICATIONS

Erika's Marine Services, (784) 485-8335/ 494-1212, F: (784) 485-8336 VHF: 68, info@ erikamarine.com

Internet Cafe, (784) 485-8326, F: (784) 485-8082

UNION MISCELLANEOUS

JT Kitesurf (784) 593-9822/430-8604, info@ kitesurfgrenadines.com

Tobago Cays Marine Park, (784) 485-8191, F: (784) 485-8192 info@tobagocays.com

UNION GENERAL YACHT SERVICES

Anchorage Yacht Club, (784) 458-8221, F: (784) 458-8365, VHF: 16/68, aycunion@ vincysurf.com, docking, laundry

Bougainvilla, (784) 458 8878/8678, laquarium@ vincysurf.com, VHF: 16, docking

Erika's Marine Services (784) 485-8335, VHF: 68, info@ erikamarine.com

UNION TECHNICAL YACHT SERVICES

Island Marine Special, (784) 458-8039, VHF: 16, mechanics

Unitech Marine Services, (784) 458-8320/527-4635, unitech@ vincysurf.com, mechanics & glass work

UNION RESTAURANTS & ACOMMODATION

Anchorage Yacht Club, (784) 458-8221, F: (784) 458-8365, VHF: 16/68, $A-B

Big Citi, (784) 458-8960/494-8424, $D

Bollhead Bar & Restaurant, (784) 593-1660, $C

Ciao Pizza, (784) 430-8630,$C

Clifton Beach Hotel, (784) 458-8235, VHF: 68, $B-C

Janti's, (784) 455-3611, happyisland@ unionisland.com $D

L'Aquarium, (784) 430-4088/458-8678, caribbeadelicacy@ yahoo.com, $B-C

Lambi, (784) 458-8549, VHF: 68, $B-C

Limelite Bar, (784) 485-8486, $D

L'Aquarium (784) 458-8311, VHF: 16, $B-D

Shark Attack, (784) 527-2694/2691, sharkattack2006@ hotmail.com, $C

Sun, Beach & Eat, (784) 531-6965/530-5913, VHF: 16, $C

The West Indies (784) 458-8911, VHF: 16, joelle@ vincysurf.com, $A-C

UNION FUN SHOPPING

Anchorage Boutique (784) 458-8221

Castello, (784) 458-8177, F: (784) 458-8732, VHF: 68

Clifton Boutique, (784) 458-8235

L'Atelier Turquoise, (784) 458-8734, anniefrance@vincysurf.com

Lully's Fishing supplies, (784) 458-8836

Mare Blu, (784) 494-8880

UNION PROVISIONING

Captain Gourmet, (784) 458-8918, F: (784) 458-8918, VHF: 08 (USA) capgourmet@ vincysurf.com

Jenny's Fruit & Veg, (784) 593-3887

Island Grown, (784) 532-2914/529 0935

UNION CHARTER

Unitech Marine Services, (784) 530-5915/ 527-4635, unitech@ vincysurf.com

Wind and Sea, Union I., Bougainvilla, T: (784) 458-8678/8678, F: (784) 458 8569 windandsea@ vincysurf.com

Grenadines Dive,
(784) 458-8138/455-
2822, VHF: 16/68, E:
gdive@ vincysurf.com

PSV RESTAURANTS
& ACCOMODATION

Petit St. Vincent Resort VHF: 16, (784)
458-8801, $A-C

GRENADA, CARRIACOU & PM

PETITE
MARTINIQUE
GENERAL
YACHT SERVICES

B&C Fuels, (473)
443-9110, Fax: (473)
443-9075, golfsierra@
hotmail.com, VHF:
16, "Golf Sierra" fuel,
water

PM
COMMUNICATIONS

Millenium Connection, (473) 443-9243,
ieshodinga @yahoo.
co.uk

PM CHANDLERY
TECHNICAL SERVICES

Clement Brothers,
T&F: (473) 443-9022

E&B Hardware, 473-
443-9086

PM RESTAURANTS
& ACCOMMODATION

Palm Beach, (473)
443-9103, VHF: 16,
efclement@yahoo.
co.uk, $C-D

**Melodie's Guest
House,** (743) 443-
9052/9093/9108, F:
(743) 443-9113

Seaside View, (473)
443-9007, F: (473)
443 9113

PM SHOPPING

**Matthew Shoppng
Center,** (473) 443-
9194

Millenium Boutique,
(473) 443-9243,
ieshabc@ hotmail.com

CARRIACOU
EMERGENCY

Customs, Carriacou,
(473) 443-7659

Hospital emergency,
774

CARRIACOU
AIRLINES

LIAT, (473) 443-7362

Bullen, (473) 443-
7468/7469, Fax: 443
8194, travel agent

CARRIACOU COMMUNICATIONS

Digisoft, (473) 443-
8955/6435, digisoft@
gmail.com

Services Unlimited,
(473) 443-8451/406-
3378, servicesunlim-
ited@spiceisle.com

CARRIACOU
GENERAL YACHT
SERVICES

Bullen, (473) 443-
7468/7469, Fax: 443
8194 vbs@spiceisle.
com, duty free fuel

My Beautiful Laundrette, (473) 403-
0164/405-1148

Shorebase Services,
443-6449

**Carriacou
Marine,** (473) 443-
6292/6940/533-8927,
info@carriacoumarine.
com

CARRIACOU
SAILMAKERS
CANVAS
CUSHIONS

In Stitches, (473)
443-8878/406-4117,
VHF: 16, asmelt@
gmaill.com

Sling's Uphostery,
(473) 403-4416

CARRIACOU
TECHNICAL
YACHT SERVICES

Dominique Wer (473)
407-1151, VHF: 16,
aluminum & stainless
(Genevieve's thera-
peutic massage)

**Hezron Wilson
Refrigeration,** (473)
443-6212

Tool Meister, (473)
445-8178, F: (473)
445-8178, tmmachine
@spiceisle.com, ma-
chine shop, mechanics

CARRIACOU
TRANSPORT

Ade's Dream, (473)
443-7317, F: (473)
443-8435, adesdea@
spiceisle.com, car
rentals

**Bubbles Turtle Dove
Taxi,** VHF:16, (473)
407-1029/443-7194

Cuthbert Snagg,
(473) 443-8293, bikes,
marine eco-tours

Linky Taxi Service,
Tel: (473) 443-7566,
Cell: (473) 406-
2457/416-5358, VHF:
16,

Lambi Queen Cycles,
(473) 443-8162, VHF:
16

CARRIACOU
RESTAURANTS &
ACCOMMODATION

Ade's Dream, (473)
443-7317, F: (473)
443-8435, $D

After Ours', (473)
443-6159, $C

**Bayside Bar and
Restaurant** (473)
443-8008, $C-D,

**Bogles Round
House,** (473) 443-
7841, $B info@ bo-
glesroundhouse. com

**Carriacou Yacht
Club,** (473) 443-6292,
F: (473) 443-6292,
VHF: 16, carriyacht@
spiceisle.com, $C-D

La Playa, (473) 410-
4216, $C-D

Lambi Queen, (473)
443-8162, VHF: 16

Lazy Turtle, 473-
443-8322, VHF: 16
auroghosh@ hotmail.
com $C-D

Le Petit Conch Shell,
(473) 443-6174/7233
$C-D

Slipway Restaurant,
(473) 443-6500, info@
slipwayrestaurant.com,
$B-C

Swampy Jo, 473-443-
8831/8760, $D

The Green Roof,
(473) 443-6399,
greenroof@ spiceisle.
com

Twilight, (473) 443-
8530, VHF: 16, $C

Victory Bar and Grill,
(473) 435-7431, $B-C

CARRIACOU FUN
SHOPPING

Fidel Productions,
(473) 435-8866/415-
0710, 443-6185,
443-7366

Simply Carriacou,
(473) 443-2029,
karen@simplycarria-
cou.com

CARRIACOU
PROVISIONING

Ade's Dream, (473)
443-7317, F: (473)
443-8435, adesdea@
spiceisle.com

After Ours', (473)
443-6159, $C

Alexis Supermarket,
(473) 443-8530

Bullen, (473) 443-
7468/9, F: 443 8194,
VHF: 16 vbs@spi-
ceisle.com

De Pastry Shop,
(473) 443-7841

Patty's Deli (473)
443-6258, shop@pat-
tysdeli.com

Twilight, (473) 443-
8530, VHF: 16

CARRIACOU DIVING

Arawak Divers (473) 443-6906/457-5112, VHF: 16, arawakdivers@spiceisle.com

Deefer Diving, (473) 443-7882, VHF: 16, info@deeferdiving.com

Lumbadive Ltd., (473) 443-8566, cell: (473) 457-4539, VHF: 16, dive@ lumbadive.com

GRENADA EMERGENCY

Emergency: police/coastguard 911

Customs, Prickly Bay, (473) 444-4509,

Customs, St. George's, (473) 440-2239/2240

Customs, Phare Bleu Marina, (473) 443-3236

Coastguard, 399

Robbie Yearwood (surgeon), Ocean House, Grand Anse (afternoon) (473) 444-1178, ho: (473) 444-5624, rosbrad@spiceisle.com

Dr. Mike Radix, (473) 444-4855/443-4379, emergency: 443-5330

Hospital, (473) 440-2051

Police, 911,

Port Authority, (473) 444-7447, VHF: 16, port

St. George's School of Medicine, (473) 444-4271

True Blue Pharmacy, (473) 444-3784

St. Augustin Medical Clinic, 440-6173-5, F:440 6176, staugms@ spiceisle.com, private hospital.

Sunsmile Dental Clinic, (473) 444-2273

Island Dental Care, (473) 437-4000, islanddentalcare @ yahoo.com

GRENADA AIRLINES

American Airlines, (473) 442-2222

British Airways, (800) 744-2997 (local 800)

BWIA, (473) 444-1221-2/4134

LIAT, (473) 440-2796-8, F: (473) 440-4166

GRENADA CHANDLERY FISHING GEAR

Budget Marine, 473-439-1983, F: 473-439-2037, budmargd@ spiceisle.com

Marine World, (473) 440-1748

Island Water World, (473) 435-2150, (473) 435-2152, sales@ islandwaterworld.com

Wholesale Yacht Part, (473) 458-6306/763-8387/ Miami: (305) 454-2971, sherri@wholesale yachtparts.com

GRENADA COMMUNICATIONS

Grenada Yacht Club, St. George's, Grenada, (473) 440-3050, VHF: 16

Boats & Harbours internet, (473) 435-8888

Fedex, (473) 440-2206

Onsite Software Support, Marquis Mall, (473) 444-3653

Renwick & Thompson, (473) 440-2198/2625, F: (473) 440-4179, renthom@ spiceisle.com, Western Union & DHL agent

Spice Island Marine Services, P.O. Box 449, St. George's, Grenada, (473) 444-4257/4342, VHF: 16, info@ spicislandmarine.com

Carenage Cafe, St george's, (473) 440-8701

GRENADA GENERAL YACHT SERVICES

Blue Water Yacht Services, (473) 435-9517/535-2583/4 VHF: 16/68, blu-h2o@ hotmail.com

Bob Goodchild Surveys, (473) 443 5784/407 4388, surveyor@flyingfish-ventures.com

Clarkes Court Bay Marina, (473) 439-2593/439-4474, VHF: 16/74, office@ccbmarina.com

Alan Hooper, (473) 440-3693/2881, surveys

Grenada Marine, (473) 443-1667, F: (473) 443-1668, Port Louis, (473) 444-1667, info @grenadamarine.com, haul out

Grenada Yacht Club, (473) 440-3050, F: (473) 440-6826, VHF: 16, gyc@spiceisle.com, marina, fuel

Henry's Safari Tours, (473) 444-5313/407-0522 F: (473) 444-4460, safari@ spiceisle.com, VHF: 68, laundry, yacht agent

Island Dreams, (473) 443-3603/ 415-2139, VHF: 74, info@ islandreamsgrenada.com, absentee yacht project management

Le Phare Bleu Marina & Resort, (473) 444-2400/ 409-7187 contact@ lepharebleu.com

Secret Harbour Marina (473) 444-4449, F: (473) 444-2090, VHF: 16,71, secretharbour@spiceisle.com, marina, fuel

Prickly Bay Marina, (473) 439-5265, F: (473) 439-5286 info@ pricklybaymarina.com, VHF: 16, marina, fuel

Port Louis Marina, (473) 435-7431/2, dockmaster (24-hour) (473) 415-0820, VHF: 14, reservations@ cnportlouismarina . com

Rock Taxi, (473) 444-5136, VHF: 16, absentee yacht management

Spice Island Marine, (473) 444-4257/3442, F: (473) 444-2816, Cell: (473) 407-4439, simco@spiceisle.com, haul-out

Spronk mega yacht Services, (473) 444-4662/407-3688/439-4369/ 443-5663, claire@ spronksprovisioning .com

Survival Anchorage, (473) 443-3957/459-3502, VHF: 16, gas refills

Tan Tan, (473) 440-1870, paint services

True Blue Inn, (473) 443 8783, F: (473) 444-5929, mail@true-blue.com, mini marina

Whisper Cove Marina, (473) 444-5296, $A-D, info@whisper-covemarina.com.

GRENADA MISCELLANEOUS

Grenada Board of Tourism, (473) 440-2279, (473) 440-6637, gbt@spiceisle.com

Grenada Chocolate Factory, (473) 442-0050, info@ grenada-chocolate.com

Grenada Golf Club, (473) 444-4128

Mayag, (473) 443-1667, mayagadmin@gmail.com

Peter Evans, (473) 444-3636, cell: (473) 441-7864, real estate & yacht broker

River Antoine Rum factory, (473) 442-7109/442-4537

GRENADA SAILMAKERS CANVAS CUSHIONS

Canvas Shop Grenada, The, (473) 443-2960, thecavasshop@spiceisle.com

Clarke's Upholstery, (473) 414-1827, v-clark-upholstery@hotmail.com

Johnny Sails & Canvas, (473) 444-1108/9619,

Neil Pryde Sails, (473) 537-5355

Turbulence, Grenada (473) 439-4495, turbsail@spiceisle.com

GRENADA TECHNICAL YACHT SERVICES

Anro Agencies, (473) 444-2220/1/444-4269, F: 473) 444-2221, anrogrenada@ spiceisle.com, Yanmar, Mariner, Mercruiser

AJS Enterprises, (473) 440-0192, yacht names

Albert Lucas, (473) 440-1281, machine shop

Carib Marine Services, (473) 414-9810/419 0000,

Cottle Boat Works, (473) 444-1070, F: (473) 444-1070, cottleboatworks@ spiceisle.com, shipwright

Dave's Gas Service, (473) 444 5571,davidbenoit@ spiceisle.com, stoves

Driftwood, (473) 459-9859, driftwood-grenada@gmail.com, woodwork

Enza Marine, T&F: 473-439-2049, cell: 473-407-3692, enzamarine@ spiceisle.com, VHF: 72, all yacht systems

Horizon Yacht Management, 473-439-1000/535-0328, info@horizongrenada.com

Lagoon Marine, (473) 440-3381, refrigeration

ModOne, (473) 439-6631/405-6631/415-2417, computers, wifi

McIntyre Bros, (473) 444-3944/5, (473) 444-2899, macford@spiceisle.com, mechanics inboard an outboard

Nauti Solutions, (473) 416-7127/7537, svmagnum@hotmail.com, mechanics

Palm Tree Marine, (473) 443-7256/419-0763, mail@palmtreemarine.com, mechanics

Protech Engineering Services, (473) 403-6371/538-3080, mncadore@gmail.com, refrigeration, stoves, appliances

Shipwrights, (473) 443-1062/407-3465, F: (473) 443-1063, info@shipwrights.com, shipwright

Subzero Air Control, (473) 440-4072/409-9376, refridge/ac

TechNick, (473) 536-1560/405-1560, technick@ spiceisle.com, welding, fabrication

Tan Tan Sam, 1-473-403-9904/444-5190, varnish, paint, polish.

Turbulence, Grenada (473) 439-4495, St. David's: (473) 443-2517, turbsail@spiceisle.com, rigging, electronics

Ultimate Filtration, (473) 440-6887, Cell: (473) 407-4989, outboards, fuel tank cleaning

Underwater Solutions, (473) 456-3927, brettfairhead@ yahoo.com

Welding Tec, (473) 537-4607, f.gweldingservices@yahoo.com

X-Marine, (473) 435-0297/415-0297/415-0180, info@xmarine.com

GRENADA TRANSPORT

Marina Taxi Association, (473) 444-1703, VHF: 16, taxi

K&J Taxi (473) 409-9621/ 440-4227, VHF: 16, kjtours@genadaexplorer.com

Grenada Adventure, 473-444-5337/ 473-535-1379, adventure@spiceisle.com

Henry's Safari Tours, (473) 444-5313, F: (473) 444-4460, safari@ spiceisle.com, VHF: 68

Maxwell Adventure Tours, (473) 444-1653, cell: (473) 406 4980, VHF: 68

McIntyre Bros, (473) 444-3944/5, (473) 444-2899, macford@spiceisle.com

Rock Taxi, (473) 444-5136, VHF: 16/10

Survival Anchorage, (473) 443-3957/459-3502

Telfor Bedeau (473) 442-6200, hiking guide

Y&R Car Rentals, (473) 444-4448, F: (473) 444-3639, Y&R@ spiceisle.com

GRENADA BANKING

CITS, (473) 440-2945, AmEx agent

National Commercial Bank (The), (473) 444-2265, (473) 444-5501, ncbgnd@spiceisle.com

GRENADA FUN SHOPPING

Ace Hardware/Napa, (473) 440-5090

Arawak Islands, (473) 444-3577, F (473) 444-3577

Big Bamboo, (473) 439-7873

Carolyn Lily, 473-435-5459

Cyber Connect, 473) 439-2355,

Fidel Productions, (473) 435-8866

Imagine, (473) 444-2554, F: (473) 444-2554, sark@spiceisle.com

Pssst, (473) 439-0787,

Tikal, (473) 440-2310, fisher@spiceisle.com

Yellow Poui Art, 473-440-3001, yellow-poui@ spiceisle.com

GRENADA PROVISIONING

Best Little Liquor Store in Town, (473) 440-2198/3422, FF: (473) 440-4179, VHF: 16 "Rhum Runner base", renthom @ spiceisle.com

Essentials, (473) 444-4662

Food Fair, (473) 440-2573, F: (473) 440-4008, hubbards @ spiceisle.com

North South Trading, (473) 444-1182, nst. wines@spiceisle.com

Merry Baker, (473) 435-6464, themerrybaker1@gmail.com

Spronk's Provisioning, (473) 407-3688/444-4662, F: (473) 444-4677

The Wine Shoppe, (473) 444-1182, nst. wines@ spiceisle.com

Phare Bleu Mini Mart, (473) 443-4232

See aslo **Blue Water Yacht Services, Henry Safari Tours and Spronk Megayacht Services** in *General Yacht Services*

GRENADA RESTAURANTS & ACCOMMODATION

1782 Bar/restaurant, (473) 435-7263, $A-D

Almost Paradise, (473) 442-0608, almostparadise@ spiceisle. com, $D

Aquarium, (473) 444-1410, aquarium@ spiceisle.com, $B-D

Bananas, (473) 439-4662, (473), F: (473) 444-4677, $B-D,

BB's Crab Back, (473) 435-7058, bbscrabback@ hotmail .com $B-C

Beachside Terrace, (473) 444-4247, F (473) 444-1234, $B-D, flambo@spiceisle.com

Bel Air Plantation & Water's Edge, 473-444-6305, belair @ spiceisle.com, $B

Calabash, (473) 444-4334, $A

Carib Sushi, (473) 439-5640, $B, caribsush i@ spiceisle.com

Charcoal, (473) 444-4745, charcoals@ spiceisle.com, $B-D

Choo Light, (473) 444-2196, $D,

Coconut Beach, (473) 444-4644, $A-B

De Big Fish, (473) 439-4401, VHF: 68, $B-D

Dodgy Dock, True Blue, 473-439-1377, $D

Dragon Bay Hideaway, 473-538-0909/435-9945, $D

Garfield's Beach Bar, G. Anse, 473-439-7700

Grenada Yacht Club, (473) 440-3050, F: (473) 440-6826, VHF: 16, $D

Helvellyn House, (473)-442-9252/418-6405, sark@spiceisle.com

Island View, (473) 443-2054, islandview@ spiceisle.com, VHF: 16

La Boulangerie, (473) 444-1131, $D papaya@ spiceisle.com

La Sagesse, (473) 444 6458, LSnature@ spiceisle.com

Little Dipper, (473) 444-5136, VHF: 10/16, $D

Mango Cottage, (473) 407-4388, mangocottagegrenada@gmail. com, accommodation

Mangrove Hide-Away, (473) 443-2782, 405-0244, $B-C

Mount hartman Estate, (473) 407-4504, reservations@ mount hartmanbay.com, $A

Museum Bistro, 473-416-7266, $D, tapas

Patrick's, (473) 440 0364/ 449 7243, $B-C

Petit Anse, (473) 442-5252, info@ petiteanse. com, $B-D

Petit Bacaye, (473) 443-2902, $B

Red Crab, (The), (473) 444-4424, crab @ spiceisle.com, $A-B

Rose Mount, (473) 444-8069, $D

Sunset View, (473) 440-5758, F: (473) 440-7001

The Beach House, (473) 444-4455, F: (473) 444-5855, beachhouse @spiceisle.com, $B

Tivigny , (473) 405-4743, info@tivigny.com, house Rental

Tropicana Inn, (473) 440-1586, $C-D

True Blue Bay, (473) 443 8783, F: (473) 444-5929, windward@ truebluebay.com, VHF: 16, $A-C

Umbrellas, (473) 439-9149, $D

GRENADA DIVING

Aquanauts, (473) 444 1126, VHF: 16, aquanauts @spiceisle.com

Dive Grenada, (473) 444 1092, info@ divegrenada.com

First Impressions, Whale watching, 473-440-3678, cell:407-1147, starwindsailing@ spiceisle.com

Scuba Tech, (473) 439-4346

GRENADA CHARTER

Horizon Yacht Charters, True Blue, Grenada, (473) 439-1000, toll free: 1-866 463-7254, F: (473) 439-1001, horizonyachts@ spiceisle.com, all kinds of charter

Footloose Charters, (473) 440-7949, (473) 440-6680, footloos@ spiceisle.com, VHF: 16, yacht agent

John Clement, (473) 406-2064, johnclement80 @hotmail. com johnclement08 @ yahoo.com

The Moorings, (473) 6661/2

OTHER SERVICES OF INTEREST

Doyle Sailmakers, 6 Crossroads, St. Philip, Barbados, (246) 423-4600, F: 246-423-4499

New Nautical Coatings, (727) 523-8053, F: (727) 523-7325

Power Boats, (868) 634-4303, F: (868) 634 4327, VHF: 72 pbmfl @powerboats.co.tt

Peake Marine, (868) 634-4427/3, F: (868) 634-4387

INTERNATIONAL CHARTER

Ed Hamilton, (207) 549 7855, F: (207) 549-7822, all kinds of charter

Sunsail, (888) 350-568, sunsail.com, all kinds of charter

The Moorings, (888)952-8420, sales@moorings.com

General Index

Cruising Guide Publications

CRUISING GUIDE TO THE VIRGIN ISLANDS
By Nancy & Simon Scott
16th Edition, 2013-2014
ISBN 978-0-944428-95-5
6 x 9, 350 pp. **$32.95**

Completely re-designed and updated style, with more Virgin Island photography and full color detailed anchorage charts, these guides have been indispensable companions for sailors and visitors to these islands since 1982. Includes a free 17 x 27 color planning chart, with aerial photos of some of the anchorages. Covers the Virgin Islands including all the U.S. and British Virgin Islands!

• GPS co-ordinates for every anchorage
• Anchoring and mooring information and fees
• Customs, immigration and National Park regulations
• Particulars on marina facilities and the amenities they offer
• Water sports-where to go and where to rent equipment
• Shore-side facilities, restaurants, beach bars, shops, provisions, internet connections

Everything you will need to help make your vacation an enjoyable and memorable experience in a concise easy-to-use format.

CRUISING GUIDE TO THE LEEWARD ISLANDS
Chris Doyle
2012-2013
ISBN 978-0-944428-93-1
6 x 9, 529 pp
$34.95

This twelfth edition covers the islands from Anguilla to Dominca, and is an essential tool for all cruisers sailing this region. Chris Doyle spends months sailing these islands to update each edition. Included are over one hundred up-to-date color sketch charts, full color aerial photos of most anchorages, island pictures, and detailed shore-side information covering services, restaurants, provisioning, travel basics and island history. Information is linked to the author's website where you can download the GPS waypoints given in the sketch charts, learn of essential updates, print town maps, and obtain links to local weather, news, and businesses.

VIRGIN ANCHORAG[
By Nancy & Simon Scott
2012 Edition
ISBN 978-0-944428-84-9
8.5 x 11, 96 pp. **$29.95**

Virgin Anchorages featu stunning color aerial p[tography of 46 of the most popular anchorages in Virgin Islands. Graphic overlays aid in navigat to safe anchorages. This is an excellent compani to Cruising Guide to the Virgin Islands.

WATERPROOF PLANNING CHART OF THE VIRGIN ISLANDS
COLOR WITH AERIAL PHOTOS
Color, 17 x 27   **$9.95**

Printed on two sides this new chart includes t U.S. & B.V.I. from St. Thomas to Anegada, incl ing anchorage and mooring locations as well as G co-ordinates, sailing routes and distances betwe waypoints. The waterproof chart is excellent the cockpit and attractive enough to hang on t wall when you get home. Designed for use with T Cruising Guide to the Virgin Islands

LEEWARD ANCHORAGES
By Chris Doyle
ISBN 0-944428-82-7
8.5 x 11, 91 pp   **$29.95**

Leeward Anchorages sho aerial photographs of the favorite anchorages from Anguilla throu Dominica with graphic overlays to illustrate da gerous and safe passages from a bird's eye vie Carefully researched and recorded by Chris Doy safe passages, markers, buoys and hazards are marked to guide you to safe, enjoyable anchorag This is a companion book to use with The Cruisi Guide to the Leeward Islands.

SAILORS GUIDE TO THE WINDWARD ISLANDS
By Chris Doyle
16th Edition,
2013-2014
ISBN 978-0-944428-94-8
6 x 9, 430 pp. **$32.95**

Revised and updated for 2013-2014, this guide features detailed sketch [ch]arts based on the author's own surveys, and [aer]ial photos of most anchorages. It also includes [cle]ar and concise navigational information. By [far] the most popular guide to the area, it covers [th]e islands from Martinique to Grenada, with [da]zzling scenic photography, unsurpassed onshore [inf]ormation, sections on exploring, provisioning, [wa]ter sports, services, restaurants and photography. [Inf]ormation is linked to the author's website where [yo]u can download town maps, GPS waypoints from [th]e sketch charts, and obtain links to local weather, [ne]ws and more.

CRUISING GUIDE TO VENEZUELA & BONAIRE
By Chris Doyle
2006
ISBN 0-944428-78-9
6 x 9, 290 pp. **$27.95**

This is the latest updated version of the only seriously researched guide [to] this area. The book includes color aerial photos [of] many anchorages, clear and concise navigational [ch]arts, with information on things to do and places [to] go while on shore. The guide is linked to the [aut]hor's website where you can download updates, [tow]n maps and much more.

CRUISING GUIDE TO TRINIDAD, TOBAGO PLUS BARBADOS AND GUYANA
By Chris Doyle
2013
ISBN 978-0-944428-96-2
6 x 9, 256 pp. **$27.95**

[Th]is updated edition has been expanded to include [Gu]yana. Including 55 sketch charts, aerial pho[to]graphs, dazzling scenic photography throughout, [un]surpassed onshore information with sections on [ex]ploring, provisioning, services and restaurants. [Th]e guide is linked to the author's website where [yo]u can download town maps, GPS waypoints given [on] the sketch charts and much more.

WINDWARD ANCHORAGES
By Chris Doyle
ISBN 0-944428-83-5
8.5 x 11, 96 pp
$29.95

Windward Anchorages is the third in the Anchorages series and a companion book to the Sailors Guide to the Windward Islands by Chris Doyle. Stunning aerial images depict anchorages from Martinique south through Dominica. These aerial images are overprinted to show the hazards to avoid, as well as, markers and buoys to guide you to the safe passages and anchorages of the Windward Islands.

CONCISE GUIDE TO CARIBBEAN WEATHER
1997 ISBN 0-9652476-1-9
6 x 9, 72 pp.
$19.95

The safest way to navigate this popular cruising area - David Jones, founder of the most successful weather net in the Caribbean, garners praise all around for his unique knowledge and clear explanations.

CRUISING GUIDE TO THE FLORIDA KEYS
By Captain Frank Papy
12th Edition, 6 x 9, 208 pp. **$19.95**

This 12th ed. is laid out in easy reference form, with a chapter devoted to each Key with color aerial photographs, 42 detailed sketch charts, along with navigational secrets. Covers Ft. Lauderdale down through the Keys and up to Tarpon Springs on the West Coast of Florida and includes facts on marinas, anchoring spots, artificial reefs, fishing information and much more.

TRICKS OF THE TRADES
By Bruce Van Sant
2001 ISBN 0-944428-62-2
6 x 9, 182 pp. **$14.95**

The author of Gentleman's Guide to Passages South widens the scope of his book to include stratagems and tips for sailors cruising aboard for the first time. Not how to sail, but how to live safely and comfortably while aboard - in short tricks he has learned during his many years of cruising.

Toll free 800-330-9542 or 727-733-5322
Fax 727-734-8179 or info@CruisingGuides.com

Advertisers Index